CAIRO

a graphic novel

VERTIGO
DC COMICS

CAIRO

a graphic novel

Written by
G. WILLOW WILSON

Art by
M.K. PERKER

Lettered by
TRAVIS LANHAM

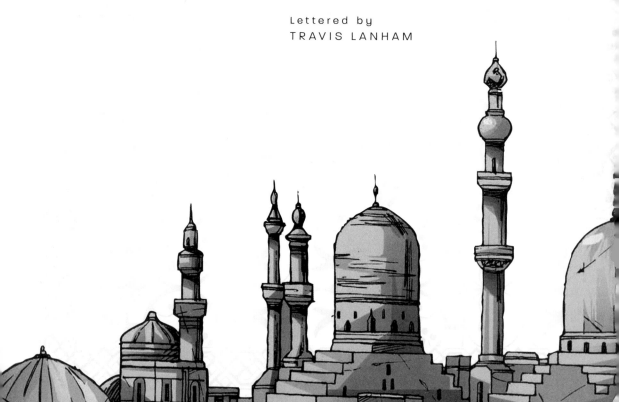

Karen Berger Sr. VP-Executive Editor
Joan Hilty Editor
Rachel Gluckstern Associate Editor
Louis Prandi Art Director
Paul Levitz President & Publisher
Georg Brewer VP-Design & DC Direct Creative
Richard Bruning Sr. VP-Creative Director
Patrick Caldon Exec. VP-Finance & Operations
Chris Caramalis VP-Finance
John Cunningham VP-Marketing
Terri Cunningham VP-Managing Editor
Alison Gill VP-Manufacturing
Hank Kanalz VP-General Manager, WildStorm
Jim Lee Editorial Director-WildStorm
Paula Lowitt Sr. VP-Business & Legal Affairs
MaryEllen McLaughlin VP-Advertising & Custom Publishing
John Nee VP-Business Development
Gregory Noveck Sr. VP-Creative Affairs
Sue Pohja VP-Book Trade Sales
Cheryl Rubin Sr. VP-Brand Management
Jeff Trojan VP-Business Development, DC Direct
Bob Wayne VP-Sales

Cover art and color by **M.K. Perker.**
Logo by **Nancy Ogami**

First printing. DC Comics, a Warner Bros. Entertainment Company.
HC ISBN: 1-4012-1140-2 978-1-4012-1140-0
SC ISBN: 1-4012-1734-6 978-1-4012-1734-1

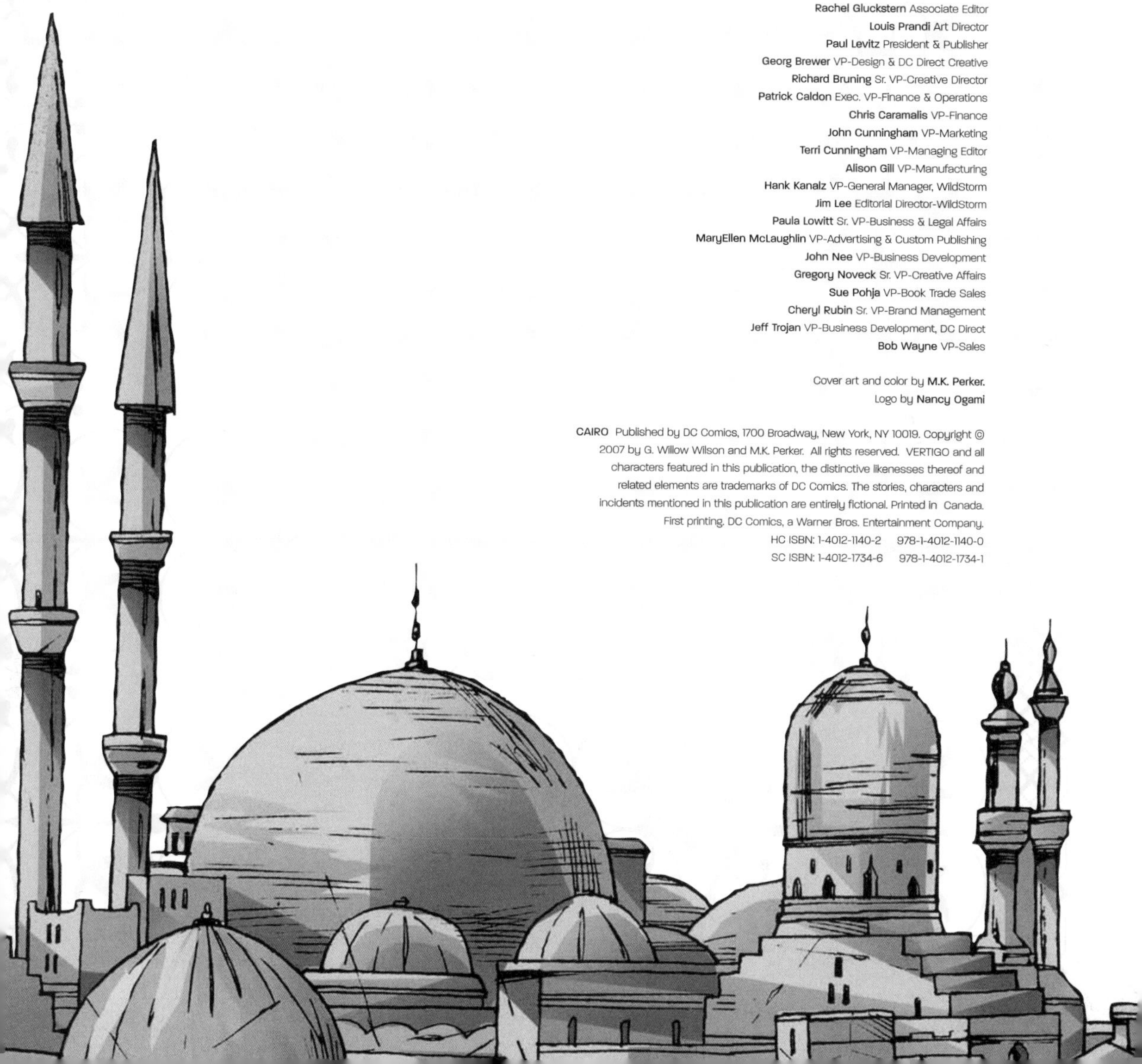

DEDICATIONS

For my sister Meredith, who knows the value of a
hookah; and for Keith Giffen, who believed in this book.

— *G. Willow Wilson*

For my mother who got me my first comic book, *Lucky
Luke*, and read it to me when I was three; and for my
father who supported me since then and never asked
whether I did my homework.

— *M.K. Perker*

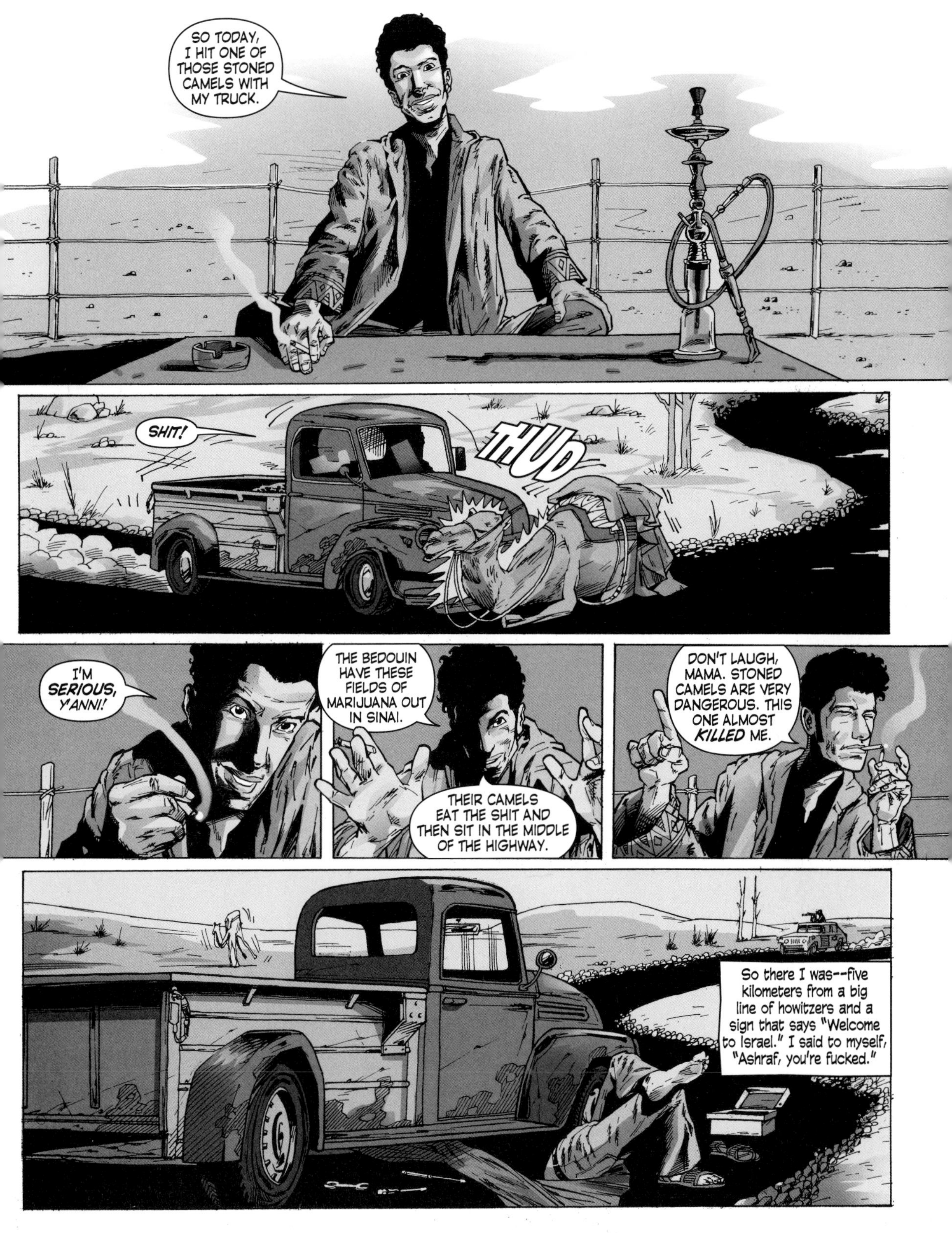
SO TODAY, I HIT ONE OF THOSE STONED CAMELS WITH MY TRUCK.
SHIT!
THUD
I'M *SERIOUS,* Y'ANNI!
THE BEDOUIN HAVE THESE FIELDS OF MARIJUANA OUT IN SINAI.
THEIR CAMELS EAT THE SHIT AND THEN SIT IN THE MIDDLE OF THE HIGHWAY.
DON'T LAUGH, MAMA. STONED CAMELS ARE VERY DANGEROUS. THIS ONE ALMOST *KILLED* ME.
So there I was--five kilometers from a big line of howitzers and a sign that says "Welcome to Israel." I said to myself, "Ashraf, you're fucked."

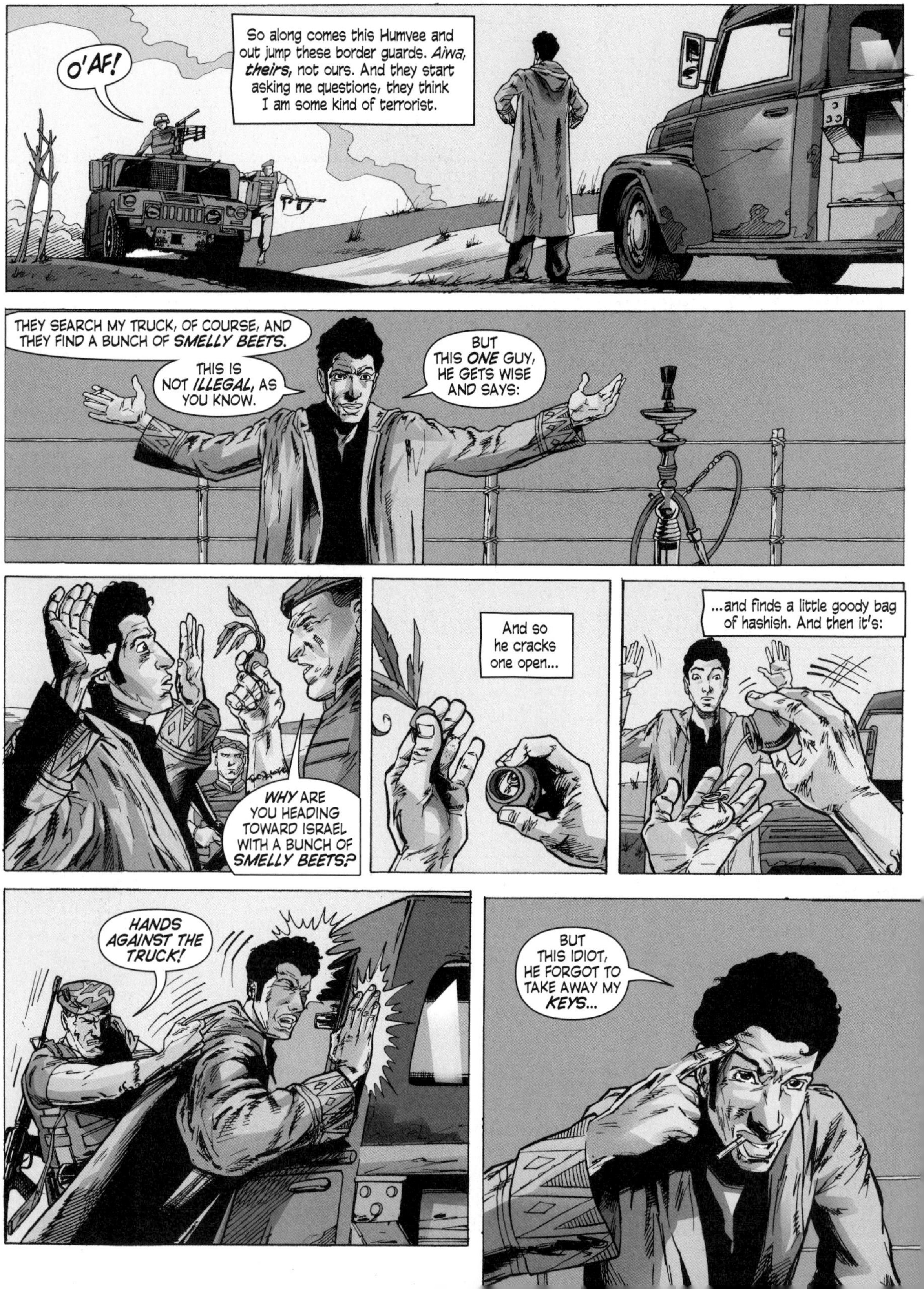

O'AF!
So along comes this Humvee and out jump these border guards. *Aiwa, **theirs,*** not ours. And they start asking me questions, they think I am some kind of terrorist.
THEY SEARCH MY TRUCK, OF COURSE, AND THEY FIND A BUNCH OF ***SMELLY BEETS.***
THIS IS NOT ***ILLEGAL,*** AS YOU KNOW.
BUT THIS ***ONE*** GUY, HE GETS WISE AND SAYS:
WHY ARE YOU HEADING TOWARD ISRAEL WITH A BUNCH OF ***SMELLY BEETS?***
And so he cracks one open...
...and finds a little goody bag of hashish. And then it's:
HANDS AGAINST THE TRUCK!
BUT THIS IDIOT, HE FORGOT TO TAKE AWAY MY ***KEYS...***

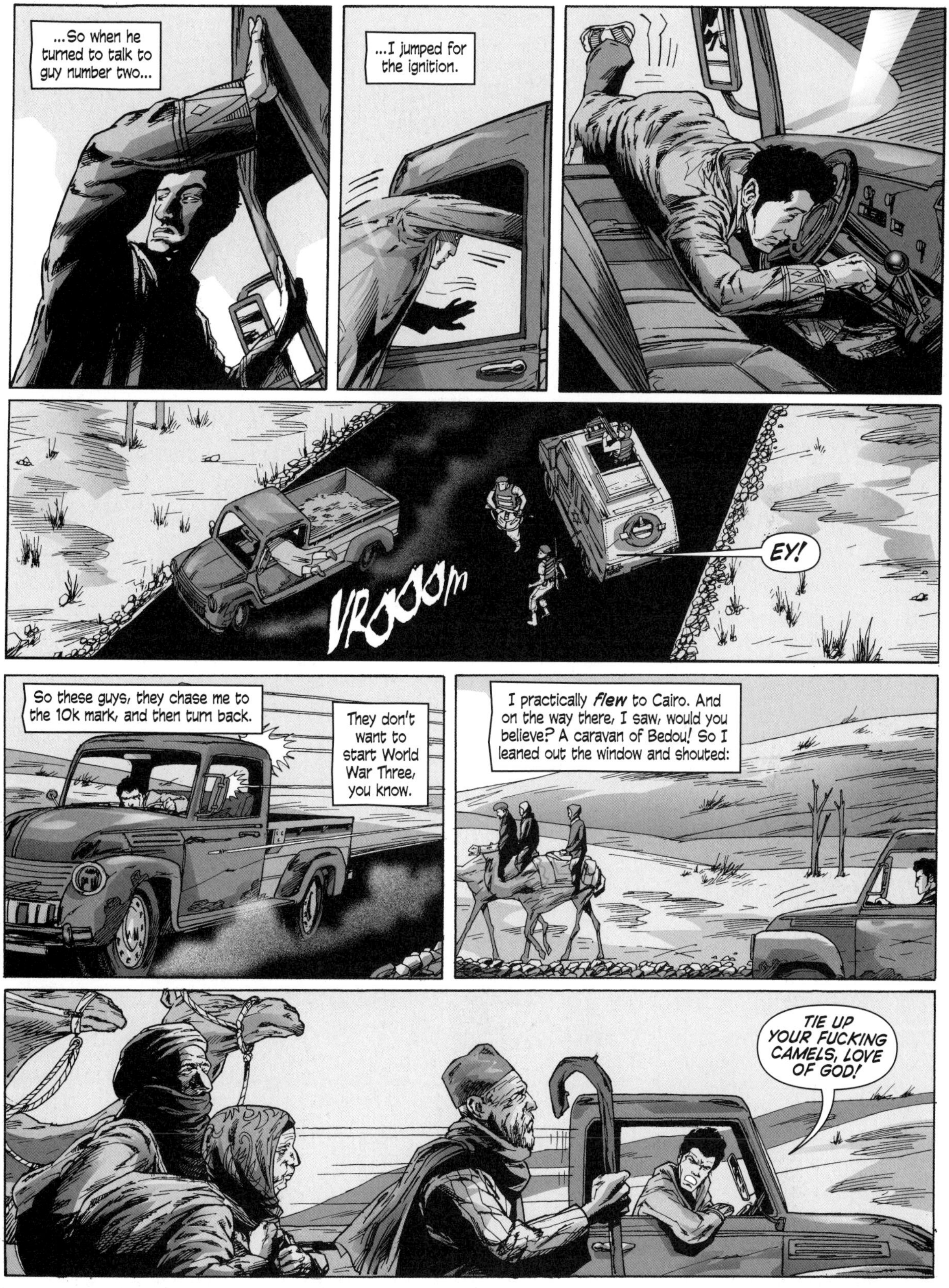
...So when he turned to talk to guy number two...
...I jumped for the ignition.
EY!
VROOOM
So these guys, they chase me to the 10k mark, and then turn back.
They don't want to start World War Three, you know.
I practically *flew* to Cairo. And on the way there, I saw, would you believe? A caravan of Bedou! So I leaned out the window and shouted:
TIE UP YOUR FUCKING CAMELS, LOVE OF GOD!

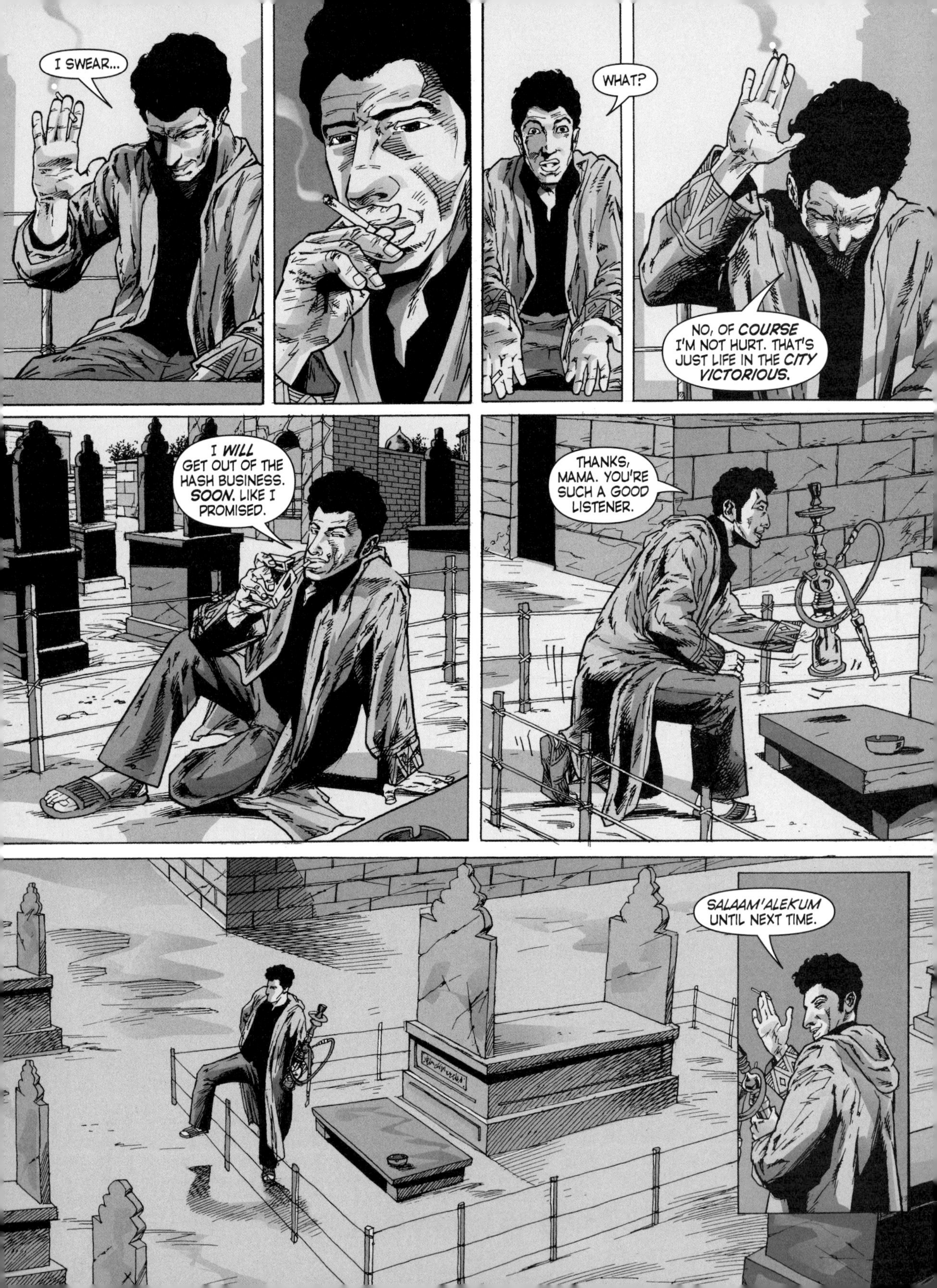
I SWEAR...
WHAT?
NO, OF COURSE I'M NOT HURT. THAT'S JUST LIFE IN THE CITY VICTORIOUS.
I WILL GET OUT OF THE HASH BUSINESS. SOON. LIKE I PROMISED.
THANKS, MAMA. YOU'RE SUCH A GOOD LISTENER.
SALAAM'ALEKUM UNTIL NEXT TIME.

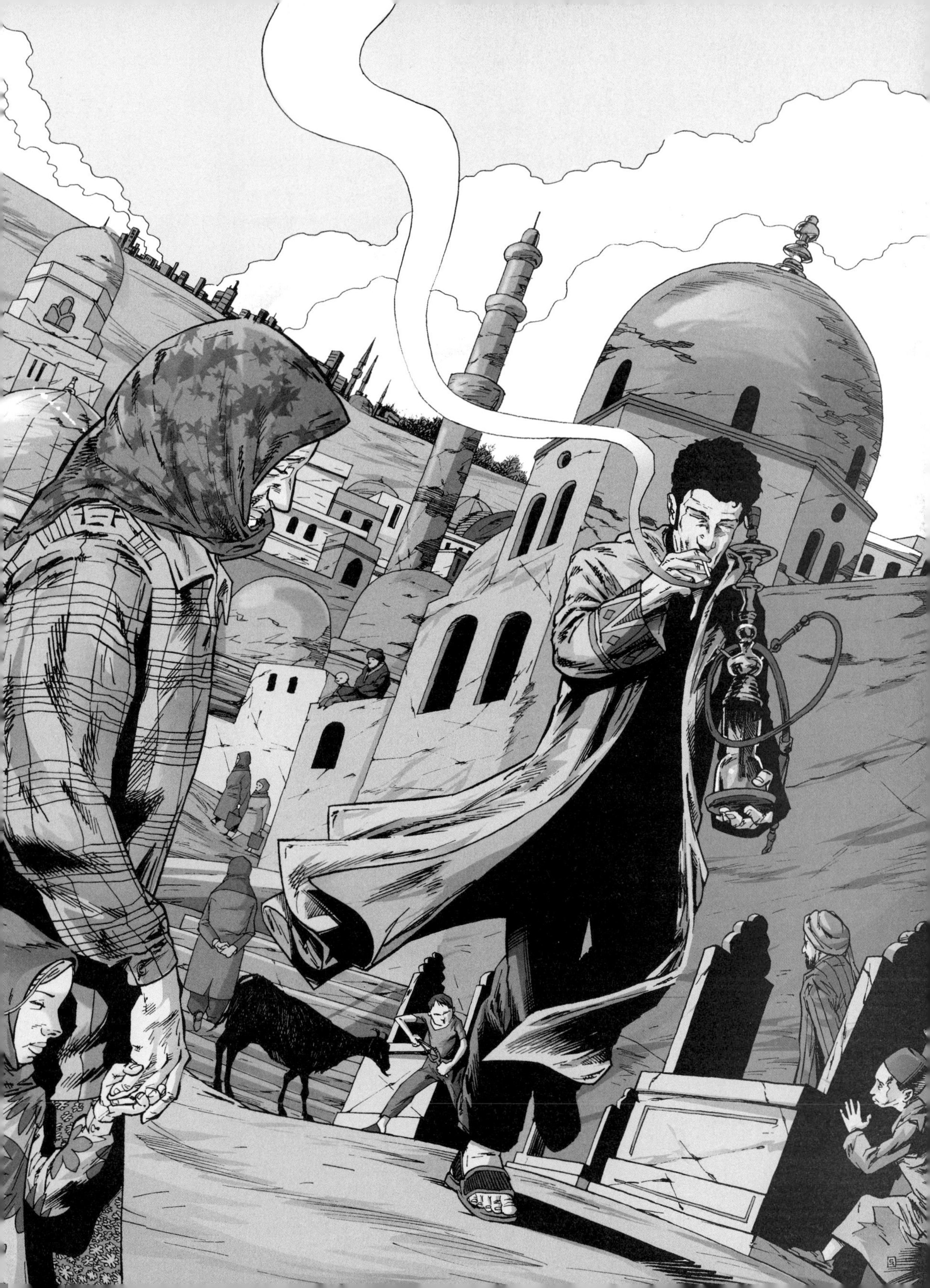

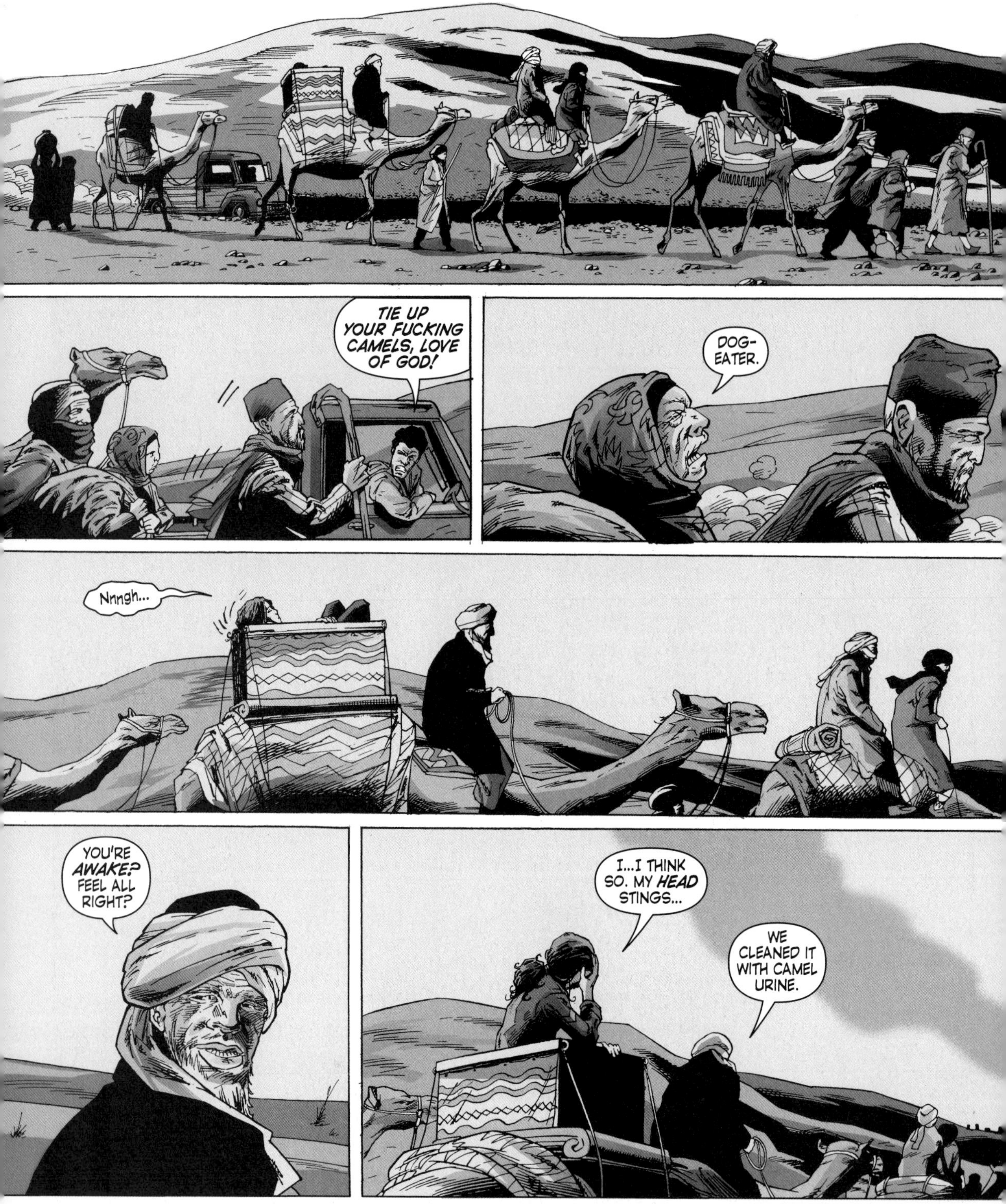
TIE UP YOUR FUCKING CAMELS, LOVE OF GOD!
DOG-EATER.
Nnngh...
YOU'RE AWAKE? FEEL ALL RIGHT?
I...I THINK SO. MY HEAD STINGS...
WE CLEANED IT WITH CAMEL URINE.

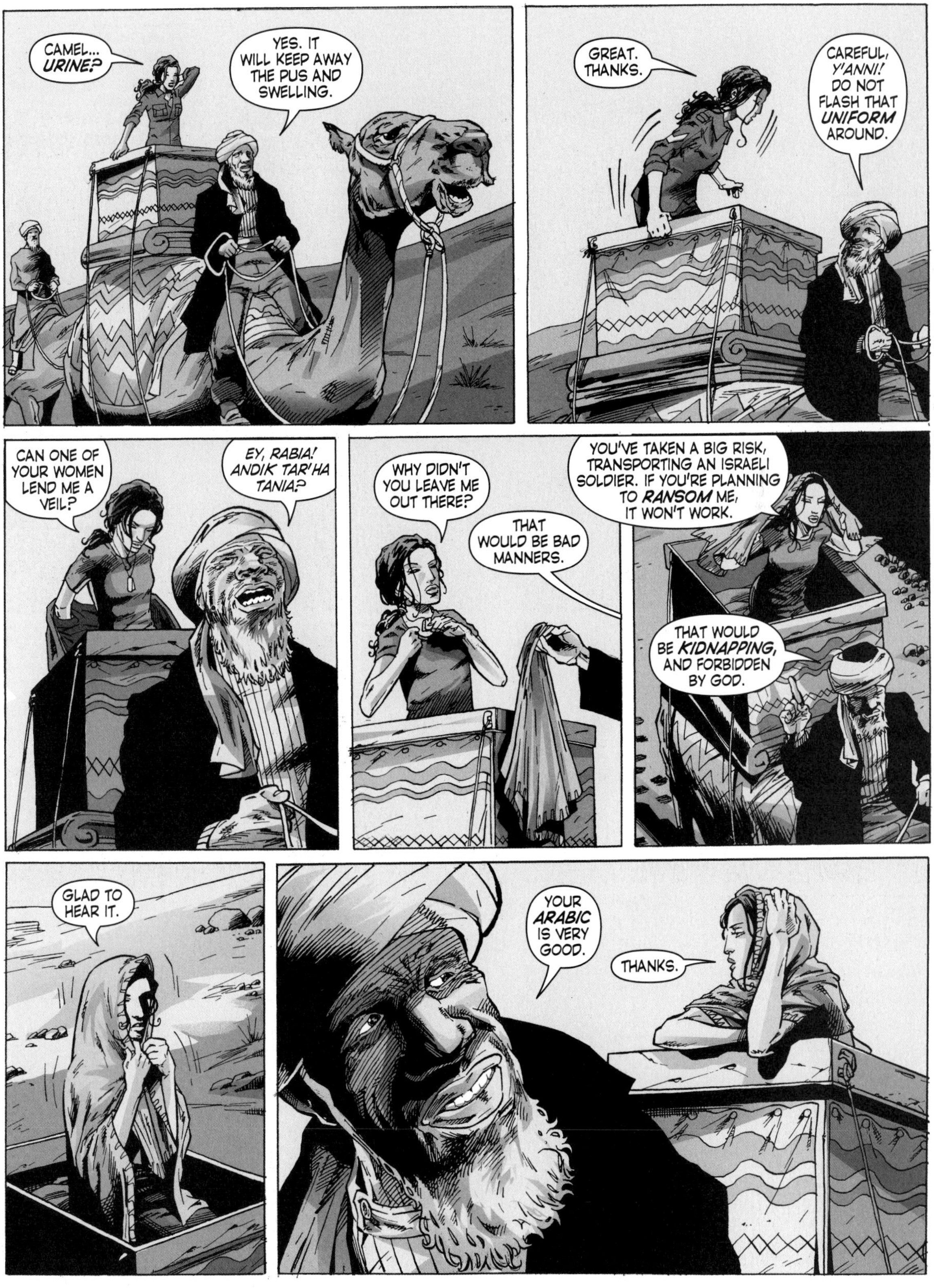
CAMEL... URINE?
YES. IT WILL KEEP AWAY THE PUS AND SWELLING.
GREAT. THANKS.
CAREFUL, Y'ANNI! DO NOT FLASH THAT UNIFORM AROUND.
CAN ONE OF YOUR WOMEN LEND ME A VEIL?
EY, RABIA! ANDIK TAR'HA TANIA?
WHY DIDN'T YOU LEAVE ME OUT THERE?
THAT WOULD BE BAD MANNERS.
YOU'VE TAKEN A BIG RISK, TRANSPORTING AN ISRAELI SOLDIER. IF YOU'RE PLANNING TO RANSOM ME, IT WON'T WORK.
THAT WOULD BE KIDNAPPING, AND FORBIDDEN BY GOD.
GLAD TO HEAR IT.
YOUR ARABIC IS VERY GOOD.
THANKS.

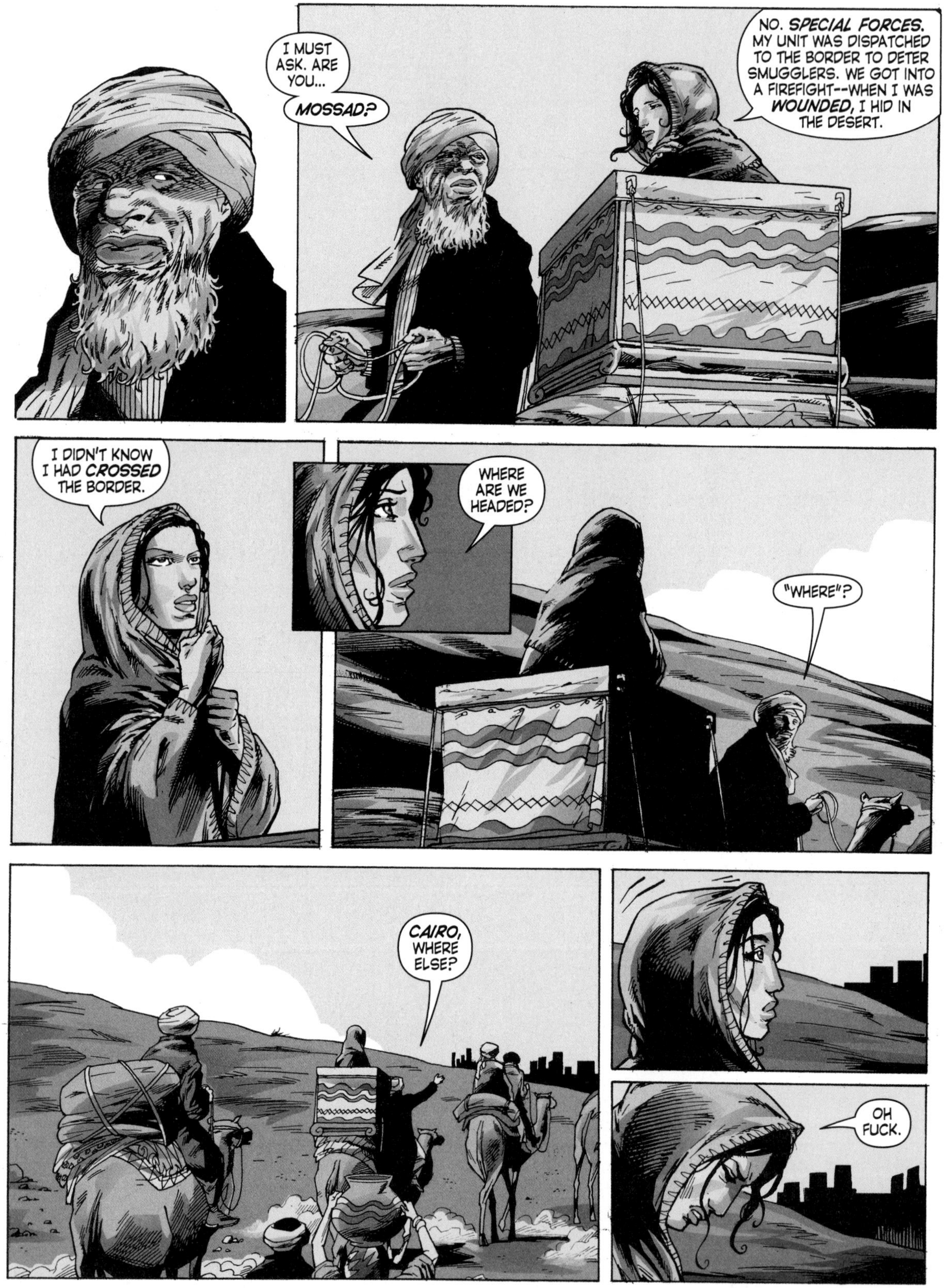
I MUST ASK. ARE YOU... MOSSAD?
NO. SPECIAL FORCES. MY UNIT WAS DISPATCHED TO THE BORDER TO DETER SMUGGLERS. WE GOT INTO A FIREFIGHT--WHEN I WAS WOUNDED, I HID IN THE DESERT.
I DIDN'T KNOW I HAD CROSSED THE BORDER.
WHERE ARE WE HEADED?
"WHERE"?
CAIRO, WHERE ELSE?
OH FUCK.

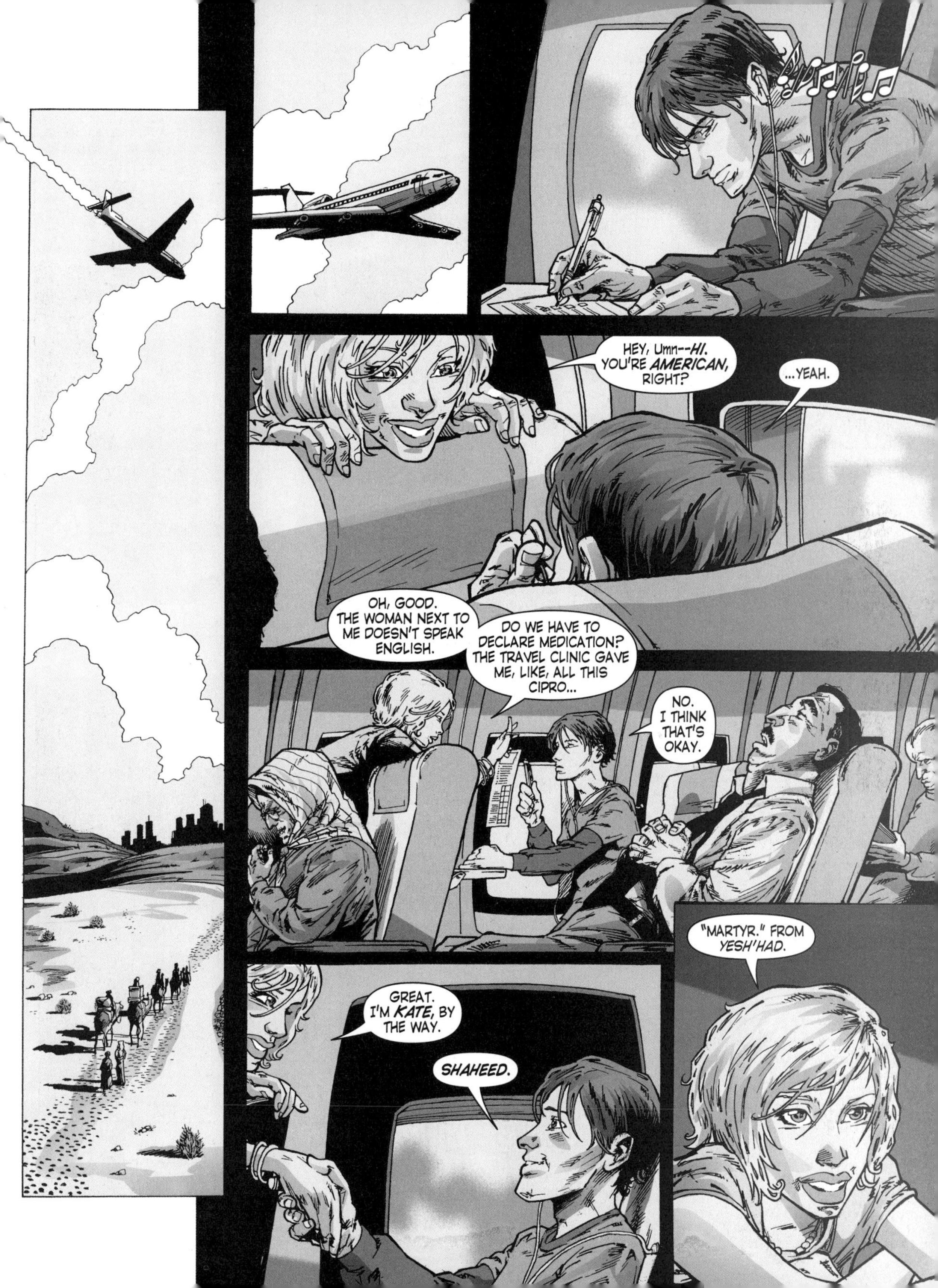
HEY, Umn--HI. YOU'RE AMERICAN, RIGHT?
...YEAH.
OH, GOOD. THE WOMAN NEXT TO ME DOESN'T SPEAK ENGLISH.
DO WE HAVE TO DECLARE MEDICATION? THE TRAVEL CLINIC GAVE ME, LIKE, ALL THIS CIPRO...
NO. I THINK THAT'S OKAY.
GREAT. I'M KATE, BY THE WAY.
SHAHEED.
"MARTYR." FROM YESH'HAD.

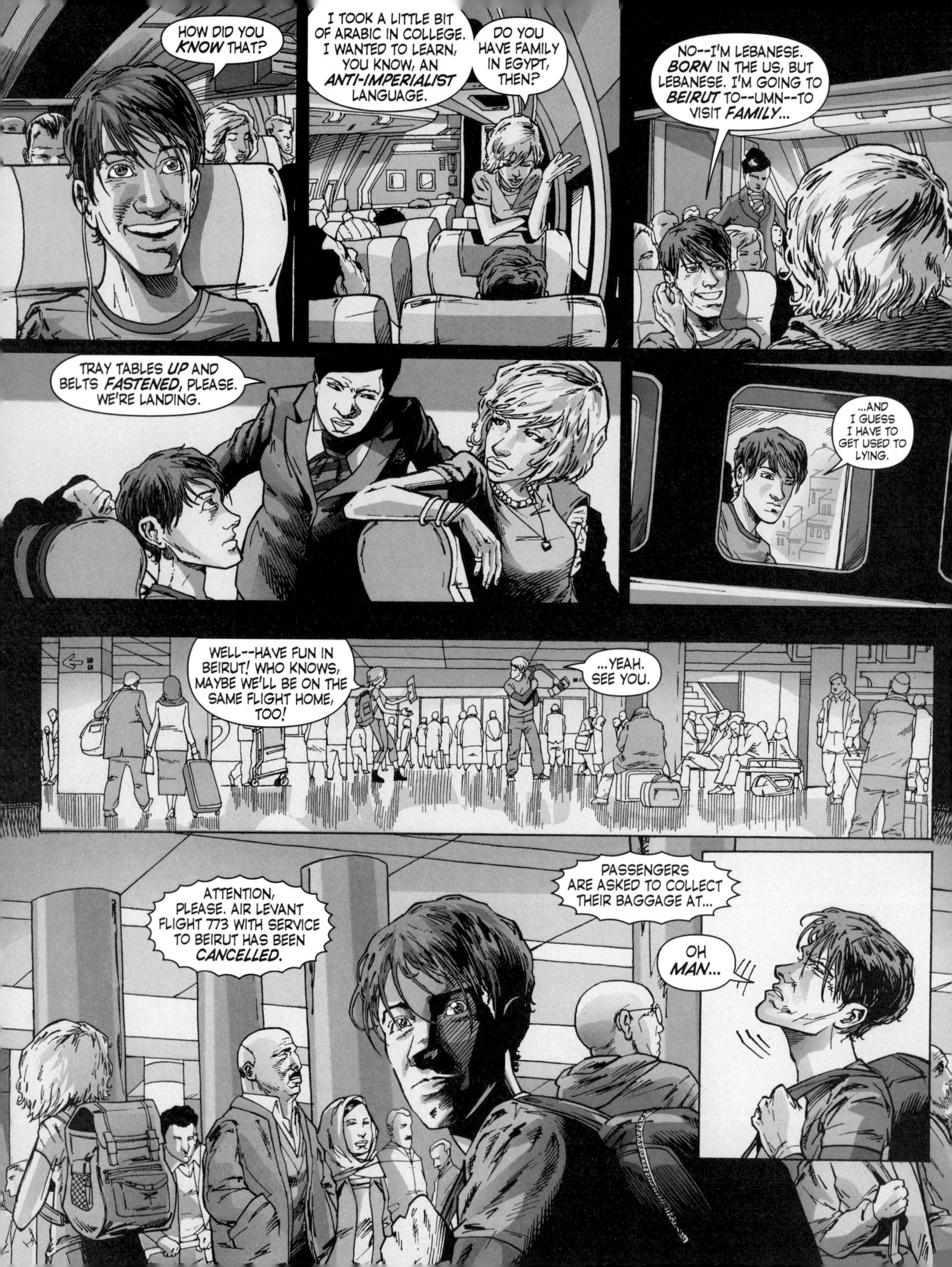
HOW DID YOU KNOW THAT?
I TOOK A LITTLE BIT OF ARABIC IN COLLEGE. I WANTED TO LEARN, YOU KNOW, AN ANTI-IMPERIALIST LANGUAGE.
DO YOU HAVE FAMILY IN EGYPT, THEN?
NO--I'M LEBANESE. BORN IN THE US, BUT LEBANESE. I'M GOING TO BEIRUT TO--UMN--TO VISIT FAMILY...
TRAY TABLES UP AND BELTS FASTENED, PLEASE. WE'RE LANDING.
...AND I GUESS I HAVE TO GET USED TO LYING.
WELL--HAVE FUN IN BEIRUT! WHO KNOWS, MAYBE WE'LL BE ON THE SAME FLIGHT HOME, TOO!
...YEAH. SEE YOU.
ATTENTION, PLEASE. AIR LEVANT FLIGHT 773 WITH SERVICE TO BEIRUT HAS BEEN CANCELLED.
PASSENGERS ARE ASKED TO COLLECT THEIR BAGGAGE AT...
OH MAN...

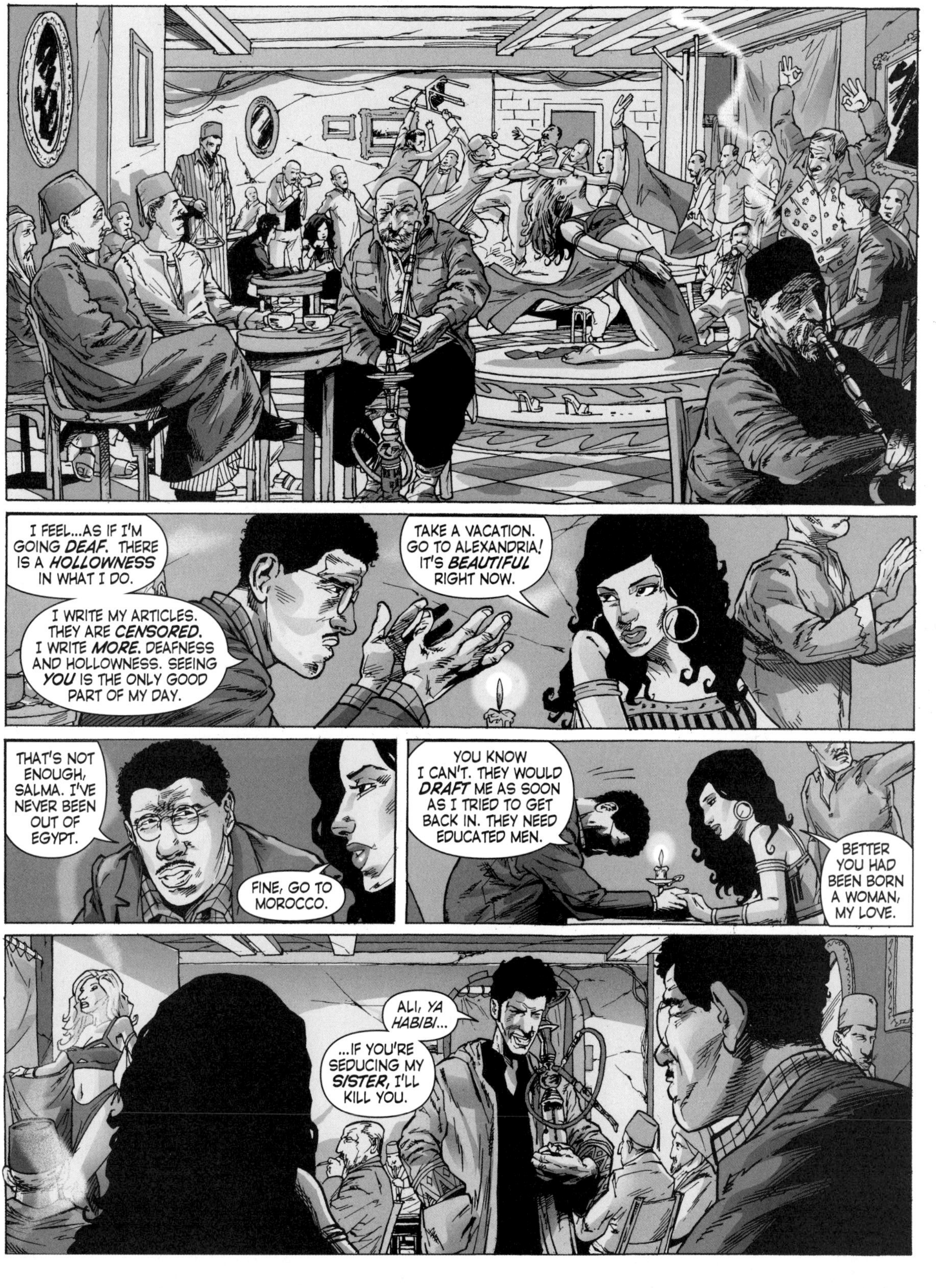
I FEEL...AS IF I'M GOING DEAF. THERE IS A HOLLOWNESS IN WHAT I DO.
I WRITE MY ARTICLES. THEY ARE CENSORED. I WRITE MORE. DEAFNESS AND HOLLOWNESS. SEEING YOU IS THE ONLY GOOD PART OF MY DAY.
TAKE A VACATION. GO TO ALEXANDRIA! IT'S BEAUTIFUL RIGHT NOW.
THAT'S NOT ENOUGH, SALMA. I'VE NEVER BEEN OUT OF EGYPT.
FINE, GO TO MOROCCO.
YOU KNOW I CAN'T. THEY WOULD DRAFT ME AS SOON AS I TRIED TO GET BACK IN. THEY NEED EDUCATED MEN.
BETTER YOU HAD BEEN BORN A WOMAN, MY LOVE.
ALI, YA HABIBI...
...IF YOU'RE SEDUCING MY SISTER, I'LL KILL YOU.

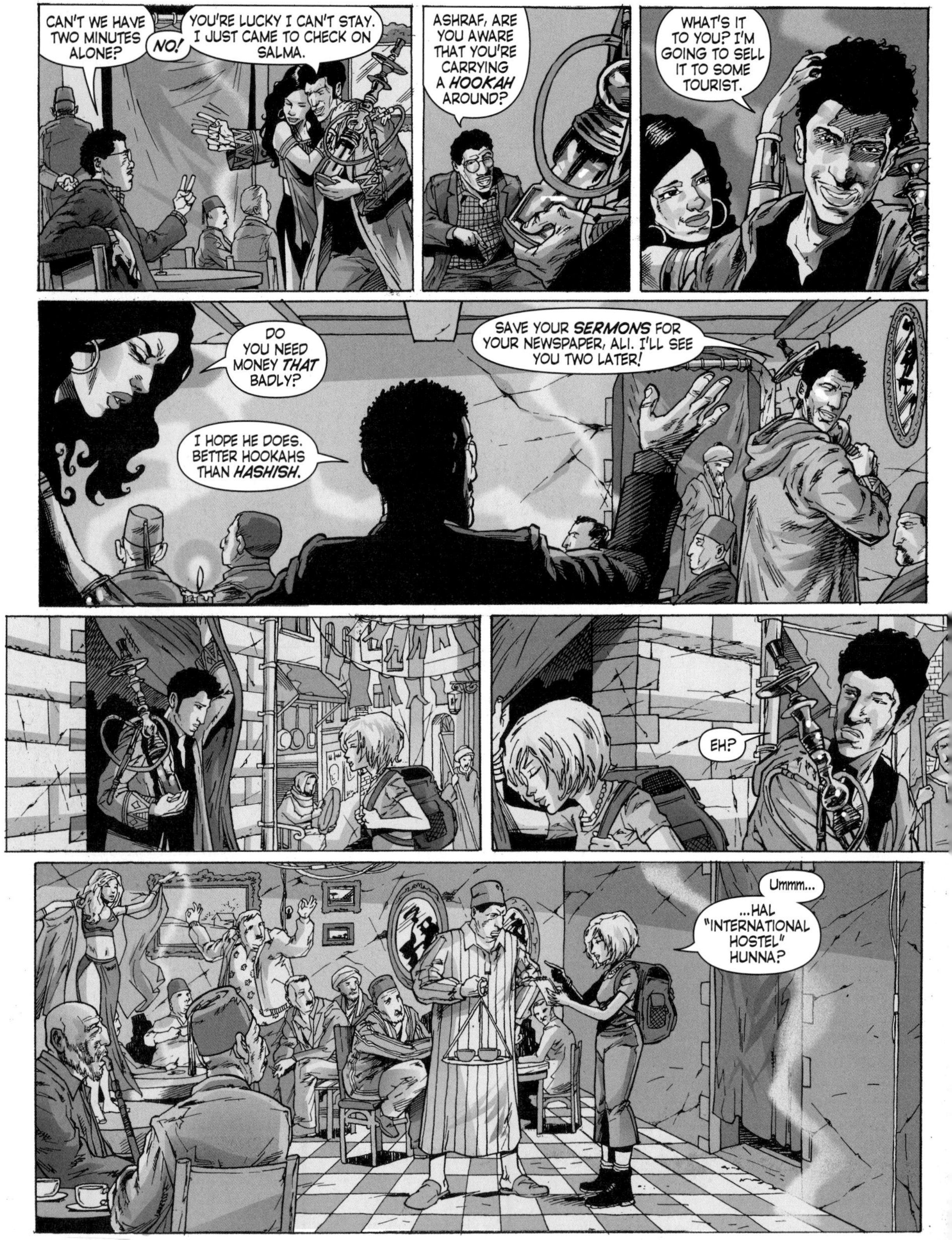
CAN'T WE HAVE TWO MINUTES ALONE?
NO!
YOU'RE LUCKY I CAN'T STAY. I JUST CAME TO CHECK ON SALMA.
ASHRAF, ARE YOU AWARE THAT YOU'RE CARRYING A HOOKAH AROUND?
WHAT'S IT TO YOU? I'M GOING TO SELL IT TO SOME TOURIST.
DO YOU NEED MONEY THAT BADLY?
I HOPE HE DOES. BETTER HOOKAHS THAN HASHISH.
SAVE YOUR SERMONS FOR YOUR NEWSPAPER, ALI. I'LL SEE YOU TWO LATER!
EH?
Ummm...
...HAL "INTERNATIONAL HOSTEL" HUNNA?

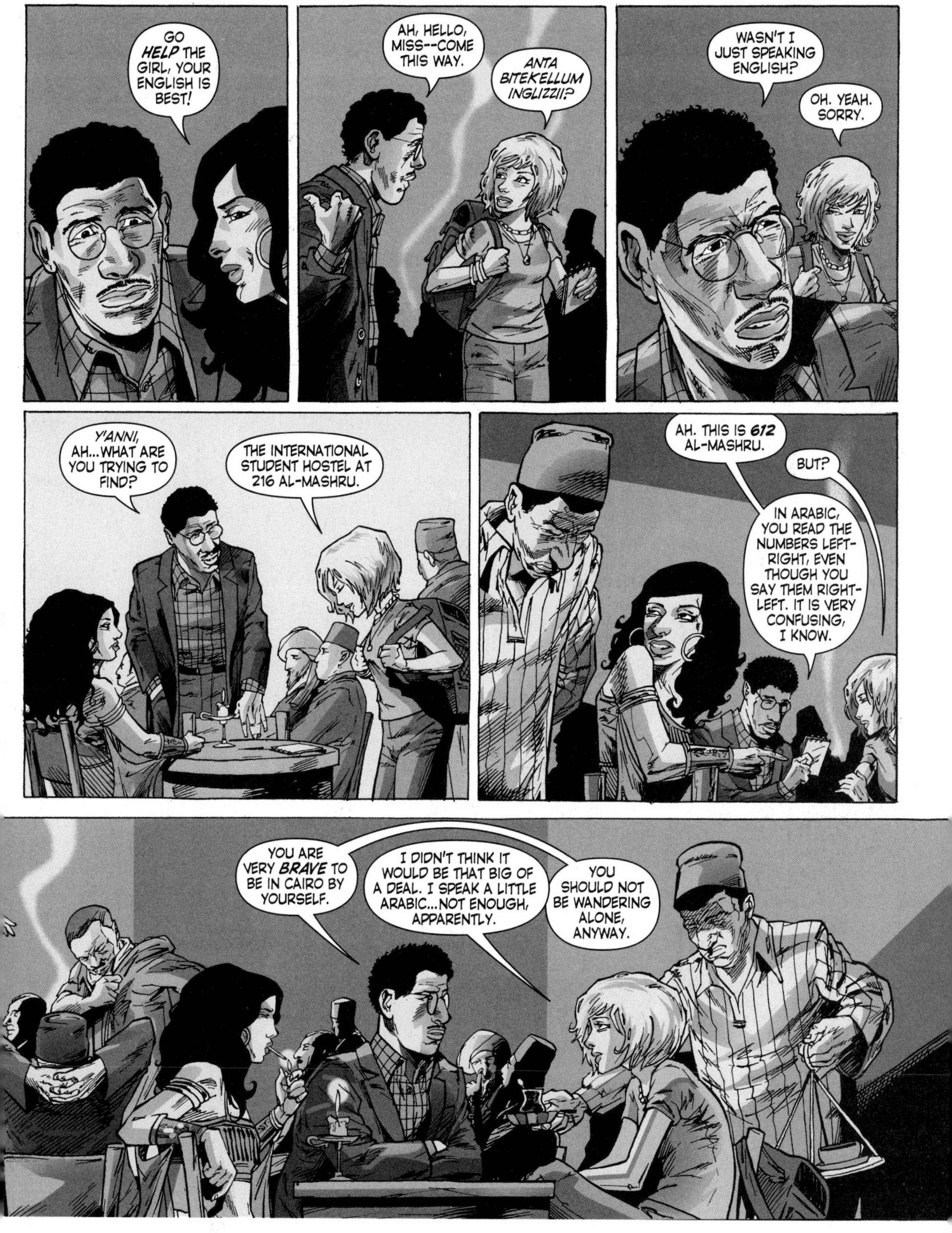
GO HELP THE GIRL, YOUR ENGLISH IS BEST!
AH, HELLO, MISS--COME THIS WAY.
ANTA BITEKELLUM INGLIZZII?
WASN'T I JUST SPEAKING ENGLISH?
OH. YEAH. SORRY.
Y'ANNI, AH...WHAT ARE YOU TRYING TO FIND?
THE INTERNATIONAL STUDENT HOSTEL AT 216 AL-MASHRU.
AH. THIS IS 612 AL-MASHRU.
BUT?
IN ARABIC, YOU READ THE NUMBERS LEFT-RIGHT, EVEN THOUGH YOU SAY THEM RIGHT-LEFT. IT IS VERY CONFUSING, I KNOW.
YOU ARE VERY BRAVE TO BE IN CAIRO BY YOURSELF.
I DIDN'T THINK IT WOULD BE THAT BIG OF A DEAL. I SPEAK A LITTLE ARABIC...NOT ENOUGH, APPARENTLY.
YOU SHOULD NOT BE WANDERING ALONE, ANYWAY.

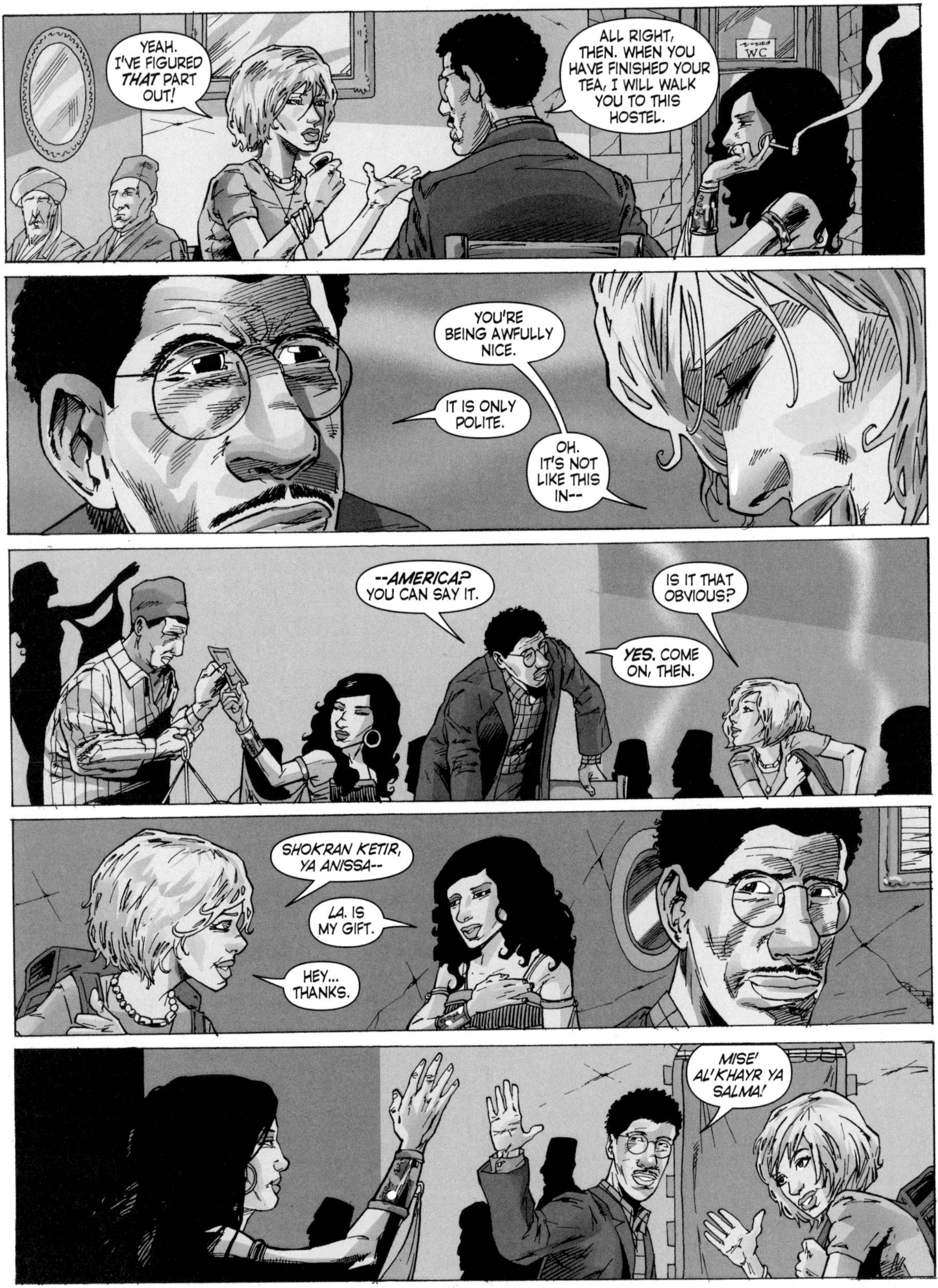
YEAH. I'VE FIGURED *THAT* PART OUT!
ALL RIGHT, THEN. WHEN YOU HAVE FINISHED YOUR TEA, I WILL WALK YOU TO THIS HOSTEL.
WC
YOU'RE BEING AWFULLY NICE.
IT IS ONLY POLITE.
OH. IT'S NOT LIKE THIS IN--
--AMERICA? YOU CAN SAY IT.
IS IT THAT OBVIOUS?
YES. COME ON, THEN.
SHOKRAN KETIR, YA ANISSA--
LA. IS MY GIFT.
HEY... THANKS.
MISE' AL'KHAYR YA SALMA!

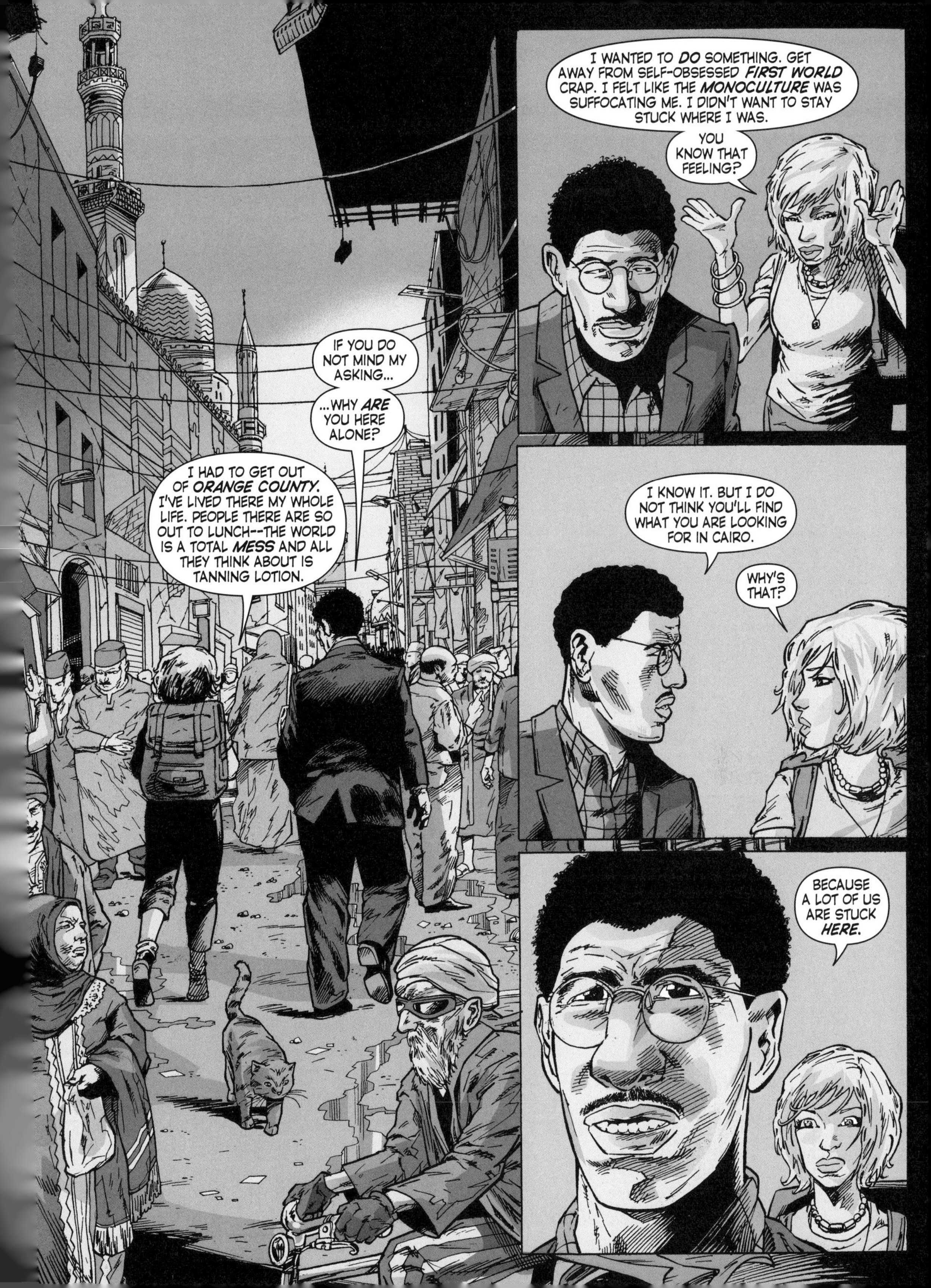
IF YOU DO NOT MIND MY ASKING...
...WHY ARE YOU HERE ALONE?
I HAD TO GET OUT OF ORANGE COUNTY. I'VE LIVED THERE MY WHOLE LIFE. PEOPLE THERE ARE SO OUT TO LUNCH--THE WORLD IS A TOTAL MESS AND ALL THEY THINK ABOUT IS TANNING LOTION.
I WANTED TO DO SOMETHING. GET AWAY FROM SELF-OBSESSED FIRST WORLD CRAP. I FELT LIKE THE MONOCULTURE WAS SUFFOCATING ME. I DIDN'T WANT TO STAY STUCK WHERE I WAS.
YOU KNOW THAT FEELING?
I KNOW IT. BUT I DO NOT THINK YOU'LL FIND WHAT YOU ARE LOOKING FOR IN CAIRO.
WHY'S THAT?
BECAUSE A LOT OF US ARE STUCK HERE.

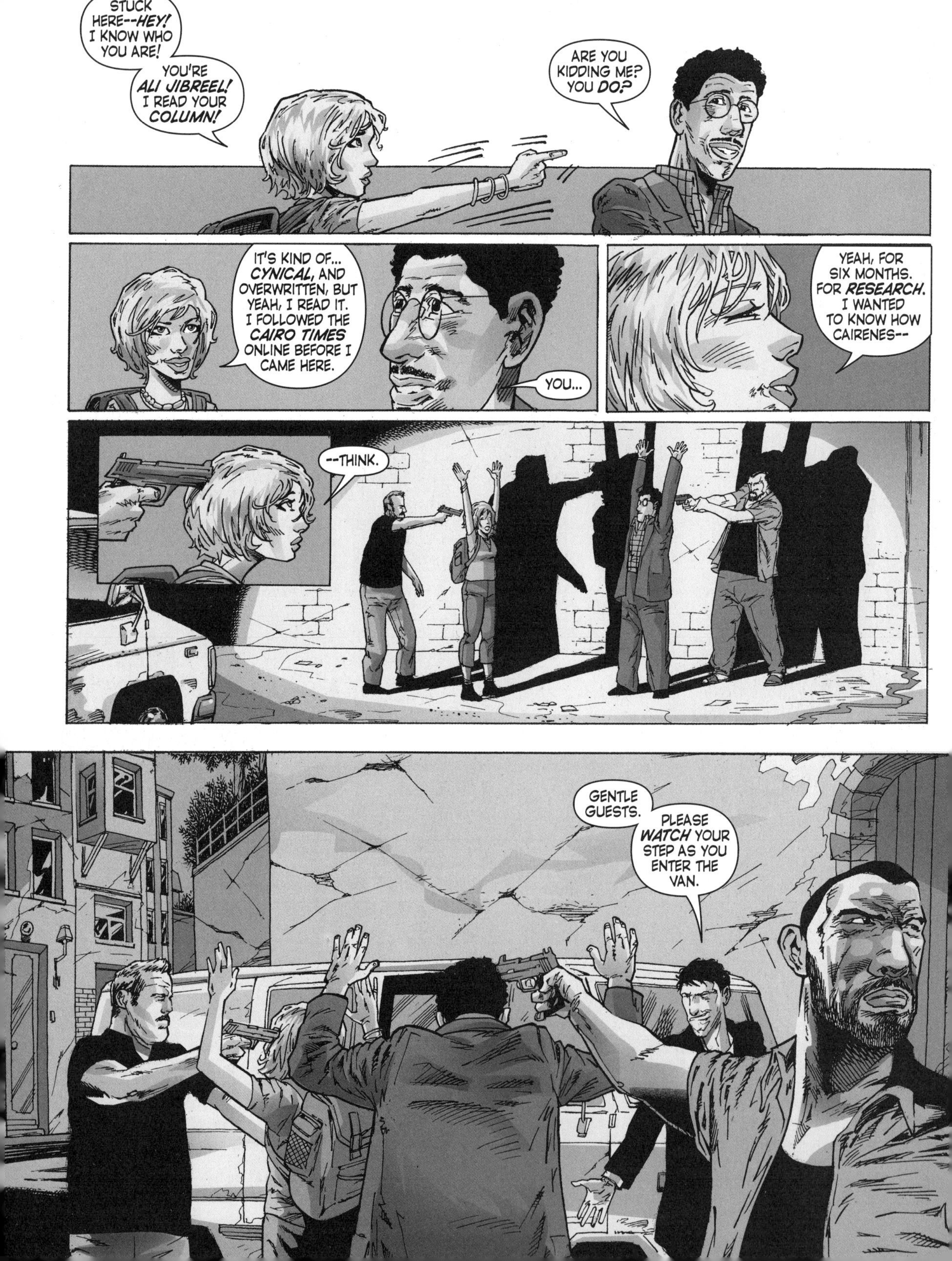

STUCK HERE--HEY! I KNOW WHO YOU ARE!
YOU'RE ALI JIBREEL! I READ YOUR COLUMN!
ARE YOU KIDDING ME? YOU DO?
IT'S KIND OF... CYNICAL, AND OVERWRITTEN, BUT YEAH, I READ IT. I FOLLOWED THE CAIRO TIMES ONLINE BEFORE I CAME HERE.
YOU...
YEAH, FOR SIX MONTHS. FOR RESEARCH. I WANTED TO KNOW HOW CAIRENES--
--THINK.
GENTLE GUESTS.
PLEASE WATCH YOUR STEP AS YOU ENTER THE VAN.

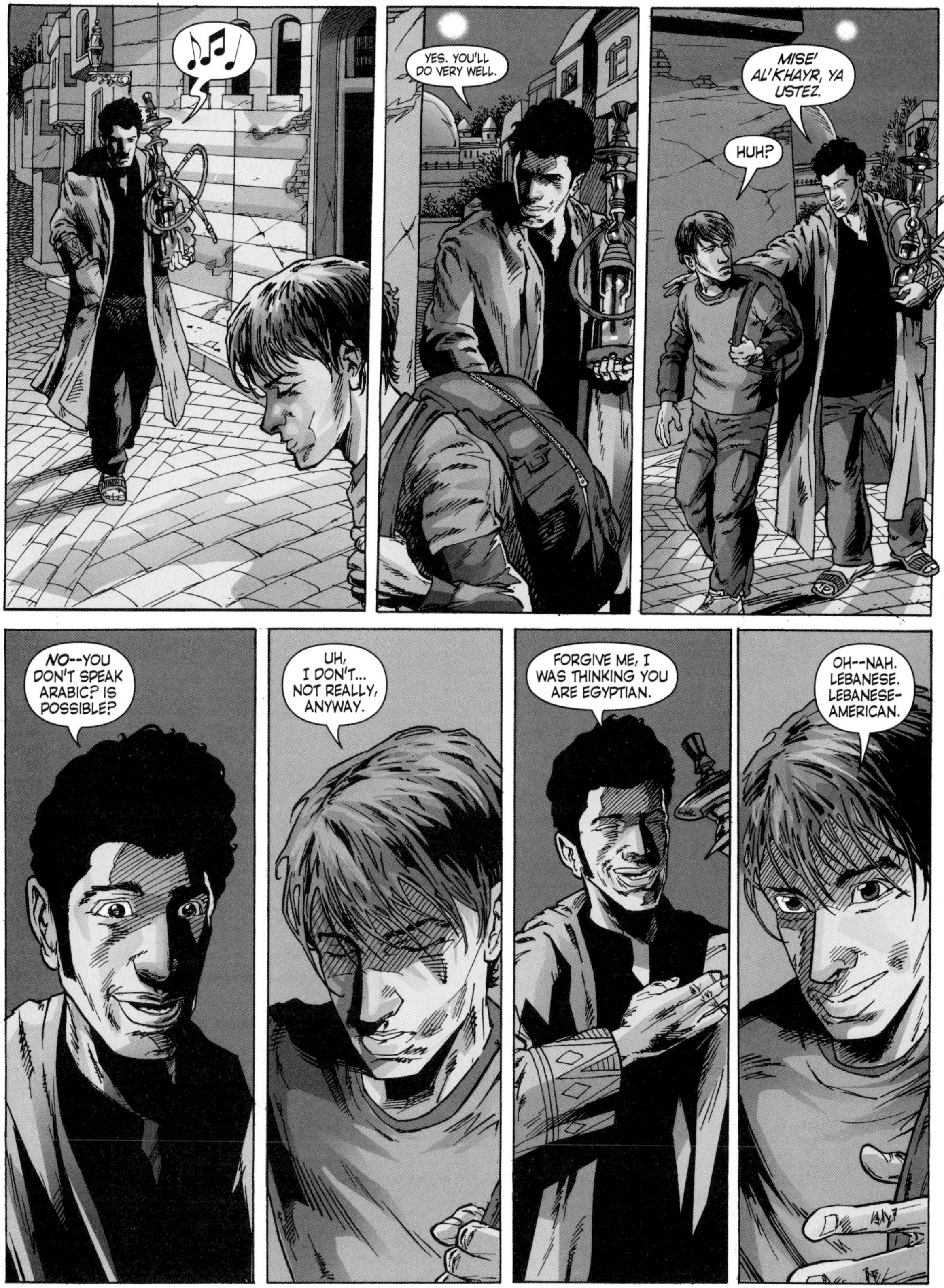
YES. YOU'LL DO VERY WELL.
MISE' AL'KHAYR, YA USTEZ.
HUH?
NO--YOU DON'T SPEAK ARABIC? IS POSSIBLE?
UH, I DON'T... NOT REALLY, ANYWAY.
FORGIVE ME, I WAS THINKING YOU ARE EGYPTIAN.
OH--NAH. LEBANESE. LEBANESE-AMERICAN.

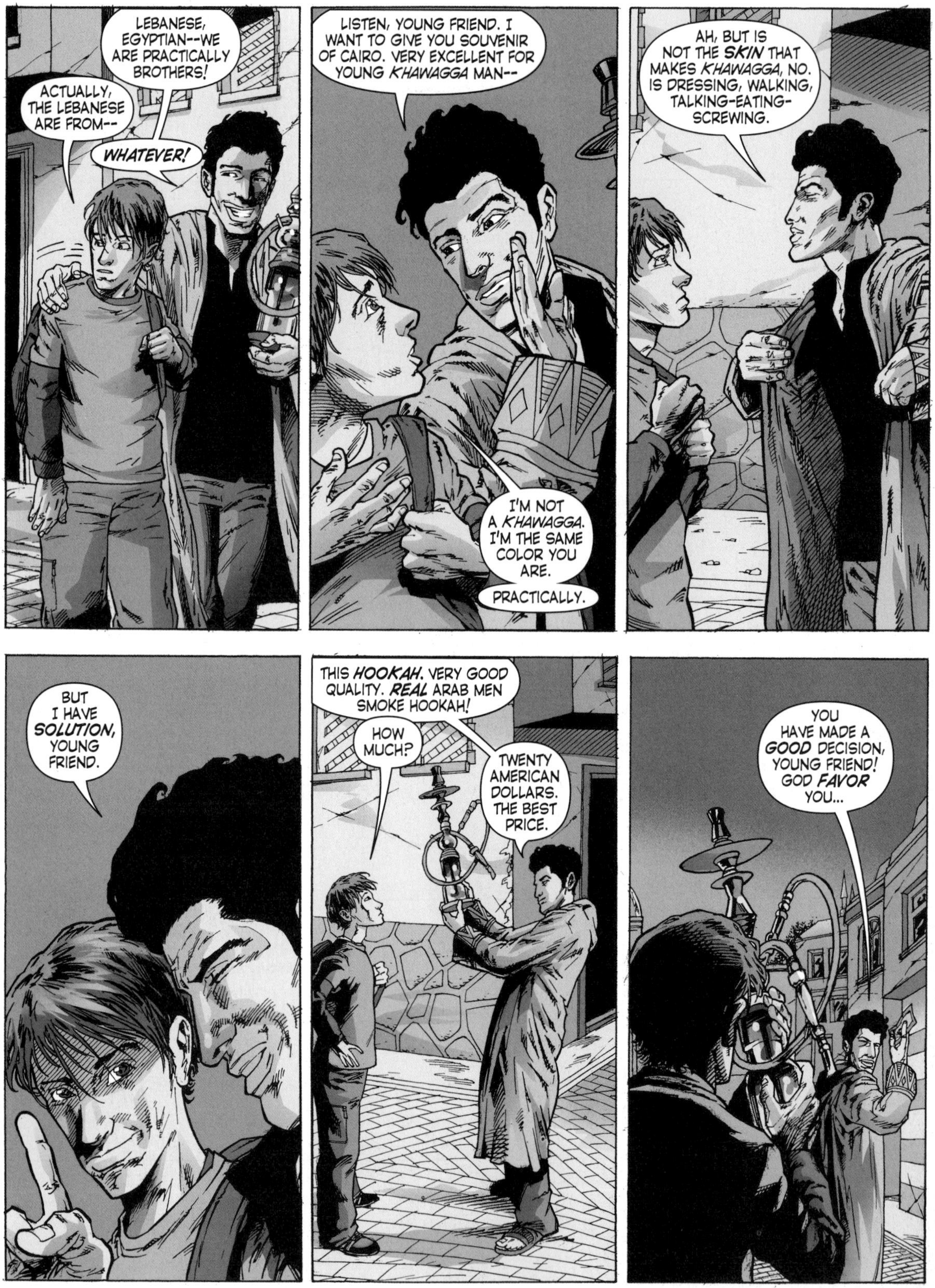
LEBANESE, EGYPTIAN--WE ARE PRACTICALLY BROTHERS!
ACTUALLY, THE LEBANESE ARE FROM--
WHATEVER!
LISTEN, YOUNG FRIEND. I WANT TO GIVE YOU SOUVENIR OF CAIRO. VERY EXCELLENT FOR YOUNG KHAWAGGA MAN--
I'M NOT A KHAWAGGA. I'M THE SAME COLOR YOU ARE.
PRACTICALLY.
AH, BUT IS NOT THE SKIN THAT MAKES KHAWAGGA, NO. IS DRESSING, WALKING, TALKING-EATING-SCREWING.
BUT I HAVE SOLUTION, YOUNG FRIEND.
THIS HOOKAH. VERY GOOD QUALITY. REAL ARAB MEN SMOKE HOOKAH!
HOW MUCH?
TWENTY AMERICAN DOLLARS. THE BEST PRICE.
YOU HAVE MADE A GOOD DECISION, YOUNG FRIEND! GOD FAVOR YOU...

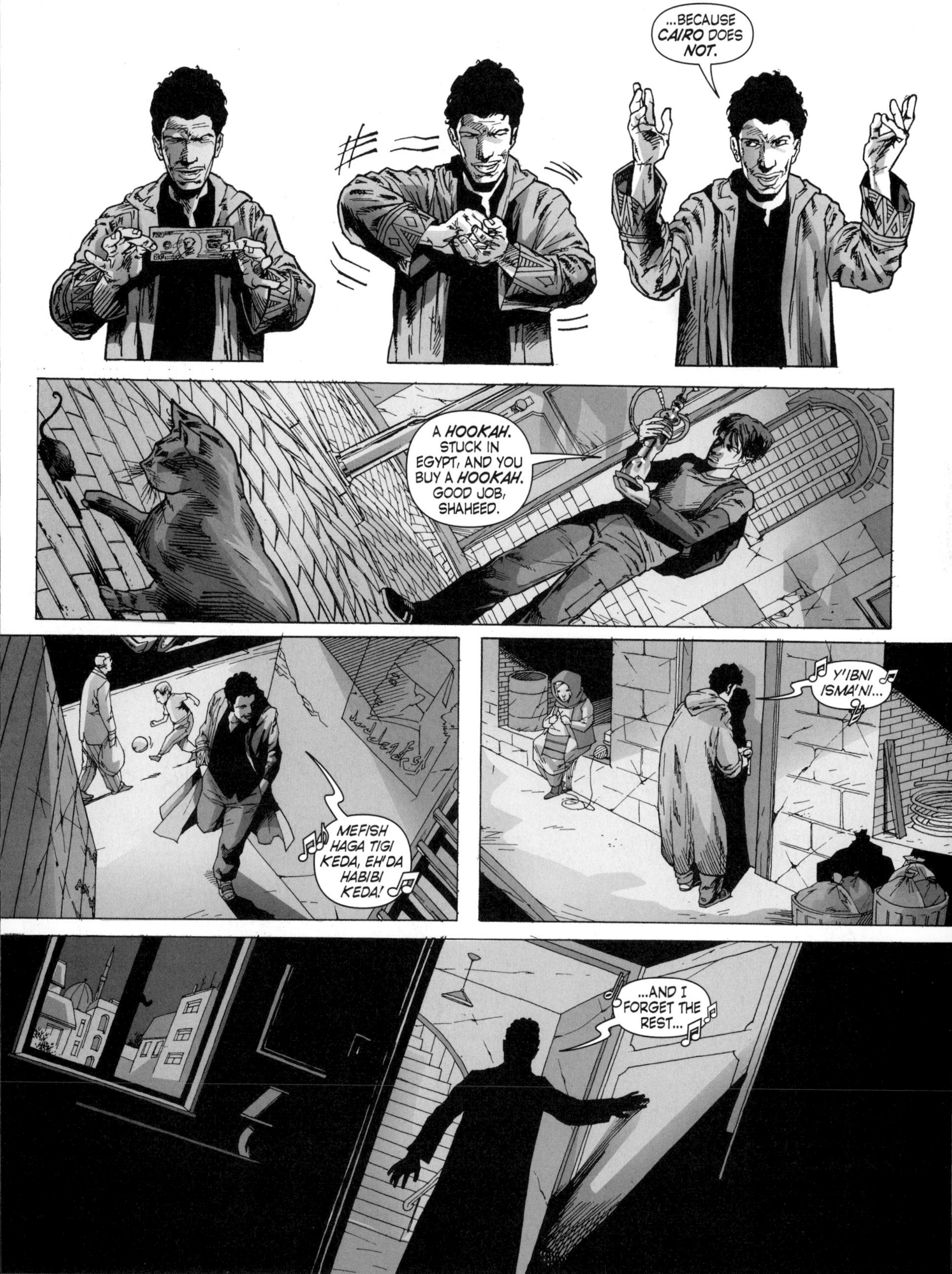
...BECAUSE CAIRO DOES NOT.
A HOOKAH. STUCK IN EGYPT, AND YOU BUY A HOOKAH. GOOD JOB, SHAHEED.
MEFISH HAGA TIGI KEDA, EH'DA HABIBI KEDA!
Y'IBNI ISMA'NI...
...AND I FORGET THE REST...

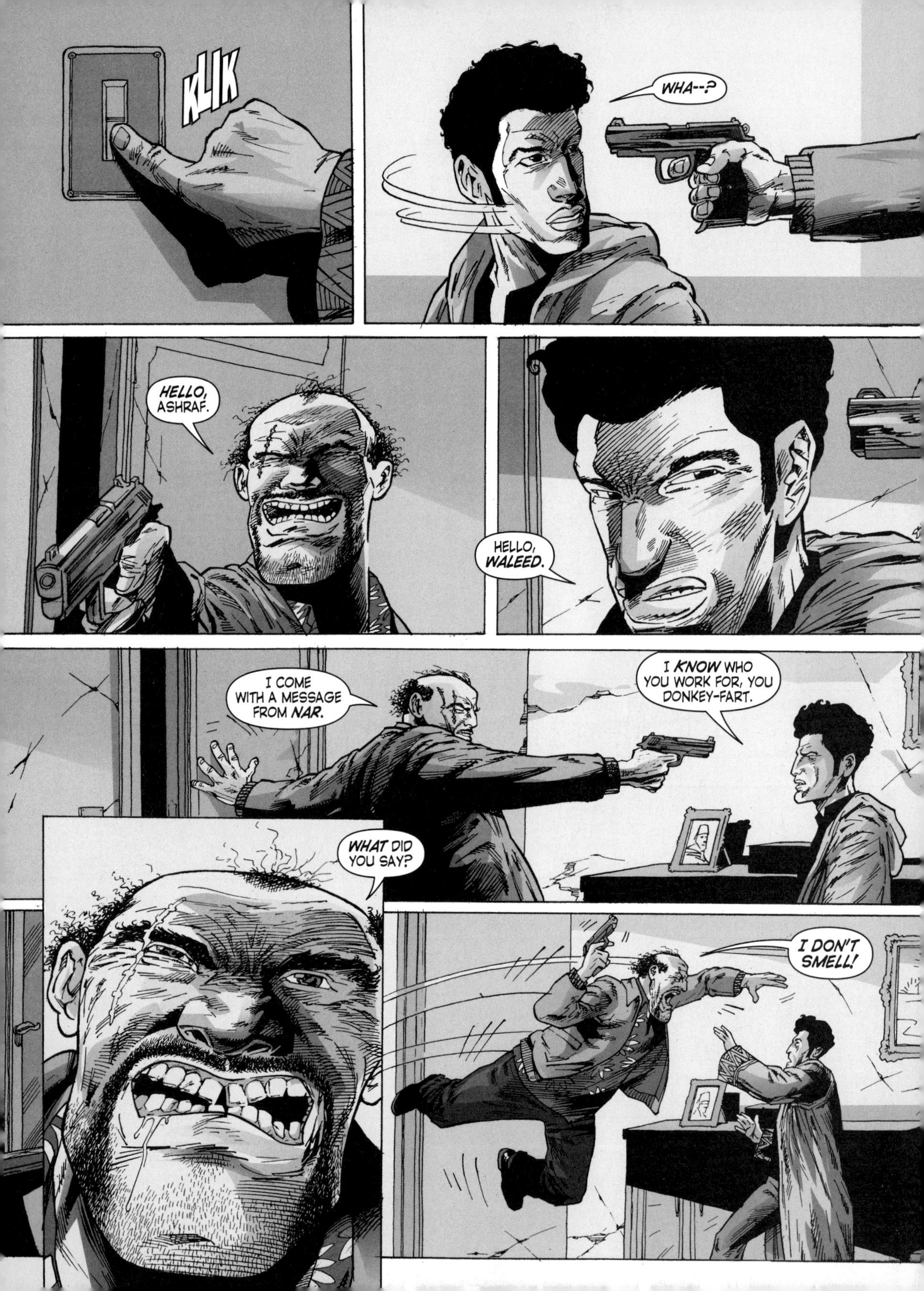
KLIK
WHA--?
HELLO, ASHRAF.
HELLO, WALEED.
I COME WITH A MESSAGE FROM NAR.
I KNOW WHO YOU WORK FOR, YOU DONKEY-FART.
WHAT DID YOU SAY?
I DON'T SMELL!

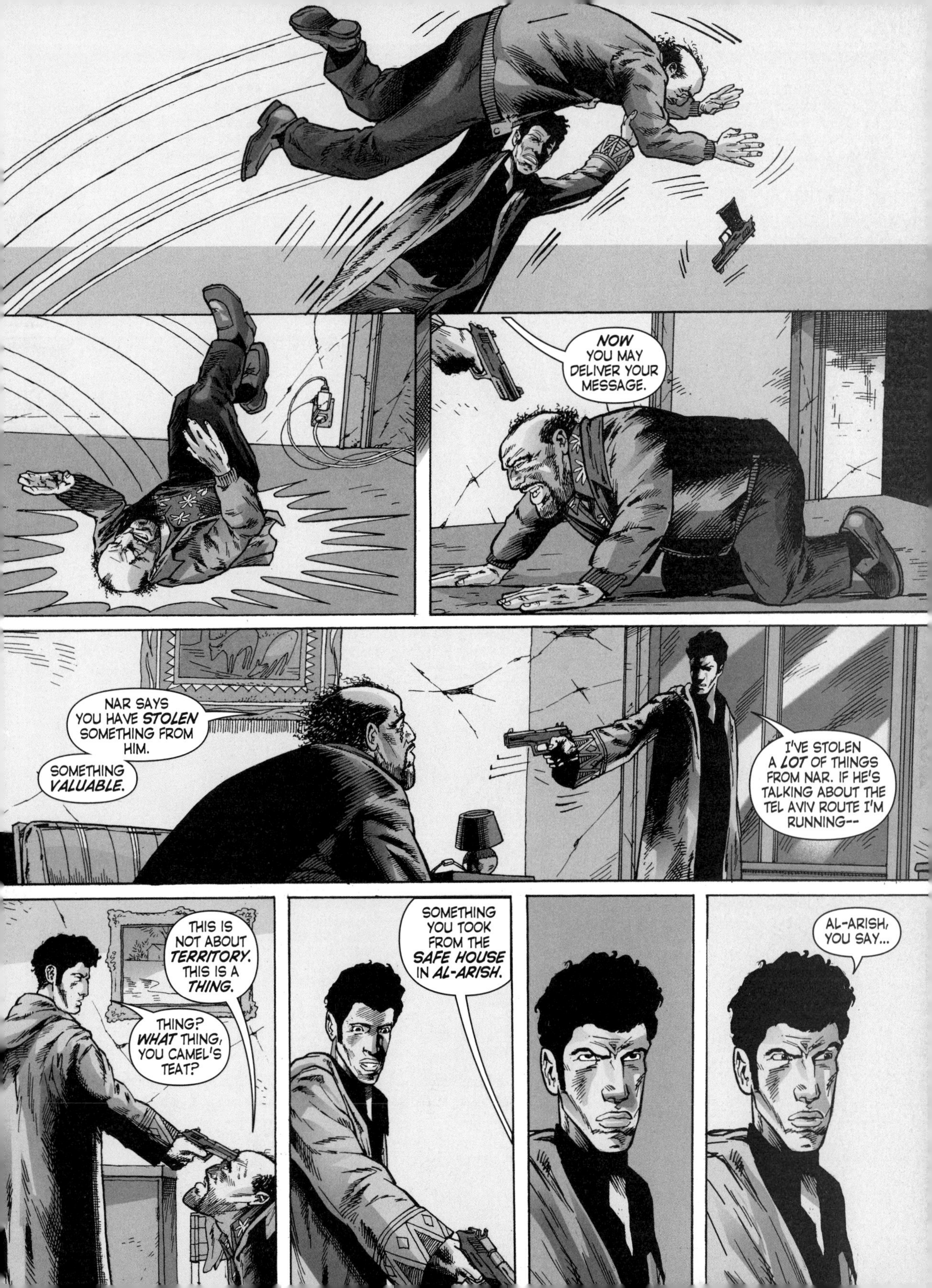
NOW YOU MAY DELIVER YOUR MESSAGE.
NAR SAYS YOU HAVE STOLEN SOMETHING FROM HIM.
SOMETHING VALUABLE.
I'VE STOLEN A LOT OF THINGS FROM NAR. IF HE'S TALKING ABOUT THE TEL AVIV ROUTE I'M RUNNING--
THIS IS NOT ABOUT TERRITORY. THIS IS A THING.
THING? WHAT THING, YOU CAMEL'S TEAT?
SOMETHING YOU TOOK FROM THE SAFE HOUSE IN AL-ARISH.
AL-ARISH, YOU SAY...

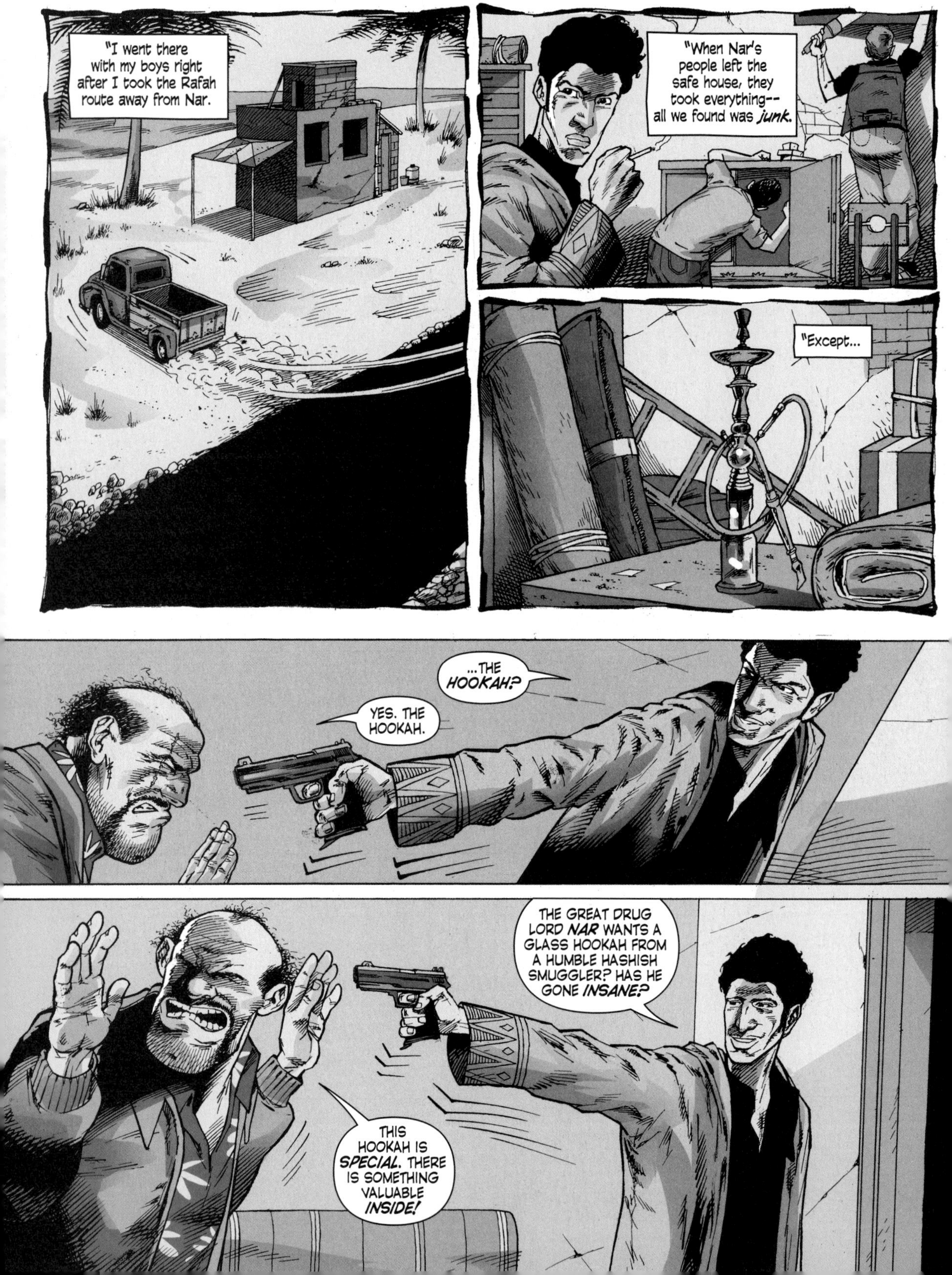
"I went there with my boys right after I took the Rafah route away from Nar.
"When Nar's people left the safe house, they took everything--all we found was *junk.*
"Except...
...THE *HOOKAH?*
YES. THE HOOKAH.
THE GREAT DRUG LORD *NAR* WANTS A GLASS HOOKAH FROM A HUMBLE HASHISH SMUGGLER? HAS HE GONE *INSANE?*
THIS HOOKAH IS *SPECIAL.* THERE IS SOMETHING VALUABLE *INSIDE!*

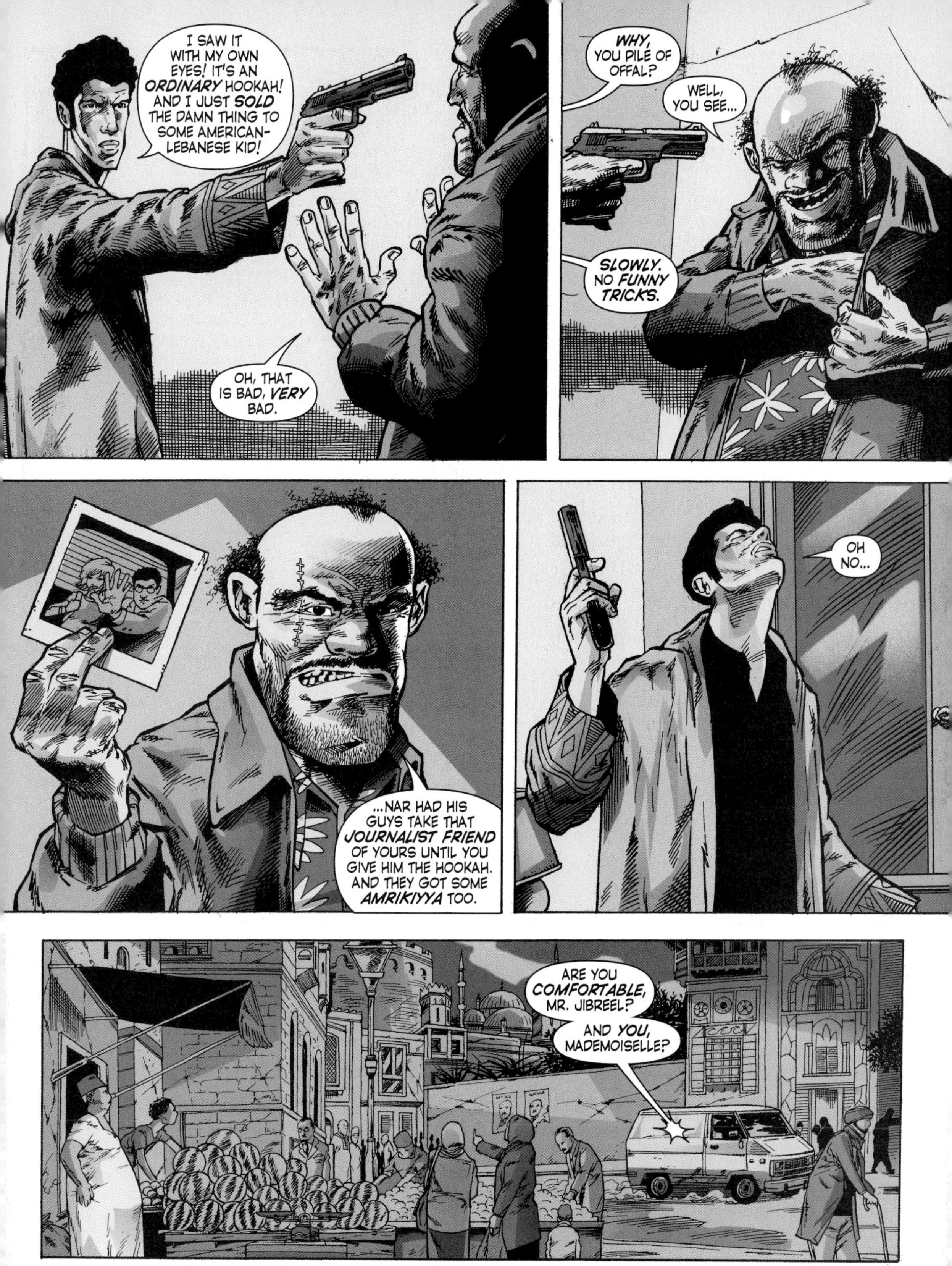
I SAW IT WITH MY OWN EYES! IT'S AN ORDINARY HOOKAH! AND I JUST SOLD THE DAMN THING TO SOME AMERICAN-LEBANESE KID!
OH, THAT IS BAD, VERY BAD.
WHY, YOU PILE OF OFFAL?
WELL, YOU SEE...
SLOWLY. NO FUNNY TRICKS.
...NAR HAD HIS GUYS TAKE THAT JOURNALIST FRIEND OF YOURS UNTIL YOU GIVE HIM THE HOOKAH. AND THEY GOT SOME AMRIKIYYA TOO.
OH NO...
ARE YOU COMFORTABLE, MR. JIBREEL?
AND YOU, MADEMOISELLE?

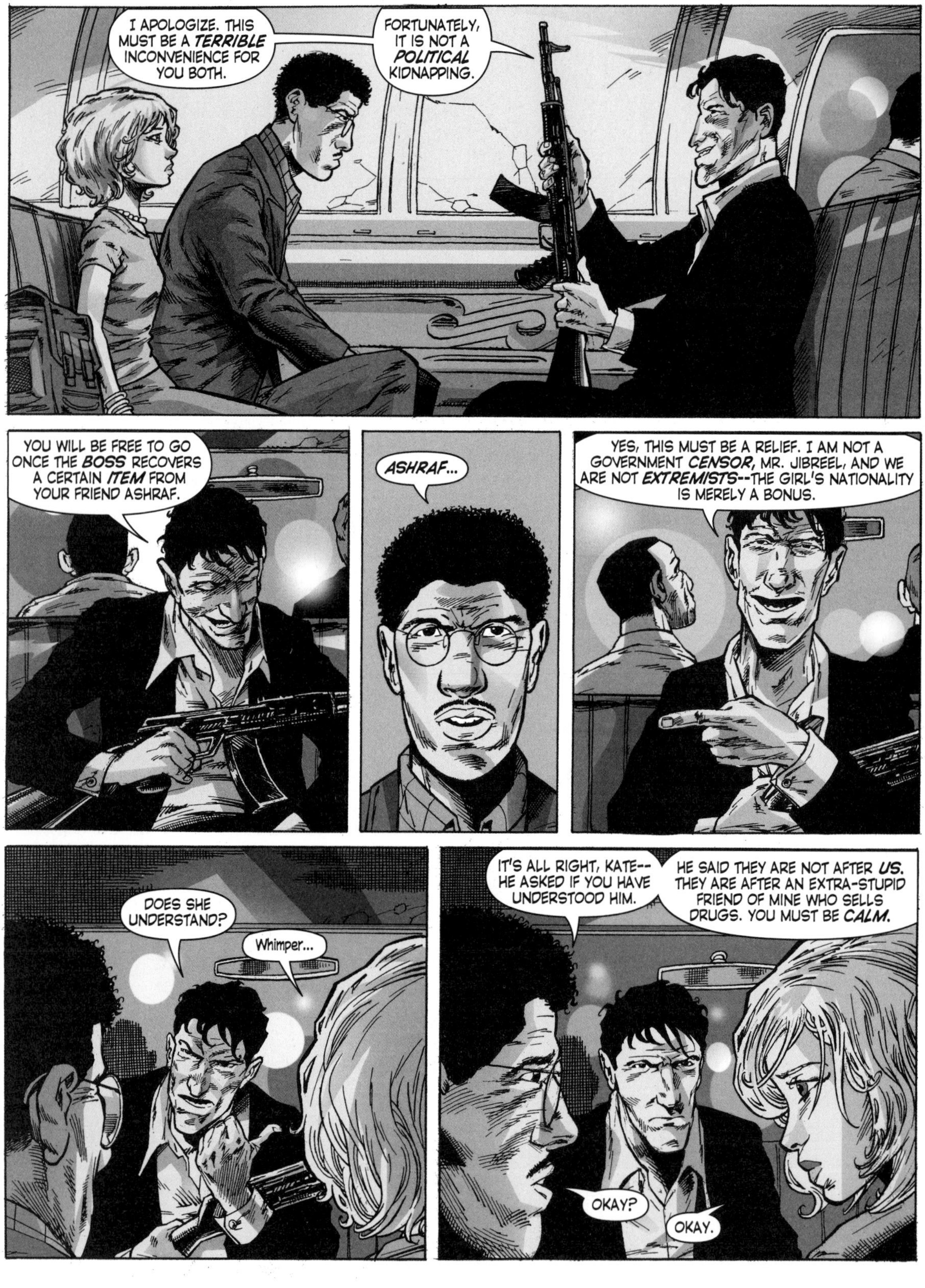
I APOLOGIZE. THIS MUST BE A TERRIBLE INCONVENIENCE FOR YOU BOTH.
FORTUNATELY, IT IS NOT A POLITICAL KIDNAPPING.
YOU WILL BE FREE TO GO ONCE THE BOSS RECOVERS A CERTAIN ITEM FROM YOUR FRIEND ASHRAF.
ASHRAF...
YES, THIS MUST BE A RELIEF. I AM NOT A GOVERNMENT CENSOR, MR. JIBREEL, AND WE ARE NOT EXTREMISTS--THE GIRL'S NATIONALITY IS MERELY A BONUS.
DOES SHE UNDERSTAND?
Whimper...
IT'S ALL RIGHT, KATE--HE ASKED IF YOU HAVE UNDERSTOOD HIM.
HE SAID THEY ARE NOT AFTER US. THEY ARE AFTER AN EXTRA-STUPID FRIEND OF MINE WHO SELLS DRUGS. YOU MUST BE CALM.
OKAY?
OKAY.

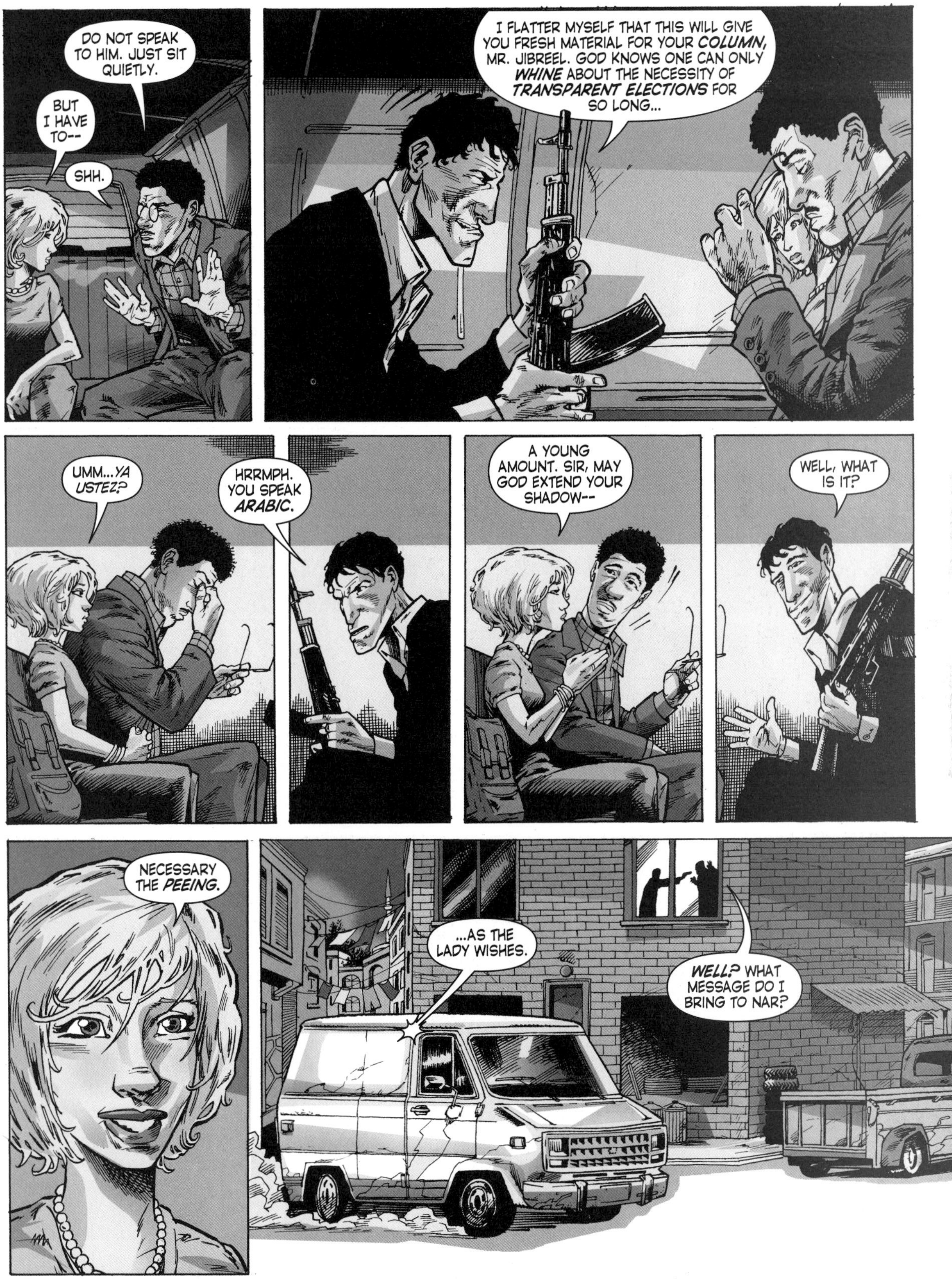
DO NOT SPEAK TO HIM. JUST SIT QUIETLY.
BUT I HAVE TO--
SHH.
I FLATTER MYSELF THAT THIS WILL GIVE YOU FRESH MATERIAL FOR YOUR COLUMN, MR. JIBREEL. GOD KNOWS ONE CAN ONLY WHINE ABOUT THE NECESSITY OF TRANSPARENT ELECTIONS FOR SO LONG...
UMM...YA USTEZ?
HRRMPH. YOU SPEAK ARABIC.
A YOUNG AMOUNT. SIR, MAY GOD EXTEND YOUR SHADOW--
WELL, WHAT IS IT?
NECESSARY THE PEEING.
...AS THE LADY WISHES.
WELL? WHAT MESSAGE DO I BRING TO NAR?

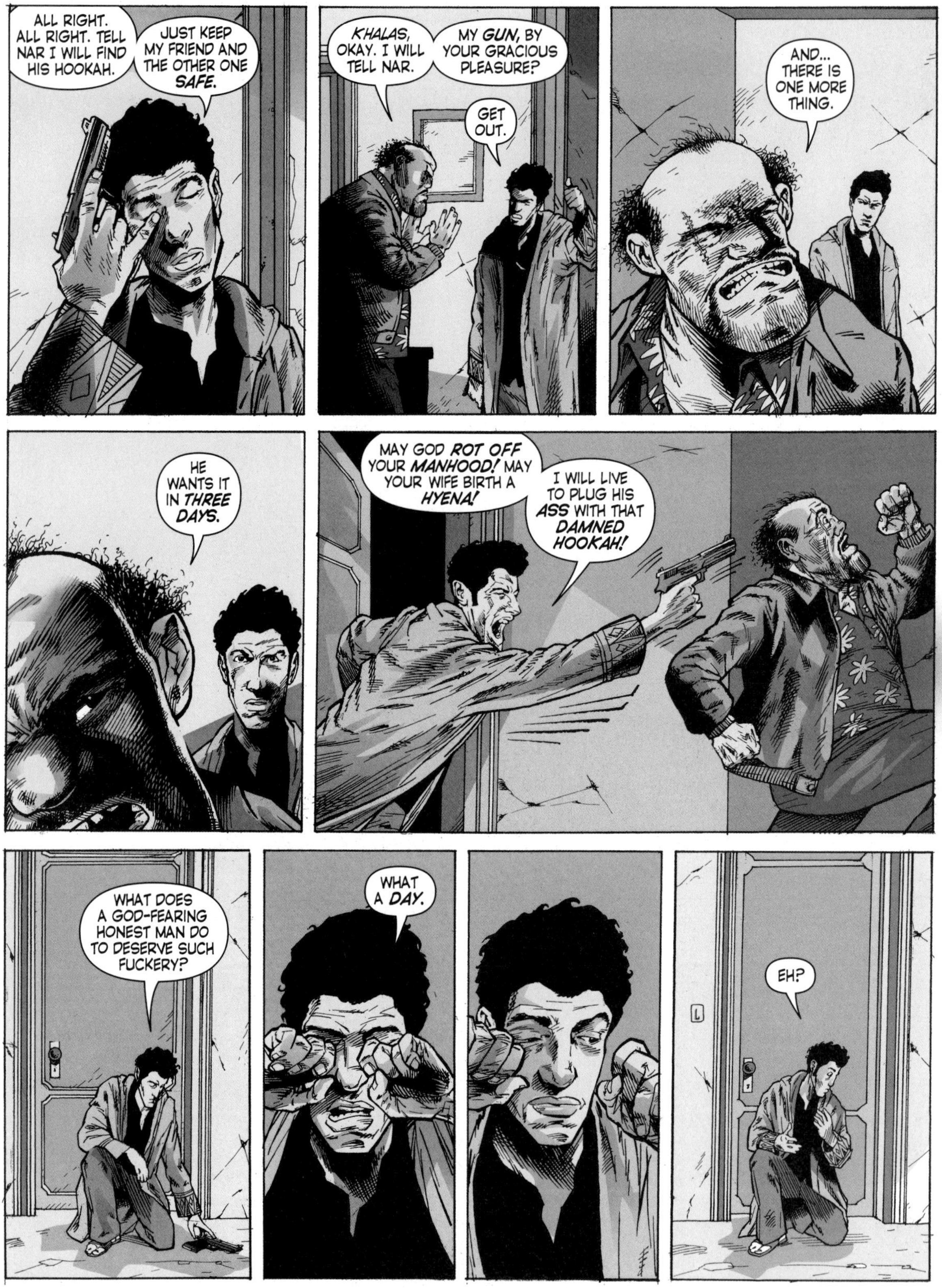
ALL RIGHT. ALL RIGHT. TELL NAR I WILL FIND HIS HOOKAH.
JUST KEEP MY FRIEND AND THE OTHER ONE SAFE.
KHALAS, OKAY. I WILL TELL NAR.
MY GUN, BY YOUR GRACIOUS PLEASURE?
GET OUT.
AND... THERE IS ONE MORE THING.
HE WANTS IT IN THREE DAYS.
MAY GOD ROT OFF YOUR MANHOOD! MAY YOUR WIFE BIRTH A HYENA!
I WILL LIVE TO PLUG HIS ASS WITH THAT DAMNED HOOKAH!
WHAT DOES A GOD-FEARING HONEST MAN DO TO DESERVE SUCH FUCKERY?
WHAT A DAY.
EH?

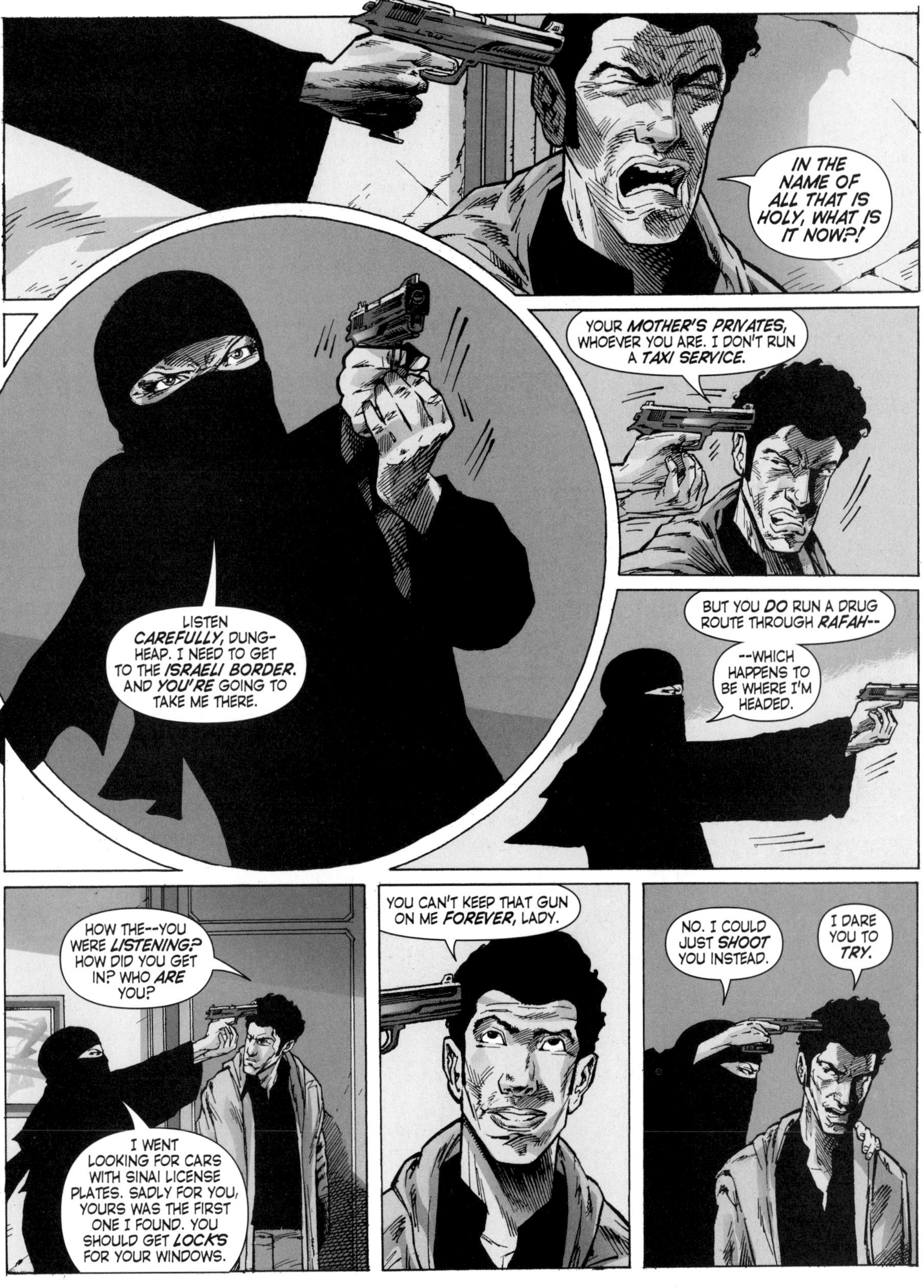
IN THE NAME OF ALL THAT IS HOLY, WHAT IS IT NOW?!
LISTEN CAREFULLY, DUNG-HEAP. I NEED TO GET TO THE ISRAELI BORDER. AND YOU'RE GOING TO TAKE ME THERE.
YOUR MOTHER'S PRIVATES, WHOEVER YOU ARE. I DON'T RUN A TAXI SERVICE.
BUT YOU DO RUN A DRUG ROUTE THROUGH RAFAH--
--WHICH HAPPENS TO BE WHERE I'M HEADED.
HOW THE--YOU WERE LISTENING? HOW DID YOU GET IN? WHO ARE YOU?
I WENT LOOKING FOR CARS WITH SINAI LICENSE PLATES. SADLY FOR YOU, YOURS WAS THE FIRST ONE I FOUND. YOU SHOULD GET LOCKS FOR YOUR WINDOWS.
YOU CAN'T KEEP THAT GUN ON ME FOREVER, LADY.
NO. I COULD JUST SHOOT YOU INSTEAD.
I DARE YOU TO TRY.

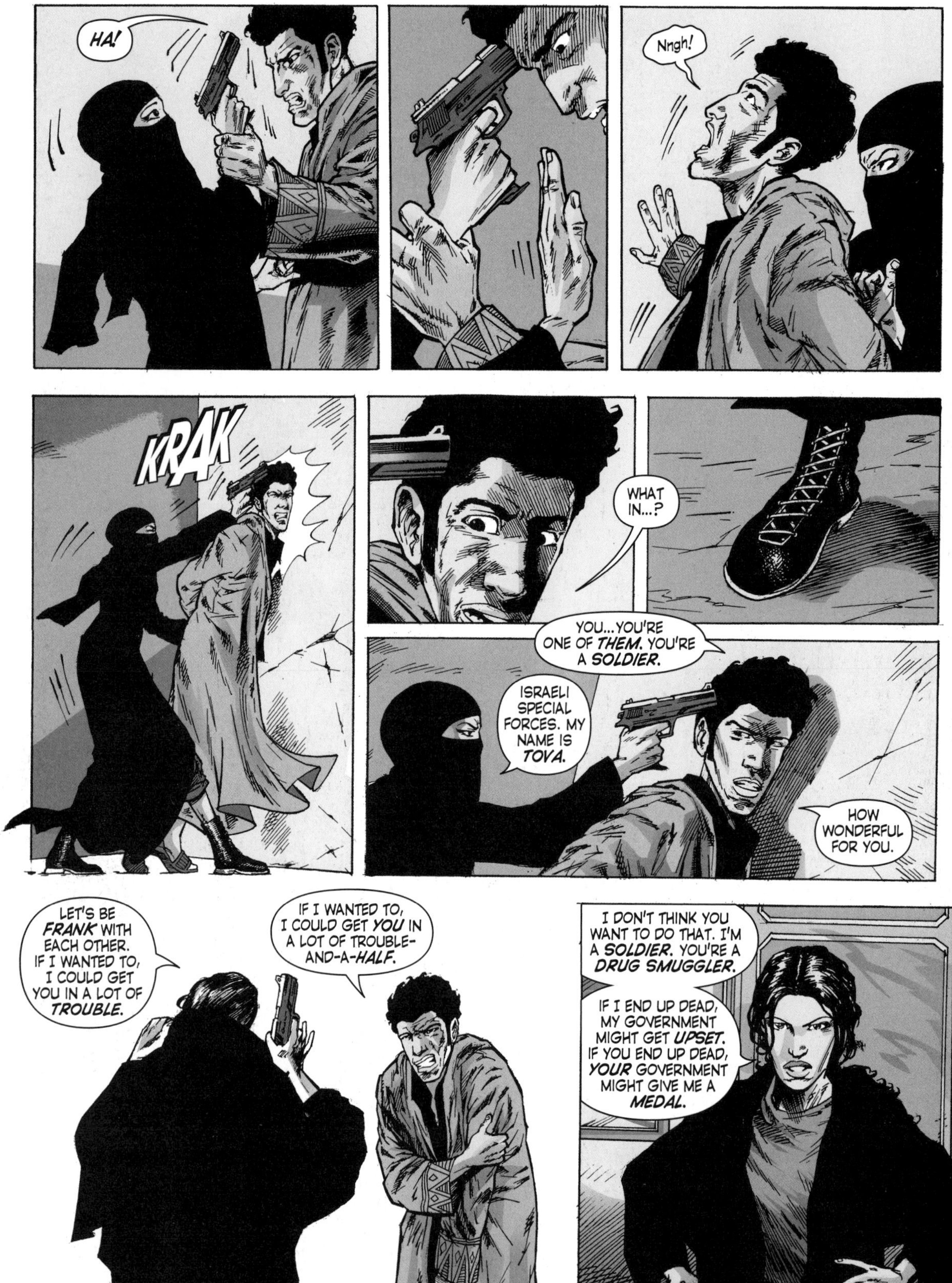
HA!
Nngh!
KRAK
WHAT IN...?
YOU...YOU'RE ONE OF THEM. YOU'RE A SOLDIER.
ISRAELI SPECIAL FORCES. MY NAME IS TOVA.
HOW WONDERFUL FOR YOU.
LET'S BE FRANK WITH EACH OTHER. IF I WANTED TO, I COULD GET YOU IN A LOT OF TROUBLE.
IF I WANTED TO, I COULD GET YOU IN A LOT OF TROUBLE-AND-A-HALF.
I DON'T THINK YOU WANT TO DO THAT. I'M A SOLDIER. YOU'RE A DRUG SMUGGLER.
IF I END UP DEAD, MY GOVERNMENT MIGHT GET UPSET. IF YOU END UP DEAD, YOUR GOVERNMENT MIGHT GIVE ME A MEDAL.

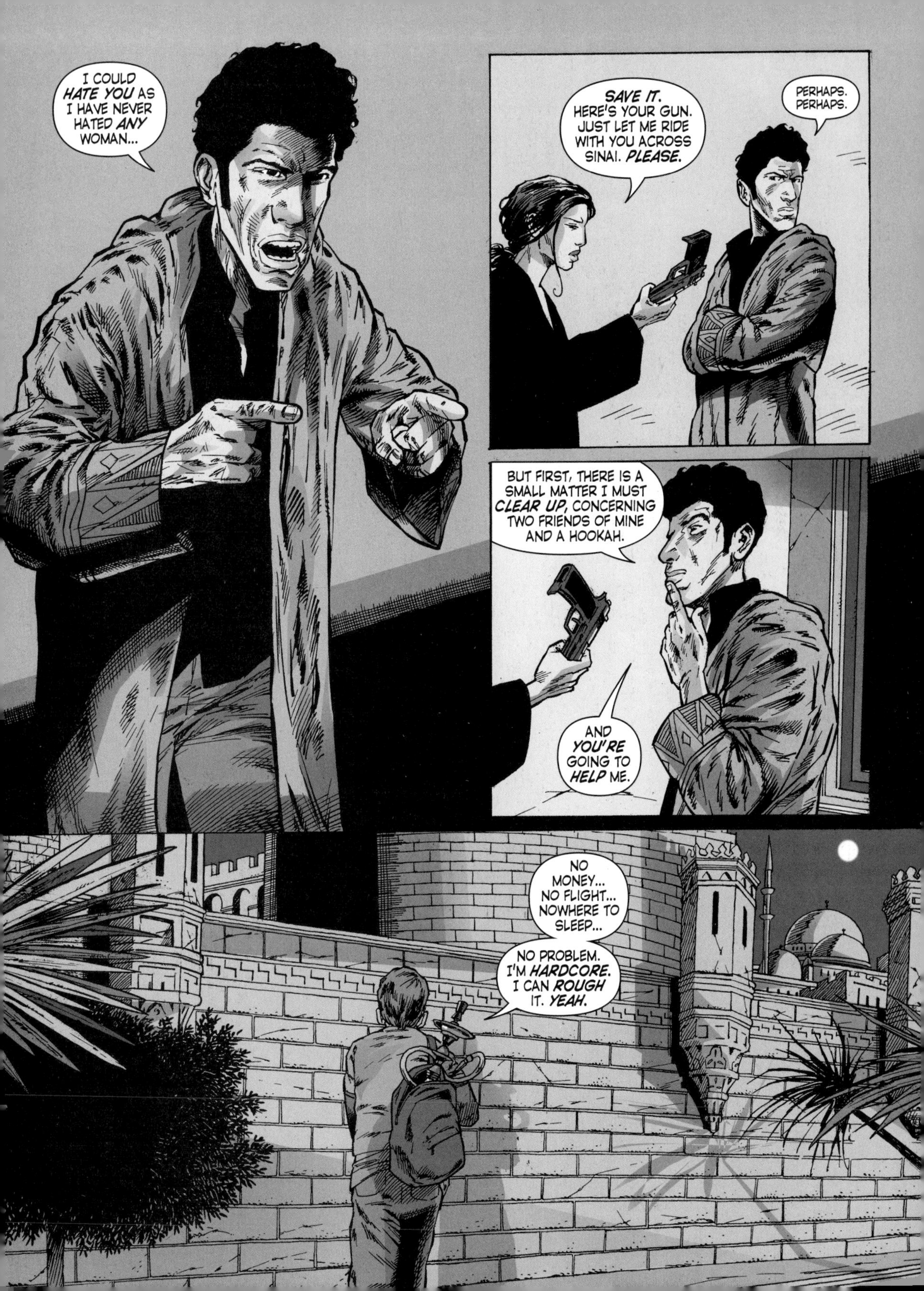
I COULD HATE YOU AS I HAVE NEVER HATED ANY WOMAN...
SAVE IT. HERE'S YOUR GUN. JUST LET ME RIDE WITH YOU ACROSS SINAI. PLEASE.
PERHAPS. PERHAPS.
BUT FIRST, THERE IS A SMALL MATTER I MUST CLEAR UP, CONCERNING TWO FRIENDS OF MINE AND A HOOKAH.
AND YOU'RE GOING TO HELP ME.
NO MONEY... NO FLIGHT... NOWHERE TO SLEEP...
NO PROBLEM. I'M HARDCORE. I CAN ROUGH IT. YEAH.

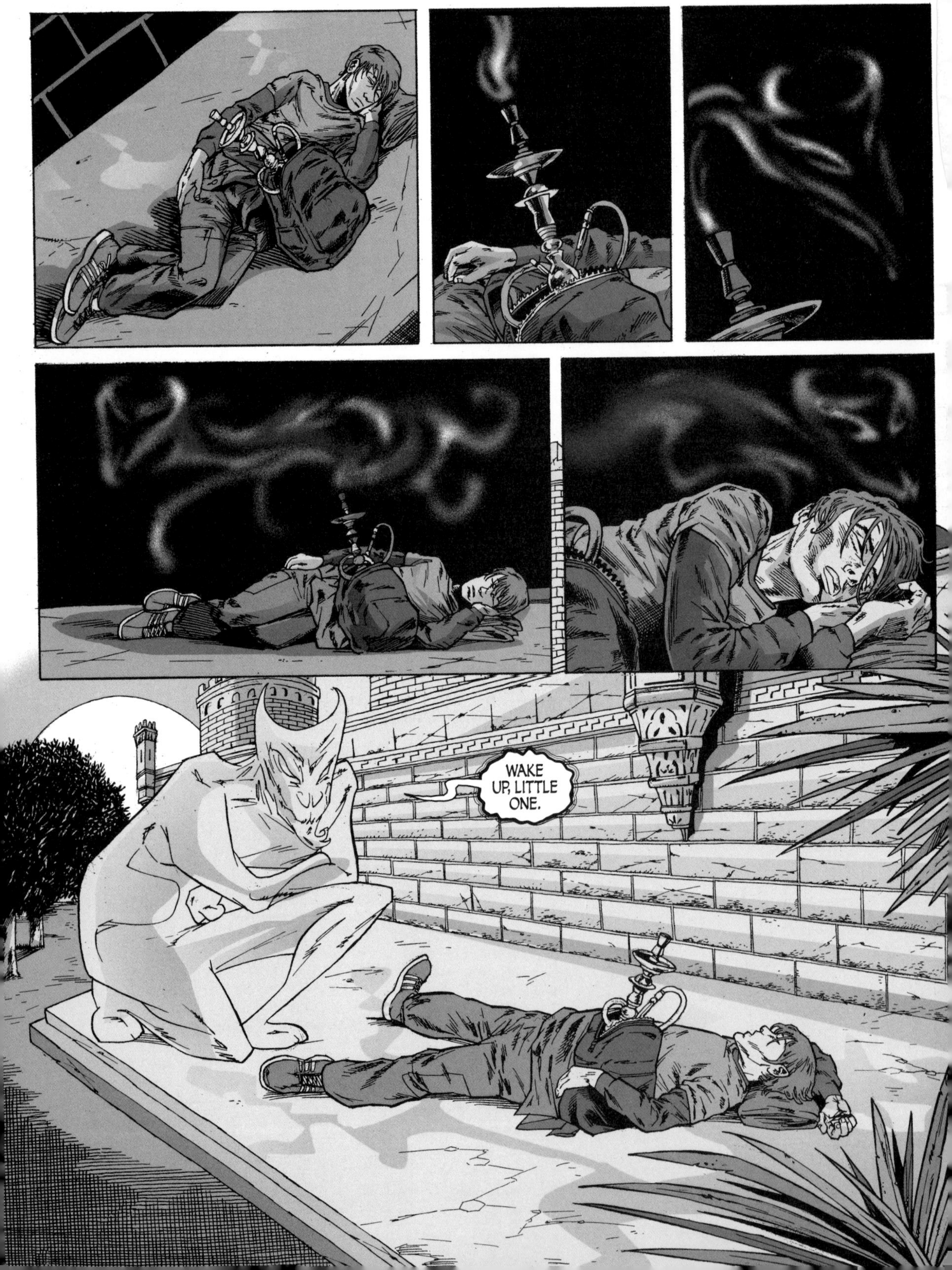
WAKE UP, LITTLE ONE.

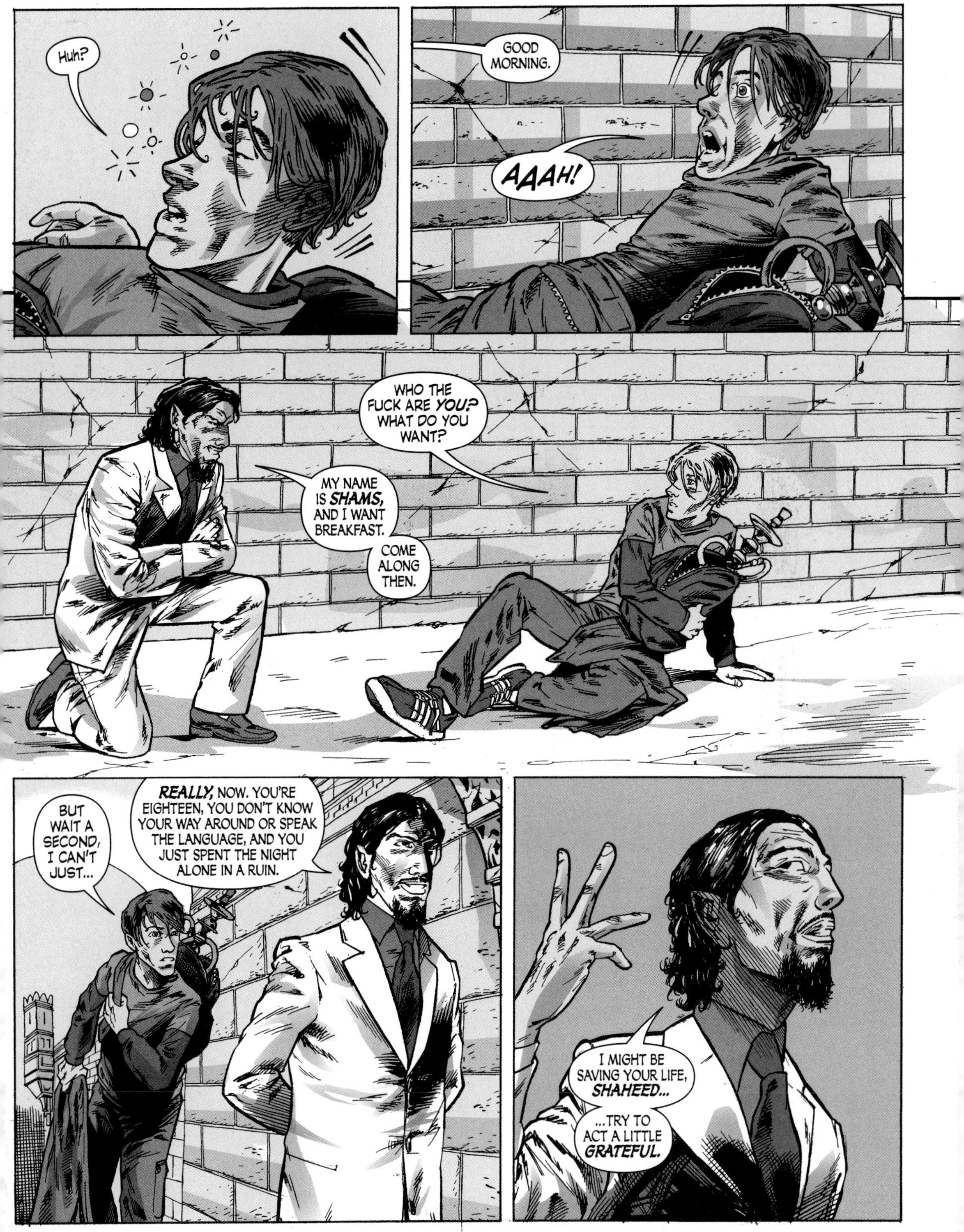
Huh?
GOOD MORNING.
AAAH!
WHO THE FUCK ARE YOU? WHAT DO YOU WANT?
MY NAME IS SHAMS, AND I WANT BREAKFAST.
COME ALONG THEN.
BUT WAIT A SECOND, I CAN'T JUST...
REALLY, NOW. YOU'RE EIGHTEEN, YOU DON'T KNOW YOUR WAY AROUND OR SPEAK THE LANGUAGE, AND YOU JUST SPENT THE NIGHT ALONE IN A RUIN.
I MIGHT BE SAVING YOUR LIFE, SHAHEED...
...TRY TO ACT A LITTLE GRATEFUL.

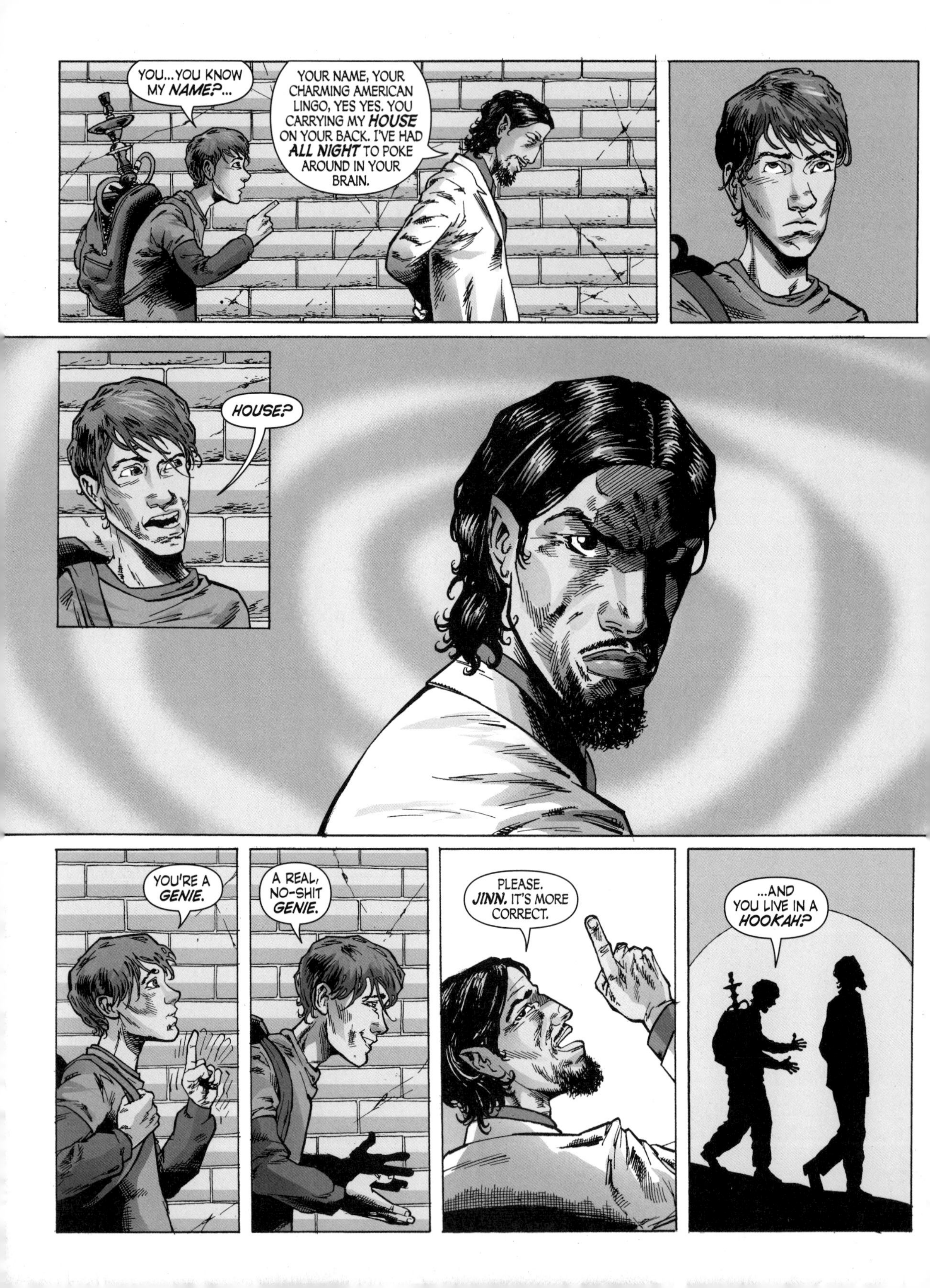
YOU...YOU KNOW MY NAME?...
YOUR NAME, YOUR CHARMING AMERICAN LINGO, YES YES. YOU CARRYING MY HOUSE ON YOUR BACK. I'VE HAD ALL NIGHT TO POKE AROUND IN YOUR BRAIN.
HOUSE?
YOU'RE A GENIE.
A REAL, NO-SHIT GENIE.
PLEASE. JINN. IT'S MORE CORRECT.
...AND YOU LIVE IN A HOOKAH?

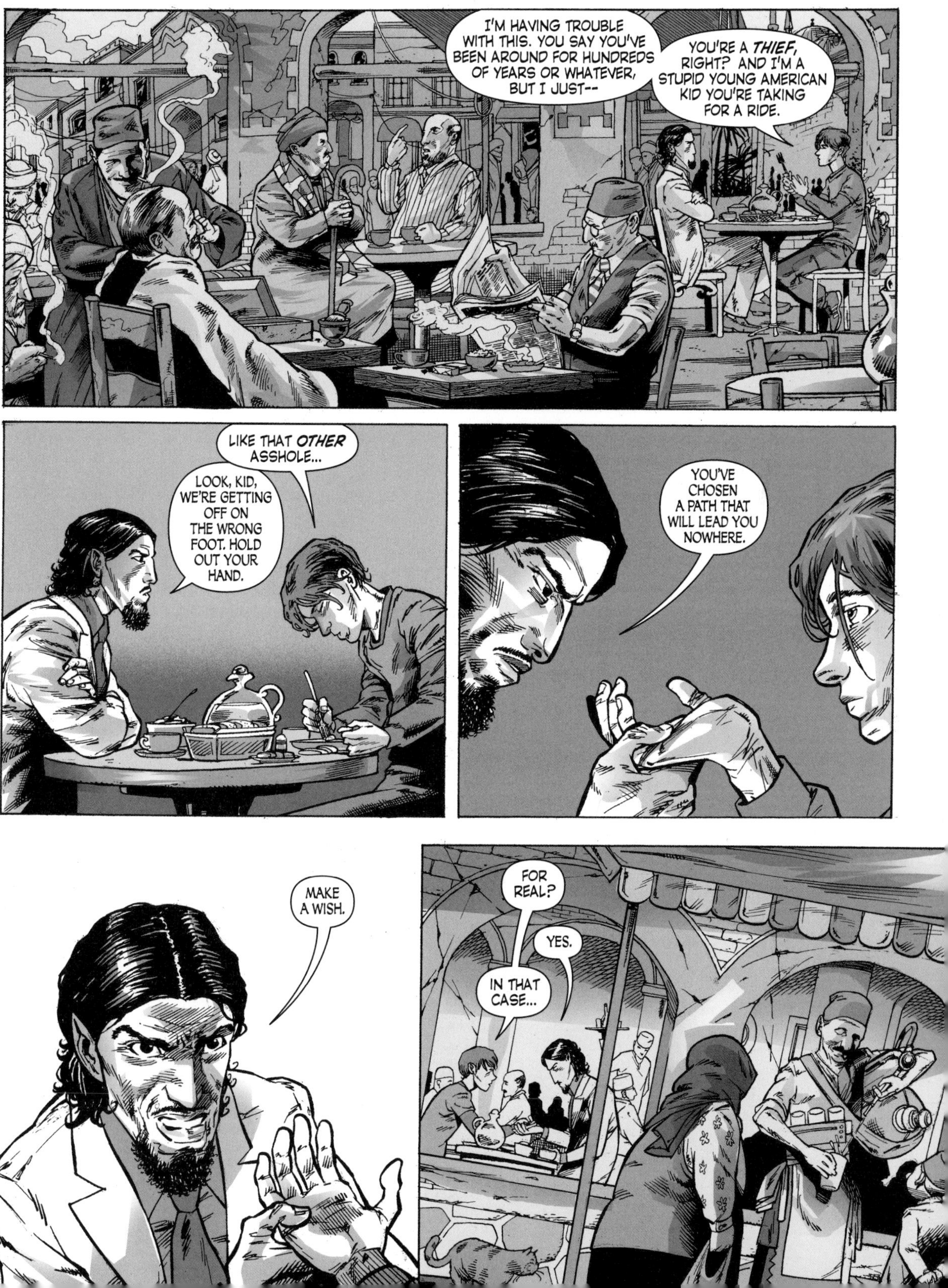
I'M HAVING TROUBLE WITH THIS. YOU SAY YOU'VE BEEN AROUND FOR HUNDREDS OF YEARS OR WHATEVER, BUT I JUST--
YOU'RE A *THIEF,* RIGHT? AND I'M A STUPID YOUNG AMERICAN KID YOU'RE TAKING FOR A RIDE.
LIKE THAT *OTHER* ASSHOLE...
LOOK, KID, WE'RE GETTING OFF ON THE WRONG FOOT. HOLD OUT YOUR HAND.
YOU'VE CHOSEN A PATH THAT WILL LEAD YOU NOWHERE.
MAKE A WISH.
FOR REAL?
YES.
IN THAT CASE...

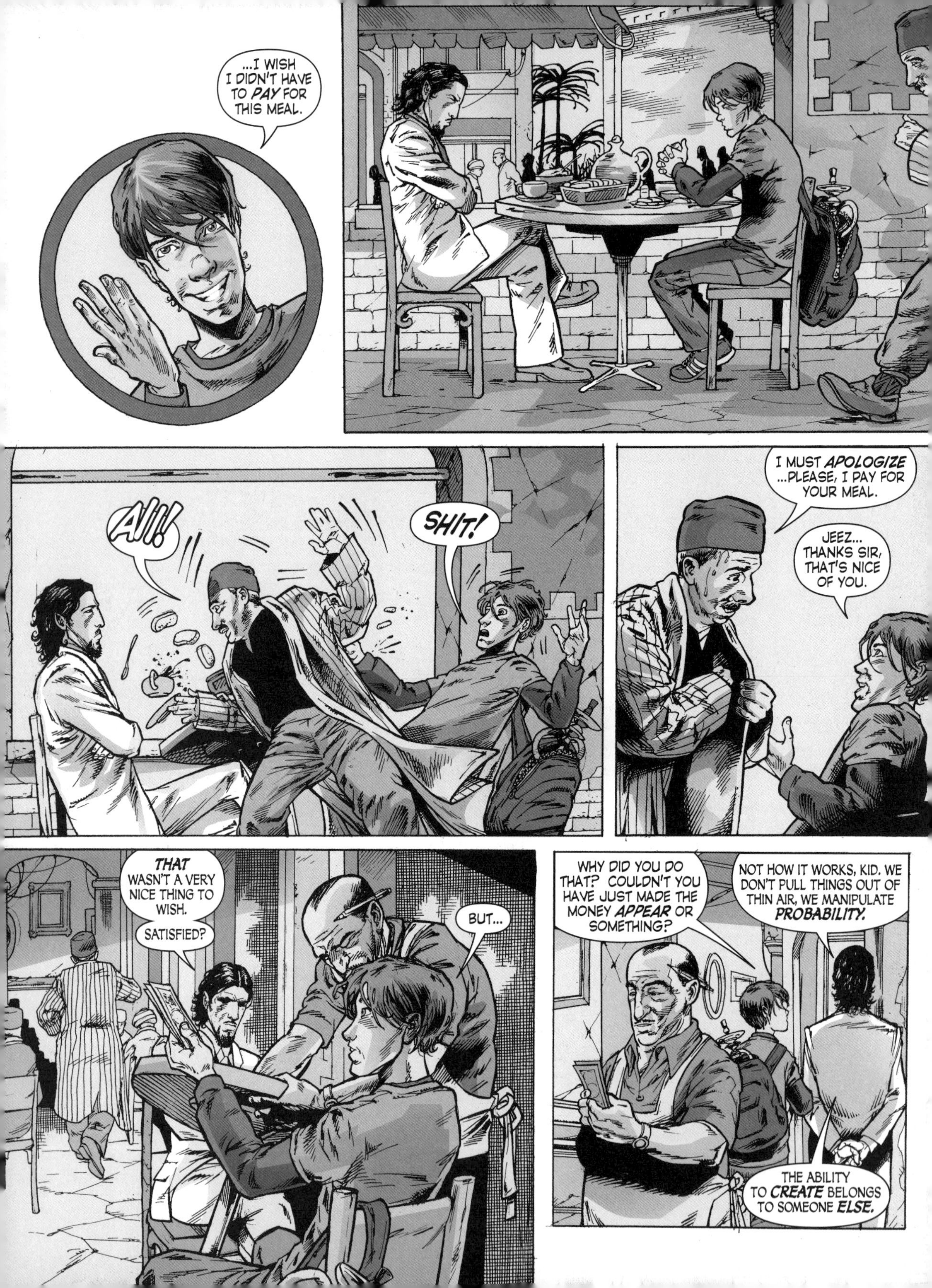

...I WISH I DIDN'T HAVE TO PAY FOR THIS MEAL.
AI!!
SHIT!
I MUST APOLOGIZE ...PLEASE, I PAY FOR YOUR MEAL.
JEEZ... THANKS SIR, THAT'S NICE OF YOU.
THAT WASN'T A VERY NICE THING TO WISH.
SATISFIED?
BUT...
WHY DID YOU DO THAT? COULDN'T YOU HAVE JUST MADE THE MONEY APPEAR OR SOMETHING?
NOT HOW IT WORKS, KID. WE DON'T PULL THINGS OUT OF THIN AIR, WE MANIPULATE PROBABILITY.
THE ABILITY TO CREATE BELONGS TO SOMEONE ELSE.

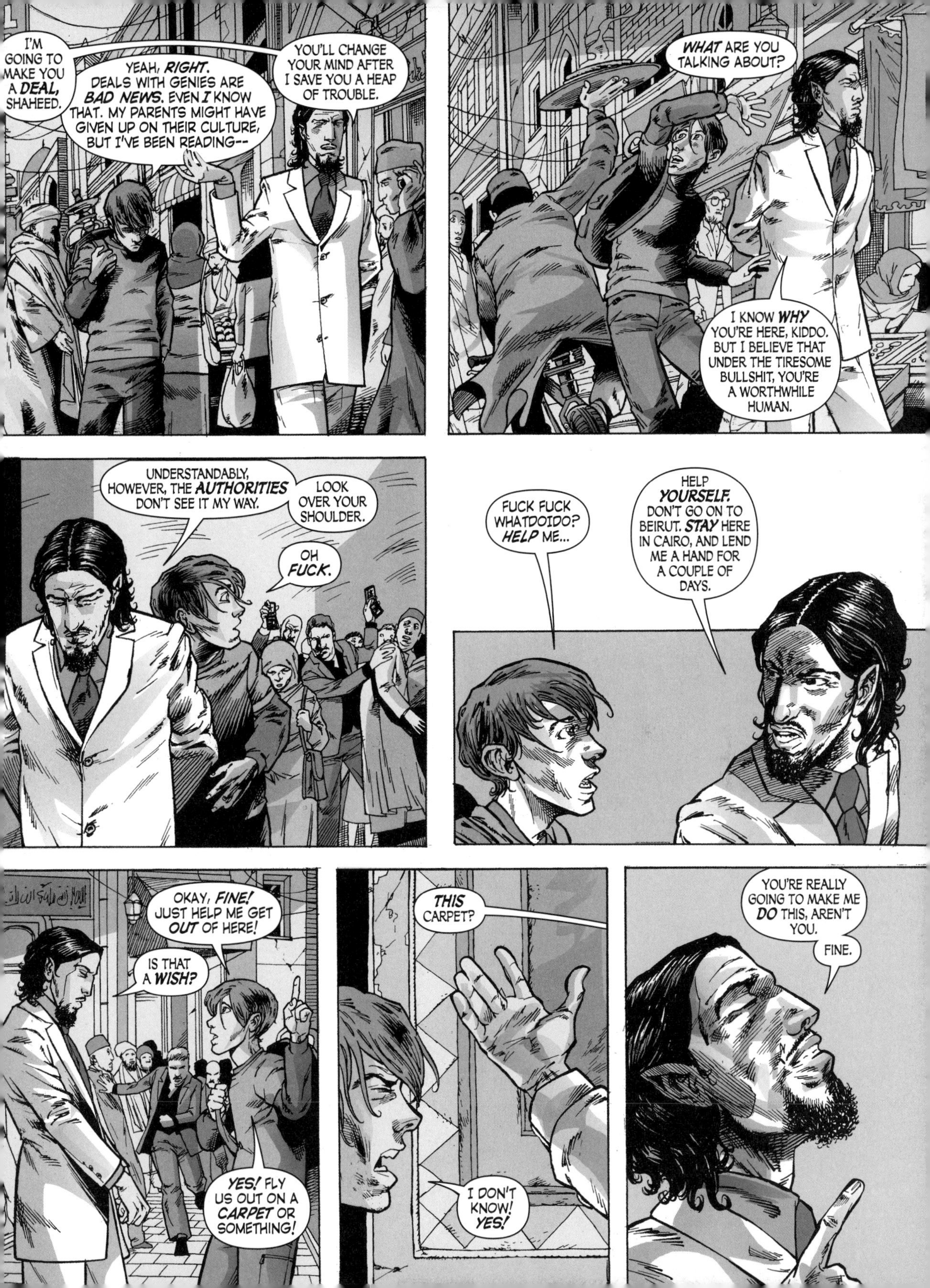
I'M GOING TO MAKE YOU A DEAL, SHAHEED.
YEAH, RIGHT. DEALS WITH GENIES ARE BAD NEWS. EVEN I KNOW THAT. MY PARENTS MIGHT HAVE GIVEN UP ON THEIR CULTURE, BUT I'VE BEEN READING--
YOU'LL CHANGE YOUR MIND AFTER I SAVE YOU A HEAP OF TROUBLE.
WHAT ARE YOU TALKING ABOUT?
I KNOW WHY YOU'RE HERE, KIDDO. BUT I BELIEVE THAT UNDER THE TIRESOME BULLSHIT, YOU'RE A WORTHWHILE HUMAN.
UNDERSTANDABLY, HOWEVER, THE AUTHORITIES DON'T SEE IT MY WAY.
LOOK OVER YOUR SHOULDER.
OH FUCK.
FUCK FUCK WHATDOIDO? HELP ME...
HELP YOURSELF. DON'T GO ON TO BEIRUT. STAY HERE IN CAIRO, AND LEND ME A HAND FOR A COUPLE OF DAYS.
OKAY, FINE! JUST HELP ME GET OUT OF HERE!
IS THAT A WISH?
YES! FLY US OUT ON A CARPET OR SOMETHING!
THIS CARPET?
I DON'T KNOW! YES!
YOU'RE REALLY GOING TO MAKE ME DO THIS, AREN'T YOU.
FINE.

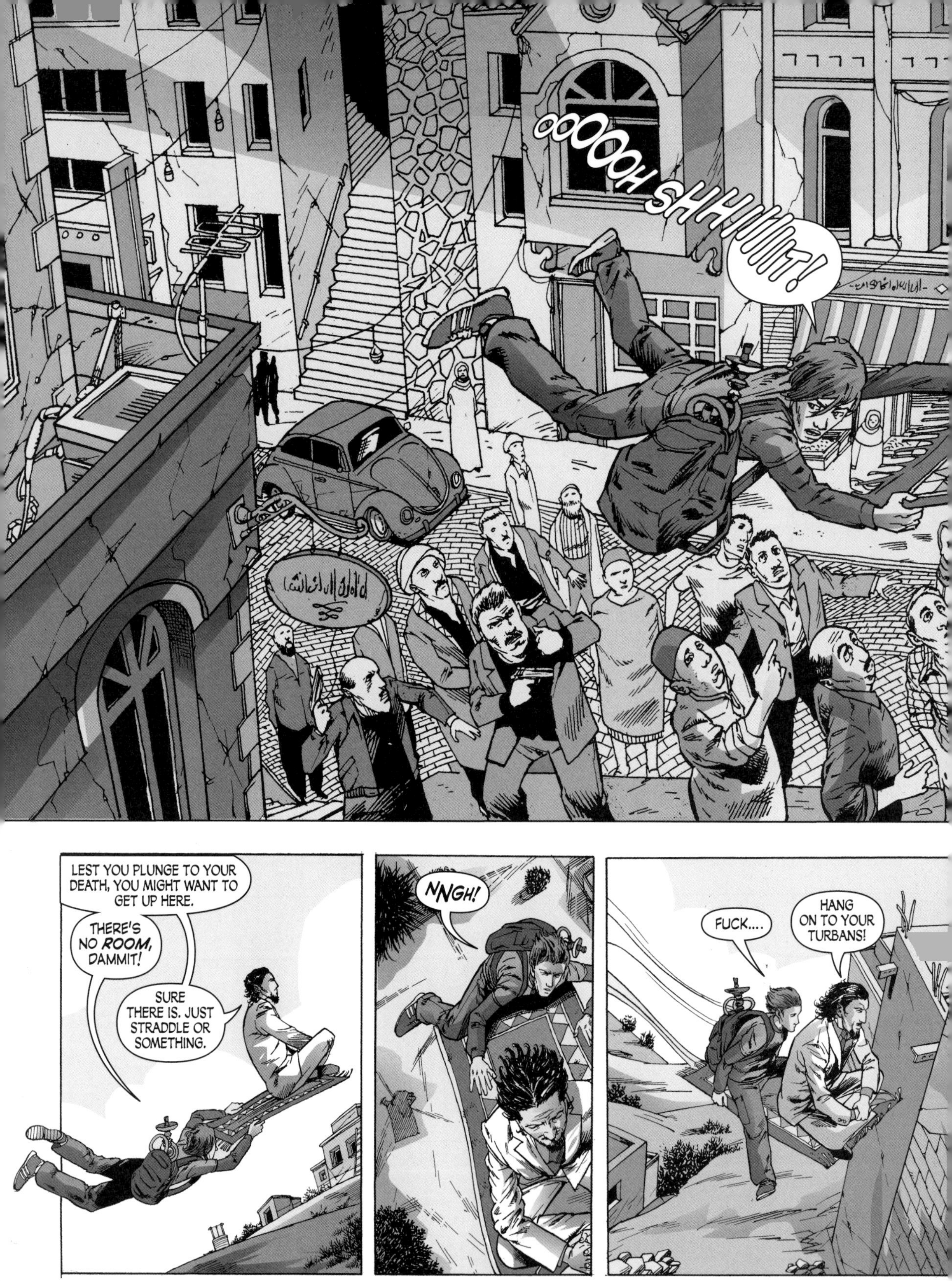
OOOOOH SHHIIIIIIT!
LEST YOU PLUNGE TO YOUR DEATH, YOU MIGHT WANT TO GET UP HERE.
THERE'S NO *ROOM,* DAMMIT!
SURE THERE IS. JUST STRADDLE OR SOMETHING.
NNGH!
FUCK....
HANG ON TO YOUR TURBANS!

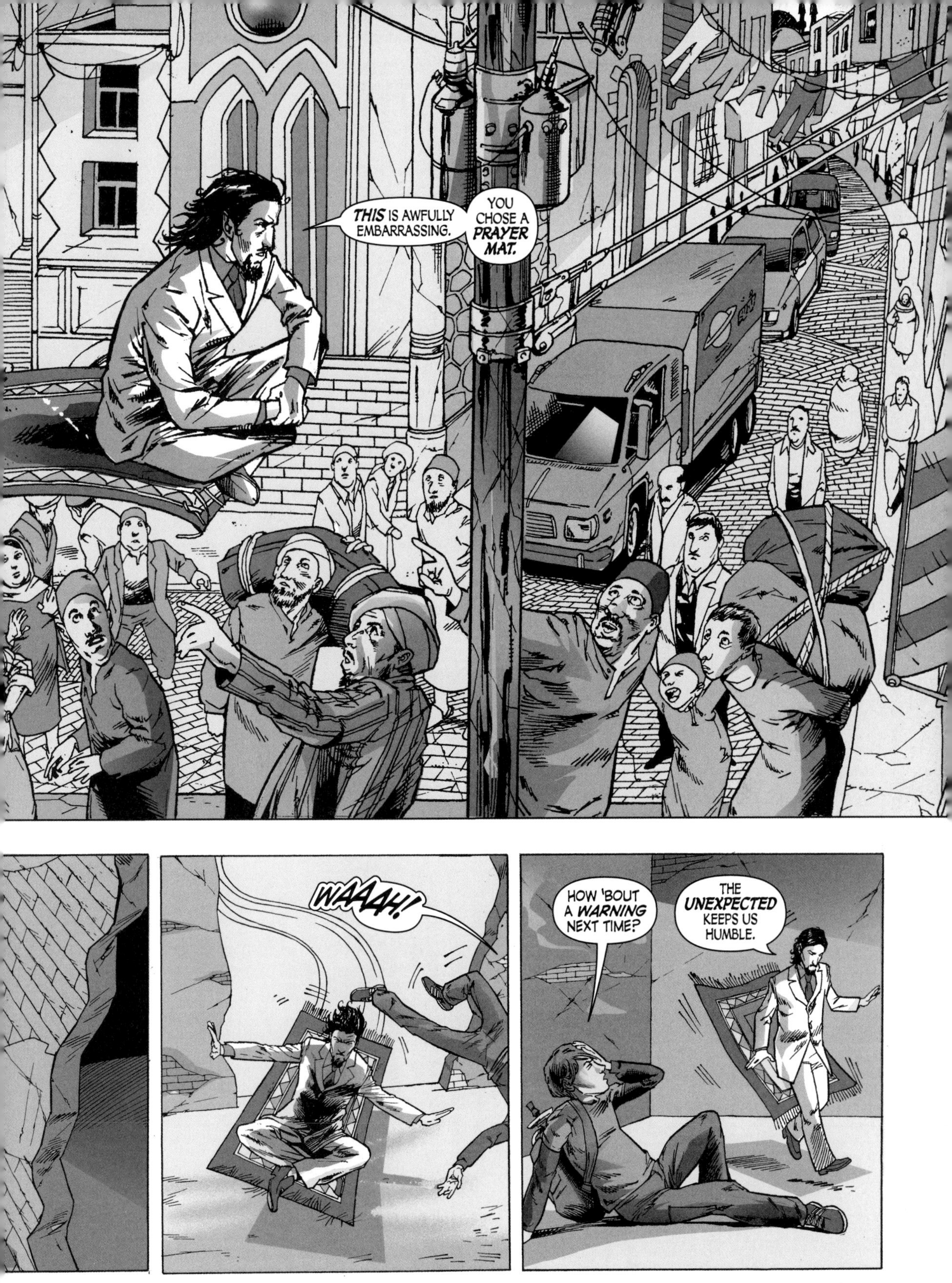
THIS IS AWFULLY EMBARRASSING.
YOU CHOSE A PRAYER MAT.
WAAAH!
HOW 'BOUT A WARNING NEXT TIME?
THE UNEXPECTED KEEPS US HUMBLE.

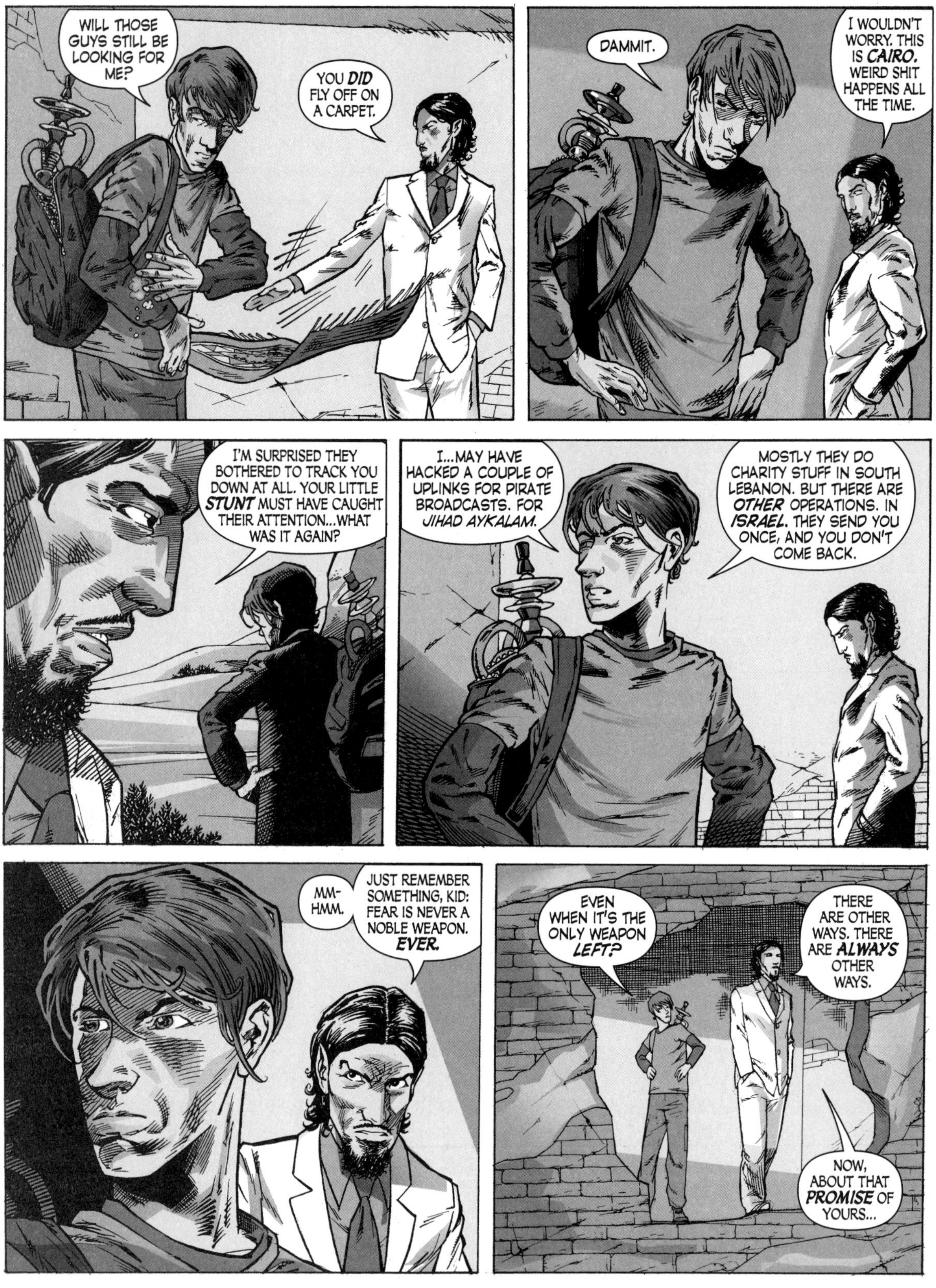
WILL THOSE GUYS STILL BE LOOKING FOR ME?
YOU DID FLY OFF ON A CARPET.
DAMMIT.
I WOULDN'T WORRY. THIS IS CAIRO. WEIRD SHIT HAPPENS ALL THE TIME.
I'M SURPRISED THEY BOTHERED TO TRACK YOU DOWN AT ALL. YOUR LITTLE STUNT MUST HAVE CAUGHT THEIR ATTENTION...WHAT WAS IT AGAIN?
I...MAY HAVE HACKED A COUPLE OF UPLINKS FOR PIRATE BROADCASTS. FOR JIHAD AYKALAM.
MOSTLY THEY DO CHARITY STUFF IN SOUTH LEBANON. BUT THERE ARE OTHER OPERATIONS. IN ISRAEL. THEY SEND YOU ONCE, AND YOU DON'T COME BACK.
MM-HMM.
JUST REMEMBER SOMETHING, KID: FEAR IS NEVER A NOBLE WEAPON. EVER.
EVEN WHEN IT'S THE ONLY WEAPON LEFT?
THERE ARE OTHER WAYS. THERE ARE ALWAYS OTHER WAYS.
NOW, ABOUT THAT PROMISE OF YOURS...

DAMMIT.

HO! WHERE'S MY PARADE? I JUST RESCUED YOUR LITTLE BEHIND.

AND YOU GAVE ME YOUR *WORD.*

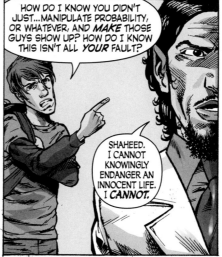

HOW DO I KNOW YOU DIDN'T JUST...MANIPULATE PROBABILITY, OR WHATEVER, AND *MAKE* THOSE GUYS SHOW UP? HOW DO I KNOW THIS ISN'T ALL *YOUR* FAULT?

SHAHEED. I CANNOT KNOWINGLY ENDANGER AN INNOCENT LIFE. I *CANNOT.*

EVEN IF IT BELONGS TO SOMEONE AS PERVERTED AND UNGRATEFUL AS YOURSELF.

IS THAT A *JINN* THING? NOT ENDANGERING A LIFE?

NO. SOMETHING ELSE.

OKAY. SO WHAT DO YOU WANT ME TO DO?

KIDDO, LET ME TELL YOU A STORY.

"Once upon a time--"

"Oh good."

"Quiet. I am telling a story."

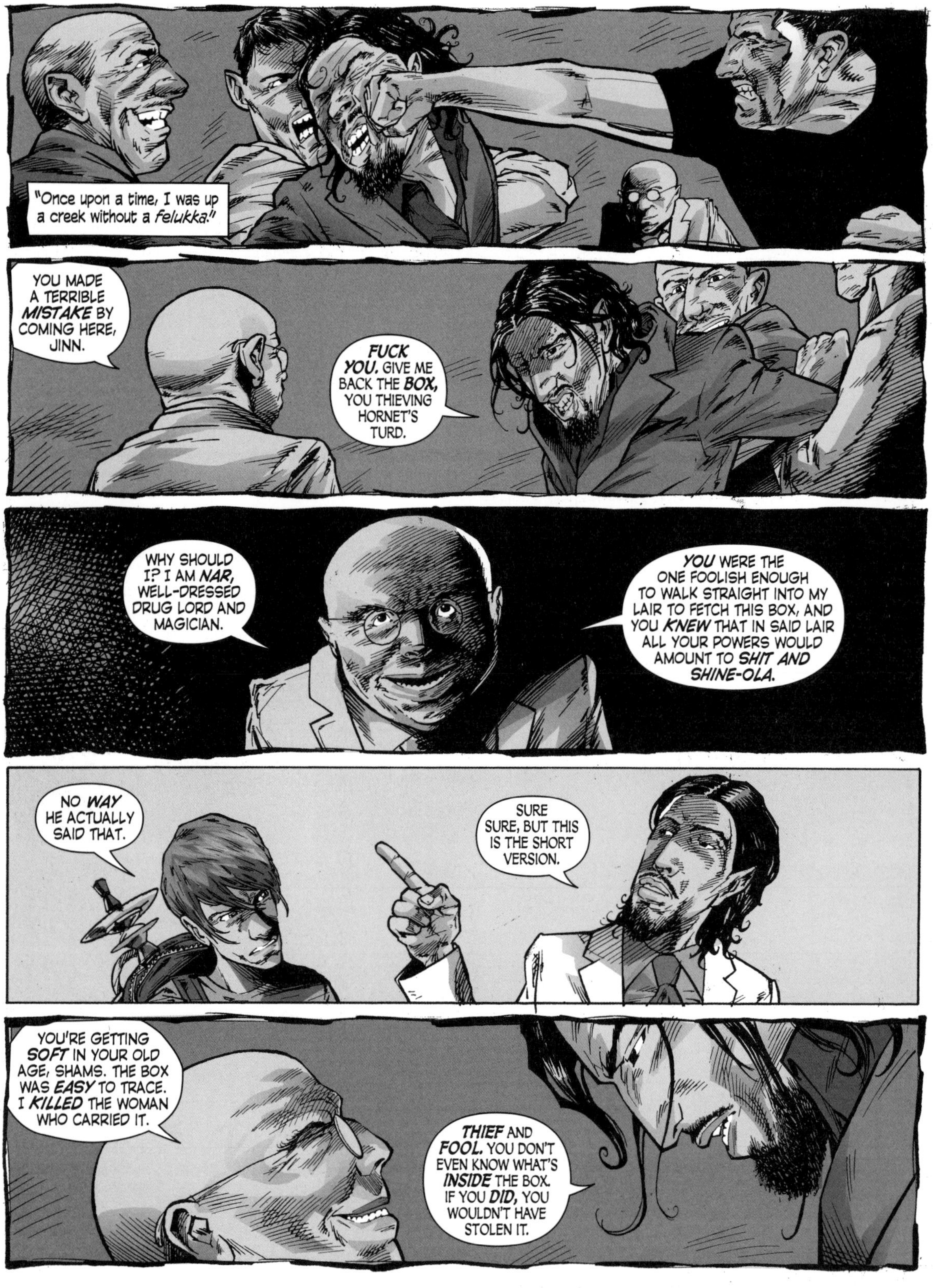
"Once upon a time, I was up a creek without a *felukka*."
YOU MADE A TERRIBLE *MISTAKE* BY COMING HERE, JINN.
FUCK YOU. GIVE ME BACK THE *BOX,* YOU THIEVING HORNET'S TURD.
WHY SHOULD I? I AM *NAR,* WELL-DRESSED DRUG LORD AND MAGICIAN.
YOU WERE THE ONE FOOLISH ENOUGH TO WALK STRAIGHT INTO MY LAIR TO FETCH THIS BOX, AND YOU *KNEW* THAT IN SAID LAIR ALL YOUR POWERS WOULD AMOUNT TO *SHIT AND SHINE-OLA.*
NO *WAY* HE ACTUALLY SAID THAT.
SURE SURE, BUT THIS IS THE SHORT VERSION.
YOU'RE GETTING *SOFT* IN YOUR OLD AGE, SHAMS. THE BOX WAS *EASY* TO TRACE. I *KILLED* THE WOMAN WHO CARRIED IT.
THIEF AND *FOOL.* YOU DON'T EVEN KNOW WHAT'S *INSIDE* THE BOX. IF YOU *DID,* YOU WOULDN'T HAVE STOLEN IT.

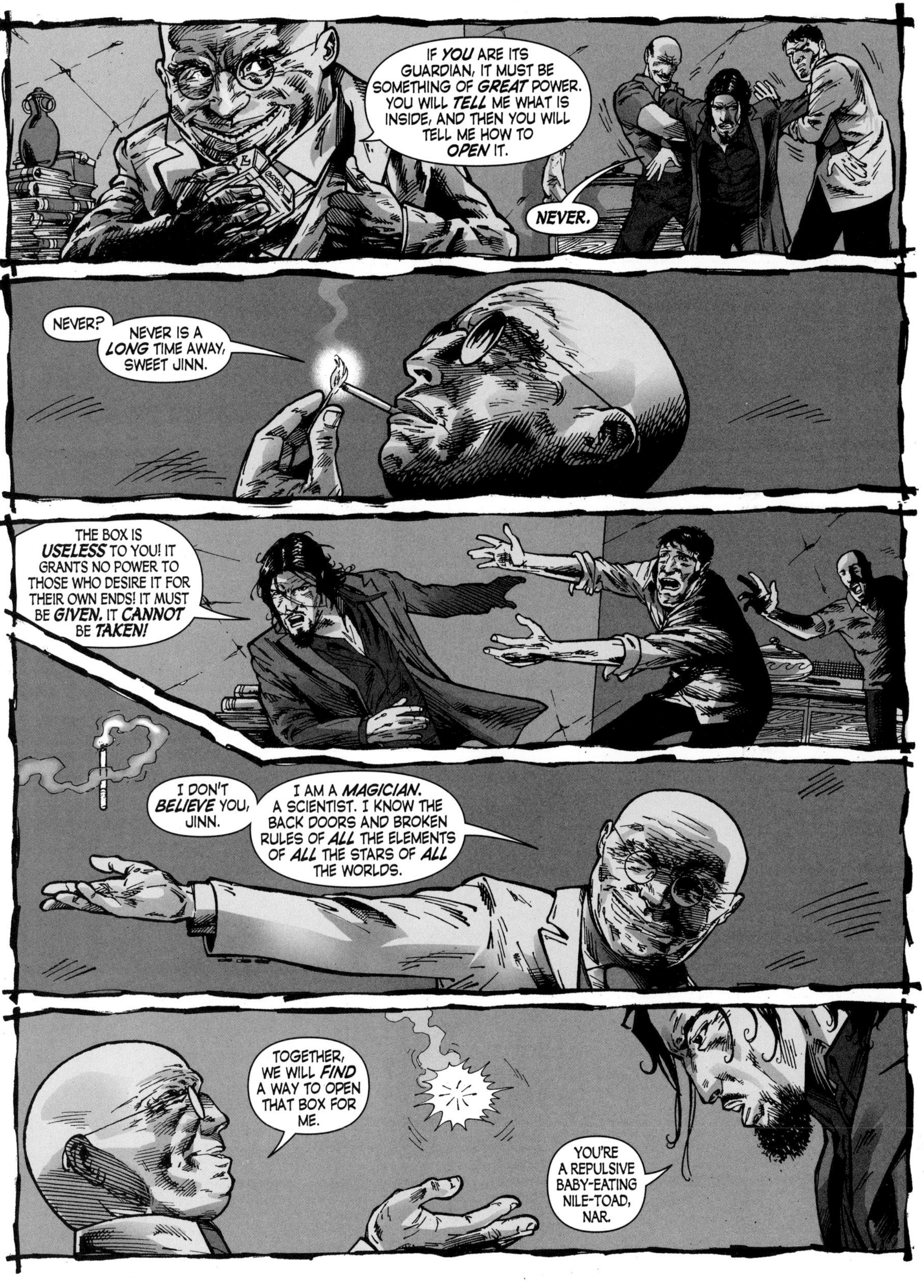
IF YOU ARE ITS GUARDIAN, IT MUST BE SOMETHING OF GREAT POWER. YOU WILL TELL ME WHAT IS INSIDE, AND THEN YOU WILL TELL ME HOW TO OPEN IT.
NEVER.
NEVER?
NEVER IS A LONG TIME AWAY, SWEET JINN.
THE BOX IS USELESS TO YOU! IT GRANTS NO POWER TO THOSE WHO DESIRE IT FOR THEIR OWN ENDS! IT MUST BE GIVEN. IT CANNOT BE TAKEN!
I DON'T BELIEVE YOU, JINN.
I AM A MAGICIAN. A SCIENTIST. I KNOW THE BACK DOORS AND BROKEN RULES OF ALL THE ELEMENTS OF ALL THE STARS OF ALL THE WORLDS.
TOGETHER, WE WILL FIND A WAY TO OPEN THAT BOX FOR ME.
YOU'RE A REPULSIVE BABY-EATING NILE-TOAD, NAR.

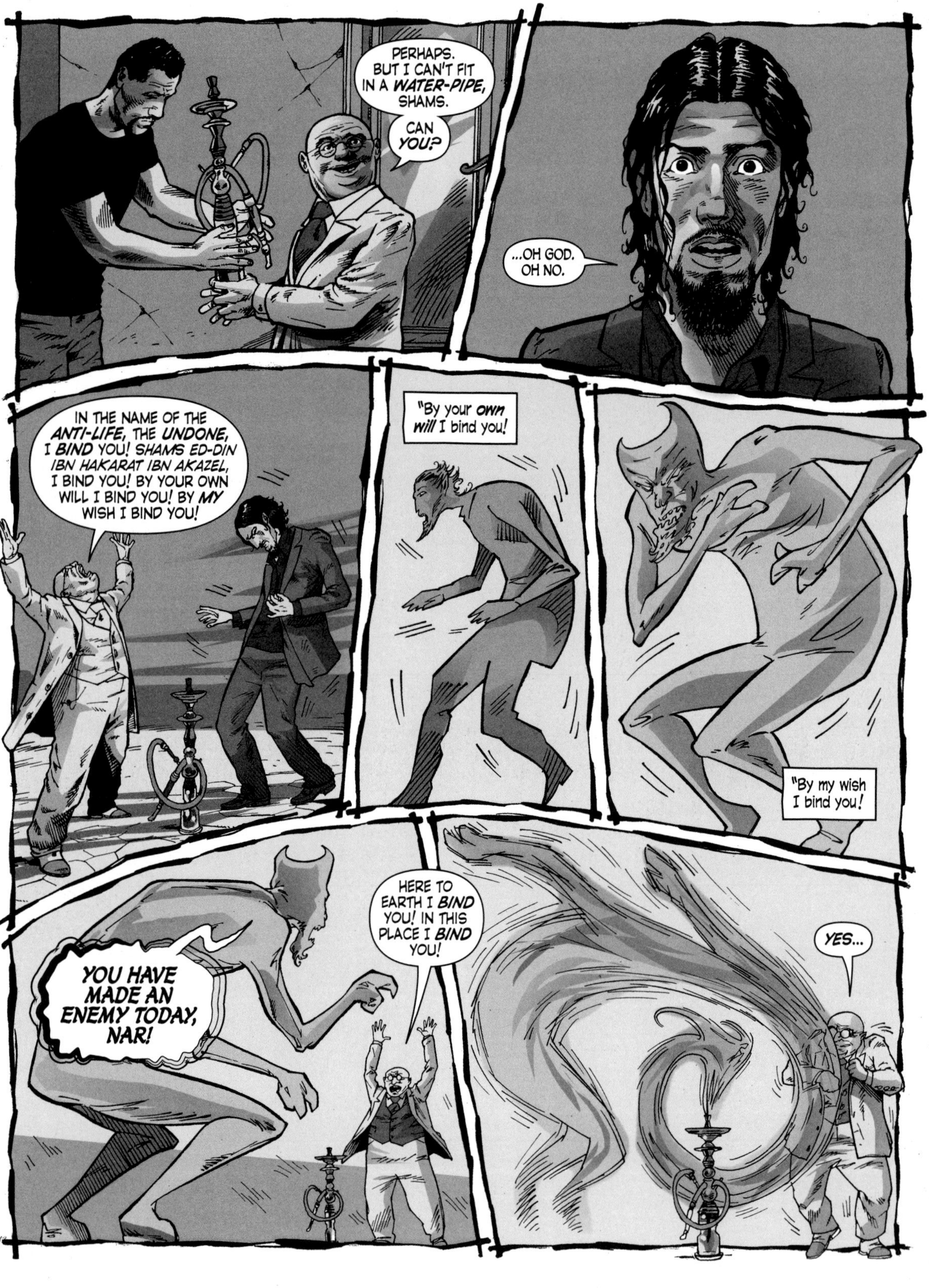
PERHAPS. BUT I CAN'T FIT IN A WATER-PIPE, SHAMS.
CAN YOU?
...OH GOD. OH NO.
IN THE NAME OF THE ANTI-LIFE, THE UNDONE, I BIND YOU! SHAMS ED-DIN IBN HAKARAT IBN AKAZEL, I BIND YOU! BY YOUR OWN WILL I BIND YOU! BY MY WISH I BIND YOU!
"By your own will I bind you!
"By my wish I bind you!
YOU HAVE MADE AN ENEMY TODAY, NAR!
HERE TO EARTH I BIND YOU! IN THIS PLACE I BIND YOU!
YES...

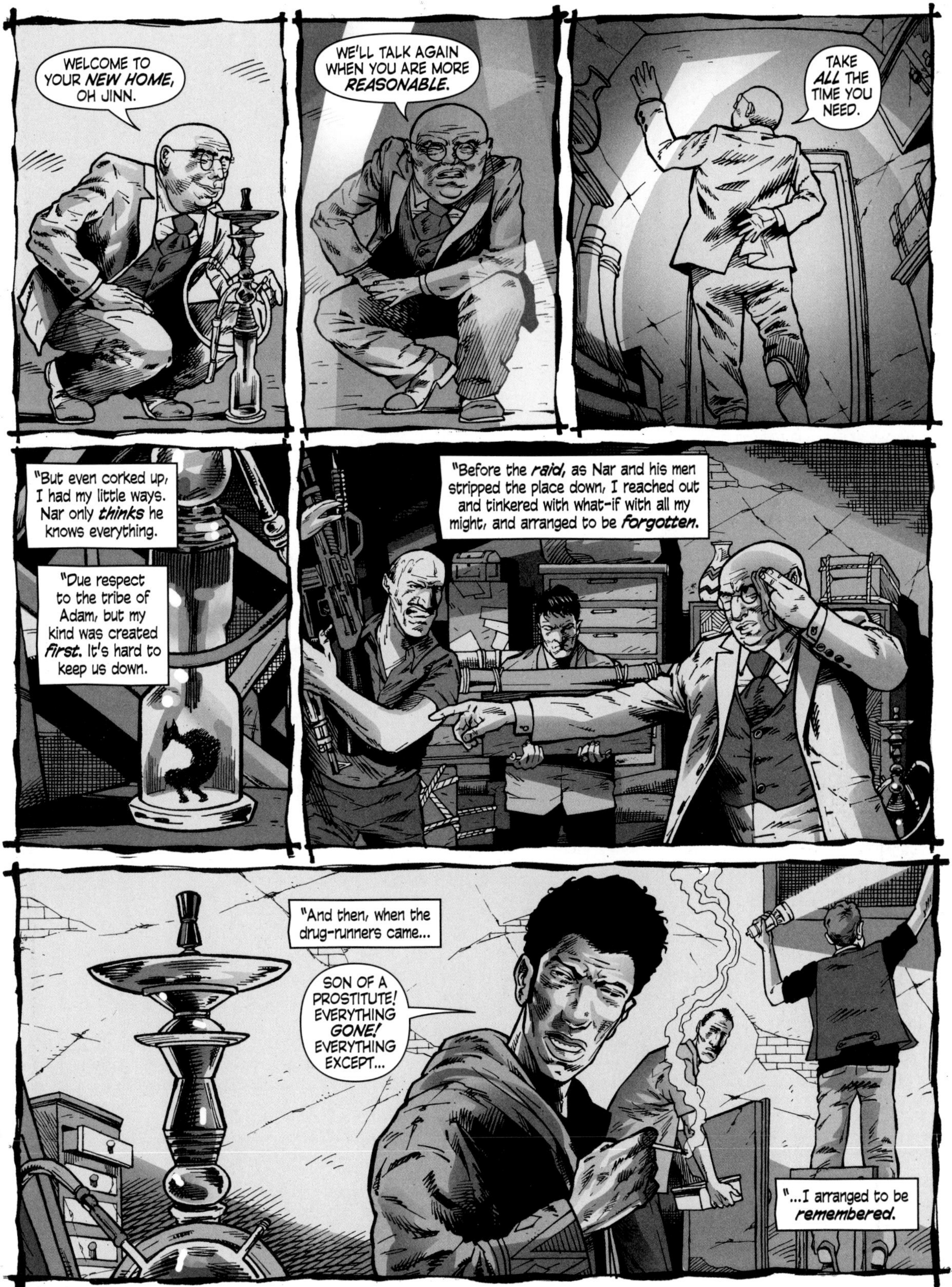
WELCOME TO YOUR NEW HOME, OH JINN.
WE'LL TALK AGAIN WHEN YOU ARE MORE REASONABLE.
TAKE ALL THE TIME YOU NEED.
"But even corked up, I had my little ways. Nar only thinks he knows everything.
"Due respect to the tribe of Adam, but my kind was created first. It's hard to keep us down.
"Before the raid, as Nar and his men stripped the place down, I reached out and tinkered with what-if with all my might, and arranged to be forgotten.
"And then, when the drug-runners came...
SON OF A PROSTITUTE! EVERYTHING GONE! EVERYTHING EXCEPT...
"...I arranged to be remembered.

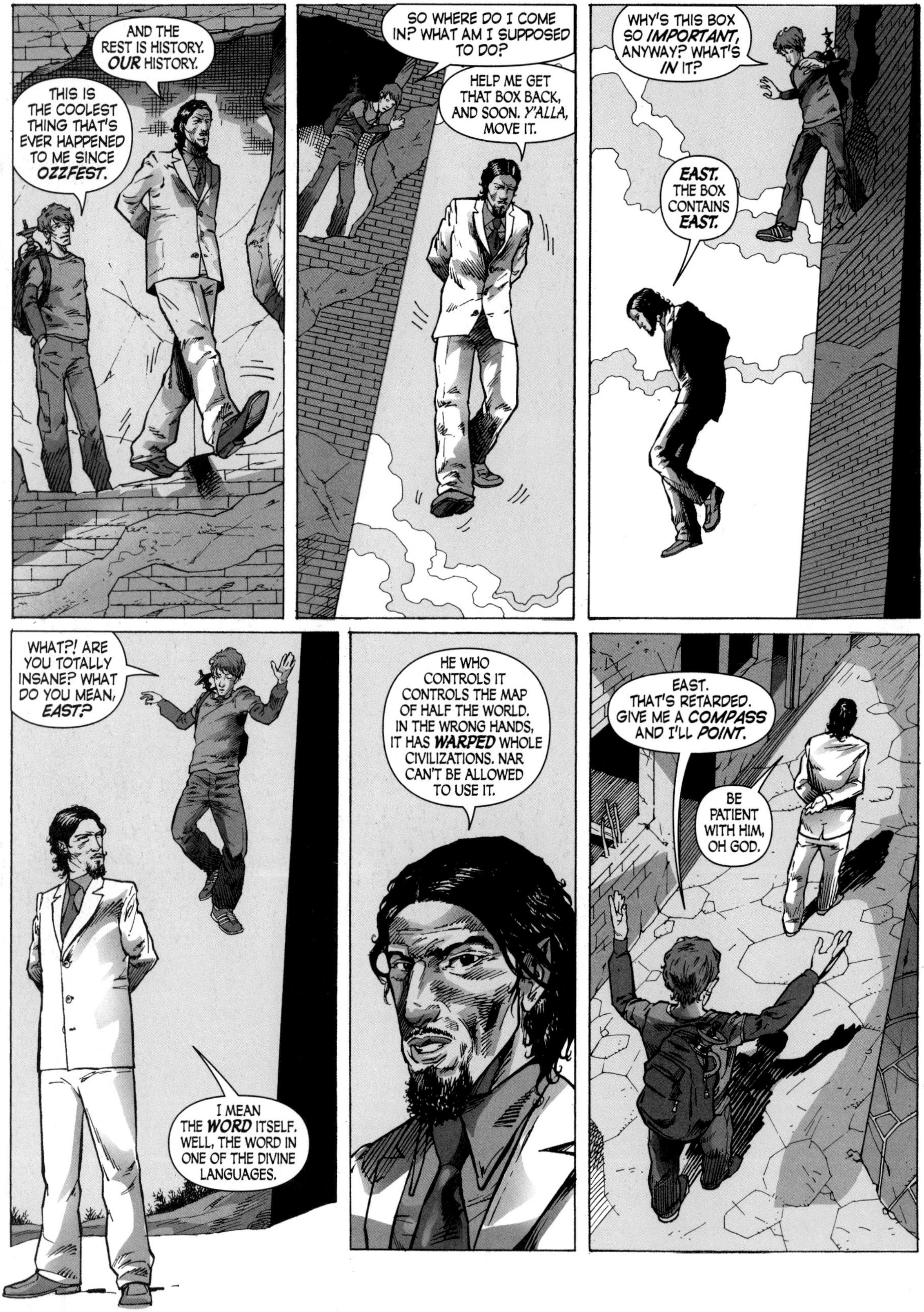

AND THE REST IS HISTORY. OUR HISTORY.
THIS IS THE COOLEST THING THAT'S EVER HAPPENED TO ME SINCE OZZFEST.
SO WHERE DO I COME IN? WHAT AM I SUPPOSED TO DO?
HELP ME GET THAT BOX BACK, AND SOON. Y'ALLA, MOVE IT.
WHY'S THIS BOX SO IMPORTANT, ANYWAY? WHAT'S IN IT?
EAST. THE BOX CONTAINS EAST.
WHAT?! ARE YOU TOTALLY INSANE? WHAT DO YOU MEAN, EAST?
I MEAN THE WORD ITSELF. WELL, THE WORD IN ONE OF THE DIVINE LANGUAGES.
HE WHO CONTROLS IT CONTROLS THE MAP OF HALF THE WORLD. IN THE WRONG HANDS, IT HAS WARPED WHOLE CIVILIZATIONS. NAR CAN'T BE ALLOWED TO USE IT.
EAST. THAT'S RETARDED. GIVE ME A COMPASS AND I'LL POINT.
BE PATIENT WITH HIM, OH GOD.

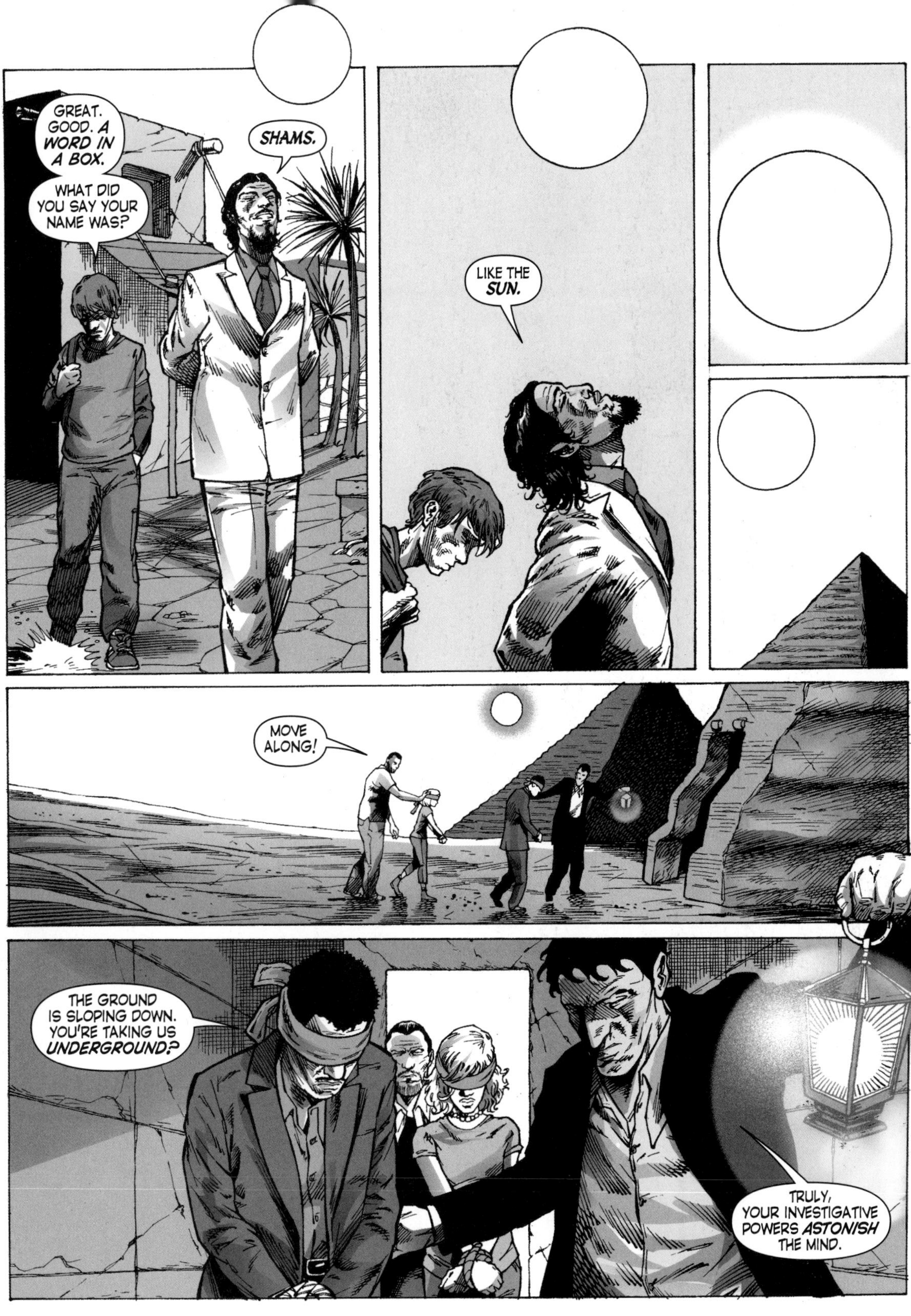
GREAT. GOOD. A WORD IN A BOX.
SHAMS.
WHAT DID YOU SAY YOUR NAME WAS?
LIKE THE SUN.
MOVE ALONG!
THE GROUND IS SLOPING DOWN. YOU'RE TAKING US UNDERGROUND?
TRULY, YOUR INVESTIGATIVE POWERS ASTONISH THE MIND.

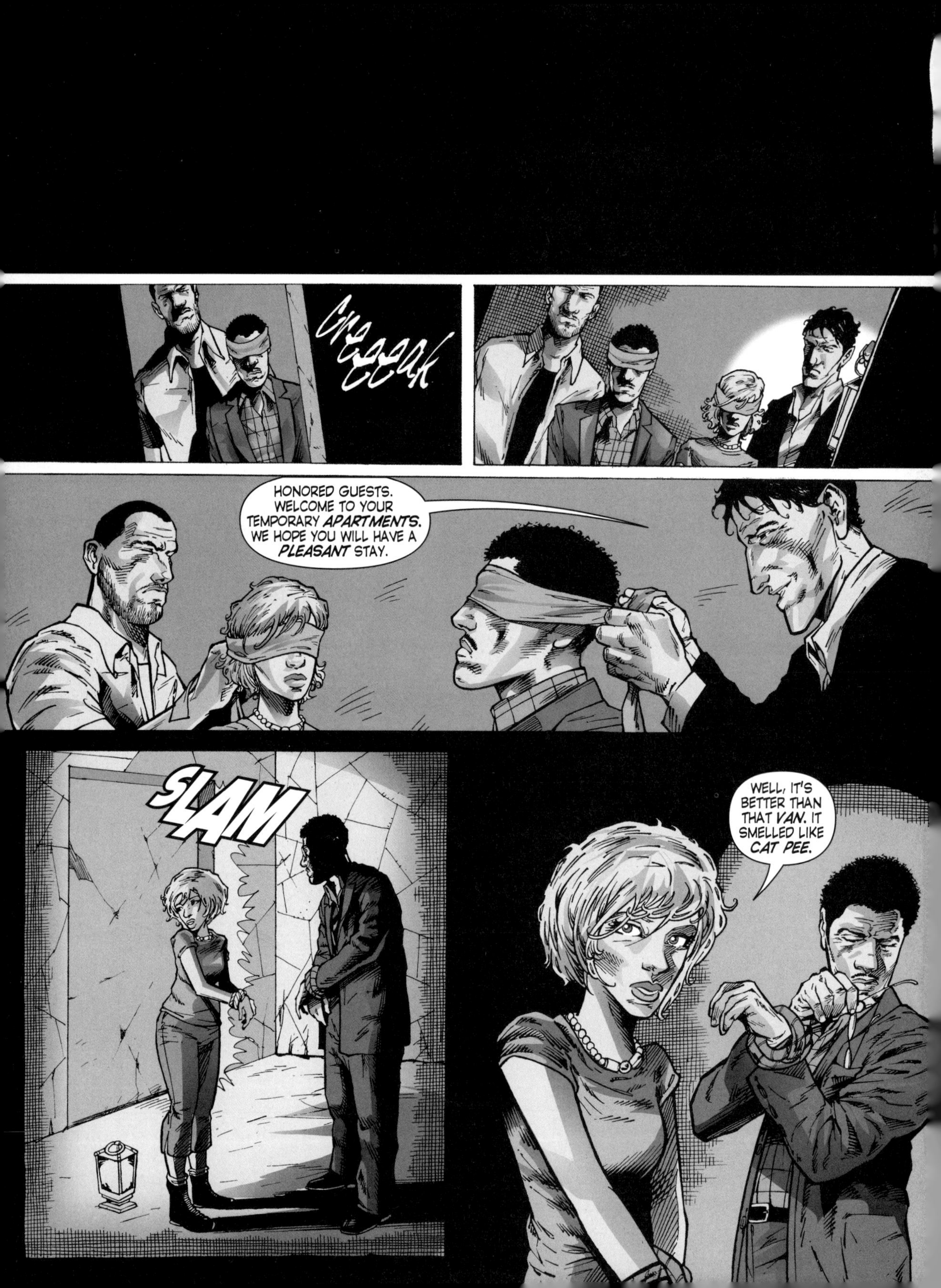
CREEEAK
HONORED GUESTS. WELCOME TO YOUR TEMPORARY APARTMENTS. WE HOPE YOU WILL HAVE A PLEASANT STAY.
SLAM
WELL, IT'S BETTER THAN THAT VAN. IT SMELLED LIKE CAT PEE.

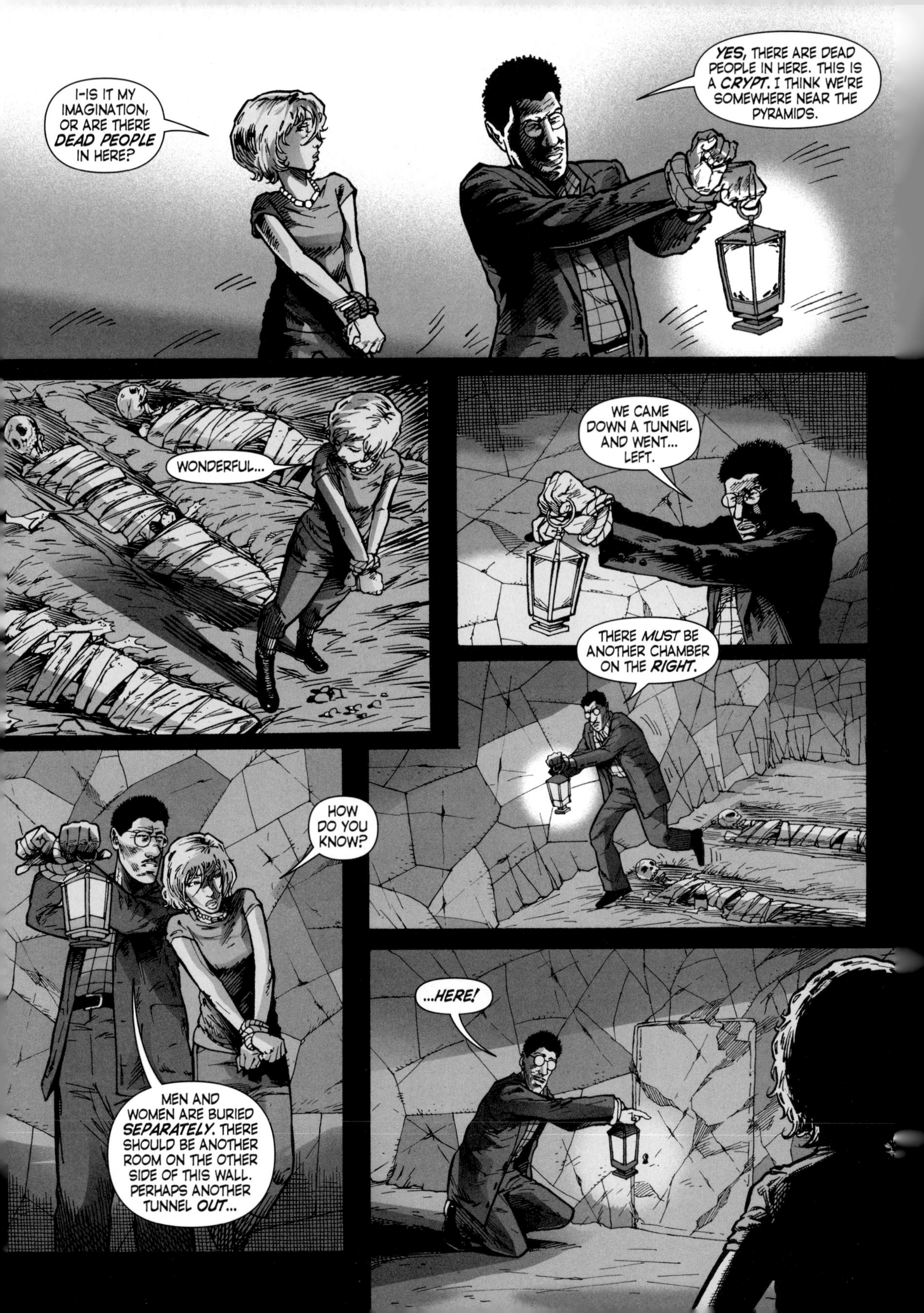
I-IS IT MY IMAGINATION, OR ARE THERE DEAD PEOPLE IN HERE?
YES, THERE ARE DEAD PEOPLE IN HERE. THIS IS A CRYPT. I THINK WE'RE SOMEWHERE NEAR THE PYRAMIDS.
WONDERFUL...
WE CAME DOWN A TUNNEL AND WENT... LEFT.
THERE MUST BE ANOTHER CHAMBER ON THE RIGHT.
HOW DO YOU KNOW?
MEN AND WOMEN ARE BURIED SEPARATELY. THERE SHOULD BE ANOTHER ROOM ON THE OTHER SIDE OF THIS WALL. PERHAPS ANOTHER TUNNEL OUT...
...HERE!

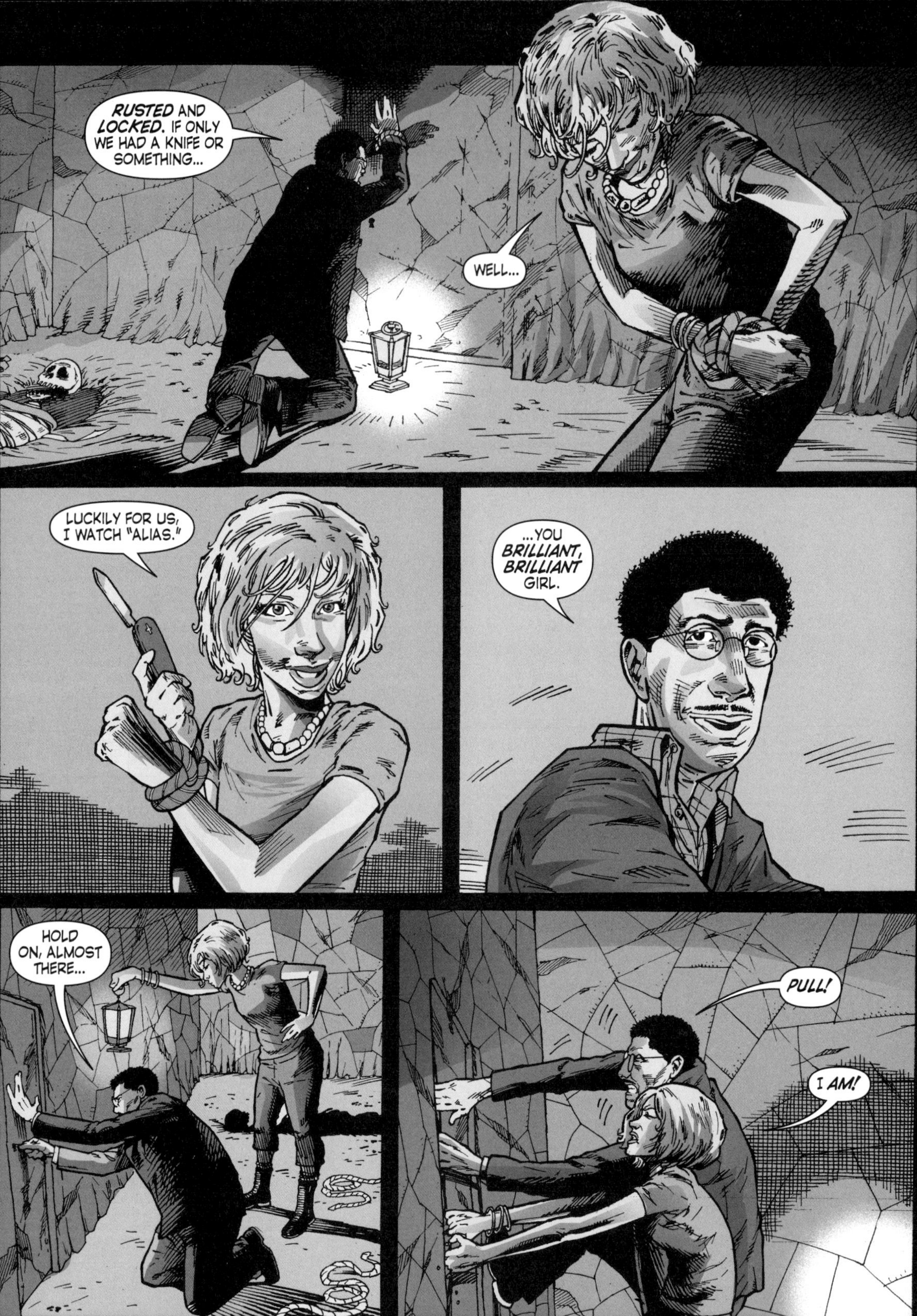
RUSTED AND LOCKED. IF ONLY WE HAD A KNIFE OR SOMETHING...
WELL...
LUCKILY FOR US, I WATCH "ALIAS."
...YOU BRILLIANT, BRILLIANT GIRL.
HOLD ON, ALMOST THERE...
PULL!
I AM!

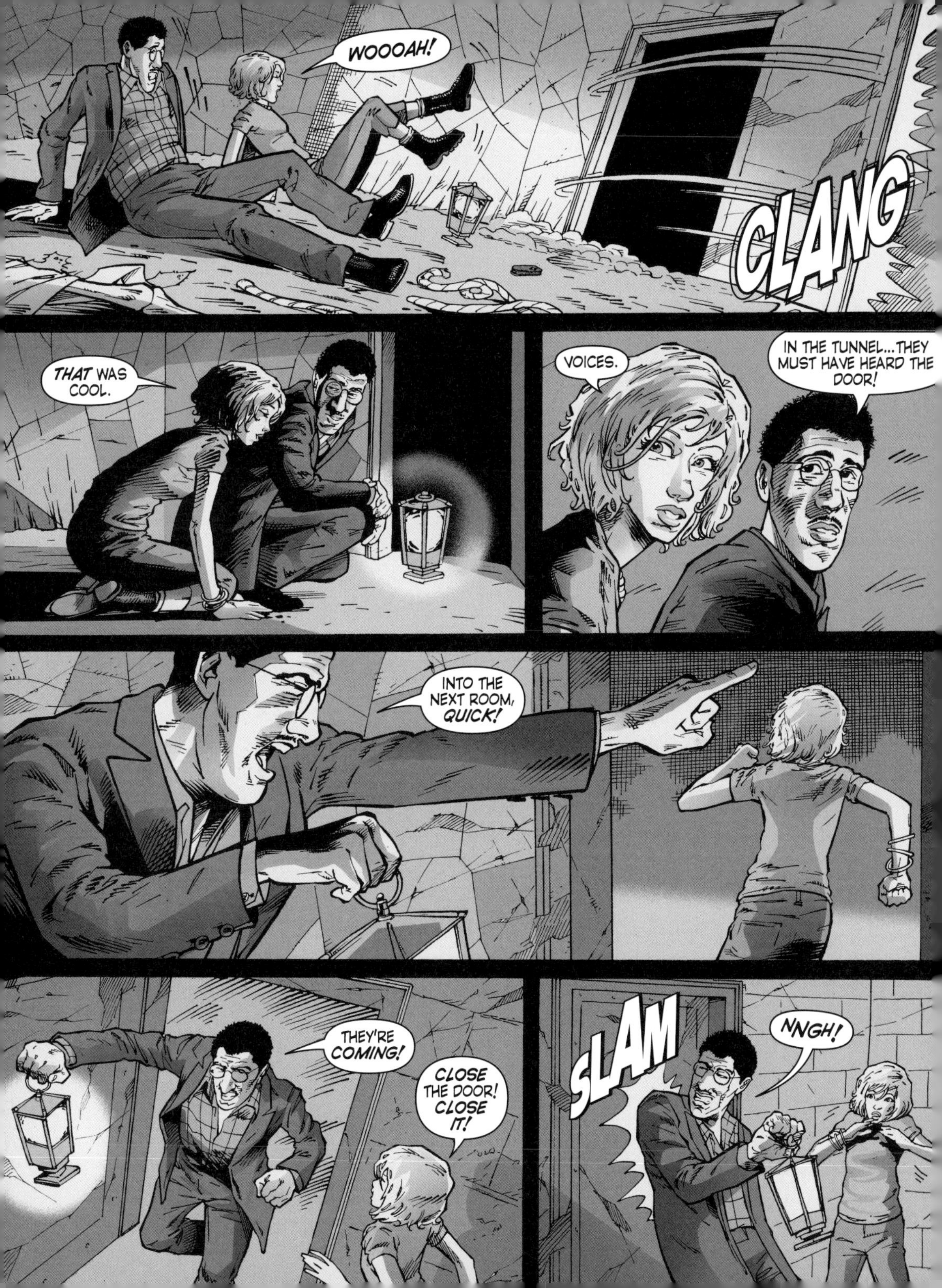
WOOOAH!
CLANG
THAT WAS COOL.
VOICES.
IN THE TUNNEL...THEY MUST HAVE HEARD THE DOOR!
INTO THE NEXT ROOM, QUICK!
THEY'RE COMING!
CLOSE THE DOOR! CLOSE IT!
SLAM
NNGH!

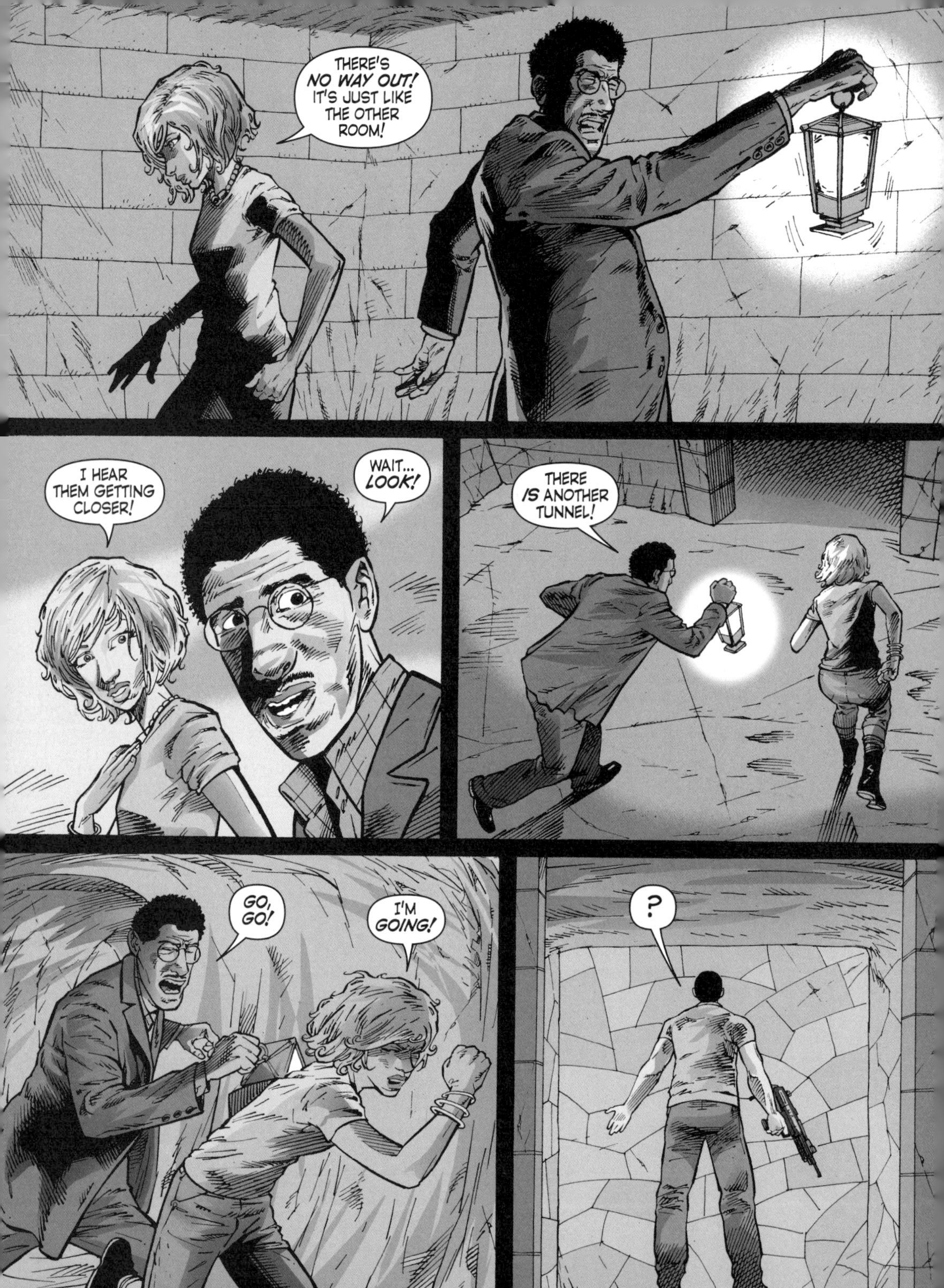
THERE'S NO WAY OUT! IT'S JUST LIKE THE OTHER ROOM!
I HEAR THEM GETTING CLOSER!
WAIT... LOOK!
THERE IS ANOTHER TUNNEL!
GO, GO!
I'M GOING!
?

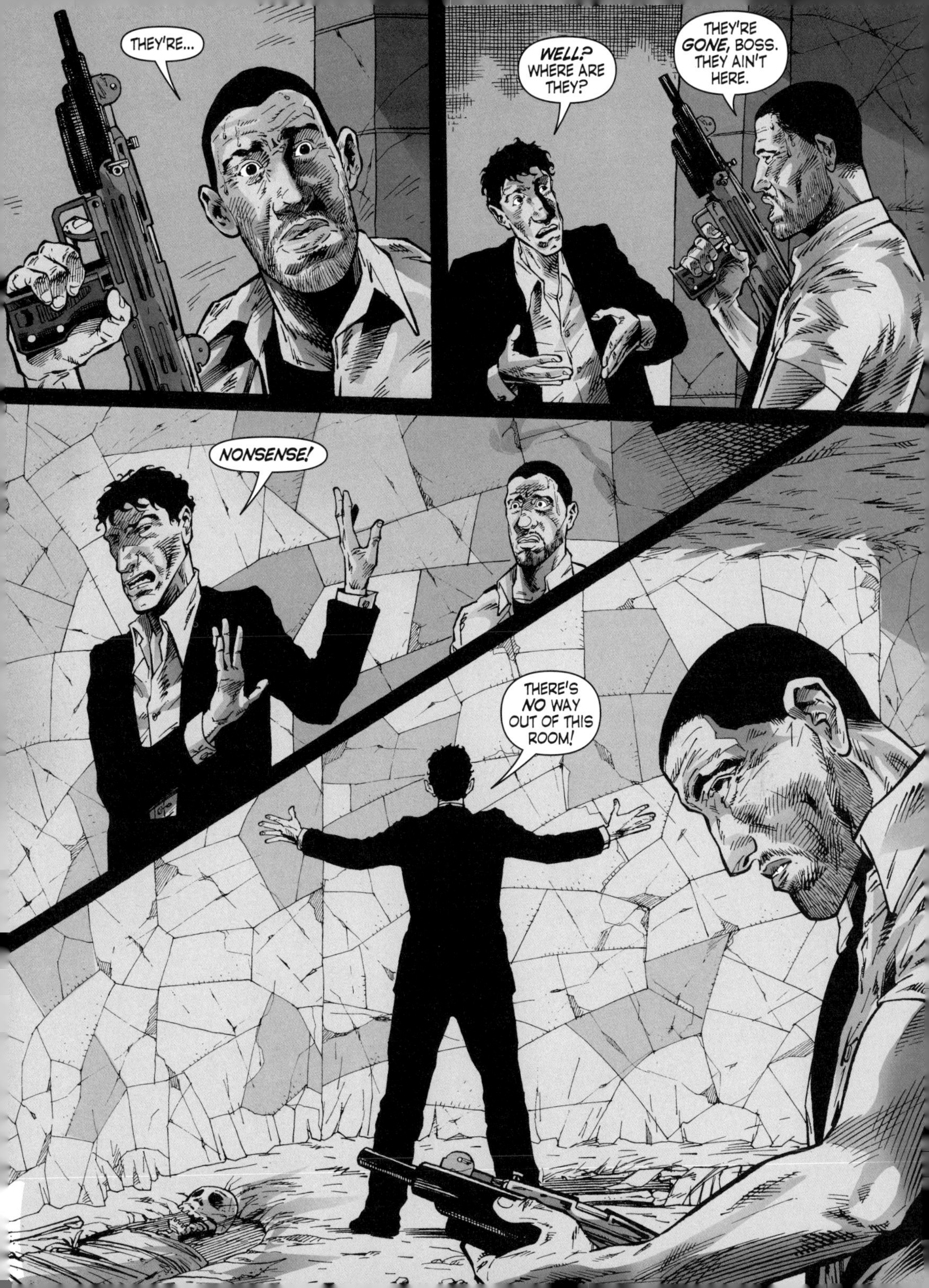
THEY'RE...
WELL? WHERE ARE THEY?
THEY'RE GONE, BOSS. THEY AIN'T HERE.
NONSENSE!
THERE'S NO WAY OUT OF THIS ROOM!

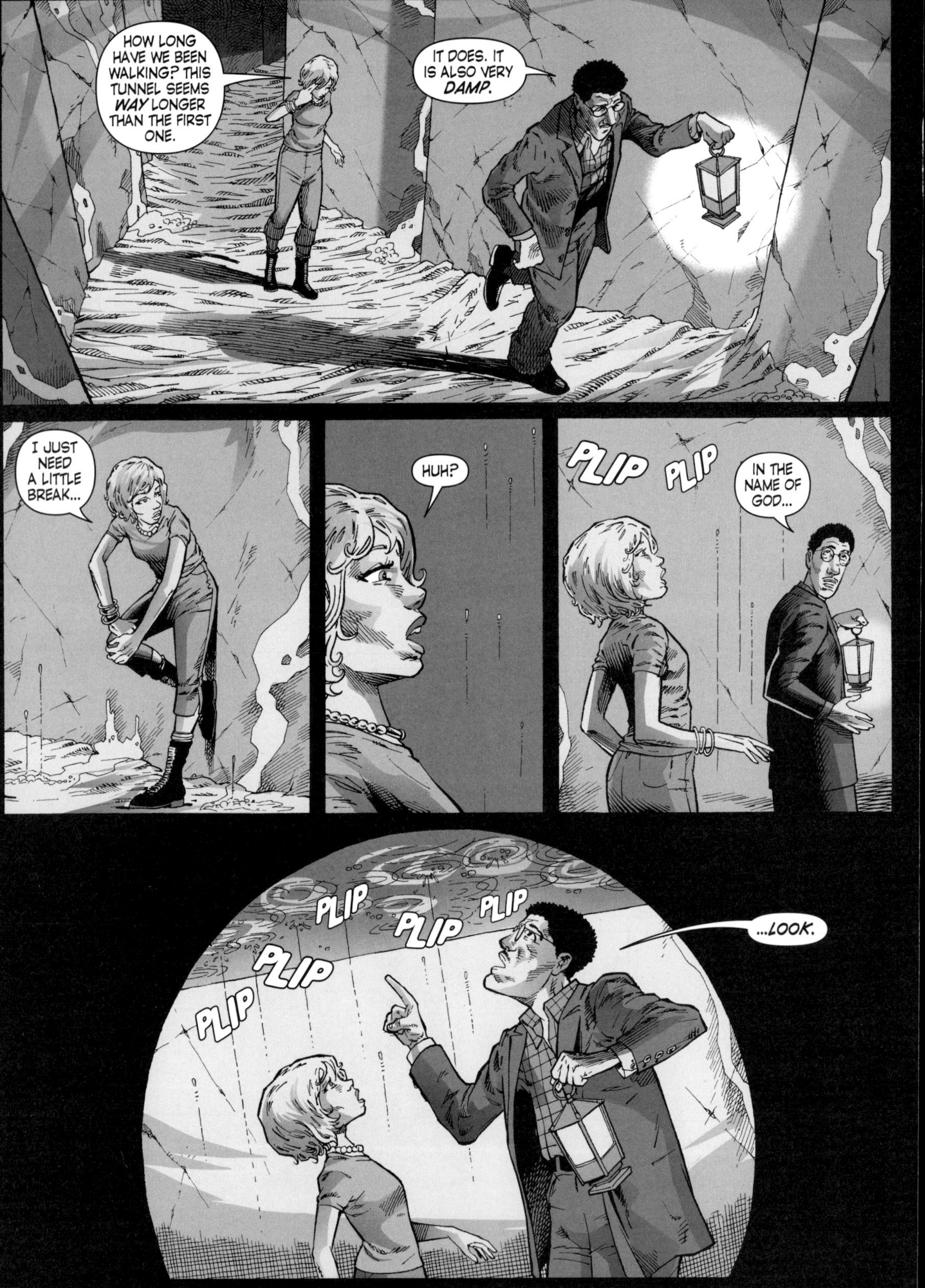

HOW LONG HAVE WE BEEN WALKING? THIS TUNNEL SEEMS WAY LONGER THAN THE FIRST ONE.
IT DOES. IT IS ALSO VERY DAMP.
I JUST NEED A LITTLE BREAK...
HUH?
PLIP PLIP
IN THE NAME OF GOD...
PLIP
PLIP
PLIP
PLIP
PLIP
...LOOK.

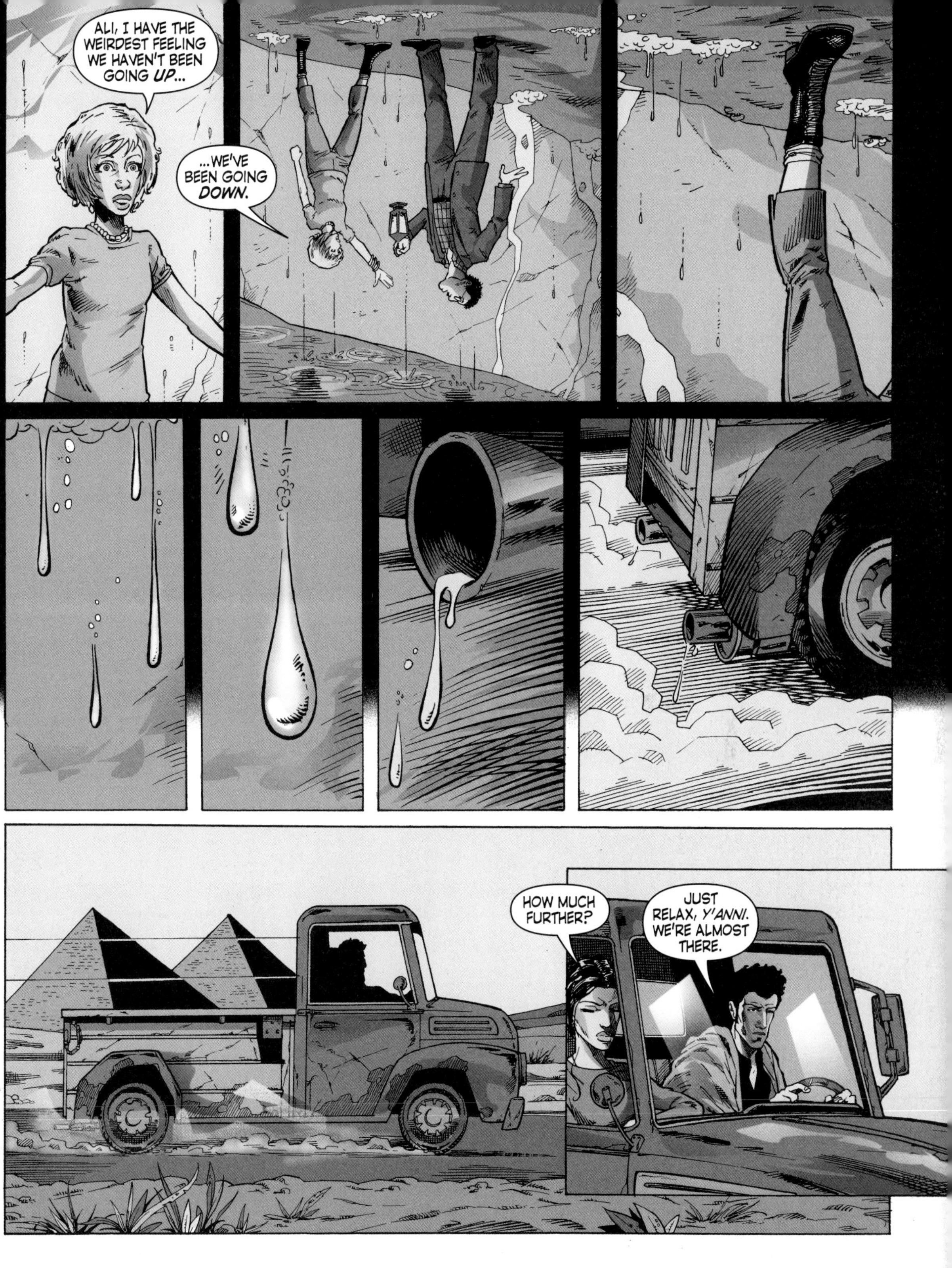
ALI, I HAVE THE WEIRDEST FEELING WE HAVEN'T BEEN GOING *UP*...
...WE'VE BEEN GOING *DOWN*.
HOW MUCH FURTHER?
JUST RELAX, *Y'ANNI*. WE'RE ALMOST THERE.

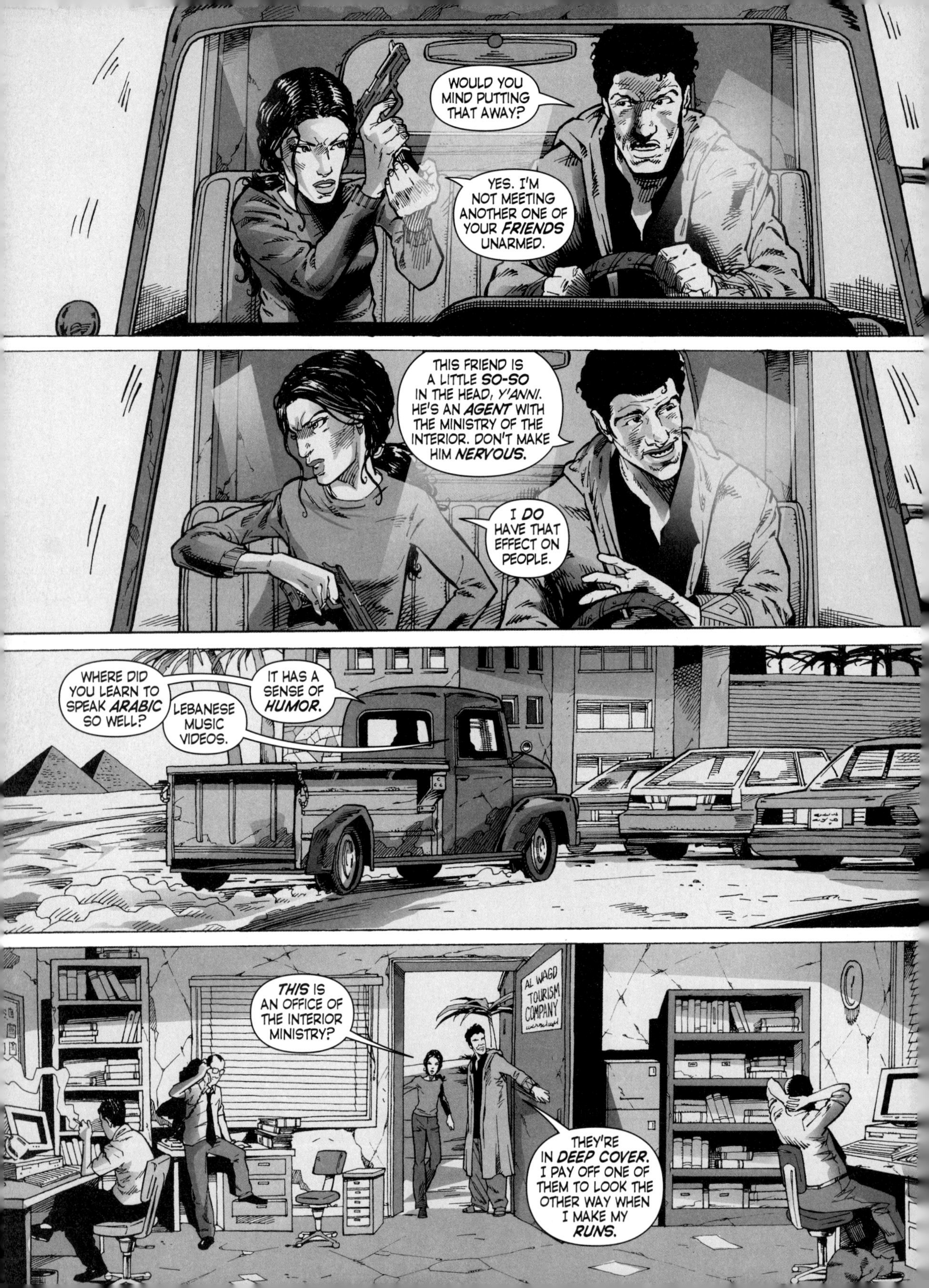
WOULD YOU MIND PUTTING THAT AWAY?
YES. I'M NOT MEETING ANOTHER ONE OF YOUR *FRIENDS* UNARMED.
THIS FRIEND IS A LITTLE *SO-SO* IN THE HEAD, *Y'ANNI*. HE'S AN *AGENT* WITH THE MINISTRY OF THE INTERIOR. DON'T MAKE HIM *NERVOUS.*
I *DO* HAVE THAT EFFECT ON PEOPLE.
WHERE DID YOU LEARN TO SPEAK *ARABIC* SO WELL?
LEBANESE MUSIC VIDEOS.
IT HAS A SENSE OF *HUMOR.*
AL WAGD TOURISM COMPANY
THIS IS AN OFFICE OF THE INTERIOR MINISTRY?
THEY'RE IN *DEEP COVER.* I PAY OFF ONE OF THEM TO LOOK THE OTHER WAY WHEN I MAKE MY *RUNS.*

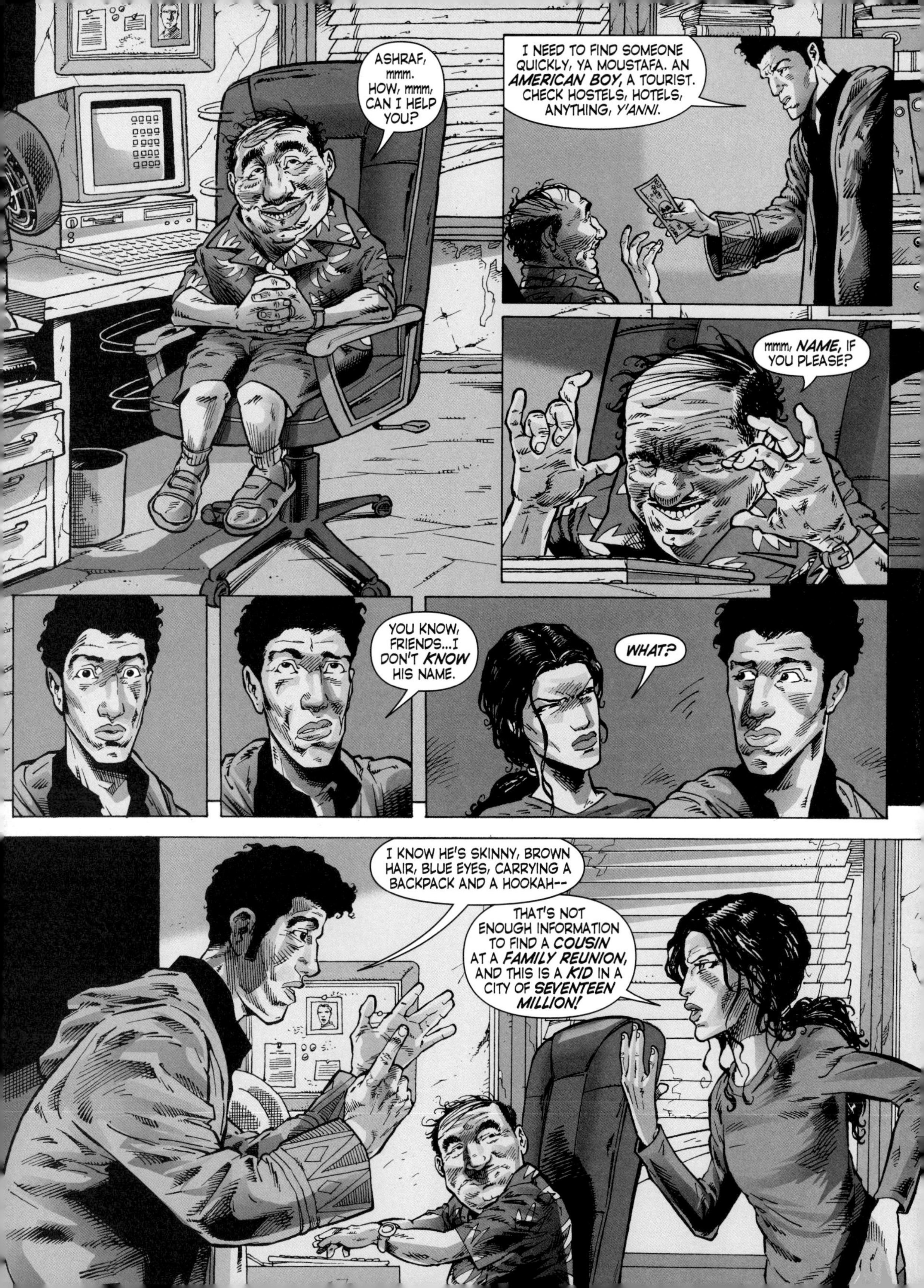
ASHRAF, mmm. HOW, mmm, CAN I HELP YOU?
I NEED TO FIND SOMEONE QUICKLY, YA MOUSTAFA. AN *AMERICAN BOY,* A TOURIST. CHECK HOSTELS, HOTELS, ANYTHING, *Y'ANNI.*
mmm, *NAME,* IF YOU PLEASE?
YOU KNOW, FRIENDS...I DON'T *KNOW* HIS NAME.
WHAT?
I KNOW HE'S SKINNY, BROWN HAIR, BLUE EYES, CARRYING A BACKPACK AND A HOOKAH--
THAT'S NOT ENOUGH INFORMATION TO FIND A *COUSIN* AT A *FAMILY REUNION,* AND THIS IS A *KID* IN A CITY OF *SEVENTEEN MILLION!*

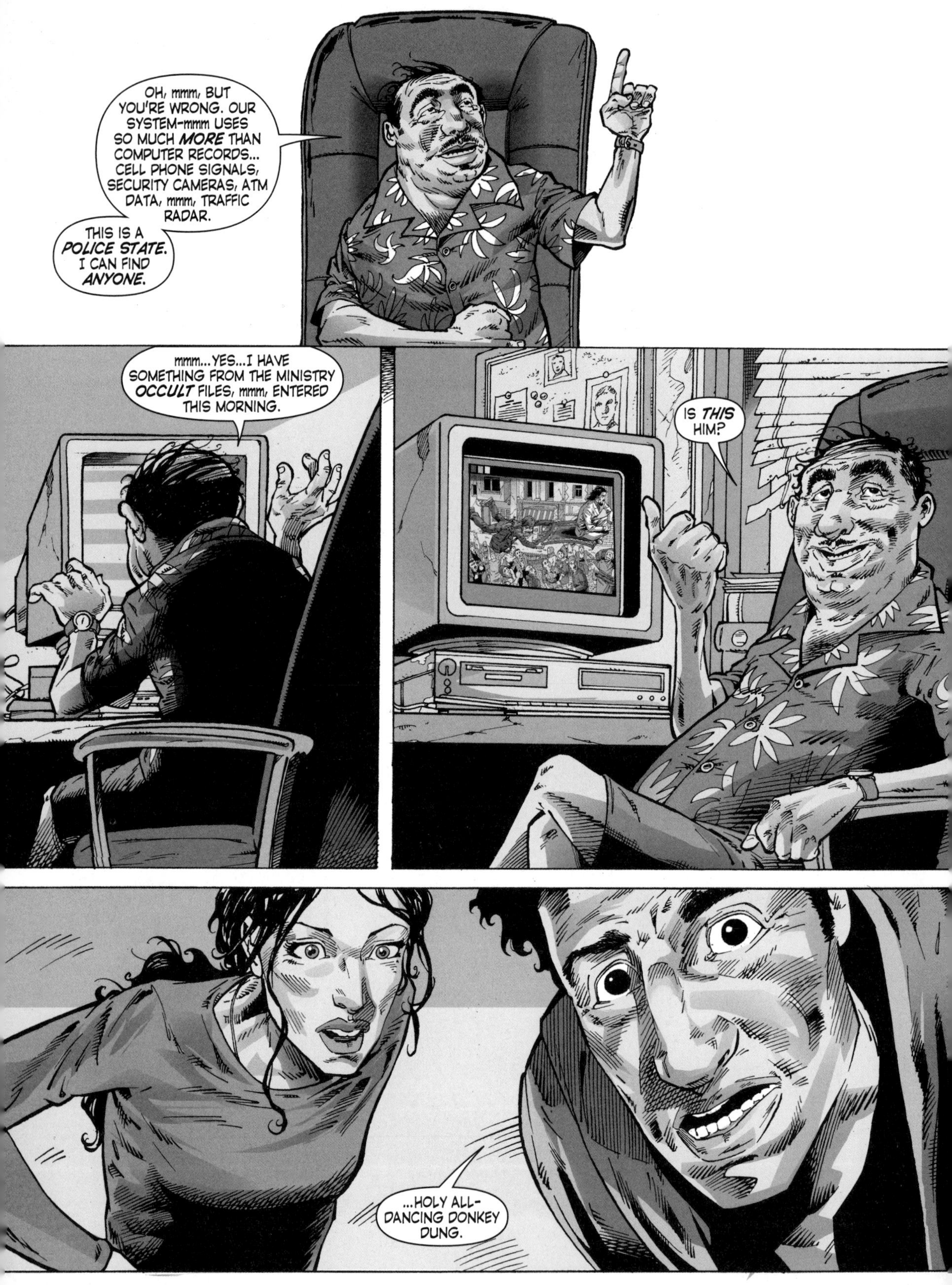
OH, mmm, BUT YOU'RE WRONG. OUR SYSTEM--mmm USES SO MUCH *MORE* THAN COMPUTER RECORDS... CELL PHONE SIGNALS, SECURITY CAMERAS, ATM DATA, mmm, TRAFFIC RADAR.
THIS IS A *POLICE STATE.* I CAN FIND *ANYONE.*
mmm...YES...I HAVE SOMETHING FROM THE MINISTRY *OCCULT* FILES, mmm, ENTERED THIS MORNING.
IS *THIS* HIM?
...HOLY ALL-DANCING DONKEY DUNG.

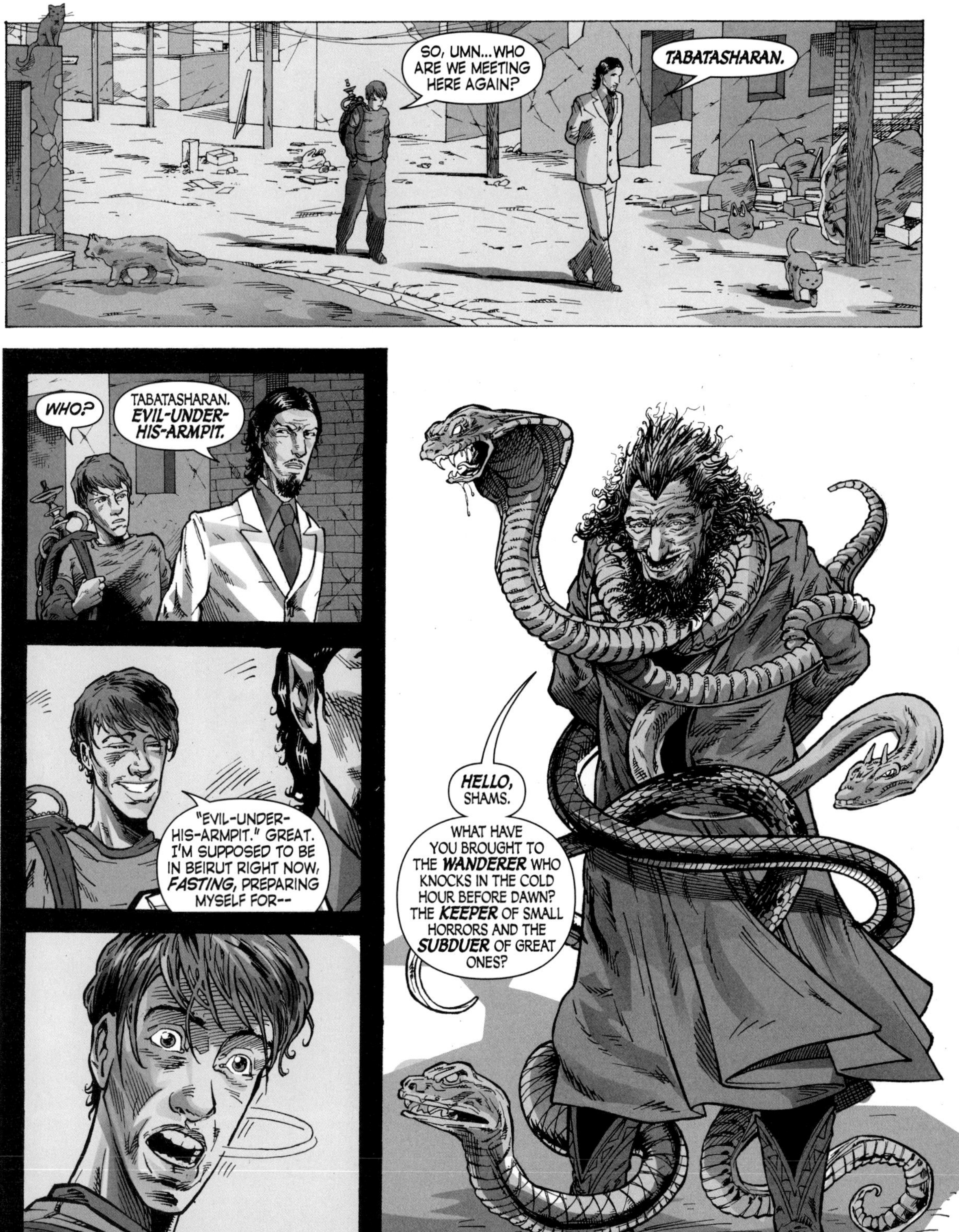
SO, UMN...WHO ARE WE MEETING HERE AGAIN?
TABATASHARAN.
WHO?
TABATASHARAN. EVIL-UNDER-HIS-ARMPIT.
"EVIL-UNDER-HIS-ARMPIT." GREAT. I'M SUPPOSED TO BE IN BEIRUT RIGHT NOW, FASTING, PREPARING MYSELF FOR--
HELLO, SHAMS.
WHAT HAVE YOU BROUGHT TO THE WANDERER WHO KNOCKS IN THE COLD HOUR BEFORE DAWN? THE KEEPER OF SMALL HORRORS AND THE SUBDUER OF GREAT ONES?

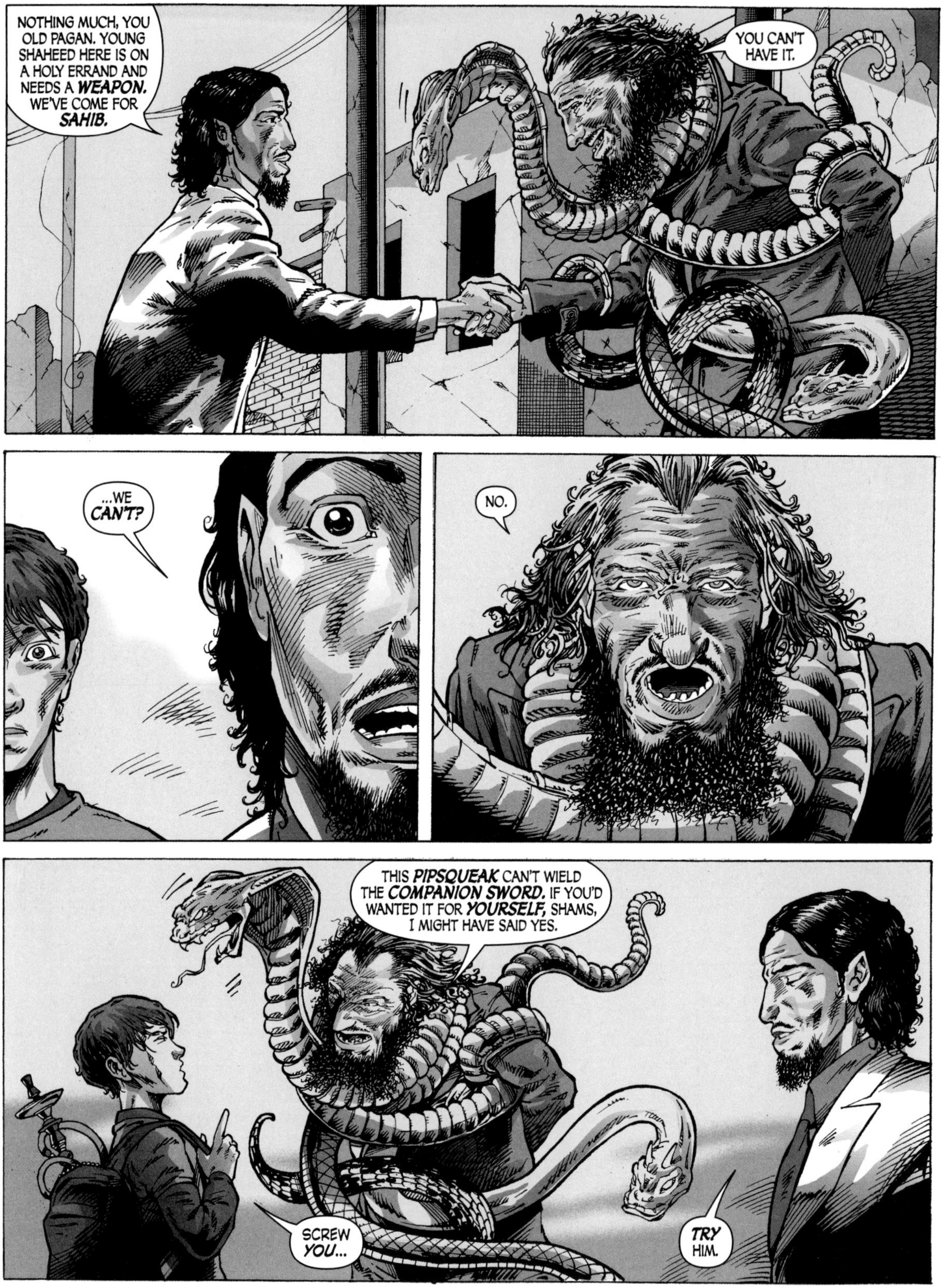
NOTHING MUCH, YOU OLD PAGAN. YOUNG SHAHEED HERE IS ON A HOLY ERRAND AND NEEDS A WEAPON. WE'VE COME FOR SAHIB.
YOU CAN'T HAVE IT.
...WE CAN'T?
NO.
THIS PIPSQUEAK CAN'T WIELD THE COMPANION SWORD. IF YOU'D WANTED IT FOR YOURSELF, SHAMS, I MIGHT HAVE SAID YES.
SCREW YOU...
TRY HIM.

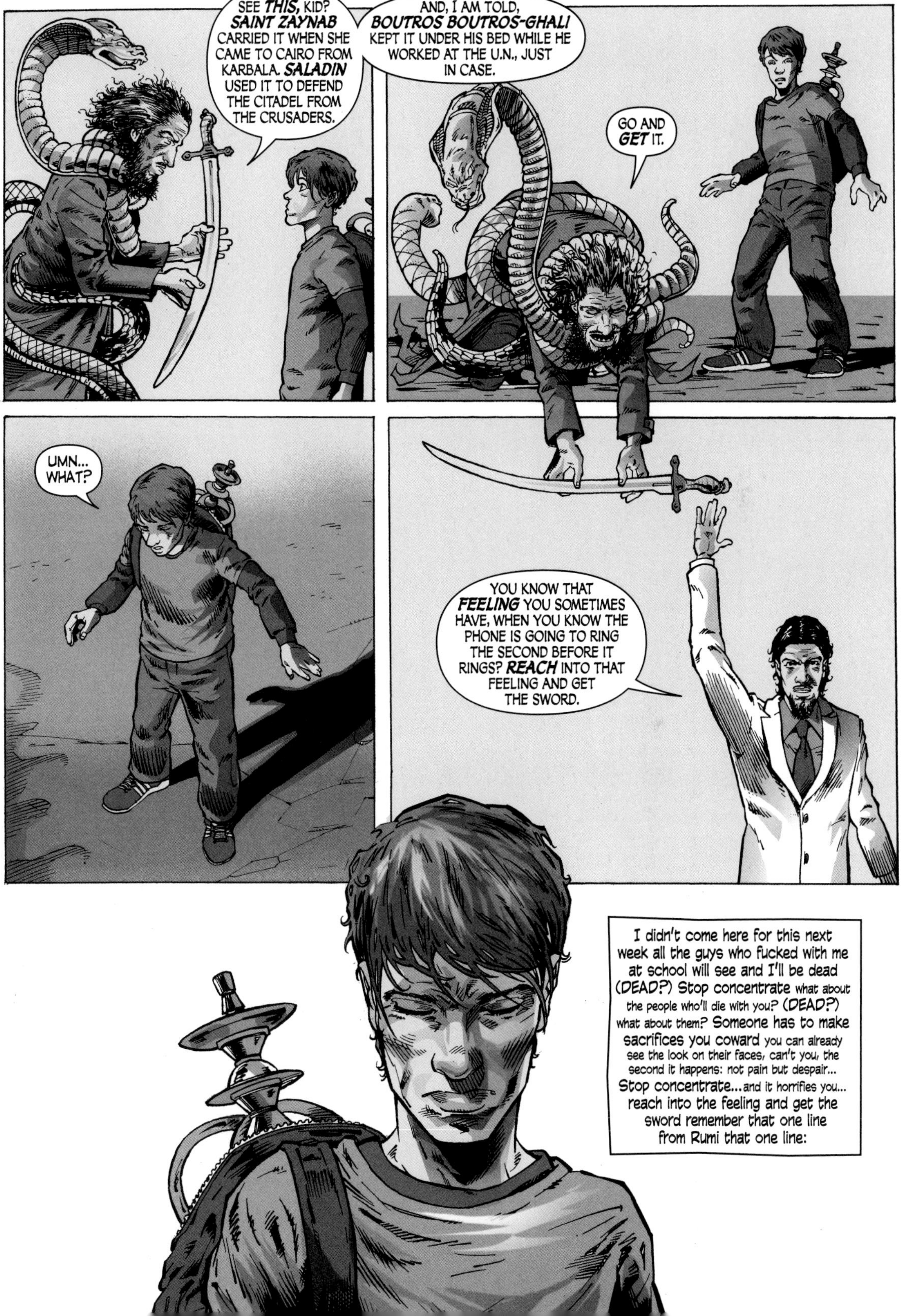
SEE THIS, KID? SAINT ZAYNAB CARRIED IT WHEN SHE CAME TO CAIRO FROM KARBALA. SALADIN USED IT TO DEFEND THE CITADEL FROM THE CRUSADERS.
AND, I AM TOLD, BOUTROS BOUTROS-GHALI KEPT IT UNDER HIS BED WHILE HE WORKED AT THE U.N., JUST IN CASE.
GO AND GET IT.
UMN... WHAT?
YOU KNOW THAT FEELING YOU SOMETIMES HAVE, WHEN YOU KNOW THE PHONE IS GOING TO RING THE SECOND BEFORE IT RINGS? REACH INTO THAT FEELING AND GET THE SWORD.
I didn't come here for this next week all the guys who fucked with me at school will see and I'll be dead (DEAD?) Stop concentrate what about the people who'll die with you? (DEAD?) what about them? Someone has to make sacrifices you coward you can already see the look on their faces, can't you, the second it happens: not pain but despair... Stop concentrate... and it horrifies you... reach into the feeling and get the sword remember that one line from Rumi that one line:

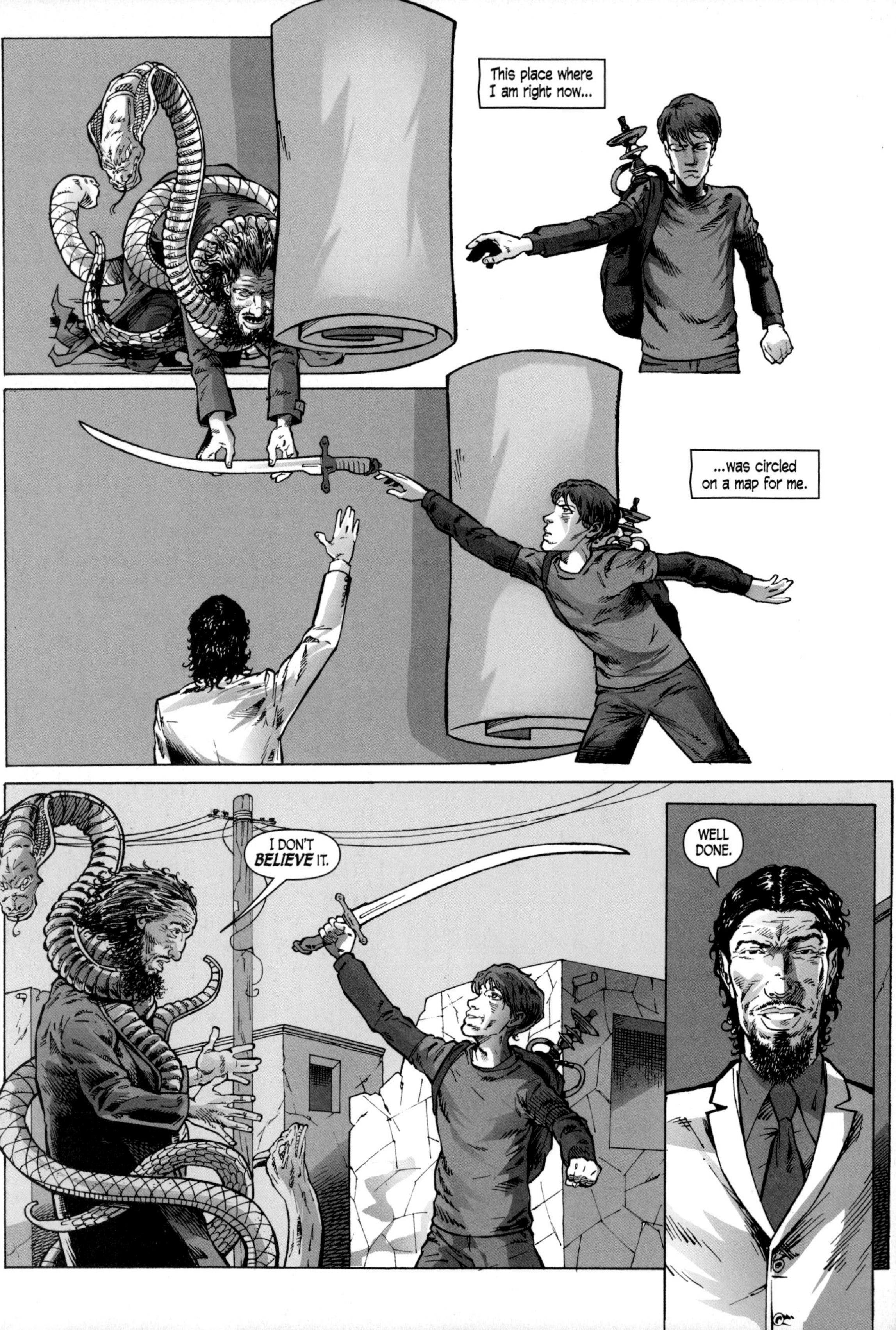

This place where I am right now...
...was circled on a map for me.
I DON'T BELIEVE IT.
WELL DONE.

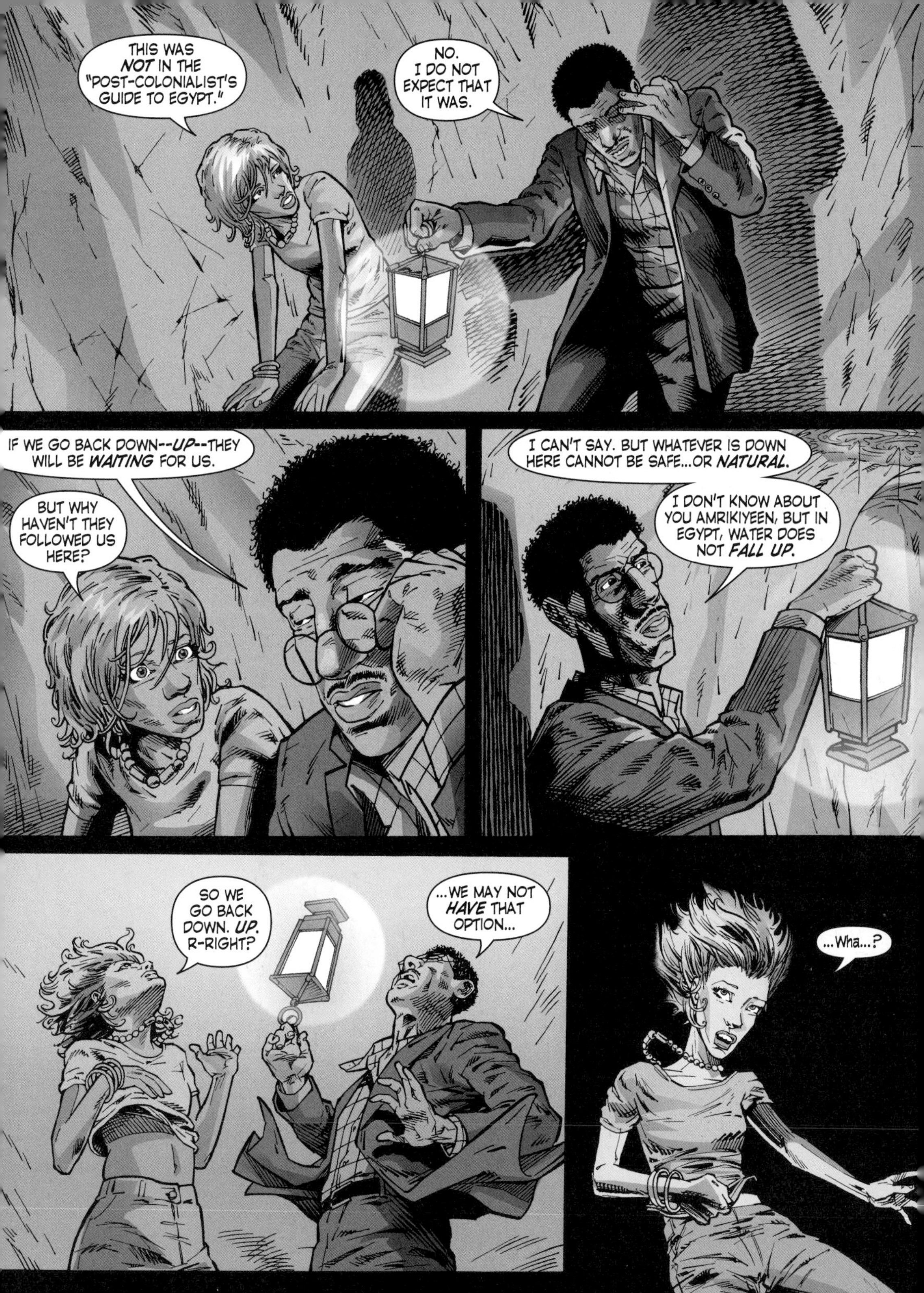
THIS WAS *NOT* IN THE "POST-COLONIALIST'S GUIDE TO EGYPT."
NO. I DO NOT EXPECT THAT IT WAS.
IF WE GO BACK DOWN--*UP*--THEY WILL BE *WAITING* FOR US.
BUT WHY HAVEN'T THEY FOLLOWED US HERE?
I CAN'T SAY. BUT WHATEVER IS DOWN HERE CANNOT BE SAFE...OR *NATURAL.*
I DON'T KNOW ABOUT YOU AMRIKIYEEN, BUT IN EGYPT, WATER DOES NOT *FALL UP.*
SO WE GO BACK DOWN. *UP.* R-RIGHT?
...WE MAY NOT *HAVE* THAT OPTION...
...Wha...?

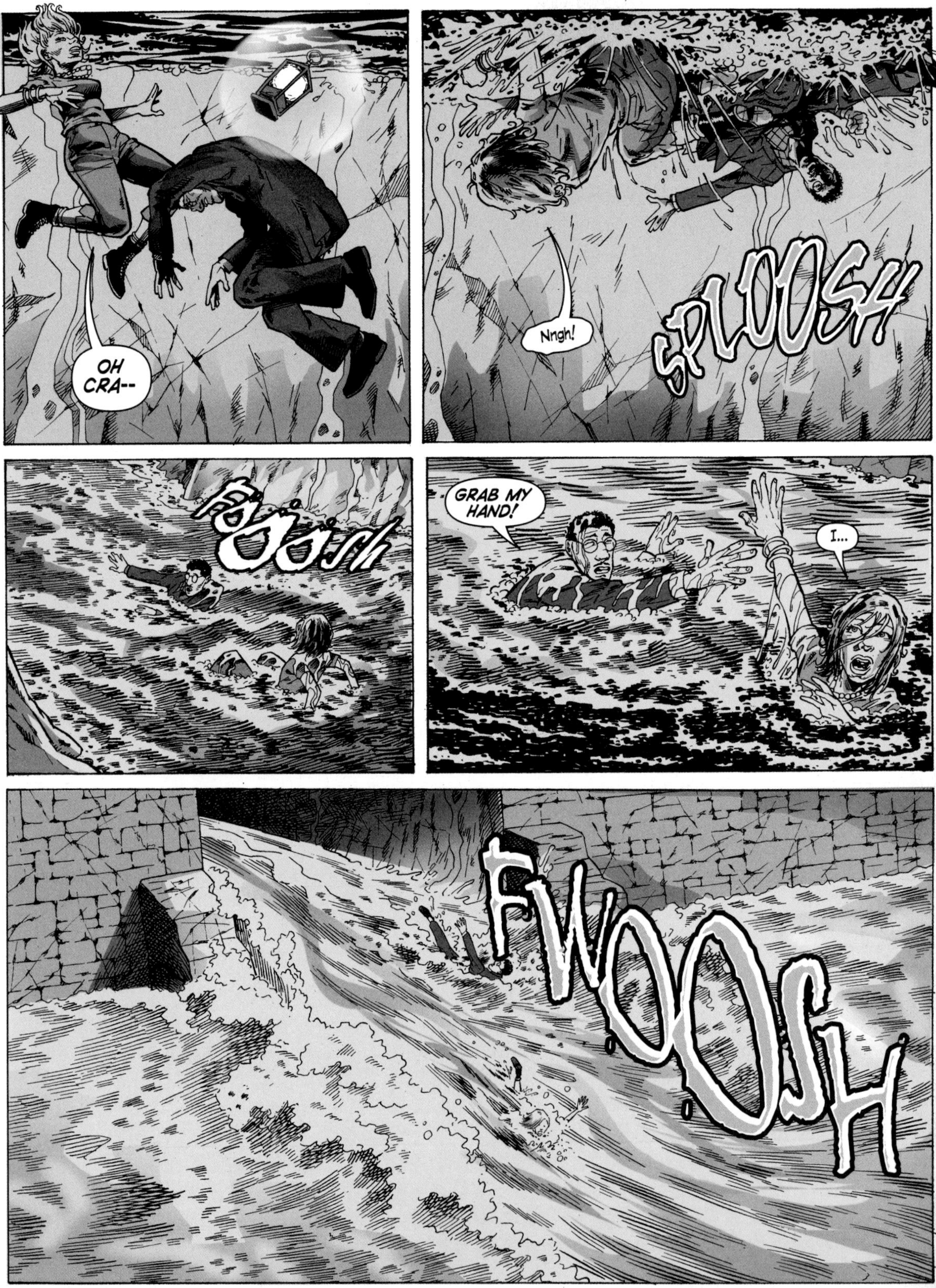
OH CRA--
Nngh!
SPLOOSH
FOOSH
GRAB MY HAND!
I...
FWOOSH

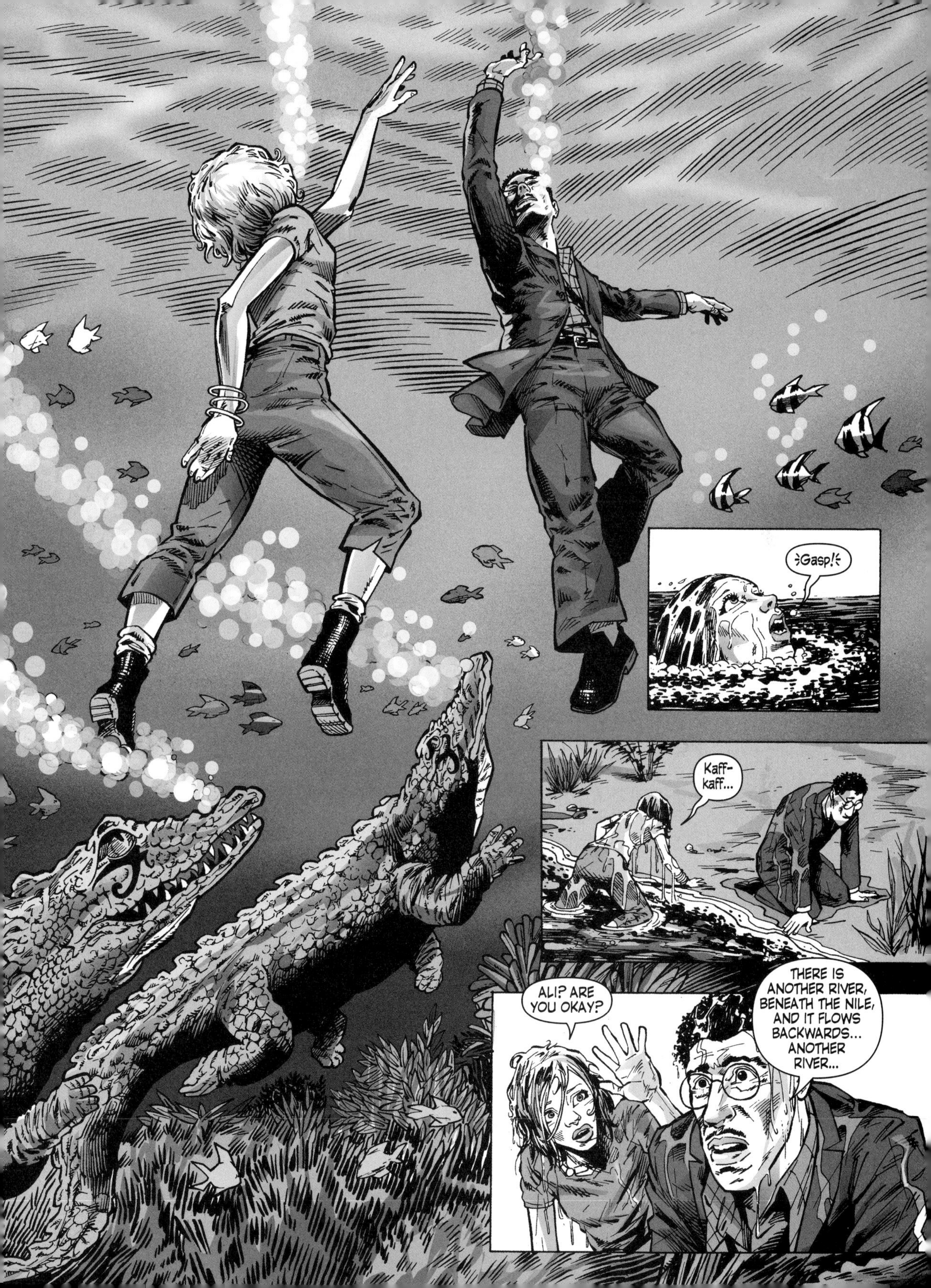
Gasp!
Kaff-kaff...
ALI? ARE YOU OKAY?
THERE IS ANOTHER RIVER, BENEATH THE NILE, AND IT FLOWS BACKWARDS... ANOTHER RIVER...

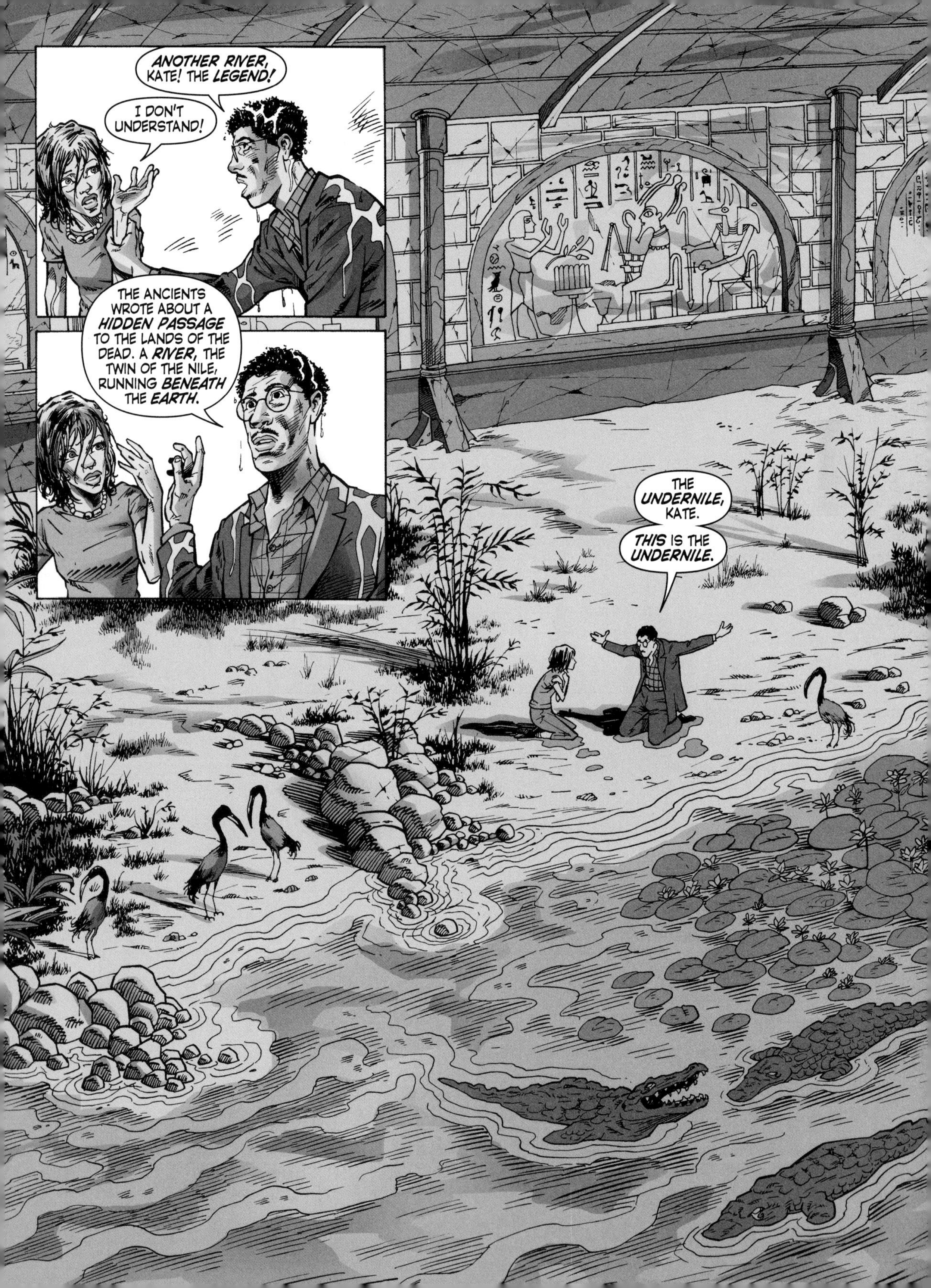
ANOTHER RIVER, KATE! THE LEGEND!
I DON'T UNDERSTAND!
THE ANCIENTS WROTE ABOUT A HIDDEN PASSAGE TO THE LANDS OF THE DEAD. A RIVER, THE TWIN OF THE NILE, RUNNING BENEATH THE EARTH.
THE UNDERNILE, KATE.
THIS IS THE UNDERNILE.

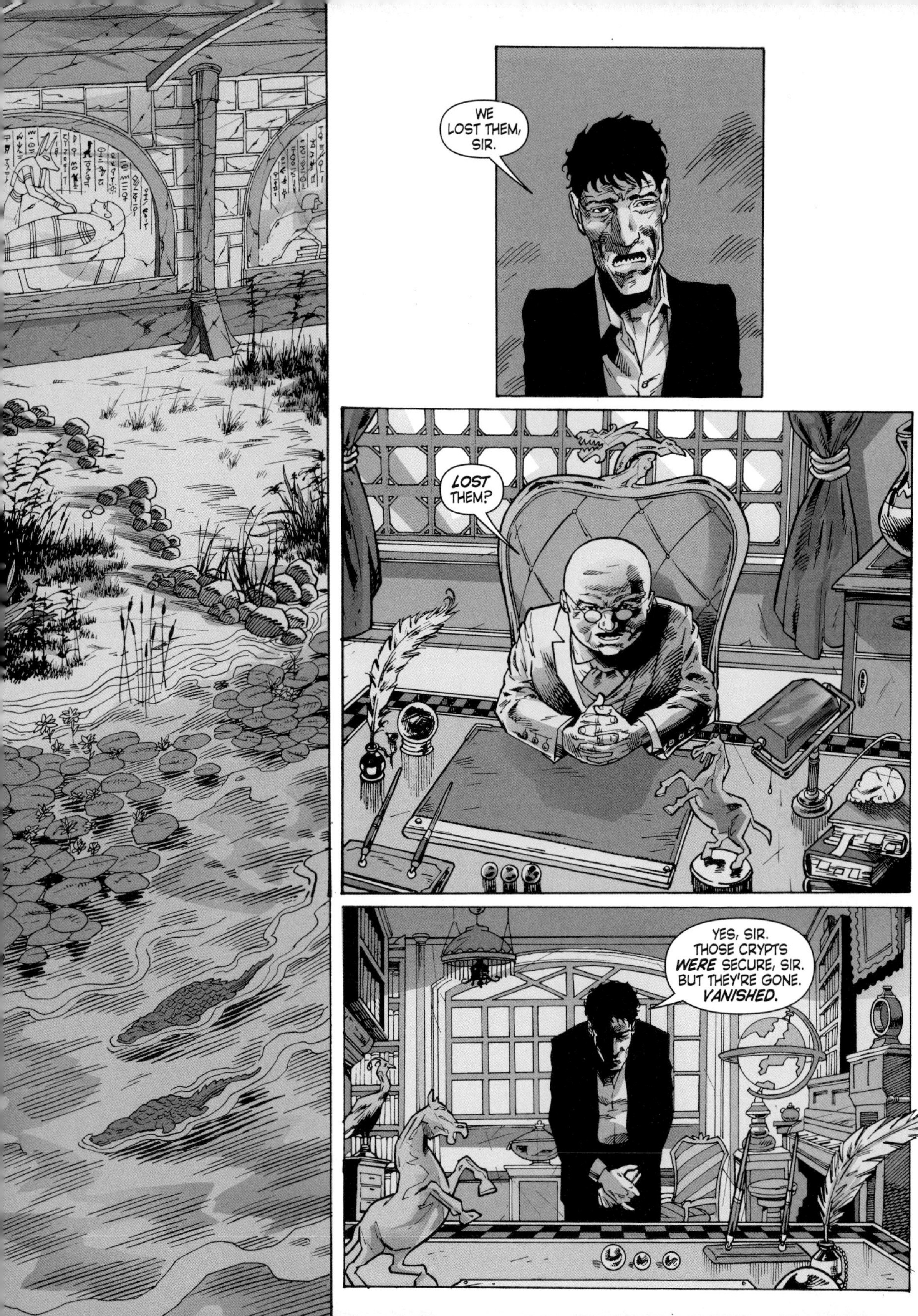
WE LOST THEM, SIR.
LOST THEM?
YES, SIR. THOSE CRYPTS WERE SECURE, SIR. BUT THEY'RE GONE. VANISHED.

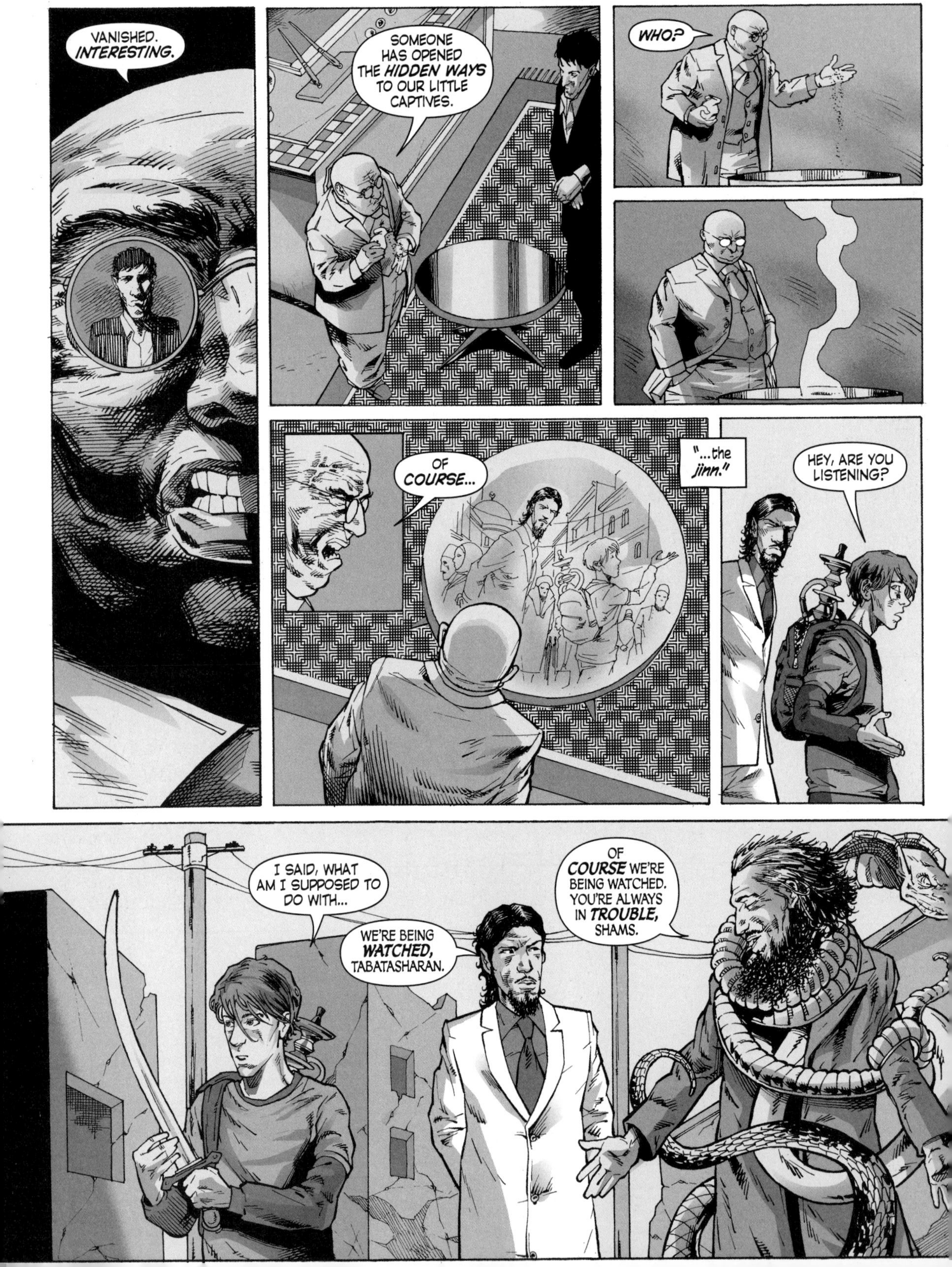
VANISHED. INTERESTING.
SOMEONE HAS OPENED THE HIDDEN WAYS TO OUR LITTLE CAPTIVES.
WHO?
OF COURSE...
"...the jinn."
HEY, ARE YOU LISTENING?
I SAID, WHAT AM I SUPPOSED TO DO WITH...
WE'RE BEING WATCHED, TABATASHARAN.
OF COURSE WE'RE BEING WATCHED. YOU'RE ALWAYS IN TROUBLE, SHAMS.

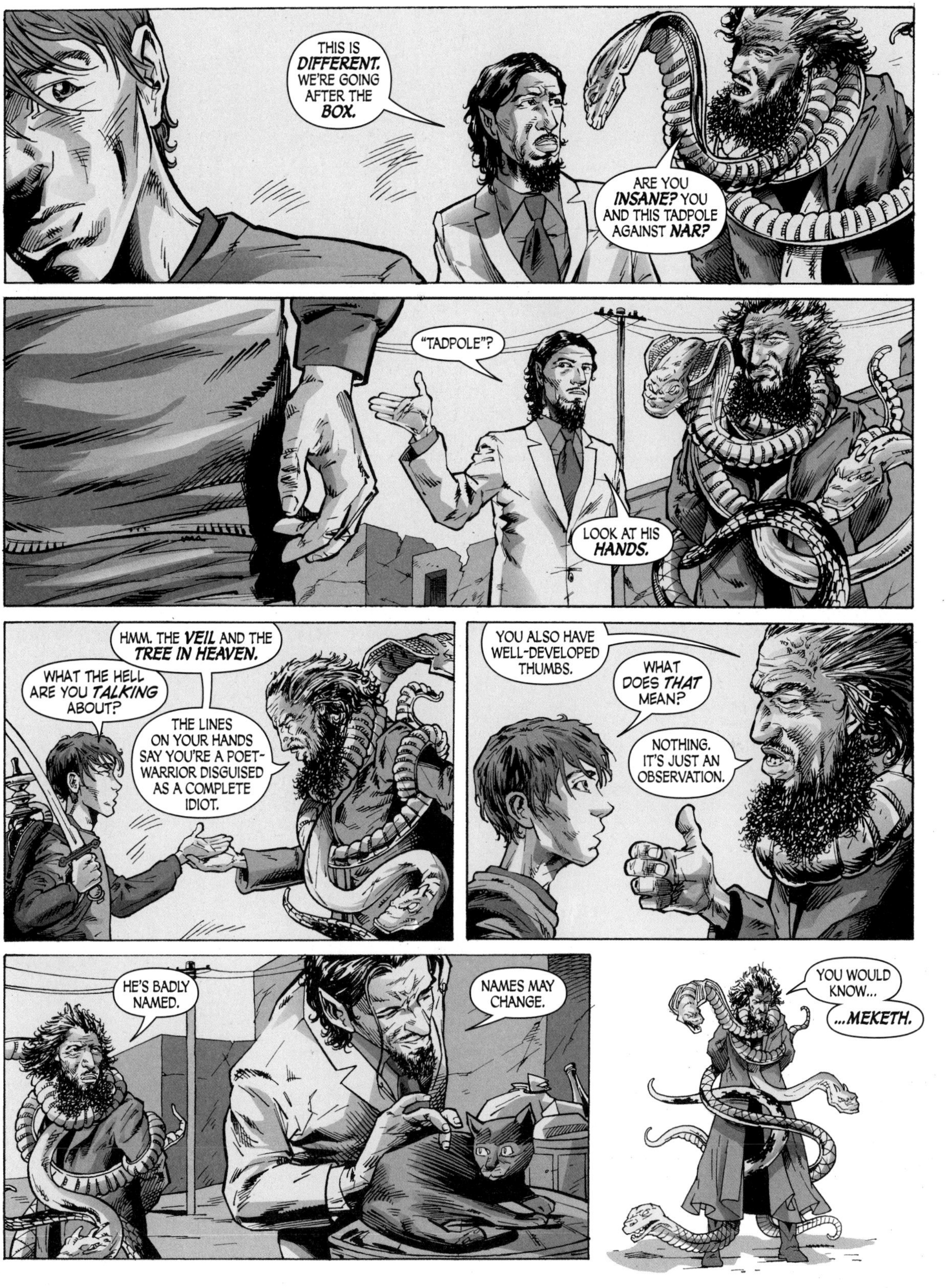
THIS IS *DIFFERENT.* WE'RE GOING AFTER THE *BOX.*
ARE YOU *INSANE?* YOU AND THIS TADPOLE AGAINST *NAR?*
"TADPOLE"?
LOOK AT HIS *HANDS.*
WHAT THE HELL ARE YOU *TALKING* ABOUT?
HMM. THE *VEIL* AND THE *TREE IN HEAVEN.*
THE LINES ON YOUR HANDS SAY YOU'RE A POET-WARRIOR DISGUISED AS A COMPLETE IDIOT.
YOU ALSO HAVE WELL-DEVELOPED THUMBS.
WHAT DOES *THAT* MEAN?
NOTHING. IT'S JUST AN OBSERVATION.
HE'S BADLY NAMED.
NAMES MAY CHANGE.
YOU WOULD KNOW...
...MEKETH.

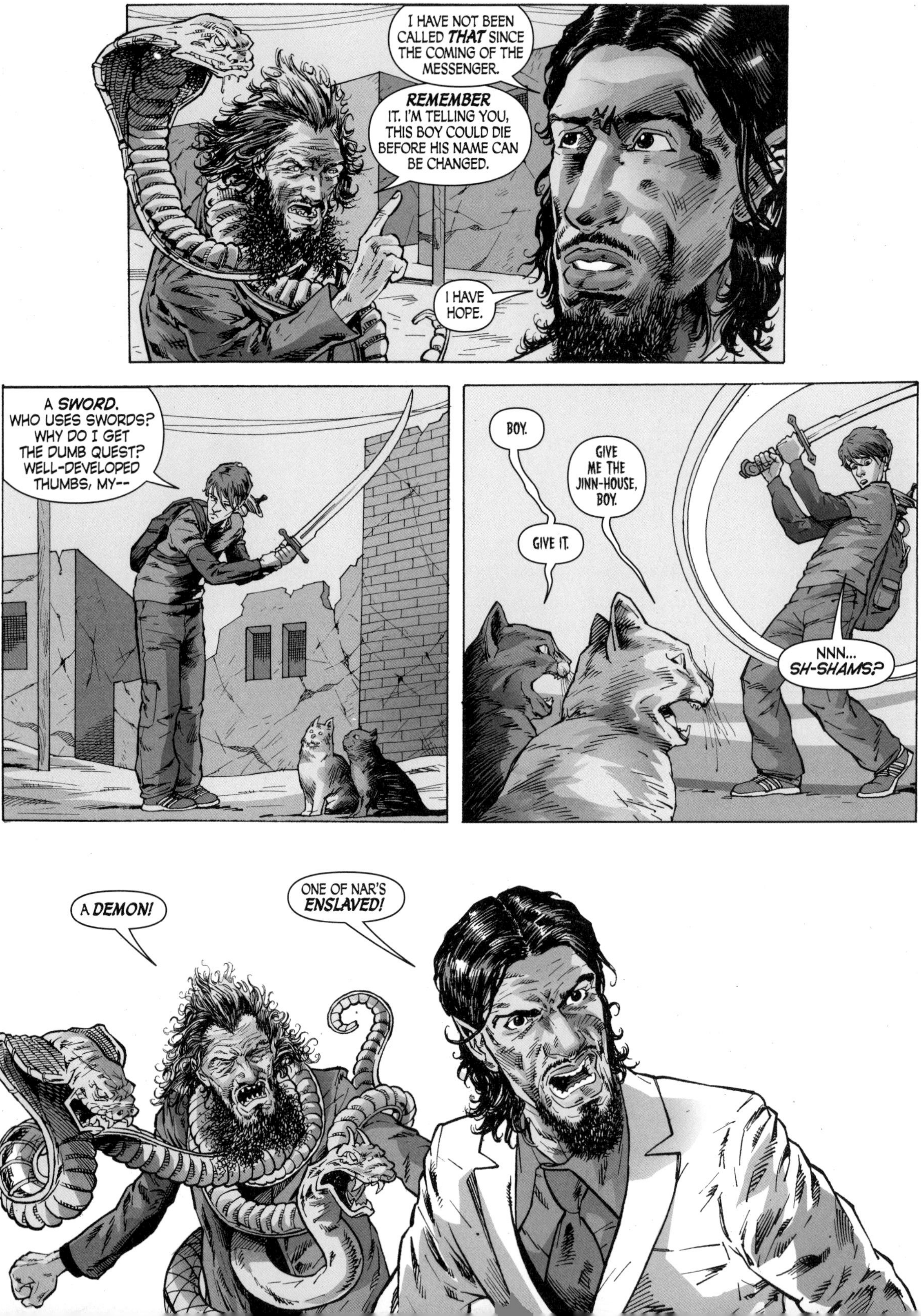
I HAVE NOT BEEN CALLED THAT SINCE THE COMING OF THE MESSENGER.
REMEMBER IT. I'M TELLING YOU, THIS BOY COULD DIE BEFORE HIS NAME CAN BE CHANGED.
I HAVE HOPE.
A SWORD. WHO USES SWORDS? WHY DO I GET THE DUMB QUEST? WELL-DEVELOPED THUMBS, MY--
BOY.
GIVE IT.
GIVE ME THE JINN-HOUSE, BOY.
NNN... SH-SHAMS?
A DEMON!
ONE OF NAR'S ENSLAVED!

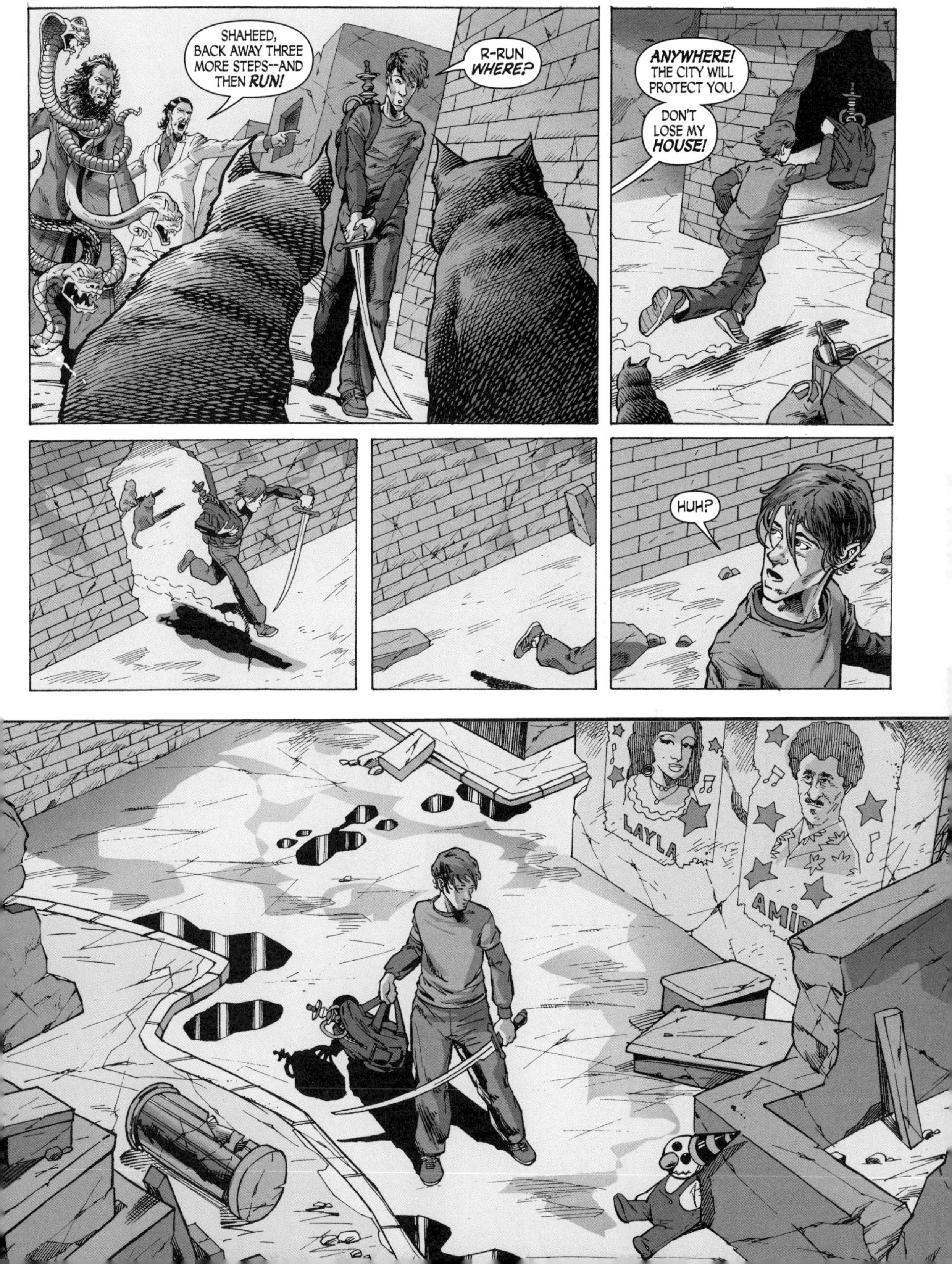
SHAHEED, BACK AWAY THREE MORE STEPS--AND THEN RUN!
R-RUN WHERE?
ANYWHERE! THE CITY WILL PROTECT YOU.
DON'T LOSE MY HOUSE!
HUH?
LAYLA
AMIR

SHE TRIES TO HIDE YOU FROM ME WITH WALLS AND OBSTACLES.

BUT THERE IS NO HIDING.

NOT HERE. NOT ANYWHERE.

LAYLA

AMI

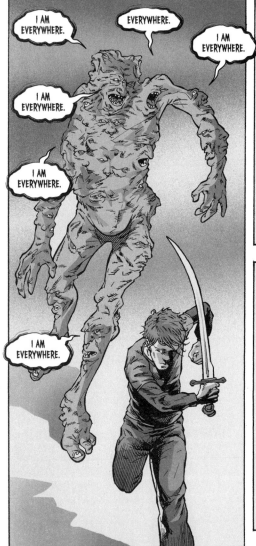

I AM EVERYWHERE.

EVERYWHERE.

I AM EVERYWHERE.

I AM EVERYWHERE.

I AM EVERYWHERE.

I AM EVERYWHERE.

GIVE ME THE JINN-HOUSE.

IT IS NAR'S BY RIGHT.

GIVE IT, OR I EAT YOUR LIVING ORGANS.

NNGH!

HAHAHA!

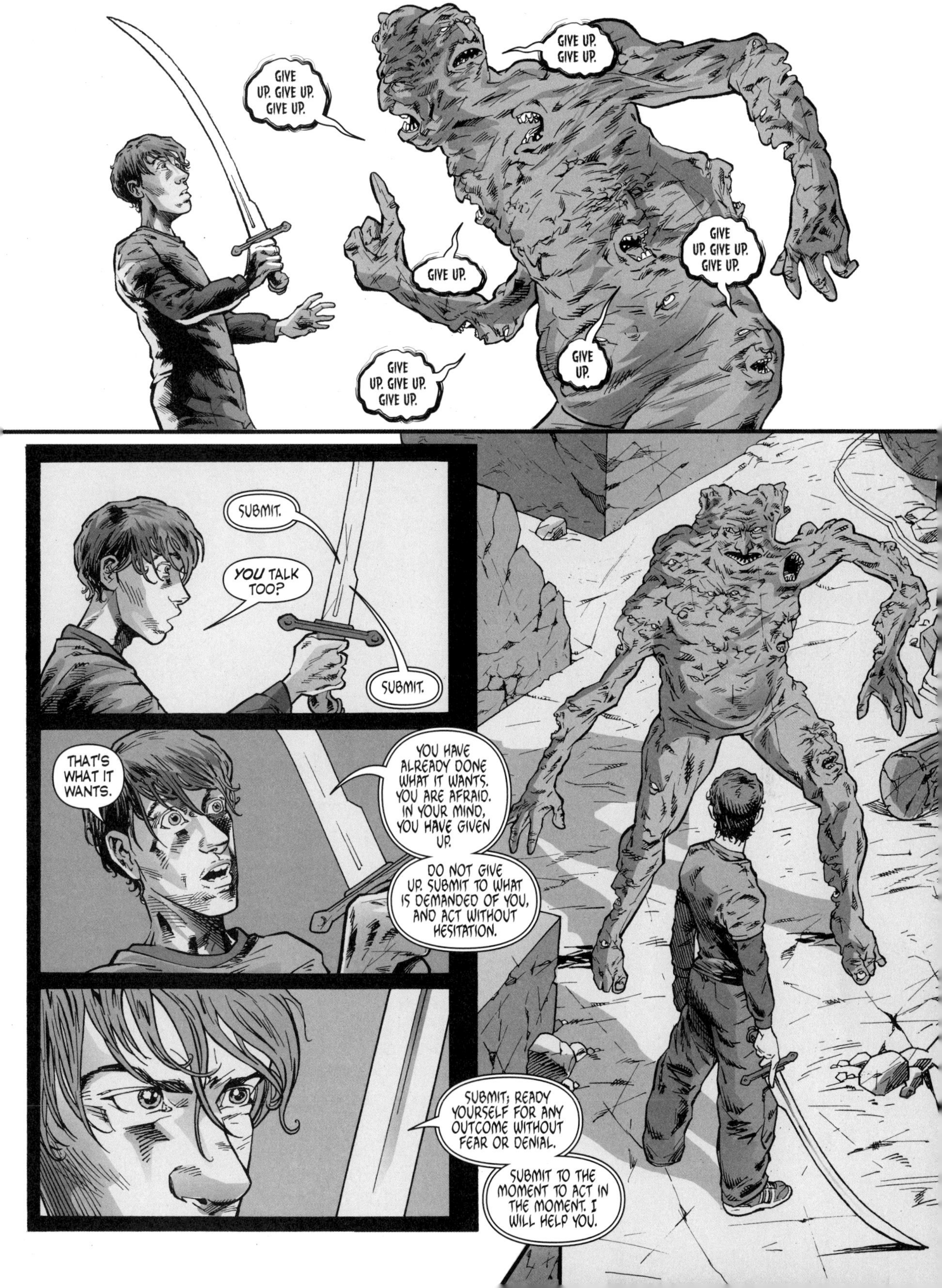
GIVE UP. GIVE UP. GIVE UP.
GIVE UP. GIVE UP.
GIVE UP.
GIVE UP. GIVE UP. GIVE UP.
GIVE UP.
GIVE UP. GIVE UP. GIVE UP.
SUBMIT.
YOU TALK TOO?
SUBMIT.
THAT'S WHAT IT WANTS.
YOU HAVE ALREADY DONE WHAT IT WANTS. YOU ARE AFRAID. IN YOUR MIND, YOU HAVE GIVEN UP.
DO NOT GIVE UP. SUBMIT TO WHAT IS DEMANDED OF YOU, AND ACT WITHOUT HESITATION.
SUBMIT; READY YOURSELF FOR ANY OUTCOME WITHOUT FEAR OR DENIAL.
SUBMIT TO THE MOMENT TO ACT IN THE MOMENT. I WILL HELP YOU.

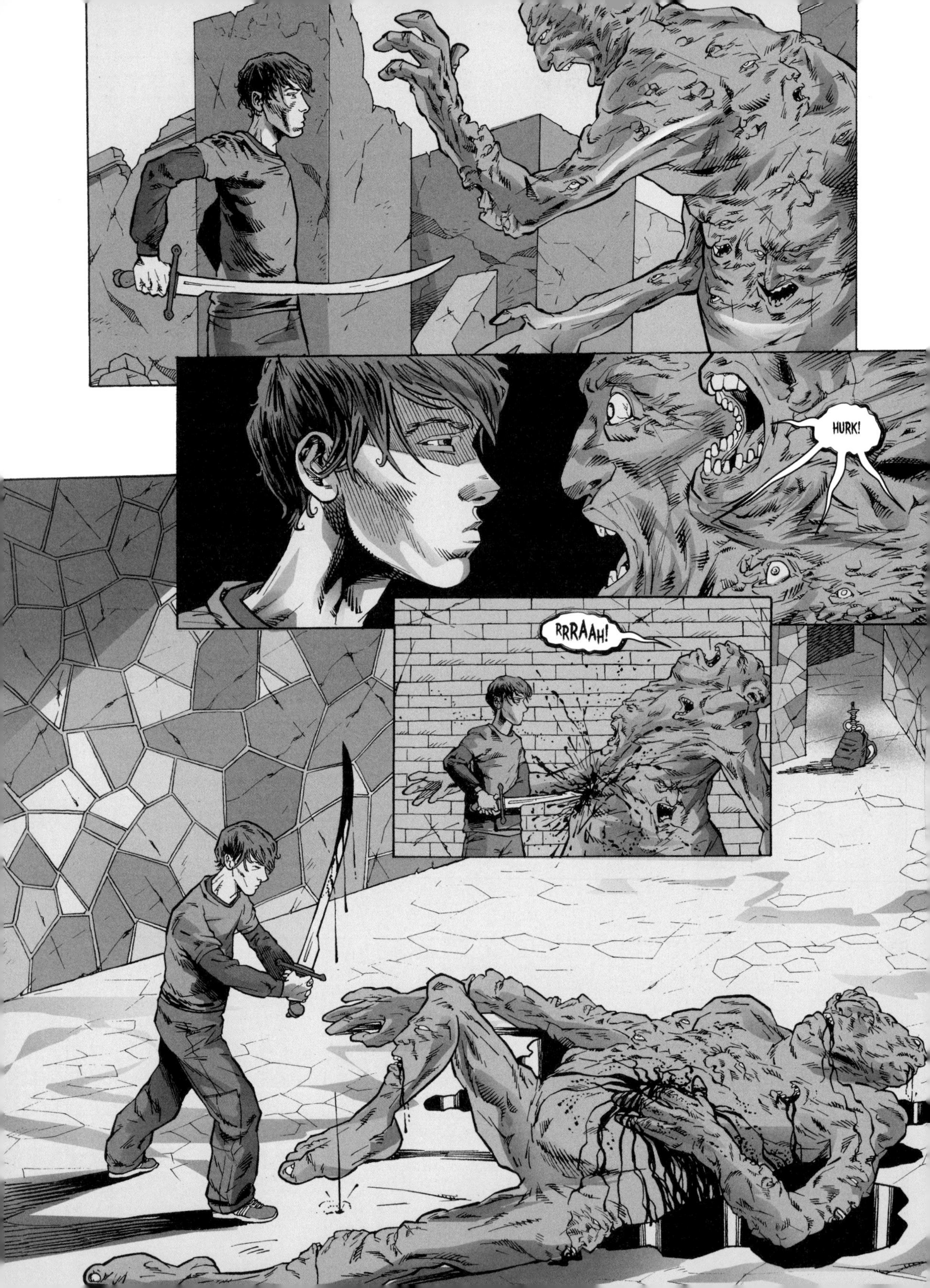
HURK!
RRRAAH!

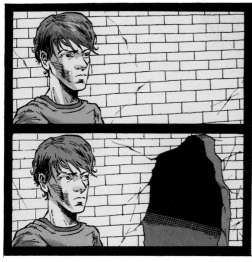

SHAHEED!

ARE YOU ALL RIGHT? ARE YOU HURT?

I--I'M FINE, I GUESS.

WELL, DAMN ME TO HELL-- THE TADPOLE'S *KILLED* A DEMON!

IT...IS NOT... OVER, SHAMS.

NAR HAS ALLIED HIMSELF WITH THE STEP STALKER... IBLIS HAS GONE INTO THE UNDERNILE TO MEET YOUR FRIENDS.

THEN I HAVE SAVED THEM FROM NAR...

...AND SENT THEM TO THEIR *DEATHS.*

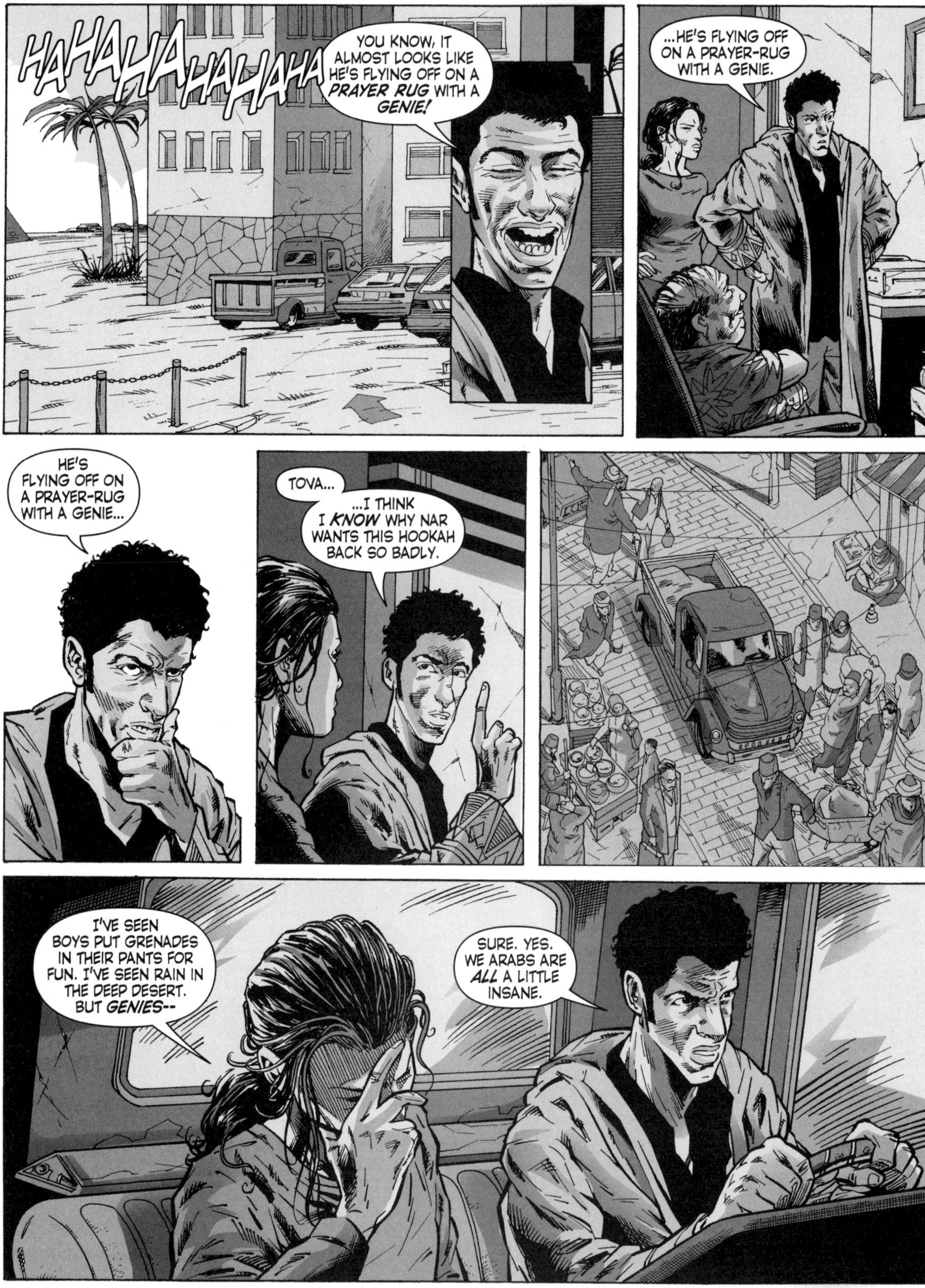
HAHAHAHAHAHAHAHA
YOU KNOW, IT ALMOST LOOKS LIKE HE'S FLYING OFF ON A PRAYER RUG WITH A GENIE!
...HE'S FLYING OFF ON A PRAYER-RUG WITH A GENIE.
HE'S FLYING OFF ON A PRAYER-RUG WITH A GENIE...
TOVA...
...I THINK I KNOW WHY NAR WANTS THIS HOOKAH BACK SO BADLY.
I'VE SEEN BOYS PUT GRENADES IN THEIR PANTS FOR FUN. I'VE SEEN RAIN IN THE DEEP DESERT. BUT GENIES--
SURE. YES. WE ARABS ARE ALL A LITTLE INSANE.

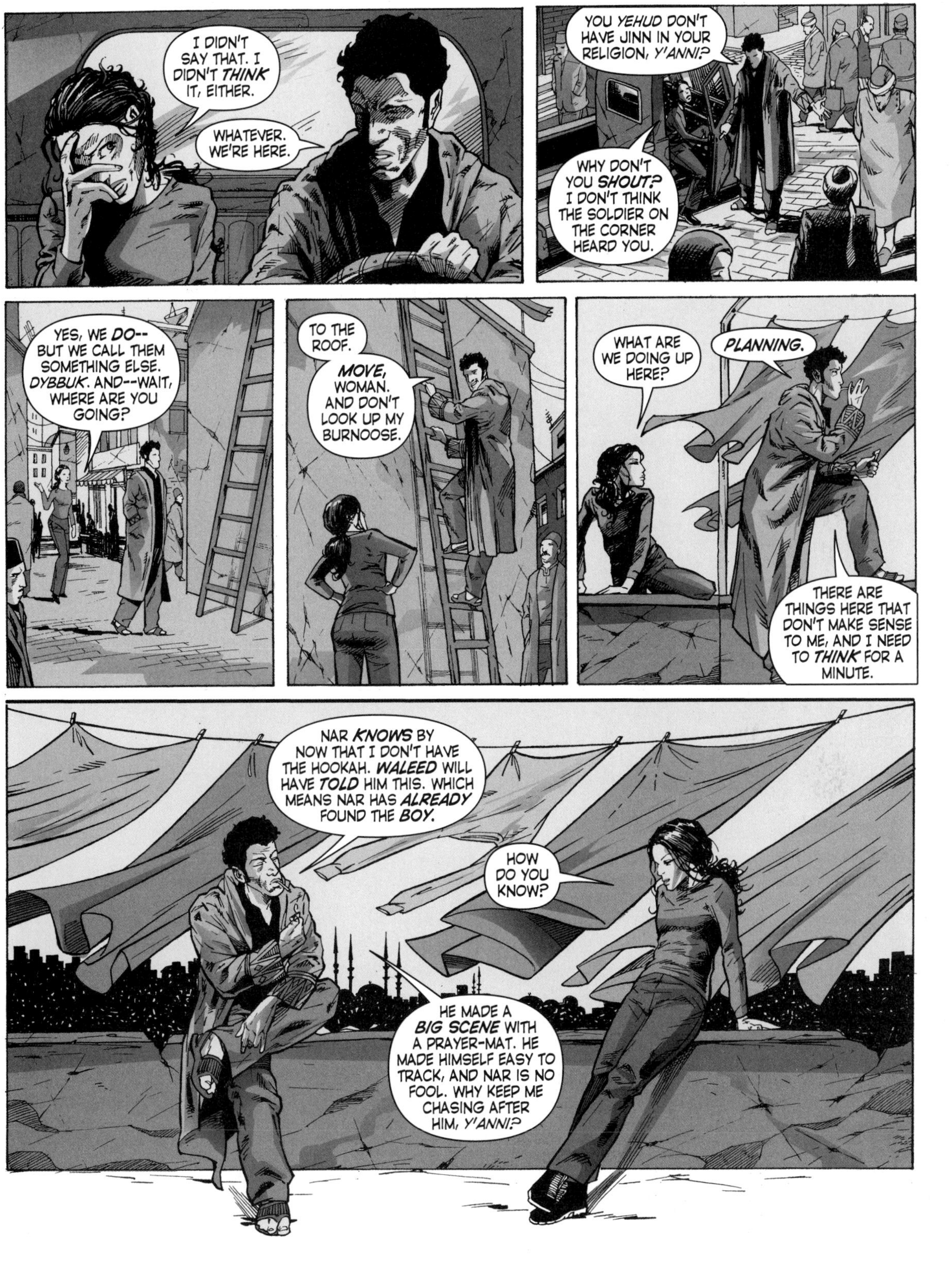
I DIDN'T SAY THAT. I DIDN'T *THINK* IT, EITHER.
WHATEVER. WE'RE HERE.
YOU *YEHUD* DON'T HAVE JINN IN YOUR RELIGION, *Y'ANNI?*
WHY DON'T YOU *SHOUT?* I DON'T THINK THE SOLDIER ON THE CORNER HEARD YOU.
YES, WE *DO*-- BUT WE CALL THEM SOMETHING ELSE. *DYBBUK*. AND--WAIT, WHERE ARE YOU GOING?
TO THE ROOF.
MOVE, WOMAN. AND DON'T LOOK UP MY BURNOOSE.
WHAT ARE WE DOING UP HERE?
PLANNING.
THERE ARE THINGS HERE THAT DON'T MAKE SENSE TO ME, AND I NEED TO *THINK* FOR A MINUTE.
NAR *KNOWS* BY NOW THAT I DON'T HAVE THE HOOKAH. *WALEED* WILL HAVE *TOLD* HIM THIS. WHICH MEANS NAR HAS *ALREADY* FOUND THE *BOY.*
HOW DO YOU KNOW?
HE MADE A *BIG SCENE* WITH A PRAYER-MAT. HE MADE HIMSELF EASY TO TRACK, AND NAR IS NO FOOL. WHY KEEP ME CHASING AFTER HIM, *Y'ANNI?*

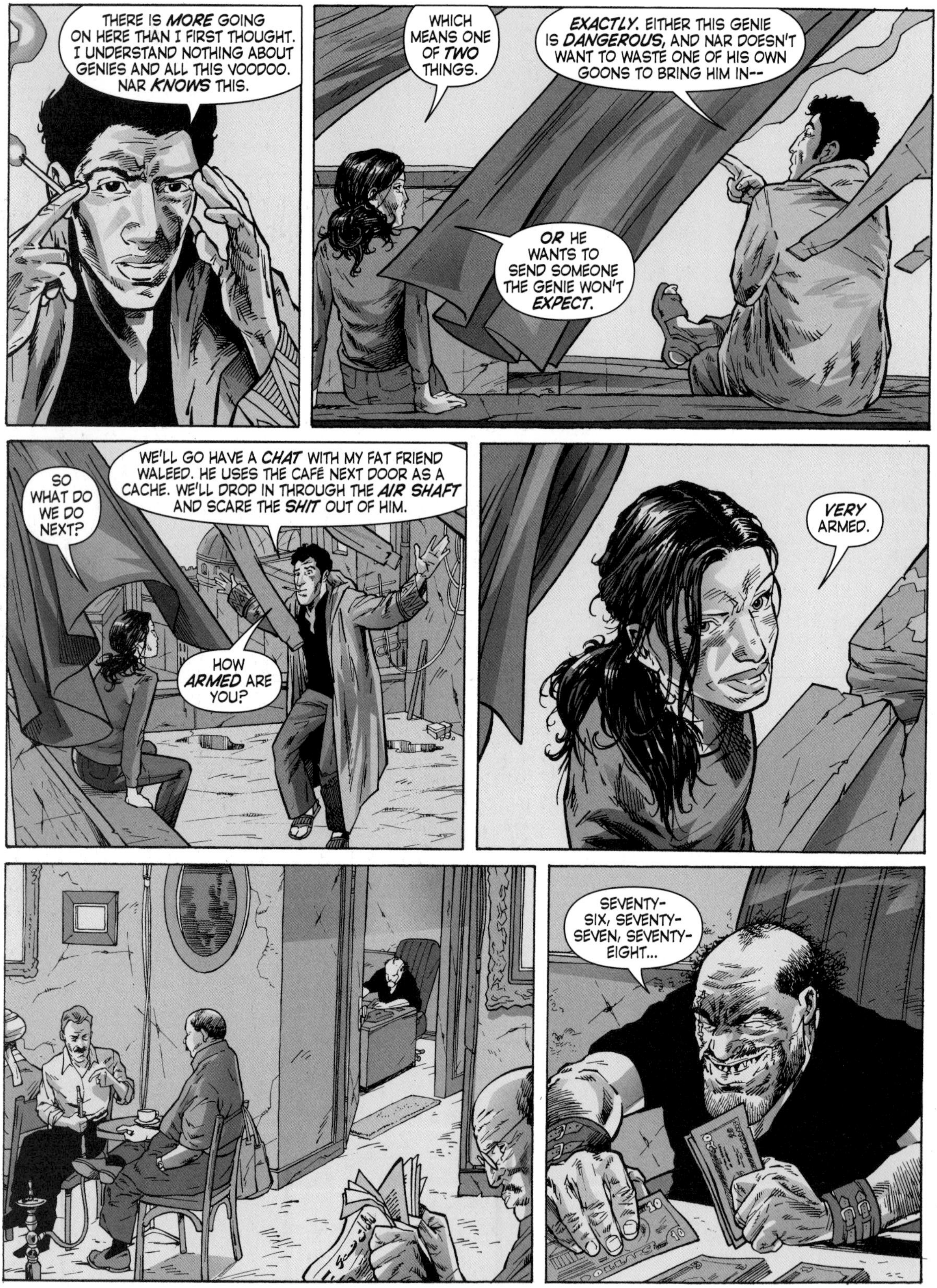
THERE IS MORE GOING ON HERE THAN I FIRST THOUGHT. I UNDERSTAND NOTHING ABOUT GENIES AND ALL THIS VOODOO. NAR KNOWS THIS.
WHICH MEANS ONE OF TWO THINGS.
EXACTLY. EITHER THIS GENIE IS DANGEROUS, AND NAR DOESN'T WANT TO WASTE ONE OF HIS OWN GOONS TO BRING HIM IN--
OR HE WANTS TO SEND SOMEONE THE GENIE WON'T EXPECT.
SO WHAT DO WE DO NEXT?
WE'LL GO HAVE A CHAT WITH MY FAT FRIEND WALEED. HE USES THE CAFÉ NEXT DOOR AS A CACHE. WE'LL DROP IN THROUGH THE AIR SHAFT AND SCARE THE SHIT OUT OF HIM.
HOW ARMED ARE YOU?
VERY ARMED.
SEVENTY-SIX, SEVENTY-SEVEN, SEVENTY-EIGHT...

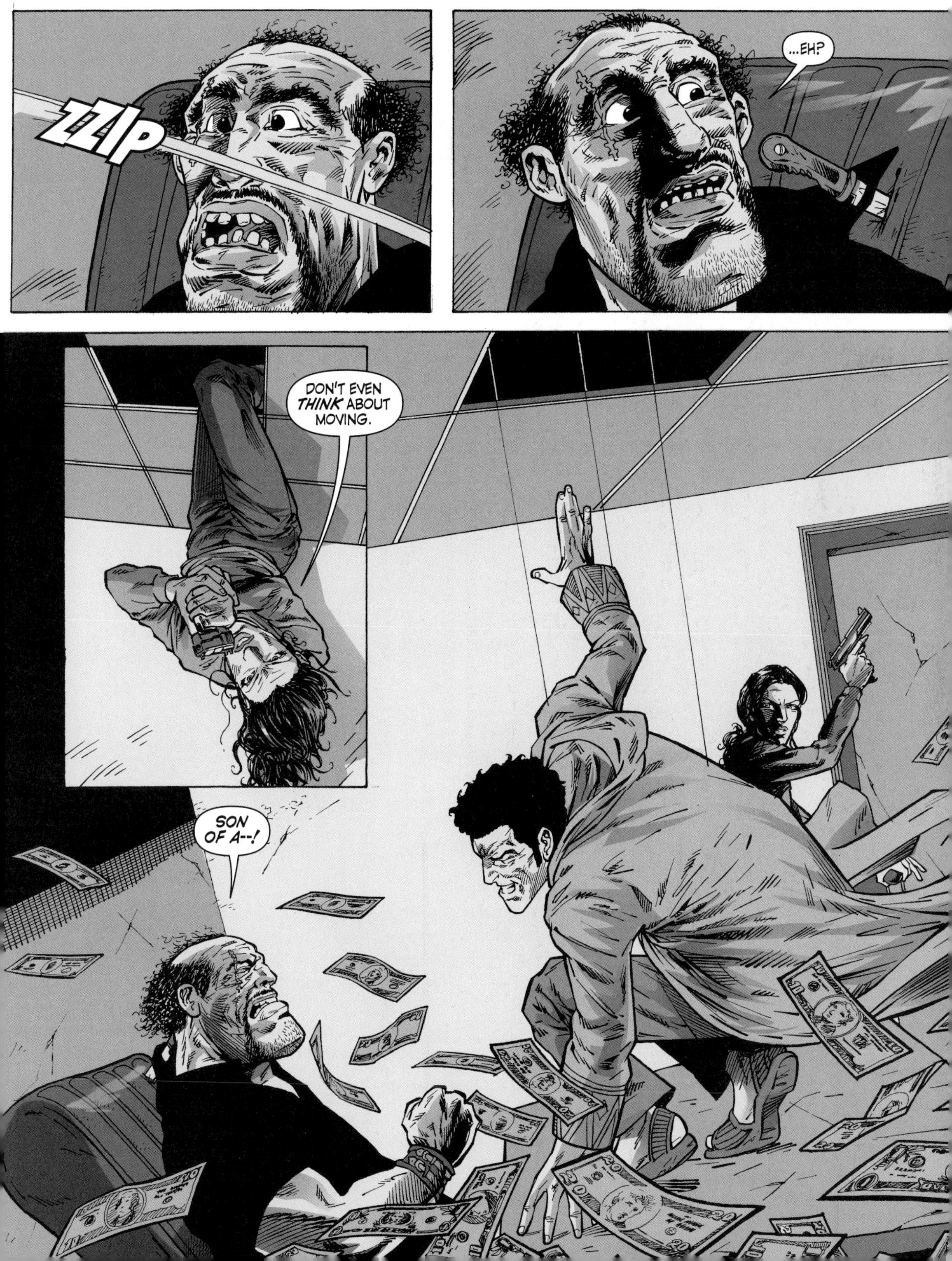
ZZIP
...EH?
DON'T EVEN *THINK* ABOUT MOVING.
SON OF A--!

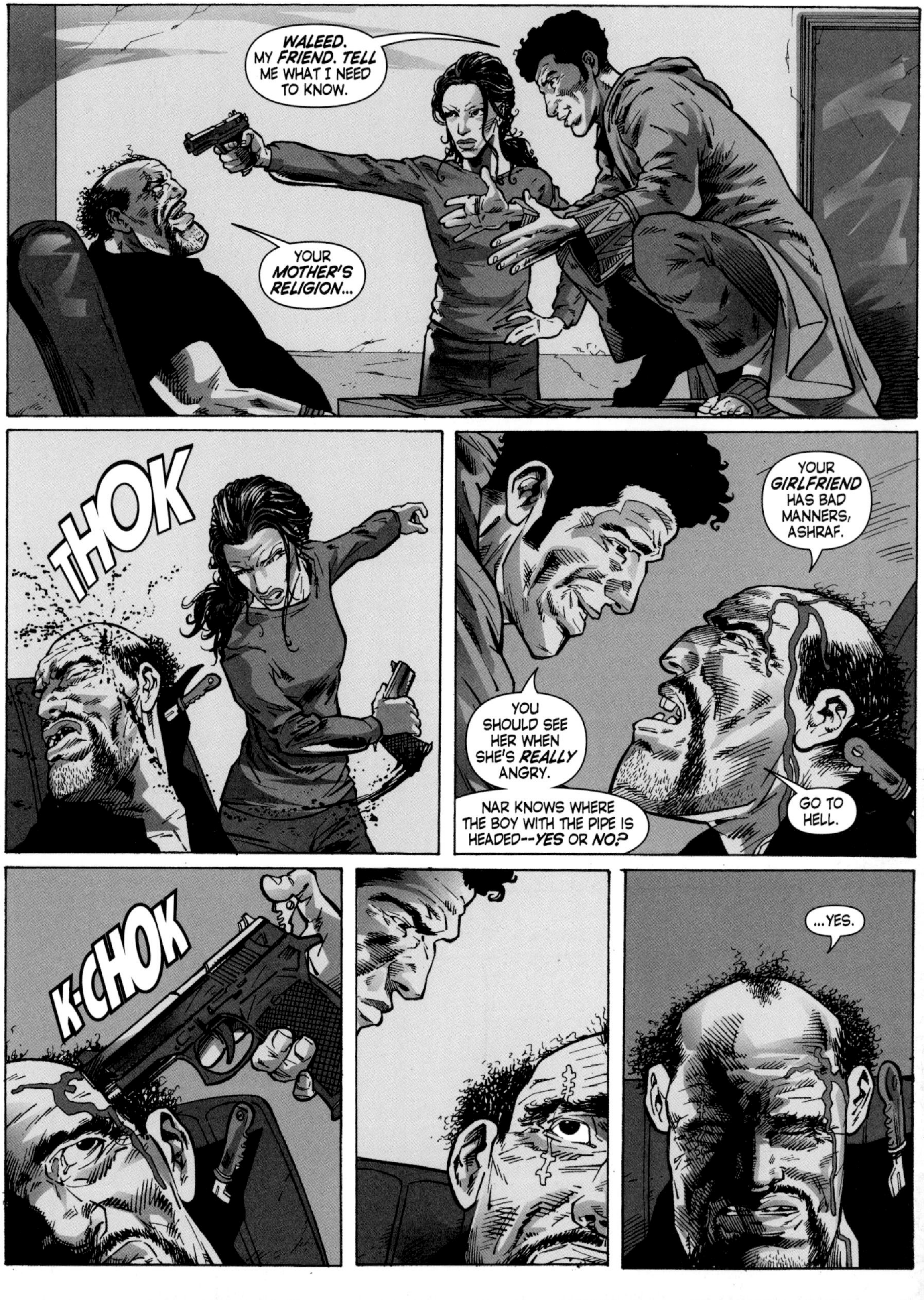
WALEED. MY FRIEND. TELL ME WHAT I NEED TO KNOW.
YOUR MOTHER'S RELIGION...
THOK
YOUR GIRLFRIEND HAS BAD MANNERS, ASHRAF.
YOU SHOULD SEE HER WHEN SHE'S REALLY ANGRY.
NAR KNOWS WHERE THE BOY WITH THE PIPE IS HEADED--YES OR NO?
GO TO HELL.
K-CHOK
...YES.

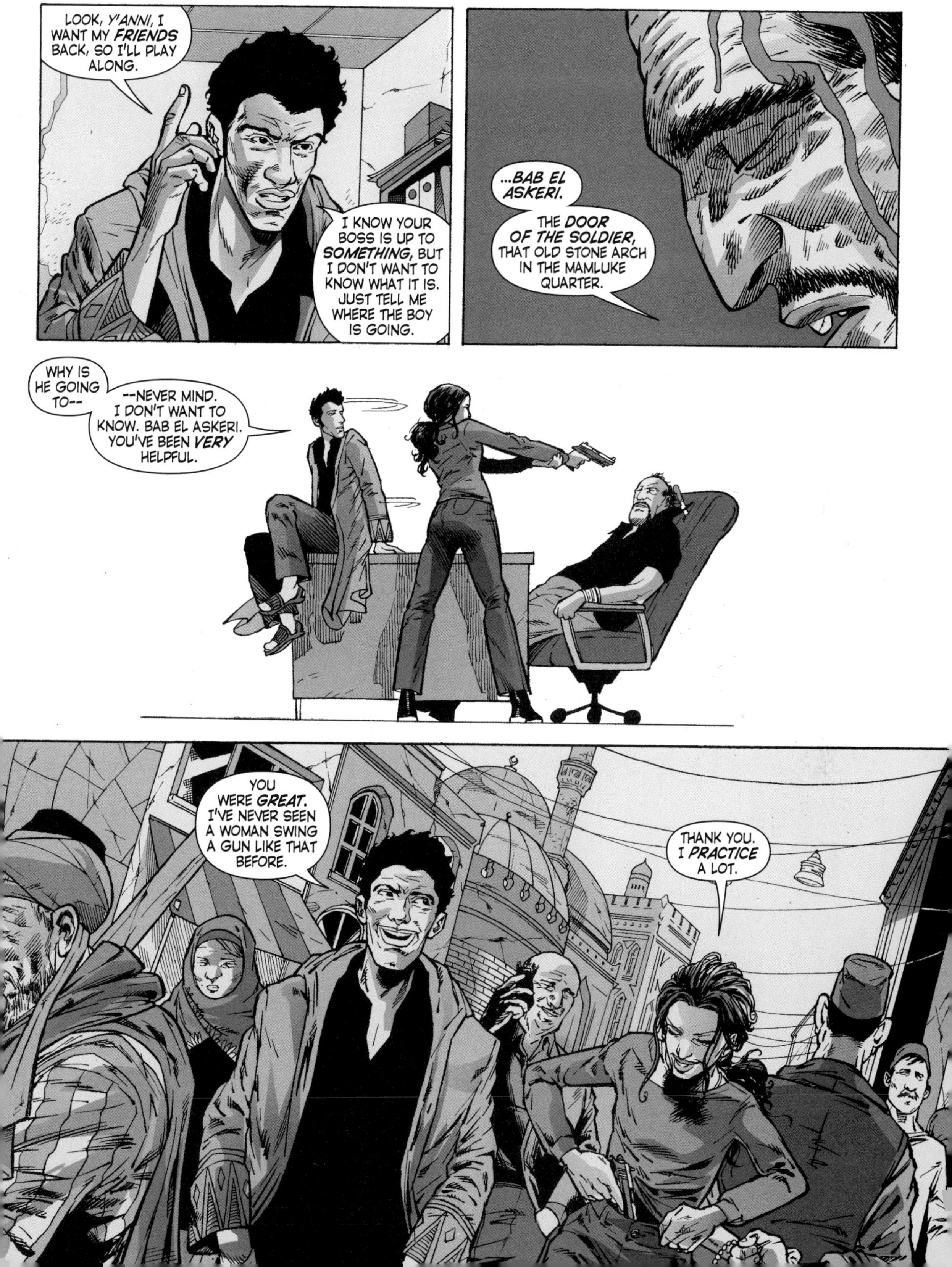
LOOK, Y'ANNI, I WANT MY FRIENDS BACK, SO I'LL PLAY ALONG.
I KNOW YOUR BOSS IS UP TO SOMETHING, BUT I DON'T WANT TO KNOW WHAT IT IS. JUST TELL ME WHERE THE BOY IS GOING.
...BAB EL ASKERI.
THE DOOR OF THE SOLDIER, THAT OLD STONE ARCH IN THE MAMLUKE QUARTER.
WHY IS HE GOING TO--
--NEVER MIND. I DON'T WANT TO KNOW. BAB EL ASKERI. YOU'VE BEEN VERY HELPFUL.
YOU WERE GREAT. I'VE NEVER SEEN A WOMAN SWING A GUN LIKE THAT BEFORE.
THANK YOU. I PRACTICE A LOT.

THIS WAS NOT SUPPOSED TO *HAPPEN.* I WAS GOING TO GET AN APARTMENT DOWNTOWN AND WRITE EDUCATIONAL PAMPHLETS FOR A HUMAN RIGHTS GROUP AND MAKE A *DIFFERENCE.*

AND NOW I'M WET. AND TIRED.

AND *STARVING.*

ME TOO.

WHAT YOU SAID, JUST BEFORE THE WORLD WENT INSANE--DO YOU *REALLY* THINK MY COLUMN IS, HOW DID YOU PUT IT, "CYNICAL AND OVERWRITTEN"?

YOU'RE BRINGING THIS UP NOW?

I WANT TO KNOW.

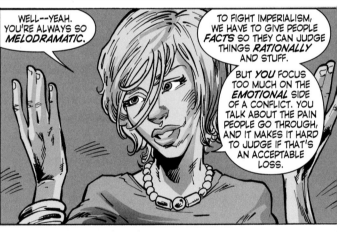

WELL--YEAH. YOU'RE ALWAYS SO *MELODRAMATIC.*

TO FIGHT IMPERIALISM, WE HAVE TO GIVE PEOPLE *FACTS* SO THEY CAN JUDGE THINGS *RATIONALLY* AND STUFF.

BUT *YOU* FOCUS TOO MUCH ON THE *EMOTIONAL* SIDE OF A CONFLICT. YOU TALK ABOUT THE PAIN PEOPLE GO THROUGH, AND IT MAKES IT HARD TO JUDGE IF THAT'S AN ACCEPTABLE LOSS.

YOU KNOW?...

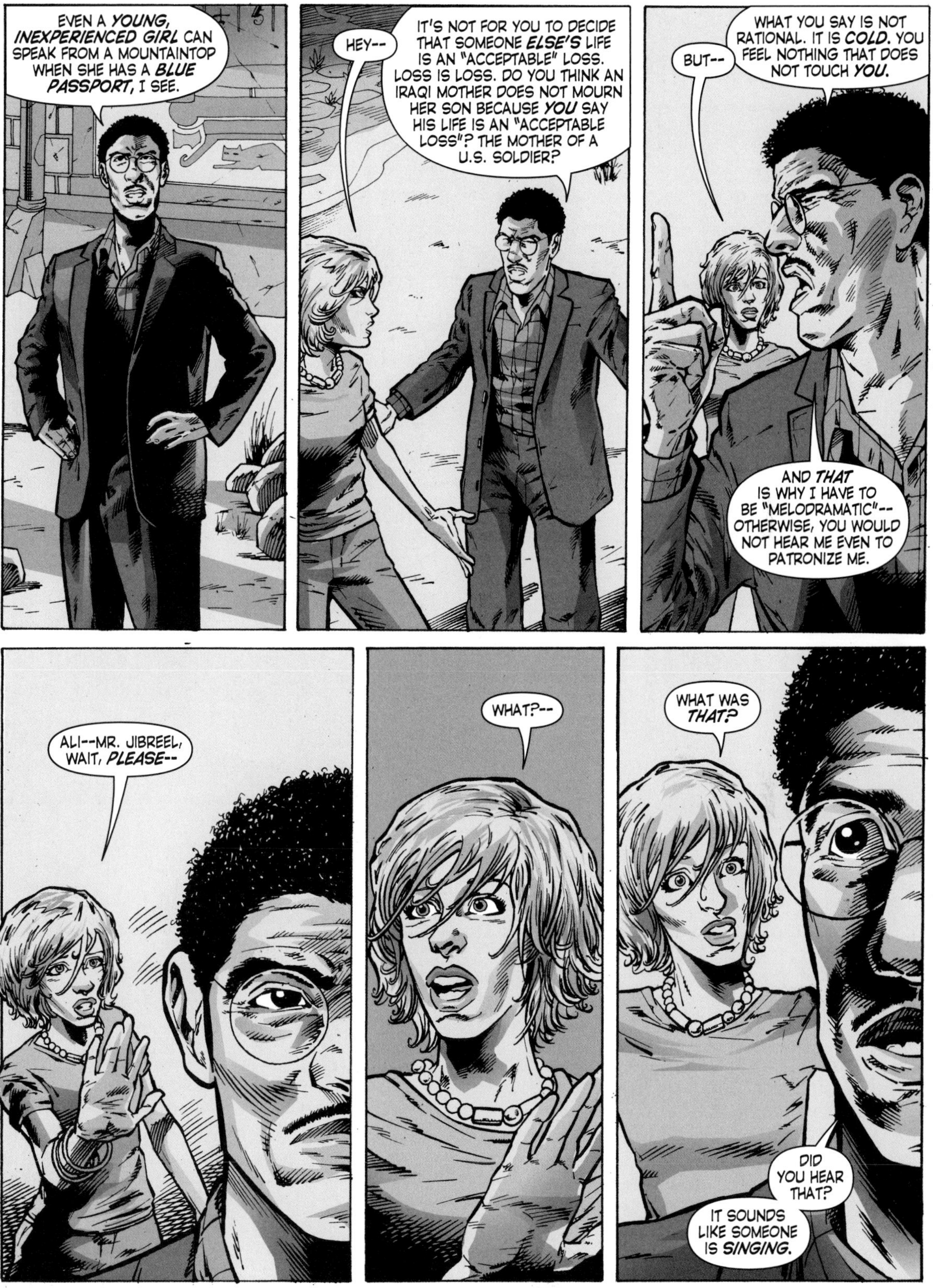
EVEN A *YOUNG, INEXPERIENCED GIRL* CAN SPEAK FROM A MOUNTAINTOP WHEN SHE HAS A *BLUE PASSPORT*, I SEE.
HEY--
IT'S NOT FOR YOU TO DECIDE THAT SOMEONE *ELSE'S* LIFE IS AN "ACCEPTABLE" LOSS. LOSS IS LOSS. DO YOU THINK AN IRAQI MOTHER DOES NOT MOURN HER SON BECAUSE *YOU* SAY HIS LIFE IS AN "ACCEPTABLE LOSS"? THE MOTHER OF A U.S. SOLDIER?
BUT--
WHAT YOU SAY IS NOT RATIONAL. IT IS *COLD.* YOU FEEL NOTHING THAT DOES NOT TOUCH *YOU.*
AND *THAT* IS WHY I HAVE TO BE "MELODRAMATIC"--OTHERWISE, YOU WOULD NOT HEAR ME EVEN TO PATRONIZE ME.
ALI--MR. JIBREEL, WAIT, *PLEASE*--
WHAT?--
WHAT WAS *THAT?*
DID YOU HEAR THAT?
IT SOUNDS LIKE SOMEONE IS *SINGING.*

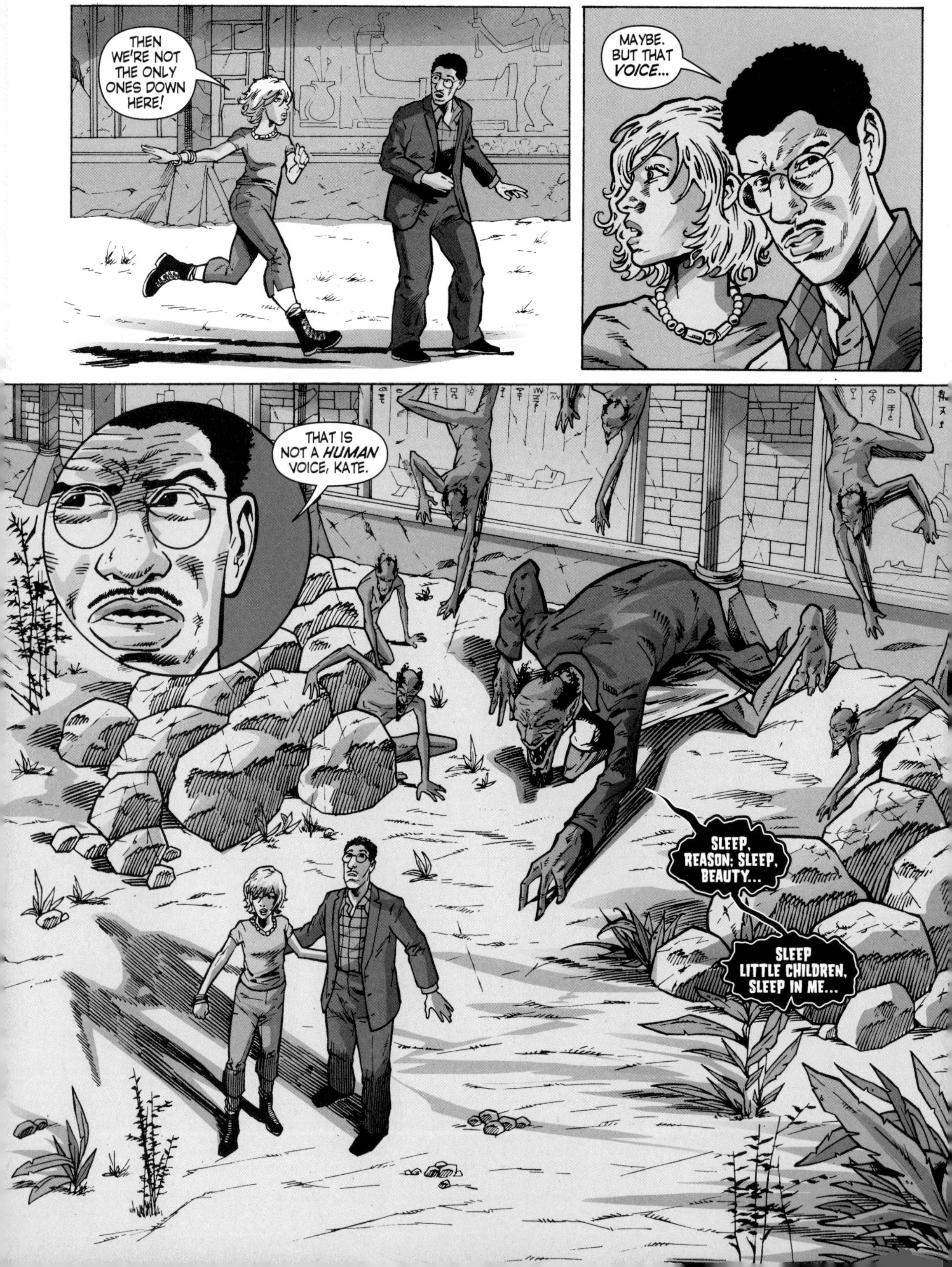
THEN WE'RE NOT THE ONLY ONES DOWN HERE!
MAYBE. BUT THAT *VOICE*...
THAT IS NOT A *HUMAN* VOICE, KATE.
SLEEP, REASON; SLEEP, BEAUTY...
SLEEP LITTLE CHILDREN, SLEEP IN ME...

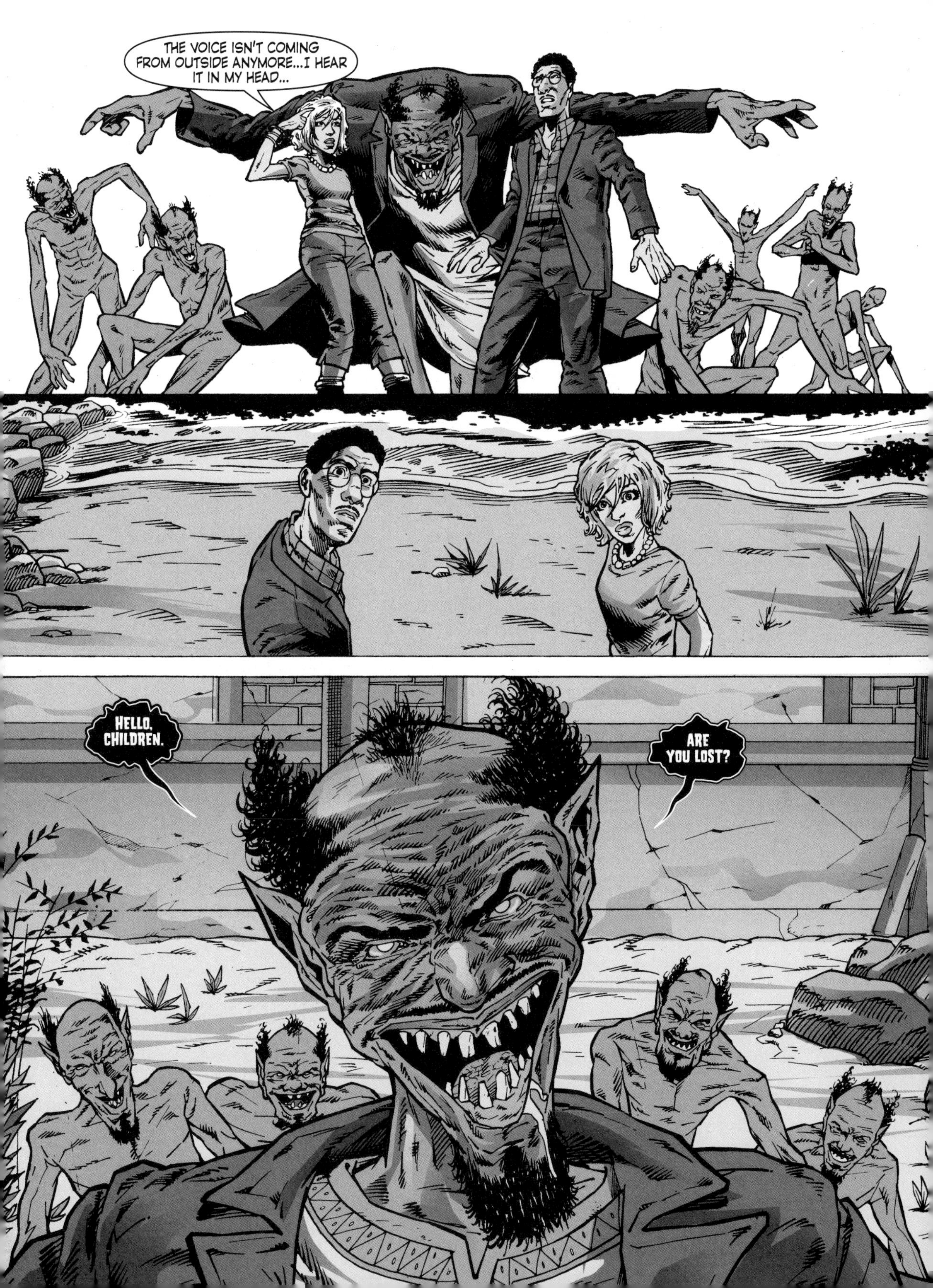
THE VOICE ISN'T COMING FROM OUTSIDE ANYMORE...I HEAR IT IN MY HEAD...
HELLO, CHILDREN.
ARE YOU LOST?

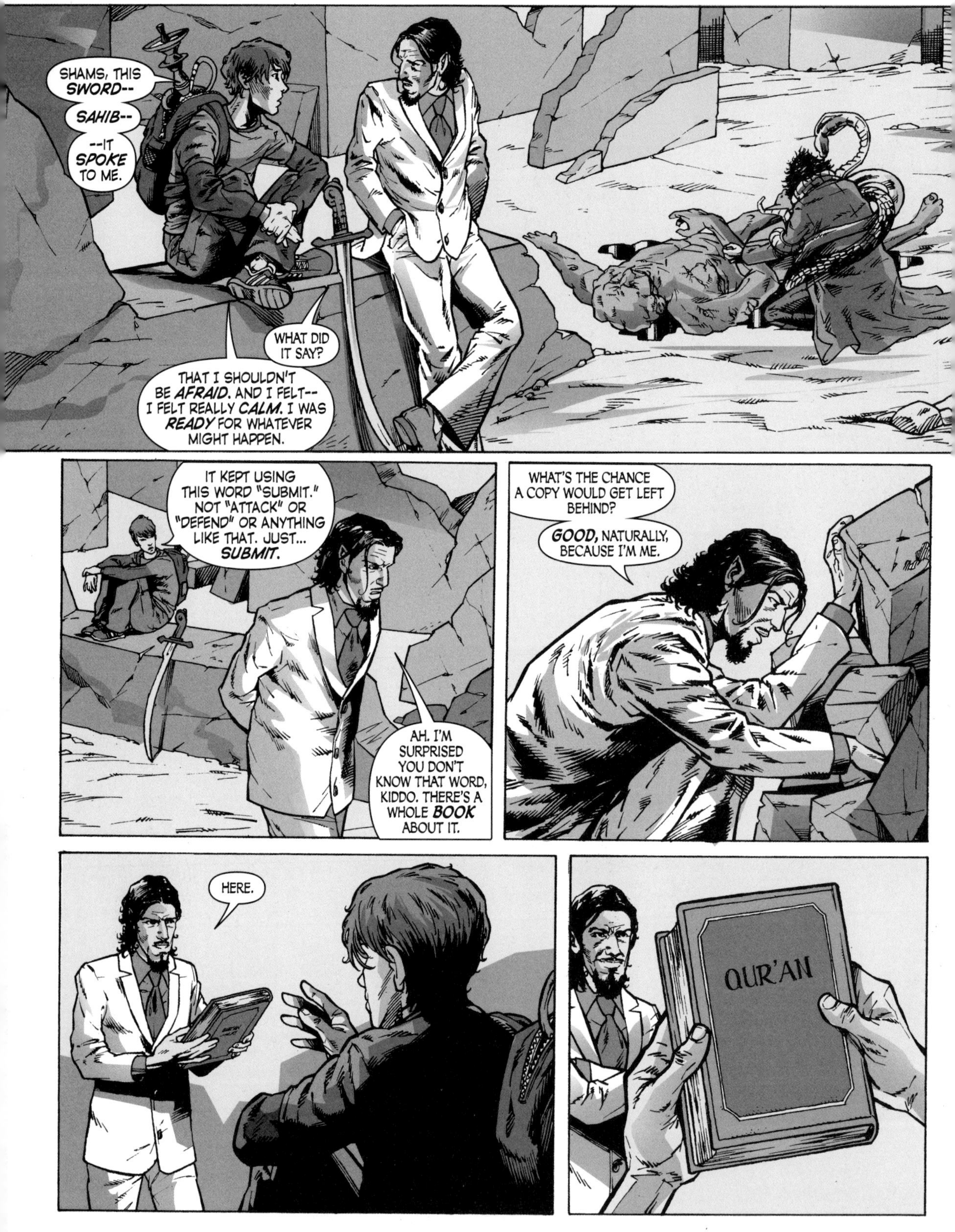
SHAMS, THIS SWORD--
SAHIB--
--IT SPOKE TO ME.
WHAT DID IT SAY?
THAT I SHOULDN'T BE AFRAID. AND I FELT-- I FELT REALLY CALM. I WAS READY FOR WHATEVER MIGHT HAPPEN.
IT KEPT USING THIS WORD "SUBMIT." NOT "ATTACK" OR "DEFEND" OR ANYTHING LIKE THAT. JUST... SUBMIT.
AH. I'M SURPRISED YOU DON'T KNOW THAT WORD, KIDDO. THERE'S A WHOLE BOOK ABOUT IT.
WHAT'S THE CHANCE A COPY WOULD GET LEFT BEHIND?
GOOD, NATURALLY, BECAUSE I'M ME.
HERE.
QUR'AN

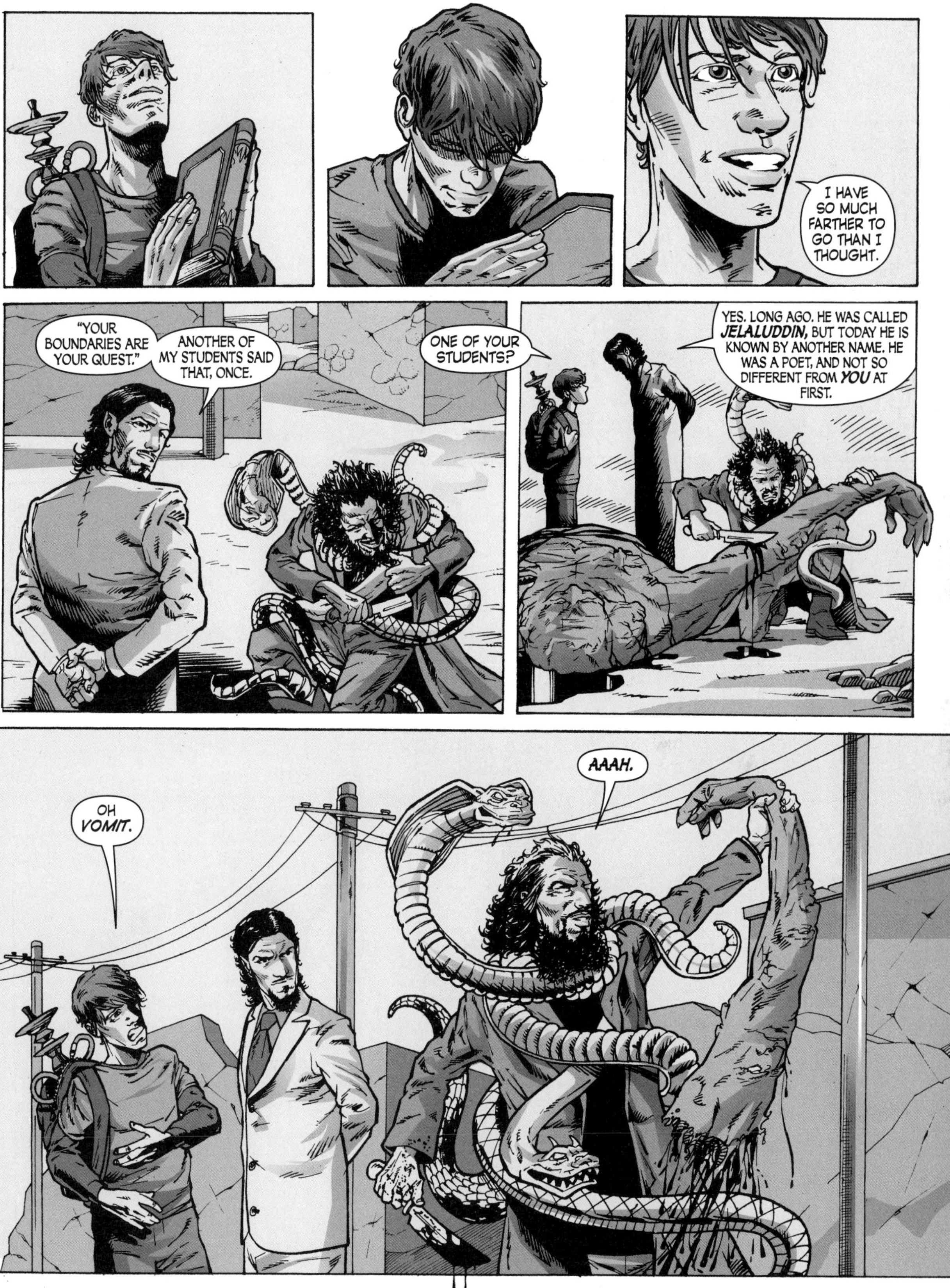
I HAVE SO MUCH FARTHER TO GO THAN I THOUGHT.
"YOUR BOUNDARIES ARE YOUR QUEST."
ANOTHER OF MY STUDENTS SAID THAT, ONCE.
ONE OF YOUR STUDENTS?
YES. LONG AGO. HE WAS CALLED JELALUDDIN, BUT TODAY HE IS KNOWN BY ANOTHER NAME. HE WAS A POET, AND NOT SO DIFFERENT FROM YOU AT FIRST.
OH VOMIT.
AAAH.

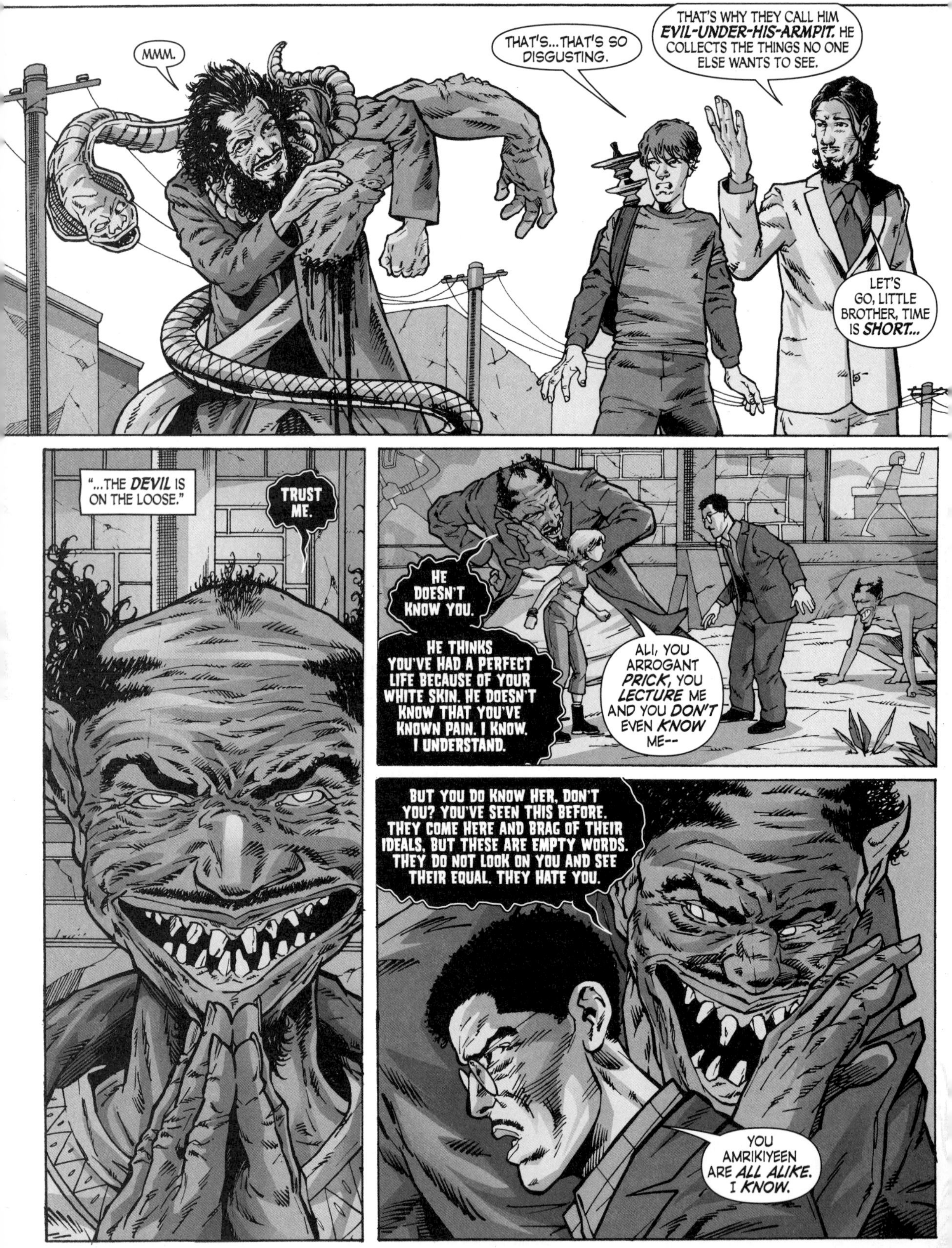
MMM.
THAT'S...THAT'S SO DISGUSTING.
THAT'S WHY THEY CALL HIM EVIL-UNDER-HIS-ARMPIT. HE COLLECTS THE THINGS NO ONE ELSE WANTS TO SEE.
LET'S GO, LITTLE BROTHER, TIME IS SHORT...
"...THE DEVIL IS ON THE LOOSE."
TRUST ME.
HE DOESN'T KNOW YOU.
HE THINKS YOU'VE HAD A PERFECT LIFE BECAUSE OF YOUR WHITE SKIN. HE DOESN'T KNOW THAT YOU'VE KNOWN PAIN. I KNOW. I UNDERSTAND.
ALI, YOU ARROGANT PRICK, YOU LECTURE ME AND YOU DON'T EVEN KNOW ME--
BUT YOU DO KNOW HER, DON'T YOU? YOU'VE SEEN THIS BEFORE. THEY COME HERE AND BRAG OF THEIR IDEALS, BUT THESE ARE EMPTY WORDS. THEY DO NOT LOOK ON YOU AND SEE THEIR EQUAL. THEY HATE YOU.
YOU AMRIKIYEEN ARE ALL ALIKE. I KNOW.

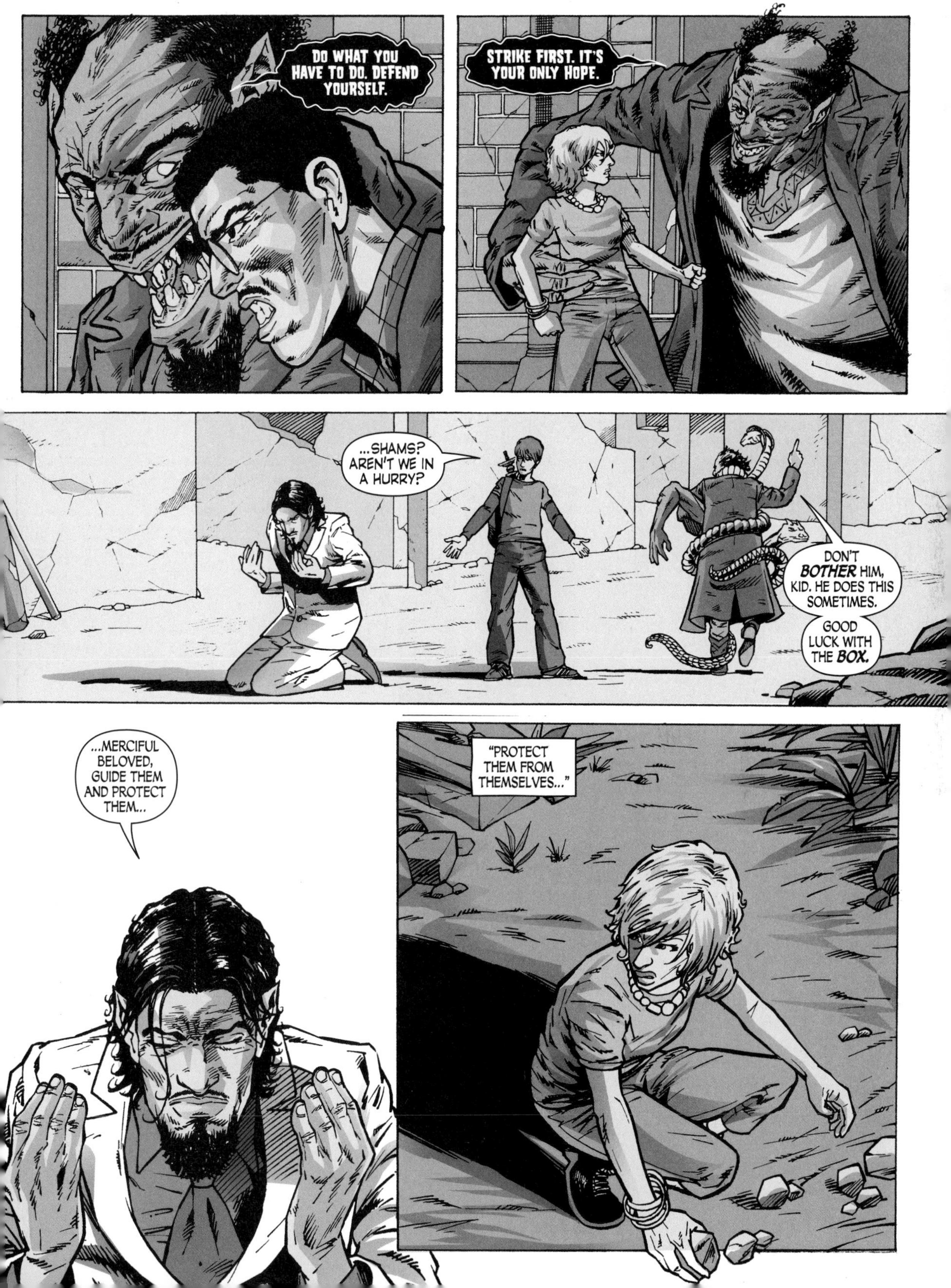
DO WHAT YOU HAVE TO DO. DEFEND YOURSELF.
STRIKE FIRST. IT'S YOUR ONLY HOPE.
...SHAMS? AREN'T WE IN A HURRY?
DON'T BOTHER HIM, KID. HE DOES THIS SOMETIMES.
GOOD LUCK WITH THE BOX.
...MERCIFUL BELOVED, GUIDE THEM AND PROTECT THEM...
"PROTECT THEM FROM THEMSELVES..."

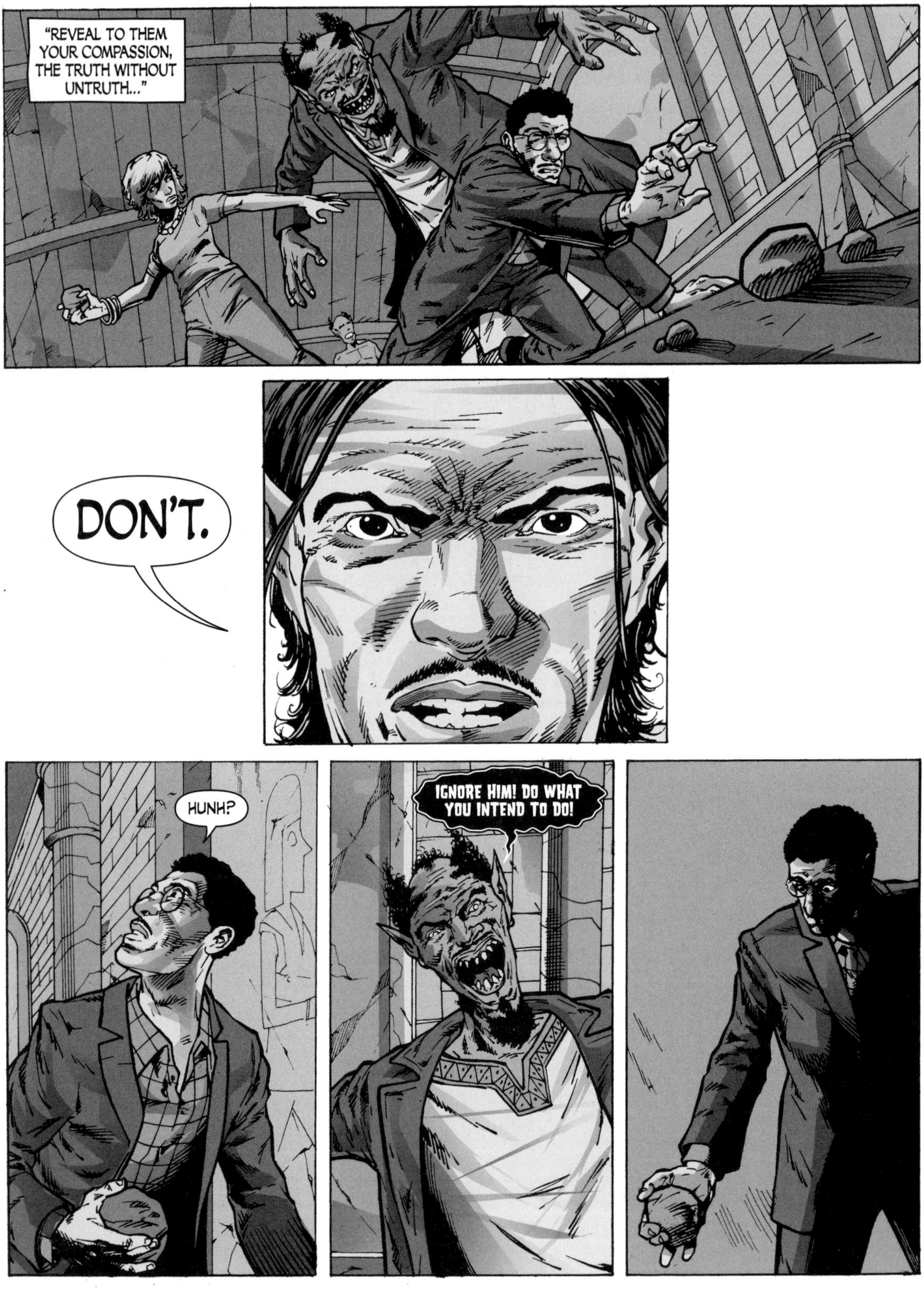
"REVEAL TO THEM YOUR COMPASSION, THE TRUTH WITHOUT UNTRUTH..."
DON'T.
HUNH?
IGNORE HIM! DO WHAT YOU INTEND TO DO!

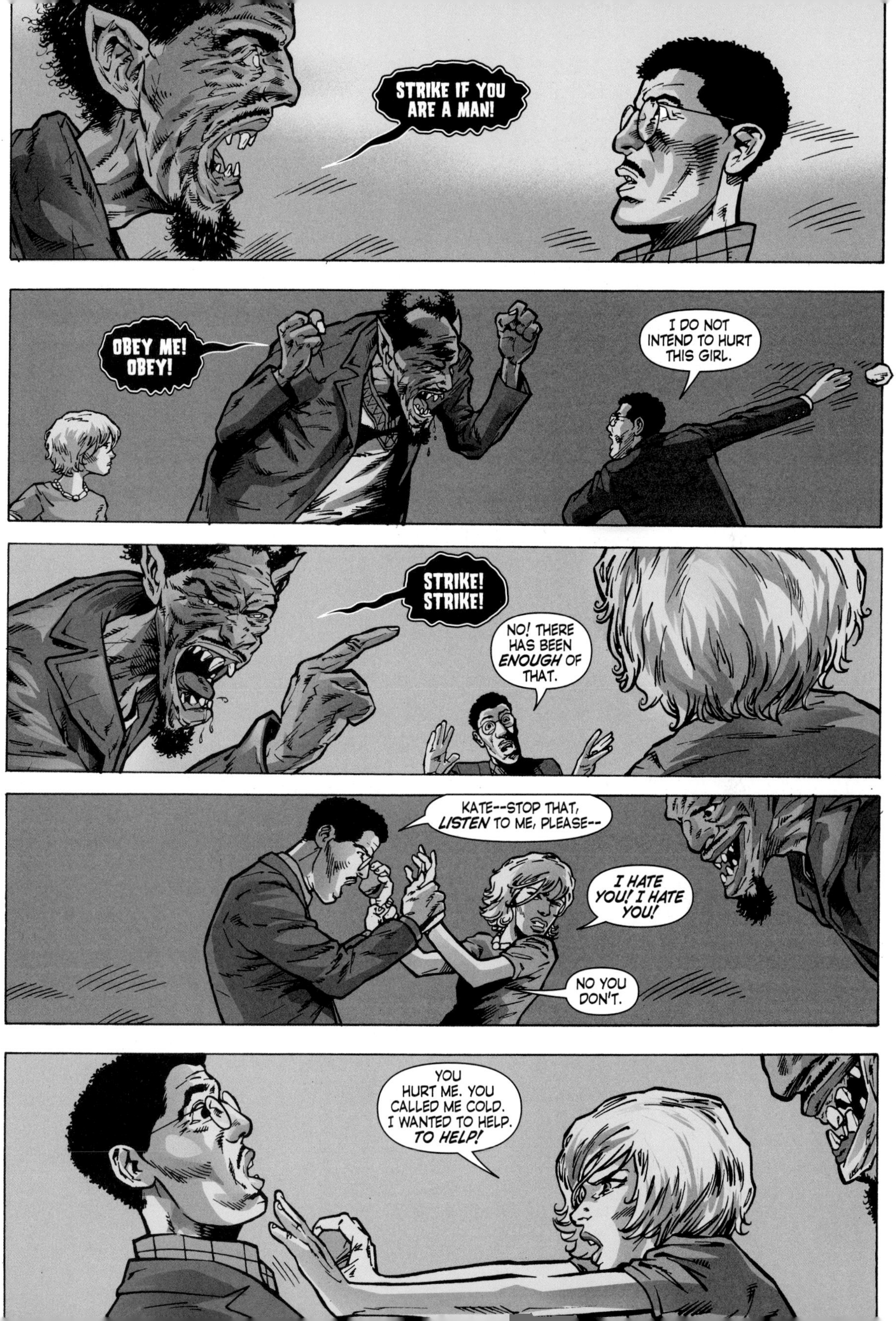
STRIKE IF YOU ARE A MAN!
OBEY ME! OBEY!
I DO NOT INTEND TO HURT THIS GIRL.
STRIKE! STRIKE!
NO! THERE HAS BEEN *ENOUGH* OF THAT.
KATE--STOP THAT, *LISTEN* TO ME, PLEASE--
I HATE YOU! I HATE YOU!
NO YOU DON'T.
YOU HURT ME. YOU CALLED ME COLD. I WANTED TO HELP. *TO HELP!*

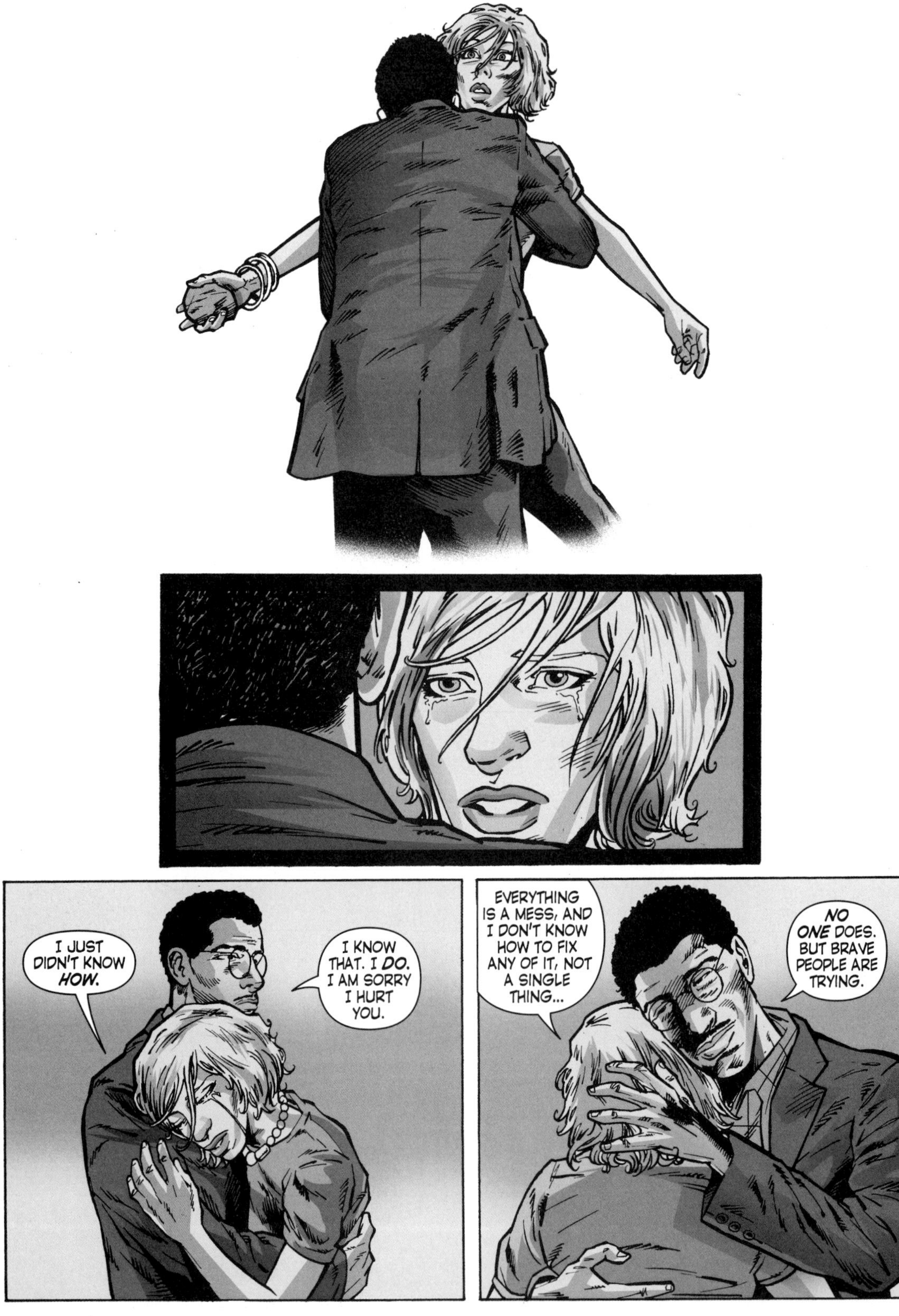
I JUST DIDN'T KNOW *HOW.*
I KNOW THAT. I *DO.* I AM SORRY I HURT YOU.
EVERYTHING IS A MESS, AND I DON'T KNOW HOW TO FIX ANY OF IT, NOT A SINGLE THING...
NO ONE DOES. BUT BRAVE PEOPLE ARE TRYING.

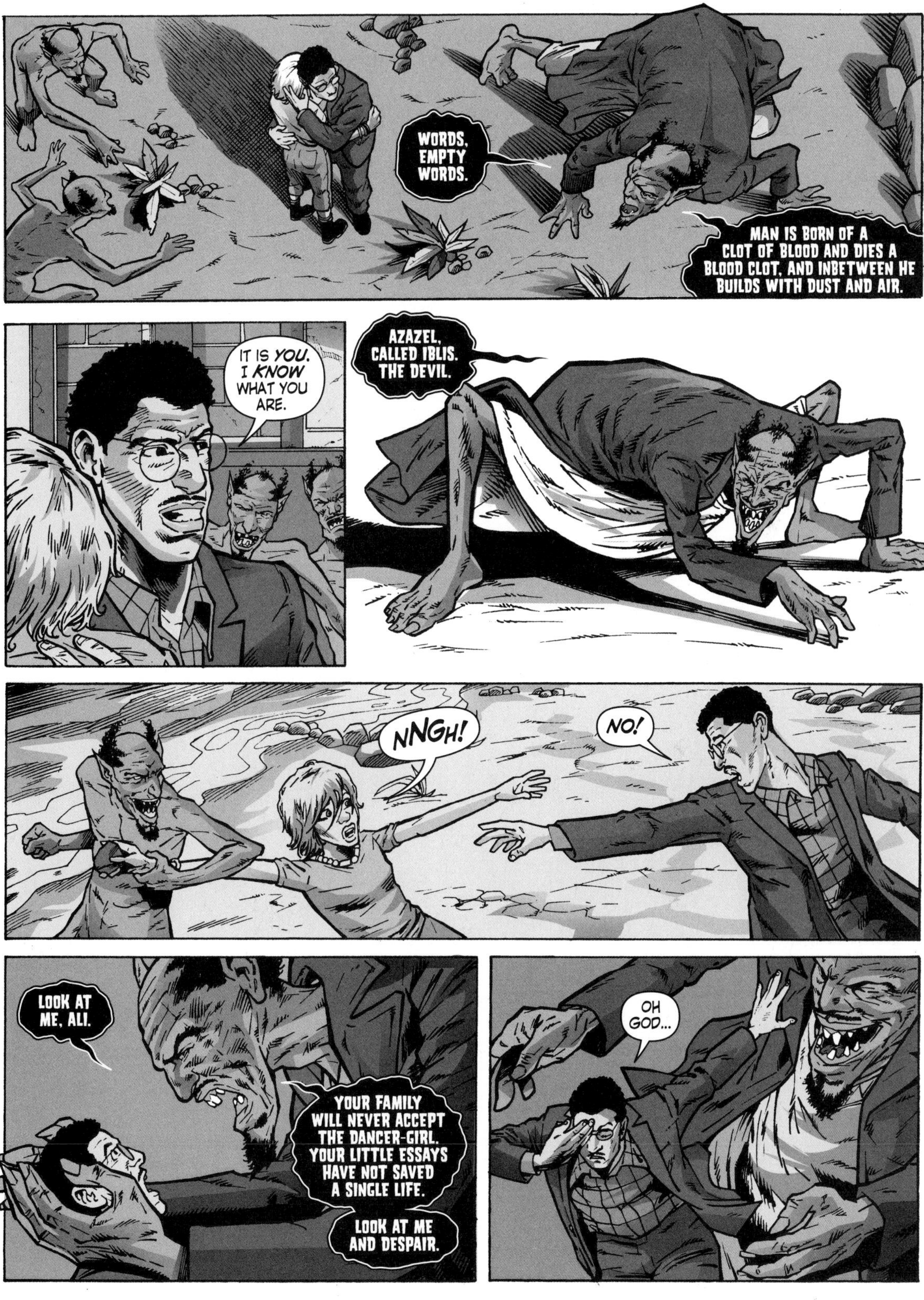
WORDS, EMPTY WORDS.
MAN IS BORN OF A CLOT OF BLOOD AND DIES A BLOOD CLOT, AND INBETWEEN HE BUILDS WITH DUST AND AIR.
IT IS YOU. I KNOW WHAT YOU ARE.
AZAZEL, CALLED IBLIS. THE DEVIL.
NNGH!
NO!
LOOK AT ME, ALI.
YOUR FAMILY WILL NEVER ACCEPT THE DANCER-GIRL. YOUR LITTLE ESSAYS HAVE NOT SAVED A SINGLE LIFE.
LOOK AT ME AND DESPAIR.
OH GOD...

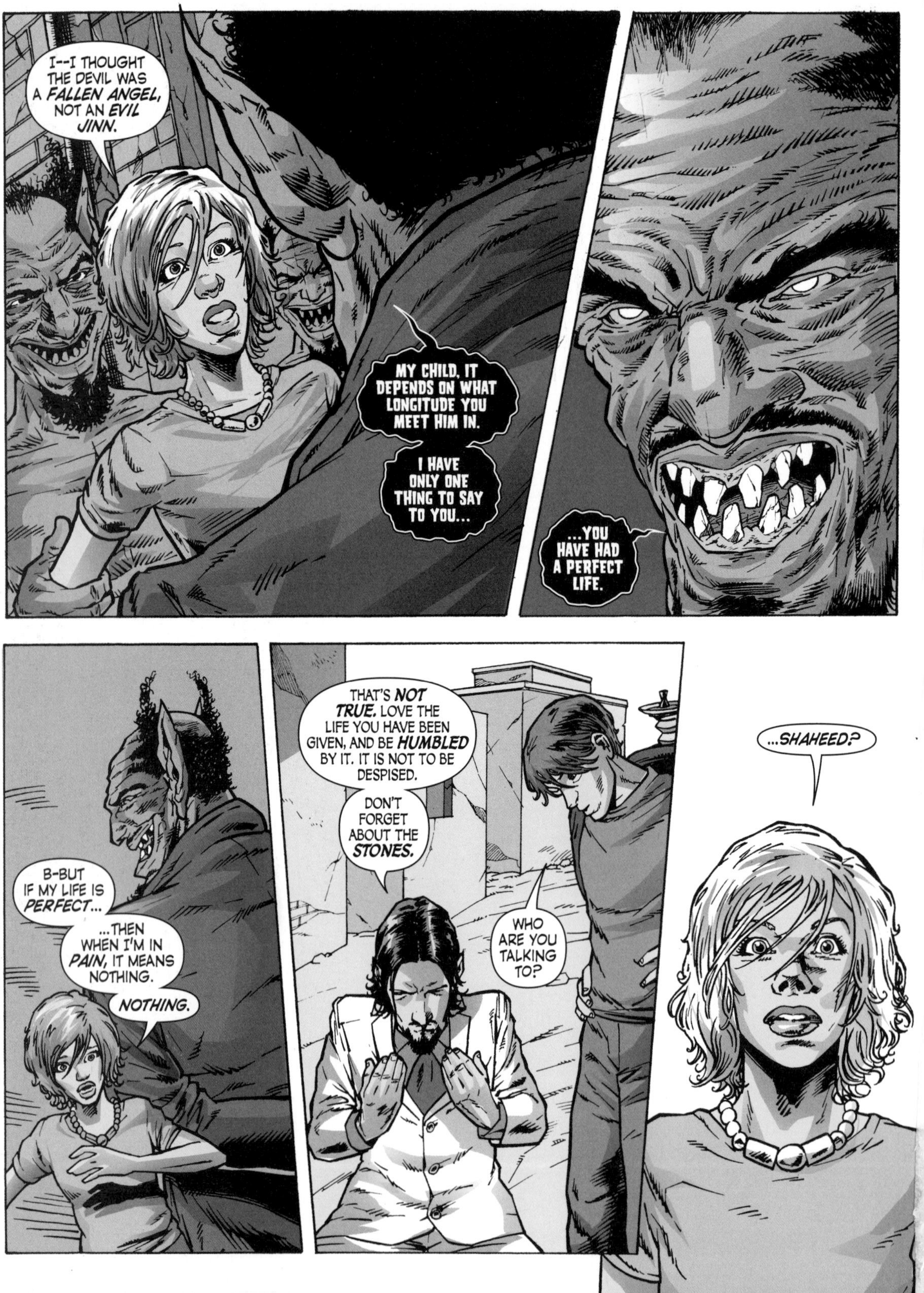

I--I THOUGHT THE DEVIL WAS A *FALLEN ANGEL*, NOT AN *EVIL JINN*.
MY CHILD, IT DEPENDS ON WHAT LONGITUDE YOU MEET HIM IN.
I HAVE ONLY ONE THING TO SAY TO YOU...
...YOU HAVE HAD A PERFECT LIFE.
B-BUT IF MY LIFE IS *PERFECT*...
...THEN WHEN I'M IN *PAIN*, IT MEANS NOTHING.
NOTHING.
THAT'S *NOT TRUE.* LOVE THE LIFE YOU HAVE BEEN GIVEN, AND BE *HUMBLED* BY IT. IT IS NOT TO BE DESPISED.
DON'T FORGET ABOUT THE *STONES.*
WHO ARE YOU TALKING TO?
...*SHAHEED?*

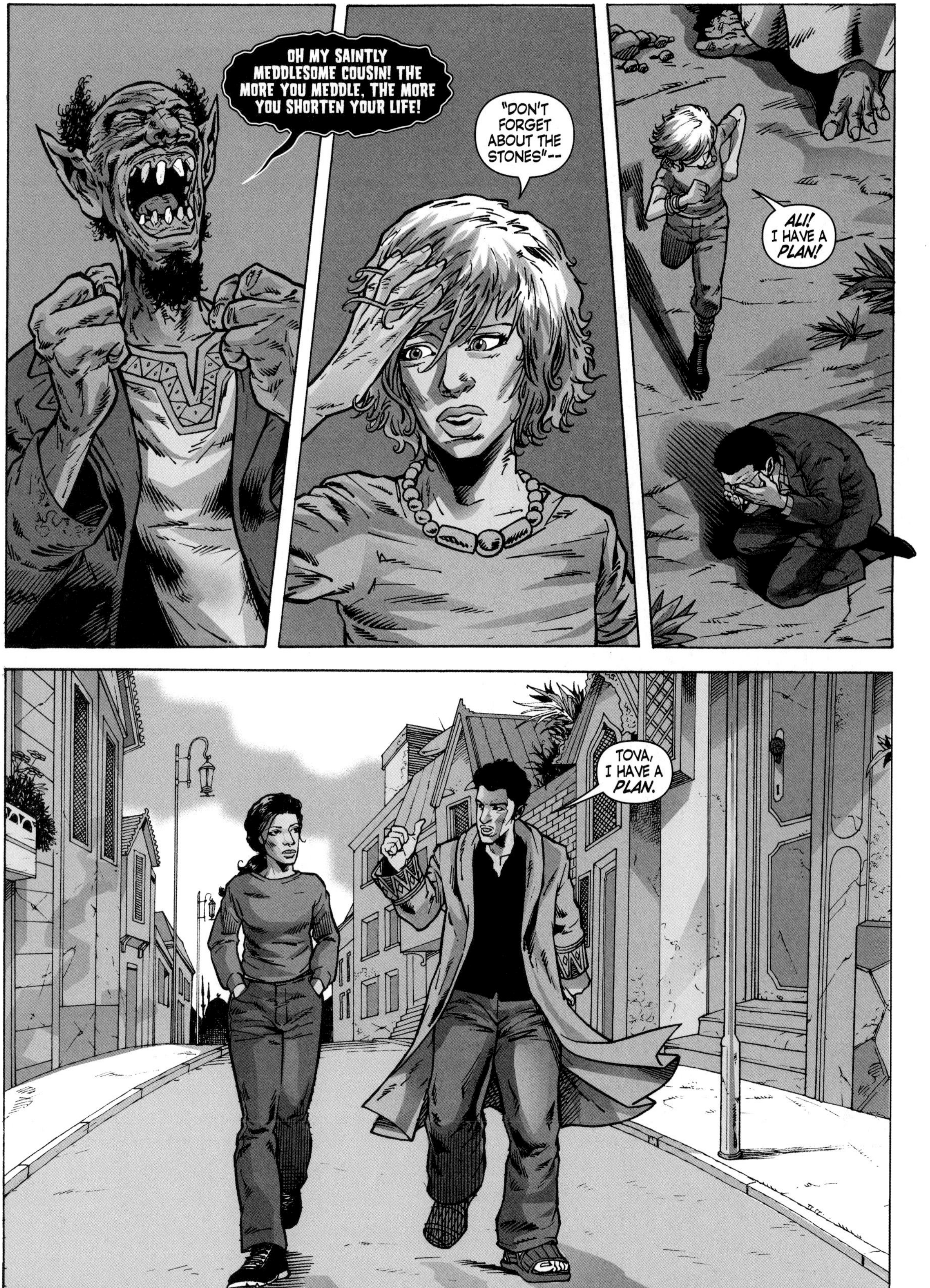
OH MY SAINTLY MEDDLESOME COUSIN! THE MORE YOU MEDDLE, THE MORE YOU SHORTEN YOUR LIFE!
"DON'T FORGET ABOUT THE STONES"--
ALI! I HAVE A PLAN!
TOVA, I HAVE A PLAN.

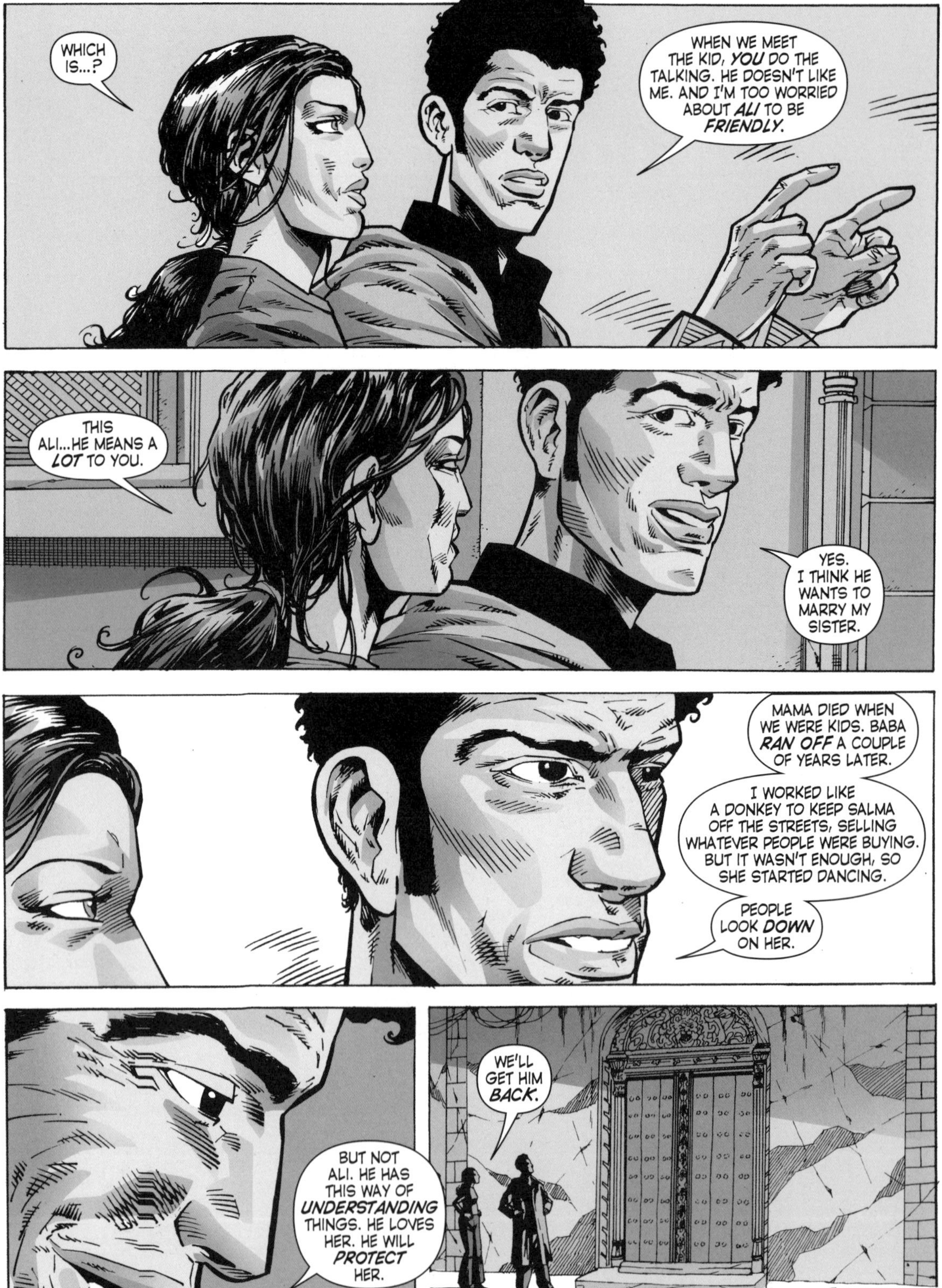
WHEN WE MEET THE KID, YOU DO THE TALKING. HE DOESN'T LIKE ME. AND I'M TOO WORRIED ABOUT ALI TO BE FRIENDLY.
WHICH IS...?
THIS ALI...HE MEANS A LOT TO YOU.
YES. I THINK HE WANTS TO MARRY MY SISTER.
MAMA DIED WHEN WE WERE KIDS. BABA RAN OFF A COUPLE OF YEARS LATER.
I WORKED LIKE A DONKEY TO KEEP SALMA OFF THE STREETS, SELLING WHATEVER PEOPLE WERE BUYING. BUT IT WASN'T ENOUGH, SO SHE STARTED DANCING.
PEOPLE LOOK DOWN ON HER.
BUT NOT ALI. HE HAS THIS WAY OF UNDERSTANDING THINGS. HE LOVES HER. HE WILL PROTECT HER.
WE'LL GET HIM BACK.

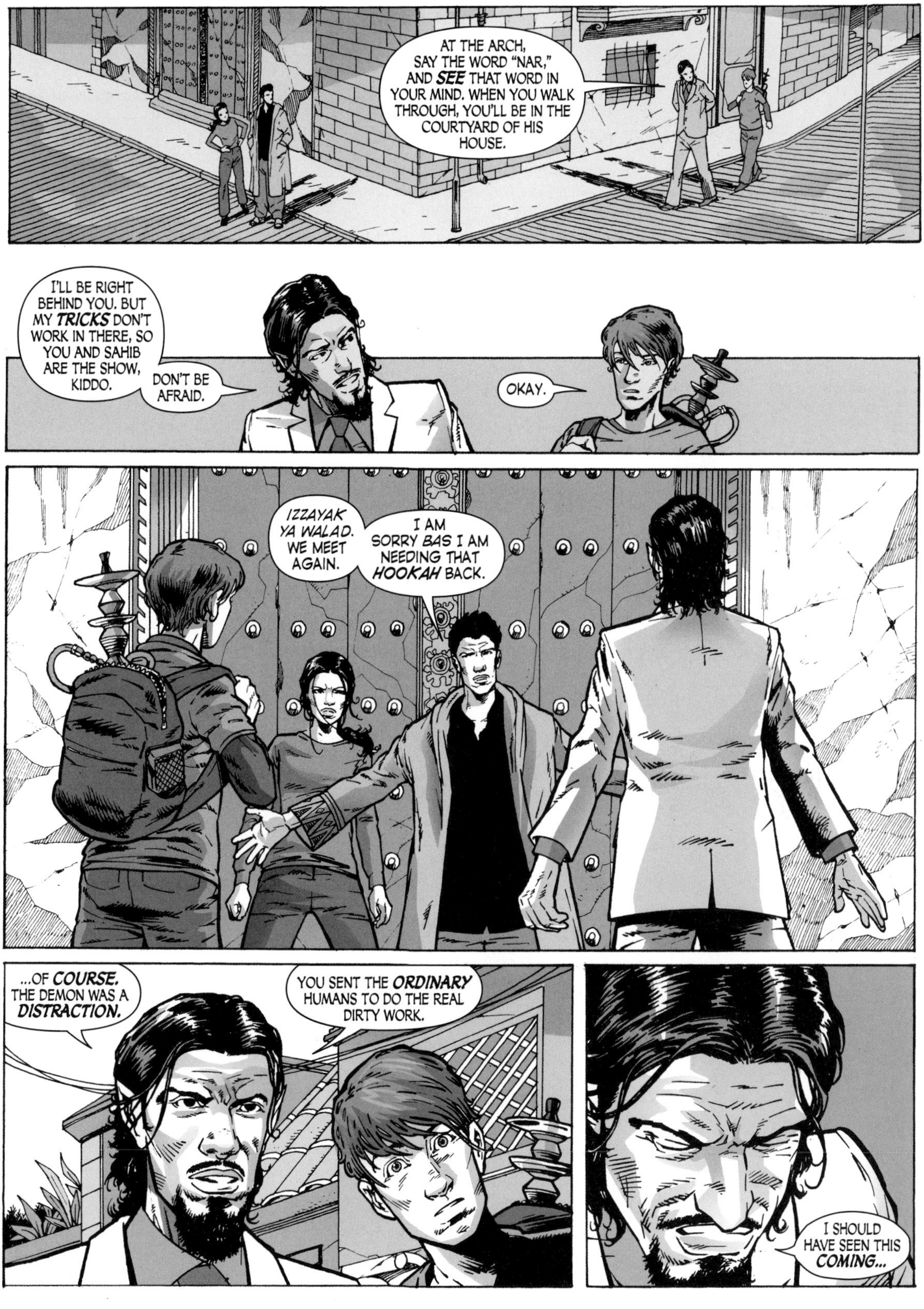
AT THE ARCH, SAY THE WORD "NAR," AND SEE THAT WORD IN YOUR MIND. WHEN YOU WALK THROUGH, YOU'LL BE IN THE COURTYARD OF HIS HOUSE.
I'LL BE RIGHT BEHIND YOU. BUT MY TRICKS DON'T WORK IN THERE, SO YOU AND SAHIB ARE THE SHOW, KIDDO.
DON'T BE AFRAID.
OKAY.
IZZAYAK YA WALAD. WE MEET AGAIN.
I AM SORRY BAS I AM NEEDING THAT HOOKAH BACK.
...OF COURSE. THE DEMON WAS A DISTRACTION.
YOU SENT THE ORDINARY HUMANS TO DO THE REAL DIRTY WORK.
I SHOULD HAVE SEEN THIS COMING...

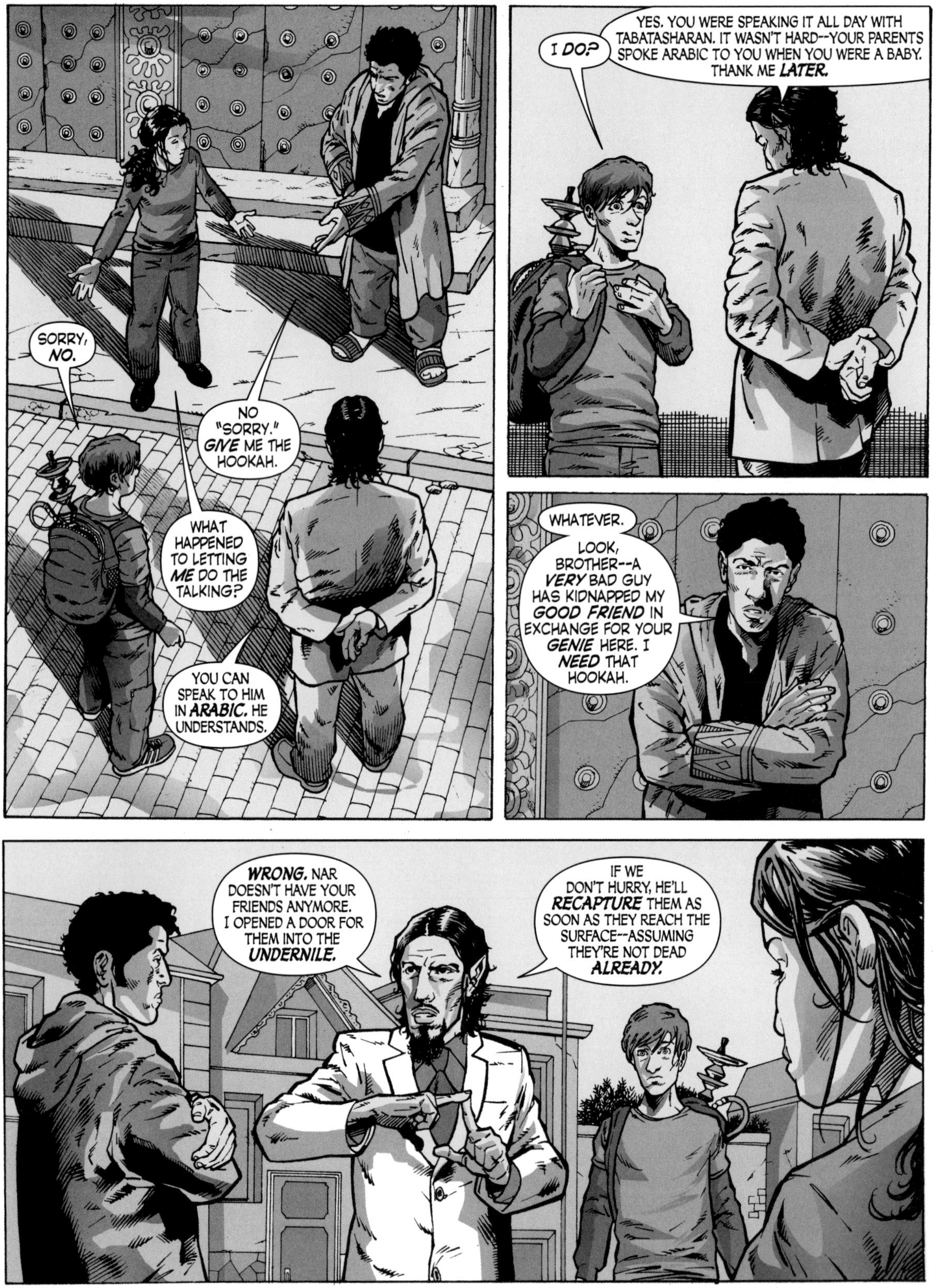
SORRY, NO.
NO "SORRY." GIVE ME THE HOOKAH.
WHAT HAPPENED TO LETTING ME DO THE TALKING?
YOU CAN SPEAK TO HIM IN ARABIC. HE UNDERSTANDS.
I DO?
YES. YOU WERE SPEAKING IT ALL DAY WITH TABATASHARAN. IT WASN'T HARD--YOUR PARENTS SPOKE ARABIC TO YOU WHEN YOU WERE A BABY. THANK ME LATER.
WHATEVER.
LOOK, BROTHER--A VERY BAD GUY HAS KIDNAPPED MY GOOD FRIEND IN EXCHANGE FOR YOUR GENIE HERE. I NEED THAT HOOKAH.
WRONG. NAR DOESN'T HAVE YOUR FRIENDS ANYMORE. I OPENED A DOOR FOR THEM INTO THE UNDERNILE.
IF WE DON'T HURRY, HE'LL RECAPTURE THEM AS SOON AS THEY REACH THE SURFACE--ASSUMING THEY'RE NOT DEAD ALREADY.

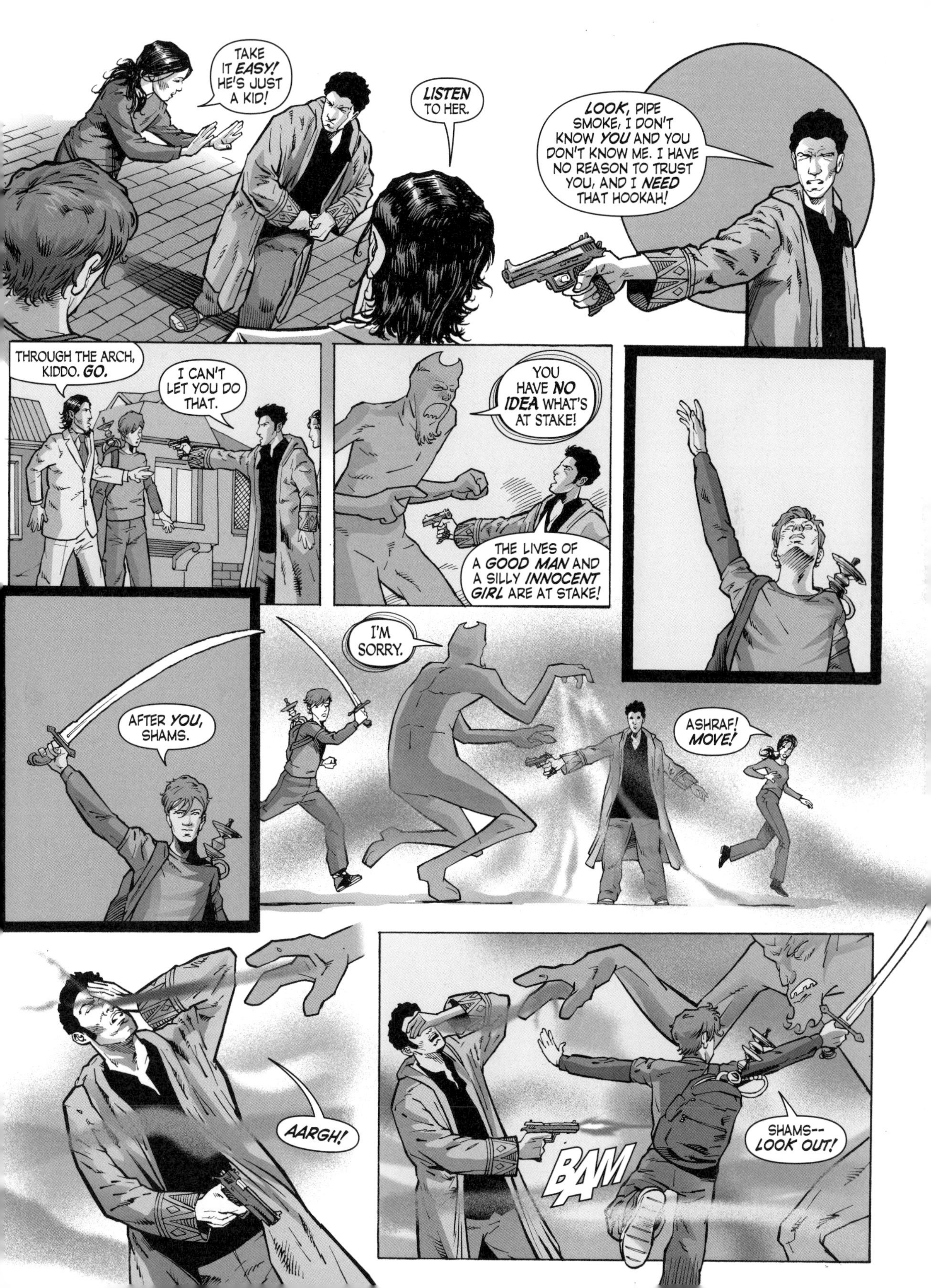
TAKE IT EASY! HE'S JUST A KID!
LISTEN TO HER.
LOOK, PIPE SMOKE, I DON'T KNOW YOU AND YOU DON'T KNOW ME. I HAVE NO REASON TO TRUST YOU, AND I NEED THAT HOOKAH!
THROUGH THE ARCH, KIDDO. GO.
I CAN'T LET YOU DO THAT.
YOU HAVE NO IDEA WHAT'S AT STAKE!
THE LIVES OF A GOOD MAN AND A SILLY INNOCENT GIRL ARE AT STAKE!
AFTER YOU, SHAMS.
I'M SORRY.
ASHRAF! MOVE!
AARGH!
BAM
SHAMS-- LOOK OUT!

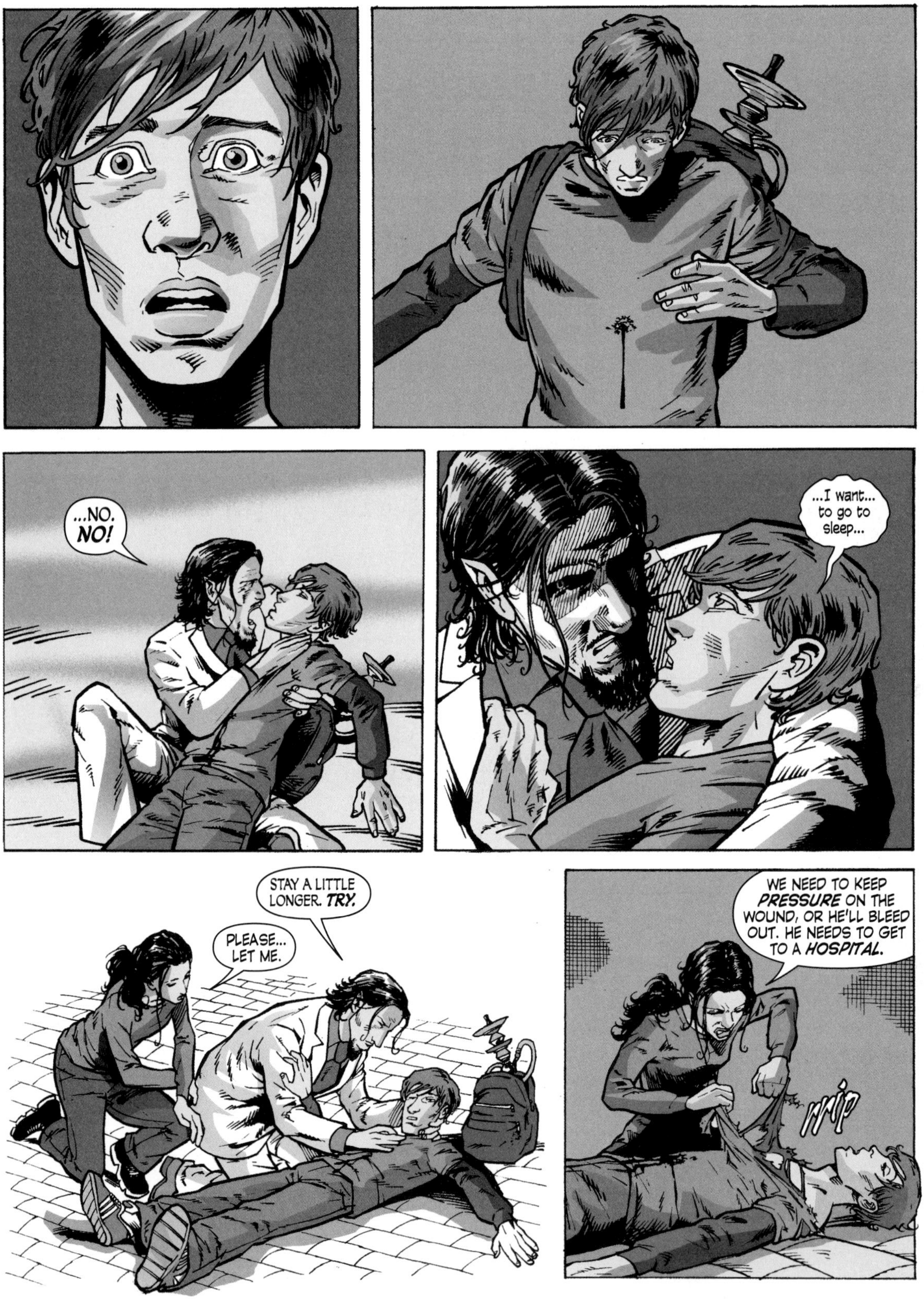
...NO. NO!
...I want... to go to sleep...
PLEASE... LET ME.
STAY A LITTLE LONGER. TRY.
WE NEED TO KEEP PRESSURE ON THE WOUND, OR HE'LL BLEED OUT. HE NEEDS TO GET TO A HOSPITAL.
rrip

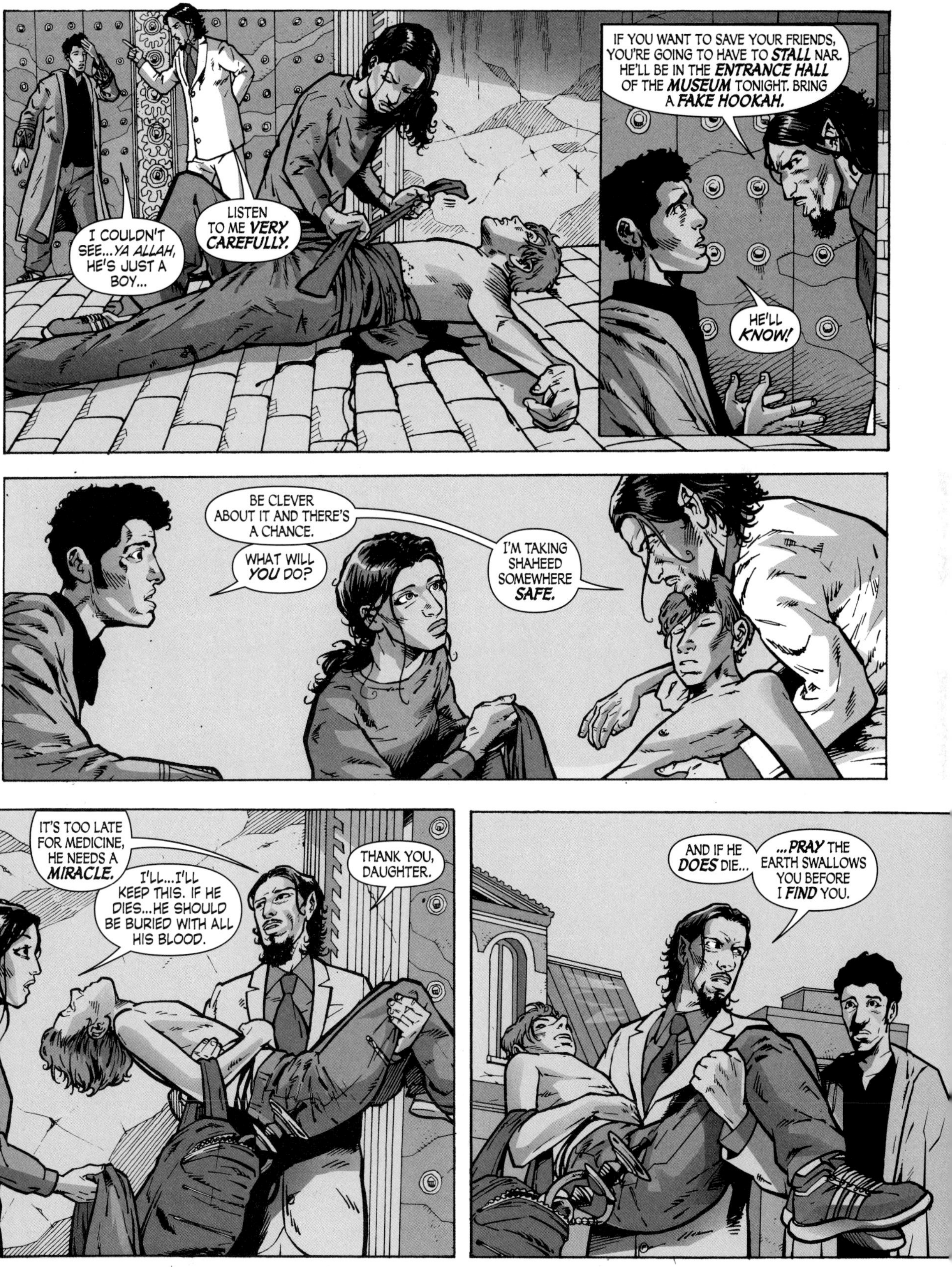
I COULDN'T SEE...YA ALLAH, HE'S JUST A BOY...
LISTEN TO ME VERY CAREFULLY.
IF YOU WANT TO SAVE YOUR FRIENDS, YOU'RE GOING TO HAVE TO STALL NAR. HE'LL BE IN THE ENTRANCE HALL OF THE MUSEUM TONIGHT. BRING A FAKE HOOKAH.
HE'LL KNOW!
BE CLEVER ABOUT IT AND THERE'S A CHANCE.
WHAT WILL YOU DO?
I'M TAKING SHAHEED SOMEWHERE SAFE.
IT'S TOO LATE FOR MEDICINE, HE NEEDS A MIRACLE.
I'LL...I'LL KEEP THIS. IF HE DIES...HE SHOULD BE BURIED WITH ALL HIS BLOOD.
THANK YOU, DAUGHTER.
AND IF HE DOES DIE...
...PRAY THE EARTH SWALLOWS YOU BEFORE I FIND YOU.

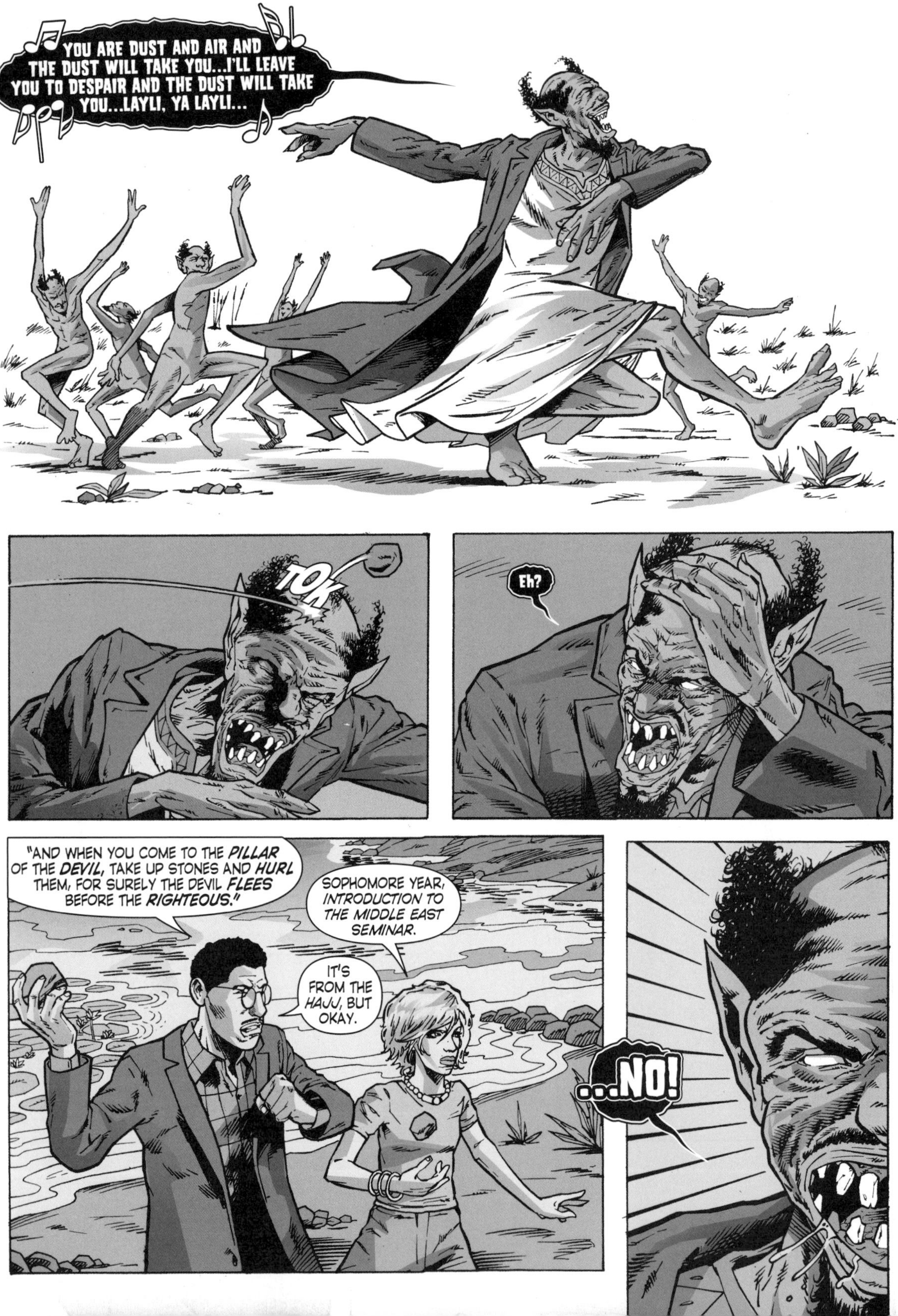
YOU ARE DUST AND AIR AND THE DUST WILL TAKE YOU...I'LL LEAVE YOU TO DESPAIR AND THE DUST WILL TAKE YOU...LAYLI, YA LAYLI...
TOK
Eh?
"AND WHEN YOU COME TO THE PILLAR OF THE DEVIL, TAKE UP STONES AND HURL THEM, FOR SURELY THE DEVIL FLEES BEFORE THE RIGHTEOUS."
SOPHOMORE YEAR, INTRODUCTION TO THE MIDDLE EAST SEMINAR.
IT'S FROM THE HAJJ, BUT OKAY.
...NO!

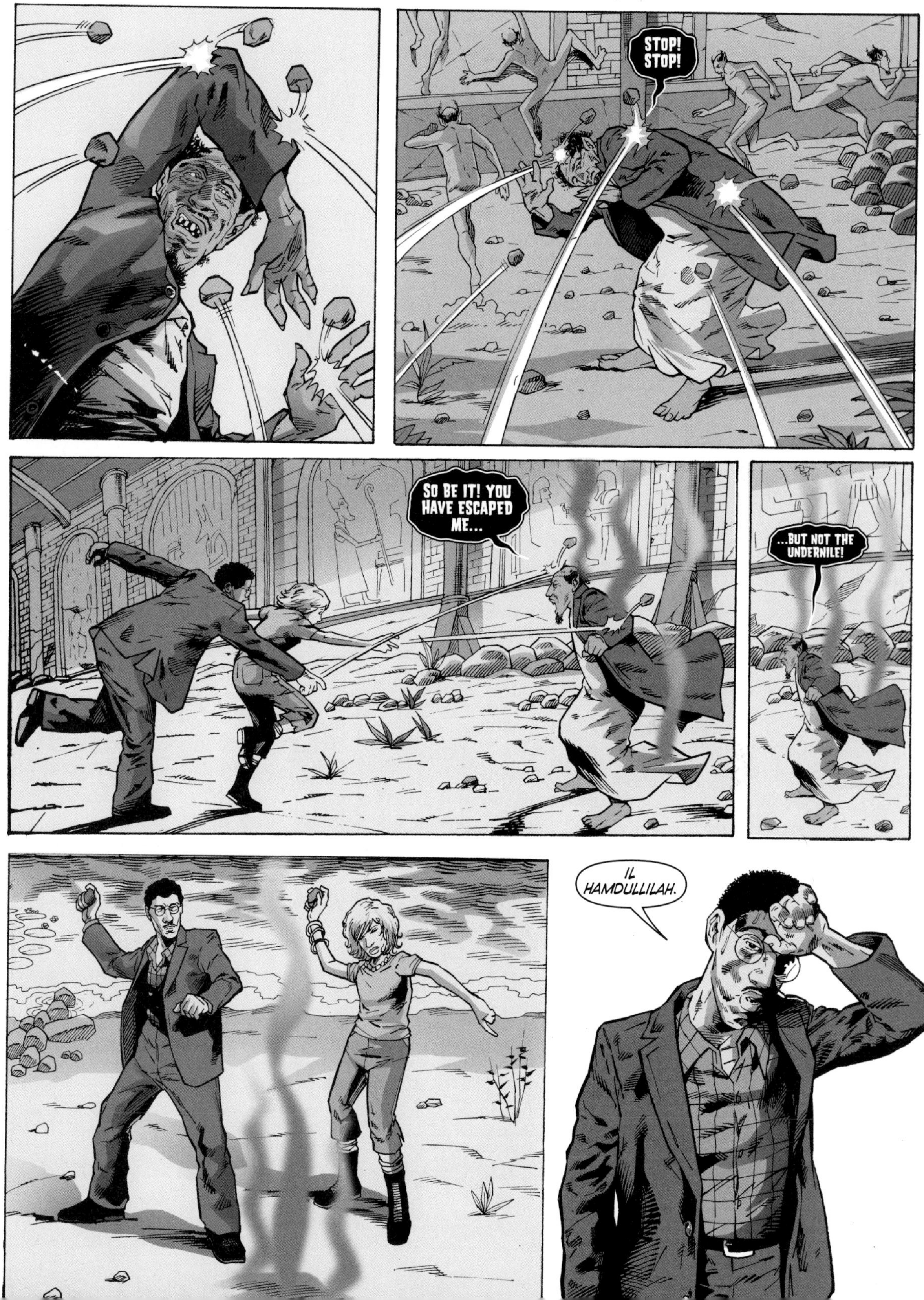
STOP! STOP!
SO BE IT! YOU HAVE ESCAPED ME...
...BUT NOT THE UNDERNILE!
IL HAMDULLILAH.

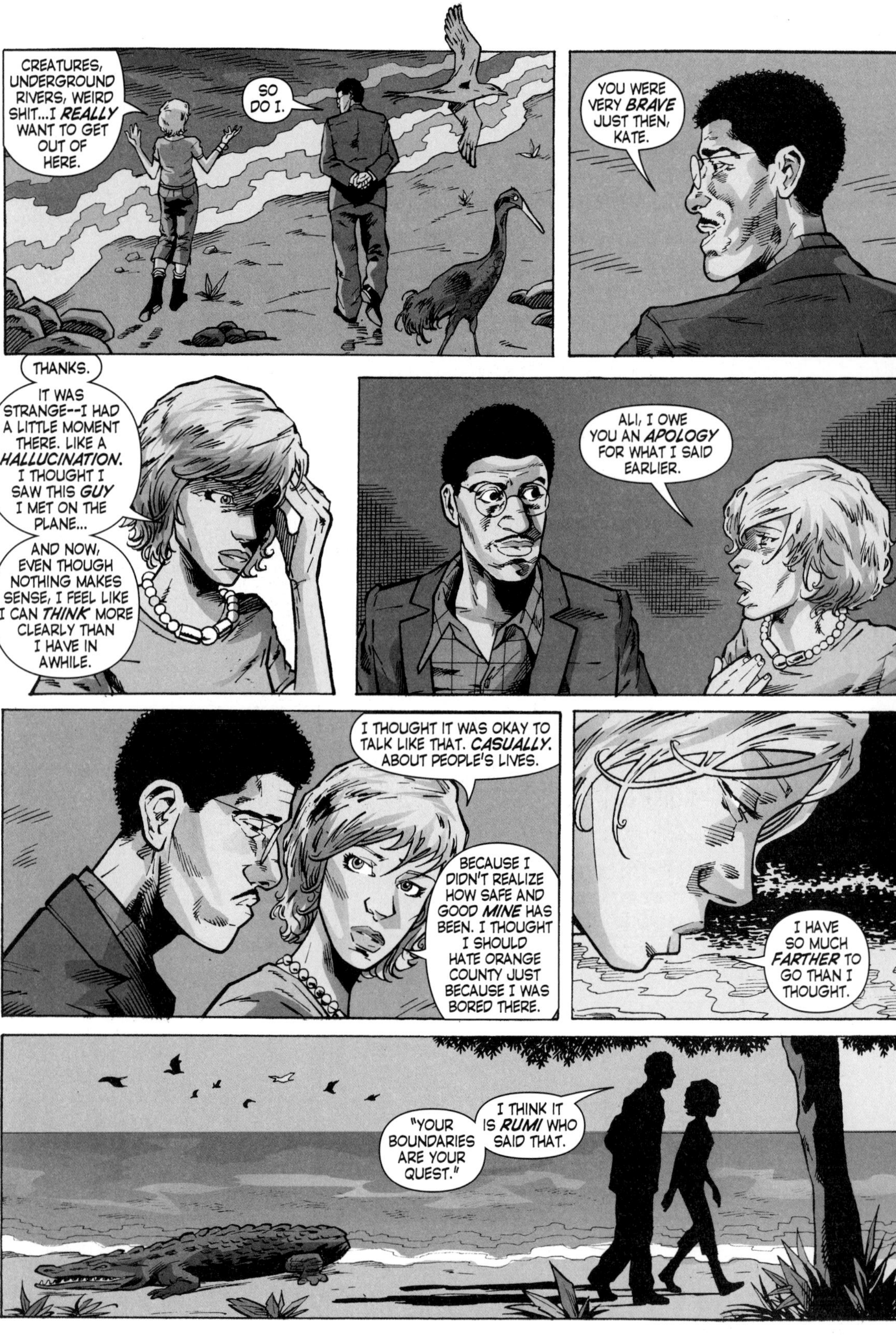
CREATURES, UNDERGROUND RIVERS, WEIRD SHIT...I *REALLY* WANT TO GET OUT OF HERE.
SO DO I.
YOU WERE VERY *BRAVE* JUST THEN, KATE.
THANKS.
IT WAS STRANGE--I HAD A LITTLE MOMENT THERE. LIKE A *HALLUCINATION*. I THOUGHT I SAW THIS *GUY* I MET ON THE PLANE...
AND NOW, EVEN THOUGH NOTHING MAKES SENSE, I FEEL LIKE I CAN *THINK* MORE CLEARLY THAN I HAVE IN AWHILE.
ALI, I OWE YOU AN *APOLOGY* FOR WHAT I SAID EARLIER.
I THOUGHT IT WAS OKAY TO TALK LIKE THAT. *CASUALLY.* ABOUT PEOPLE'S LIVES.
BECAUSE I DIDN'T REALIZE HOW SAFE AND GOOD *MINE* HAS BEEN. I THOUGHT I SHOULD HATE ORANGE COUNTY JUST BECAUSE I WAS BORED THERE.
I HAVE SO MUCH *FARTHER* TO GO THAN I THOUGHT.
"YOUR BOUNDARIES ARE YOUR QUEST."
I THINK IT IS *RUMI* WHO SAID THAT.

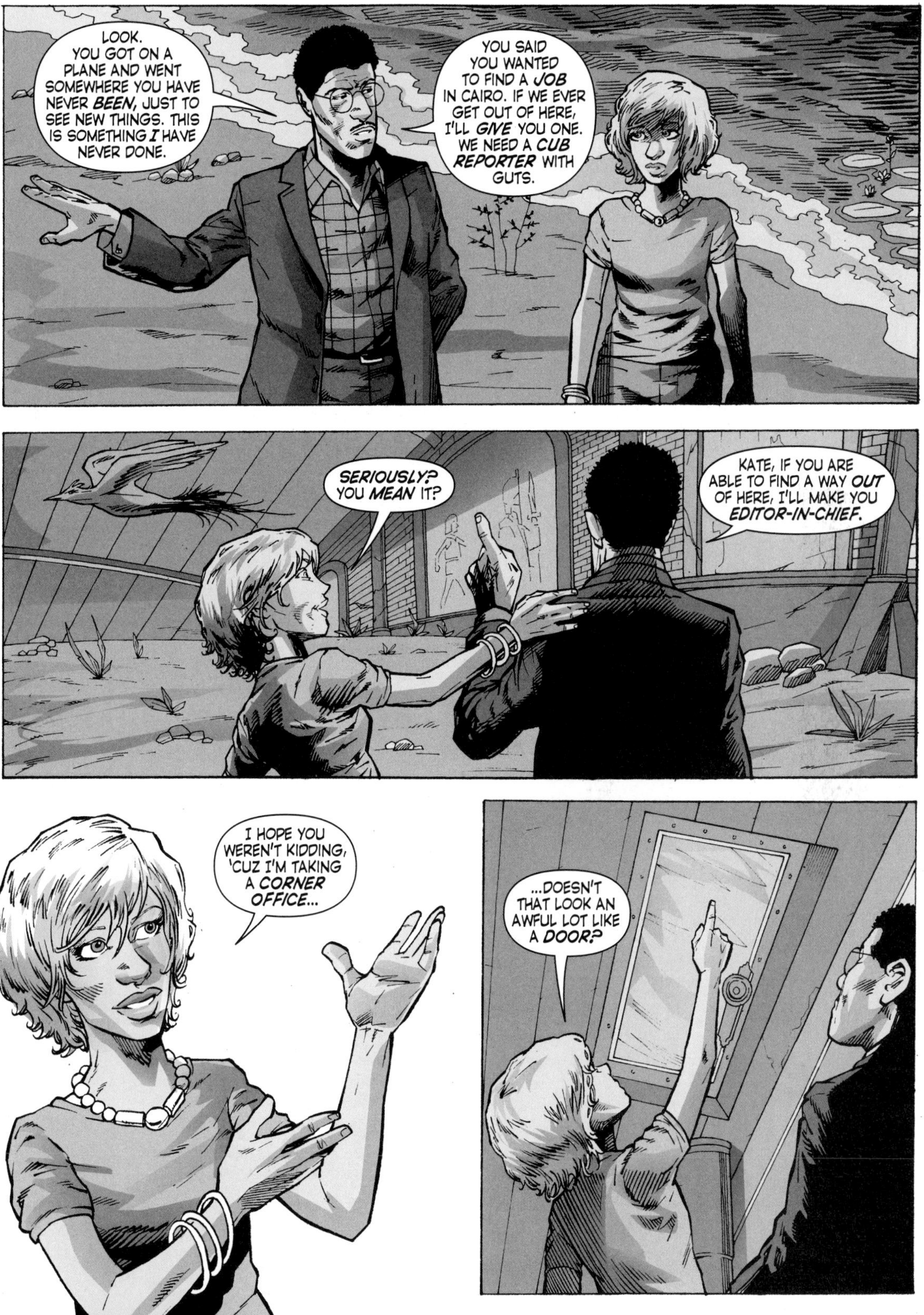
LOOK. YOU GOT ON A PLANE AND WENT SOMEWHERE YOU HAVE NEVER *BEEN,* JUST TO SEE NEW THINGS. THIS IS SOMETHING *I* HAVE NEVER DONE.
YOU SAID YOU WANTED TO FIND A *JOB* IN CAIRO. IF WE EVER GET OUT OF HERE, I'LL *GIVE* YOU ONE. WE NEED A *CUB REPORTER* WITH GUTS.
SERIOUSLY? YOU *MEAN* IT?
KATE, IF YOU ARE ABLE TO FIND A WAY *OUT* OF HERE, I'LL MAKE YOU *EDITOR-IN-CHIEF.*
I HOPE YOU WEREN'T KIDDING, 'CUZ I'M TAKING A *CORNER OFFICE*...
...DOESN'T THAT LOOK AN AWFUL LOT LIKE A *DOOR?*

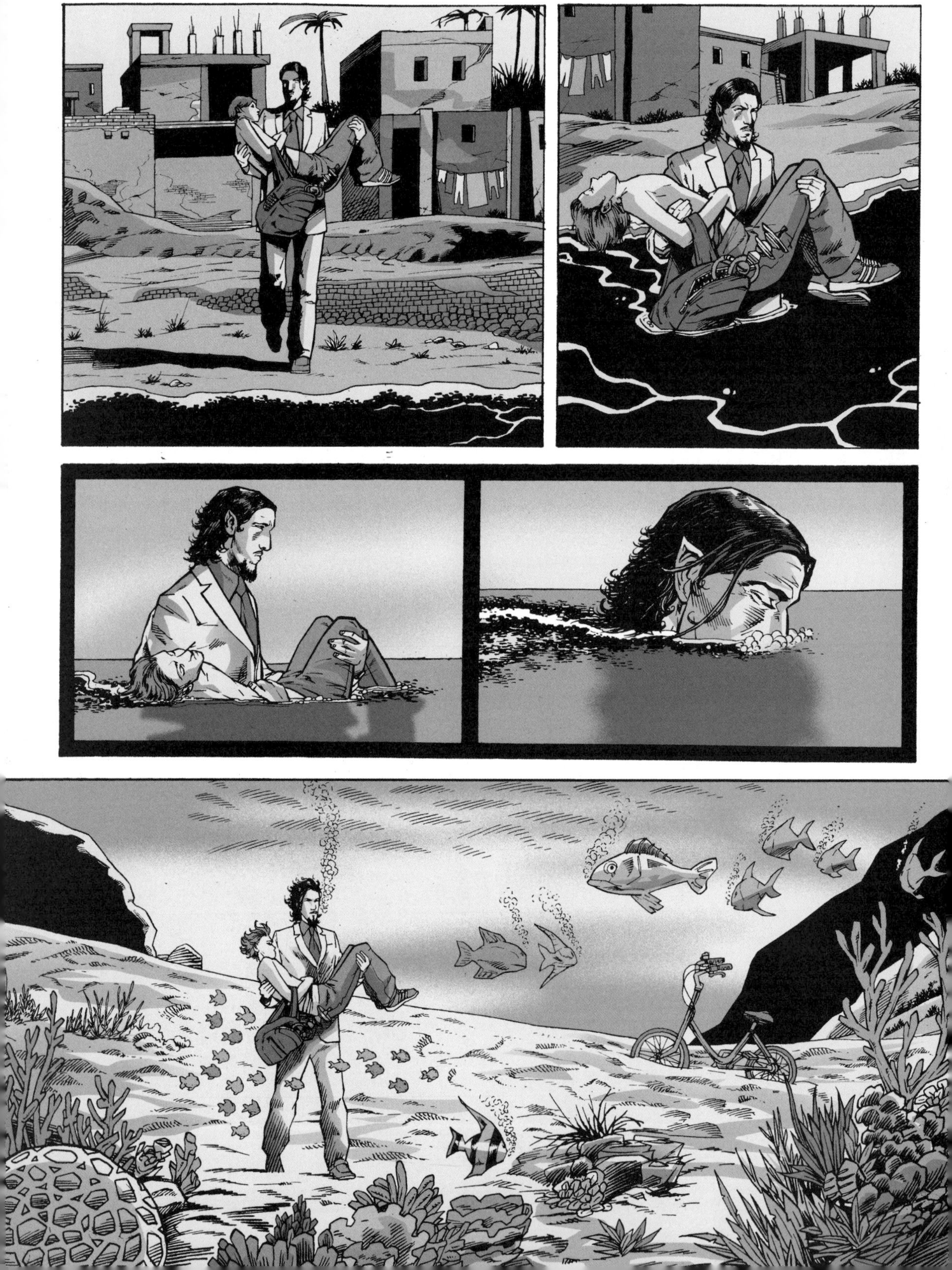

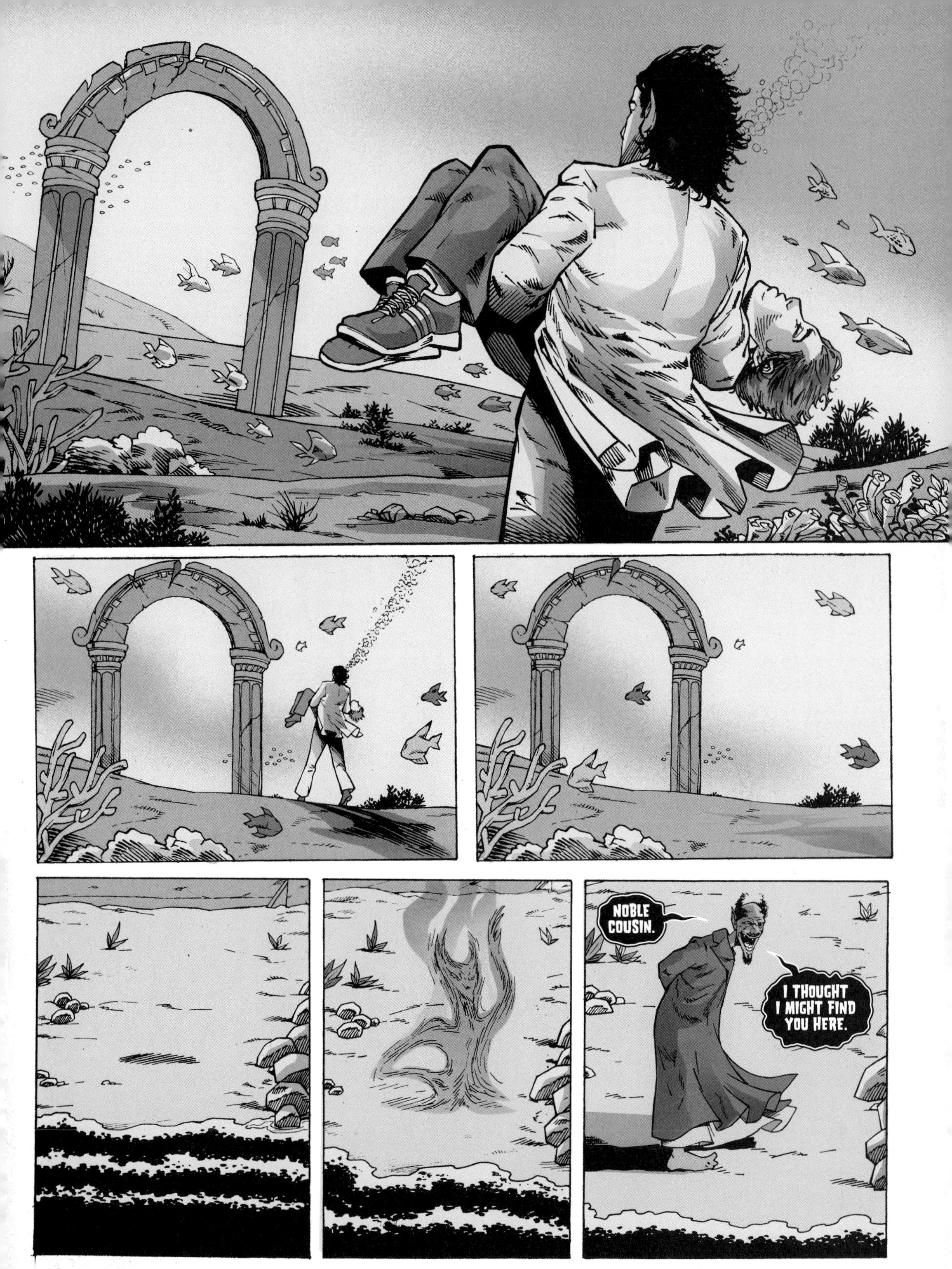
NOBLE COUSIN.
I THOUGHT I MIGHT FIND YOU HERE.

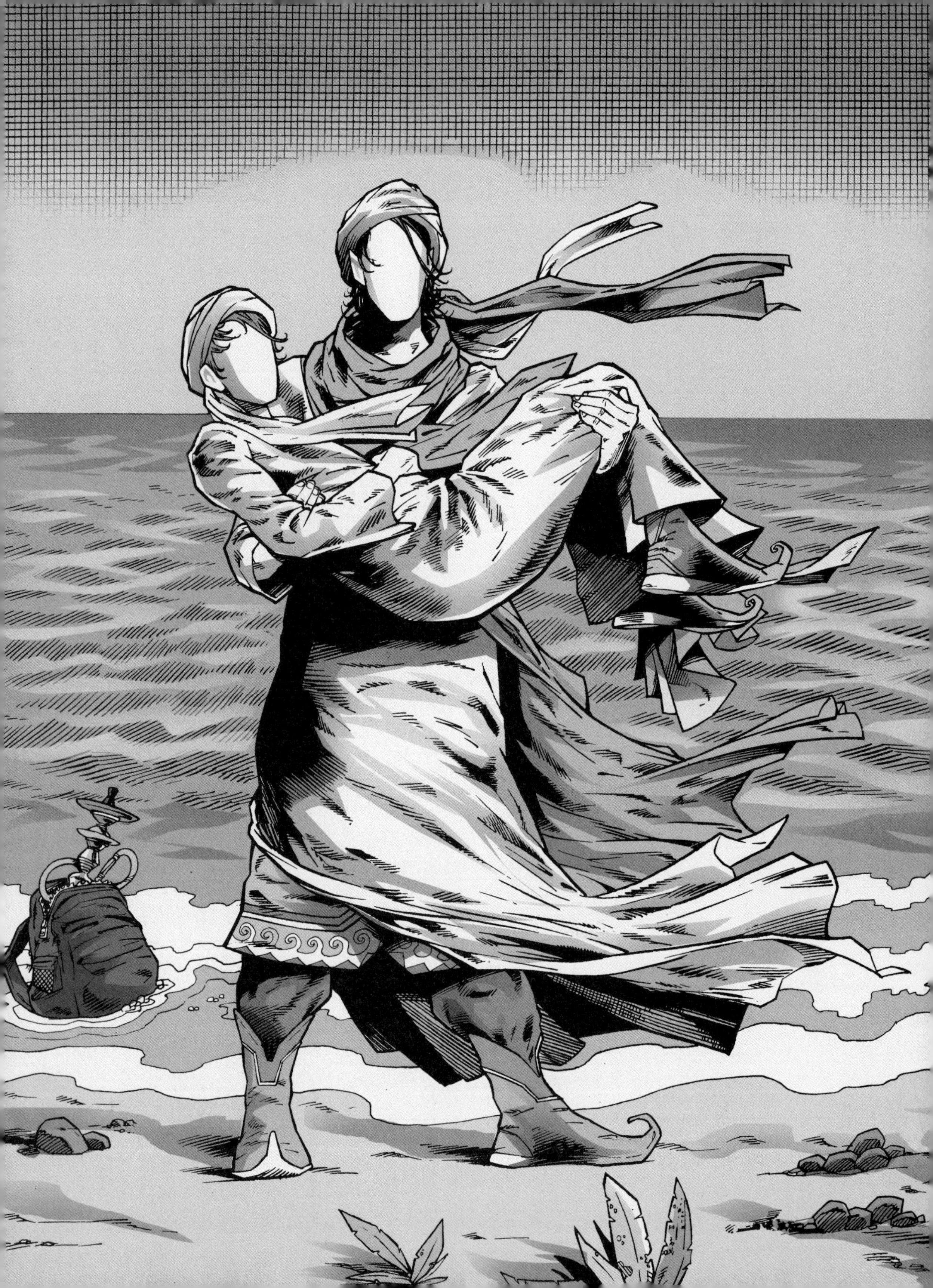

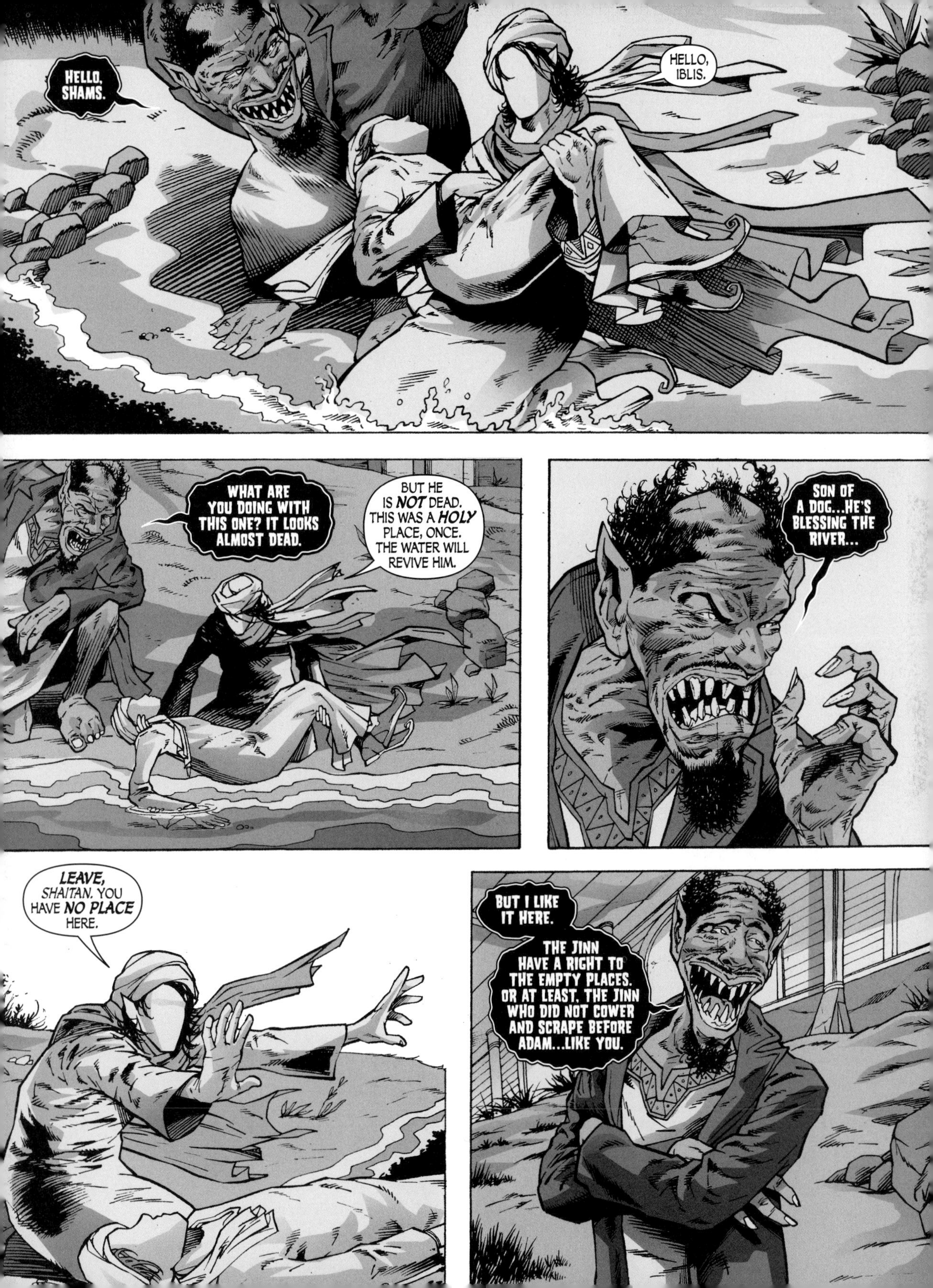
HELLO, SHAMS.
HELLO, IBLIS.
WHAT ARE YOU DOING WITH THIS ONE? IT LOOKS ALMOST DEAD.
BUT HE IS *NOT* DEAD. THIS WAS A *HOLY* PLACE, ONCE. THE WATER WILL REVIVE HIM.
SON OF A DOG...HE'S BLESSING THE RIVER...
LEAVE, *SHAITAN.* YOU HAVE *NO PLACE* HERE.
BUT I LIKE IT HERE.
THE JINN HAVE A RIGHT TO THE EMPTY PLACES. OR AT LEAST, THE JINN WHO DID NOT COWER AND SCRAPE BEFORE ADAM...LIKE YOU.

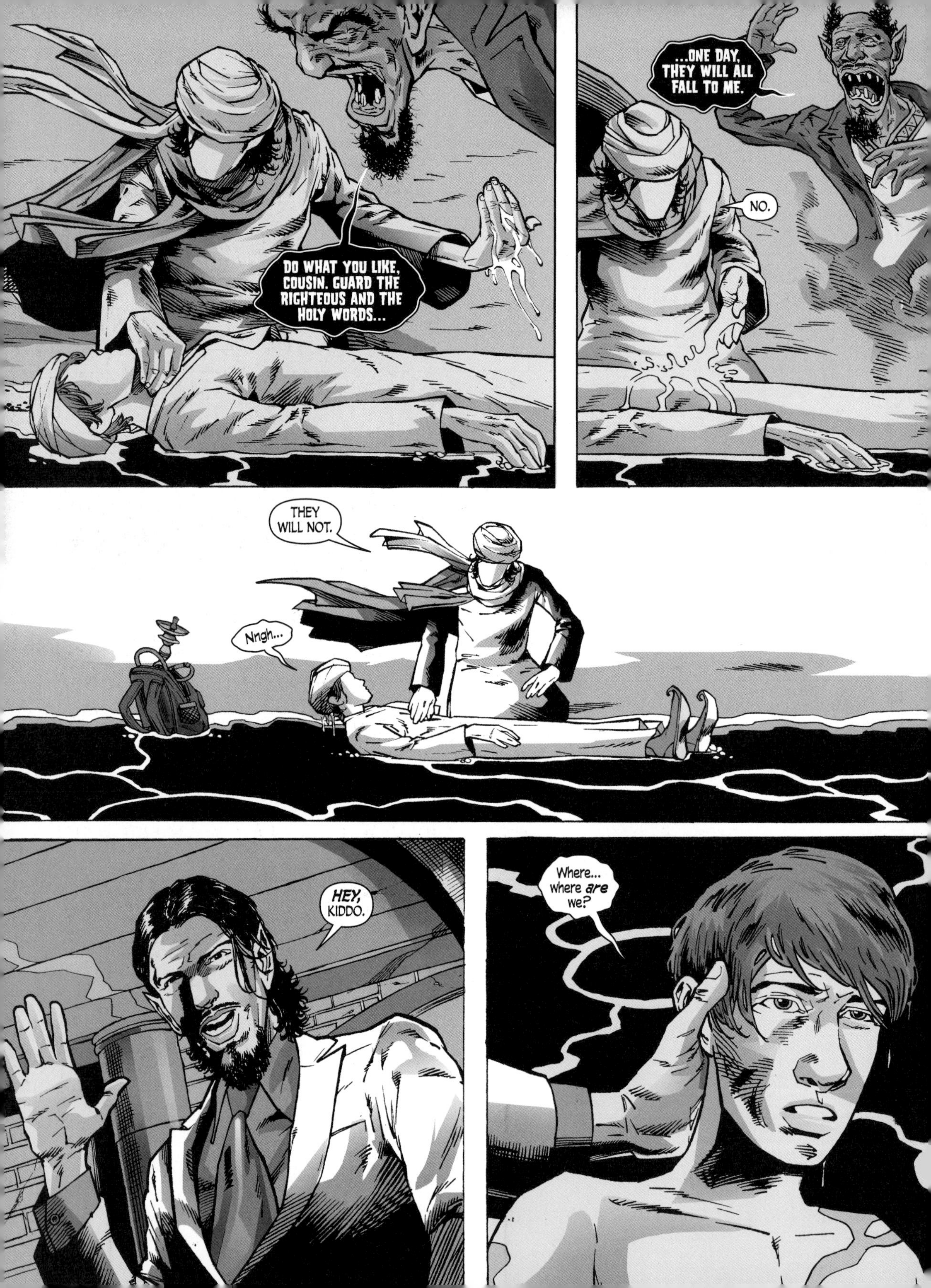
DO WHAT YOU LIKE, COUSIN. GUARD THE RIGHTEOUS AND THE HOLY WORDS...
...ONE DAY, THEY WILL ALL FALL TO ME.
NO.
THEY WILL NOT.
Nngh...
HEY, KIDDO.
Where... where are we?

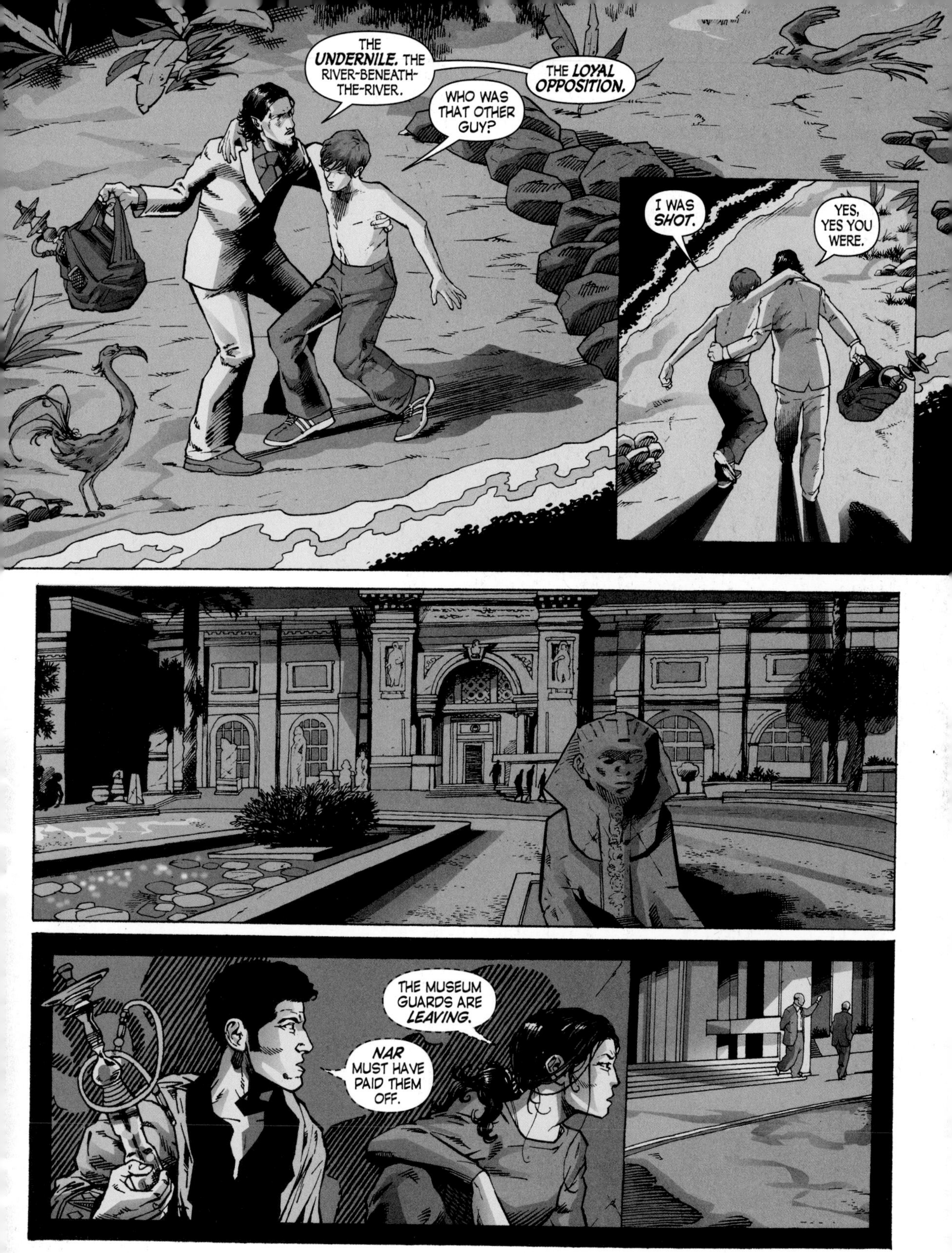
THE UNDERNILE. THE RIVER-BENEATH-THE-RIVER.
THE LOYAL OPPOSITION.
WHO WAS THAT OTHER GUY?
I WAS SHOT.
YES, YES YOU WERE.
THE MUSEUM GUARDS ARE LEAVING.
NAR MUST HAVE PAID THEM OFF.

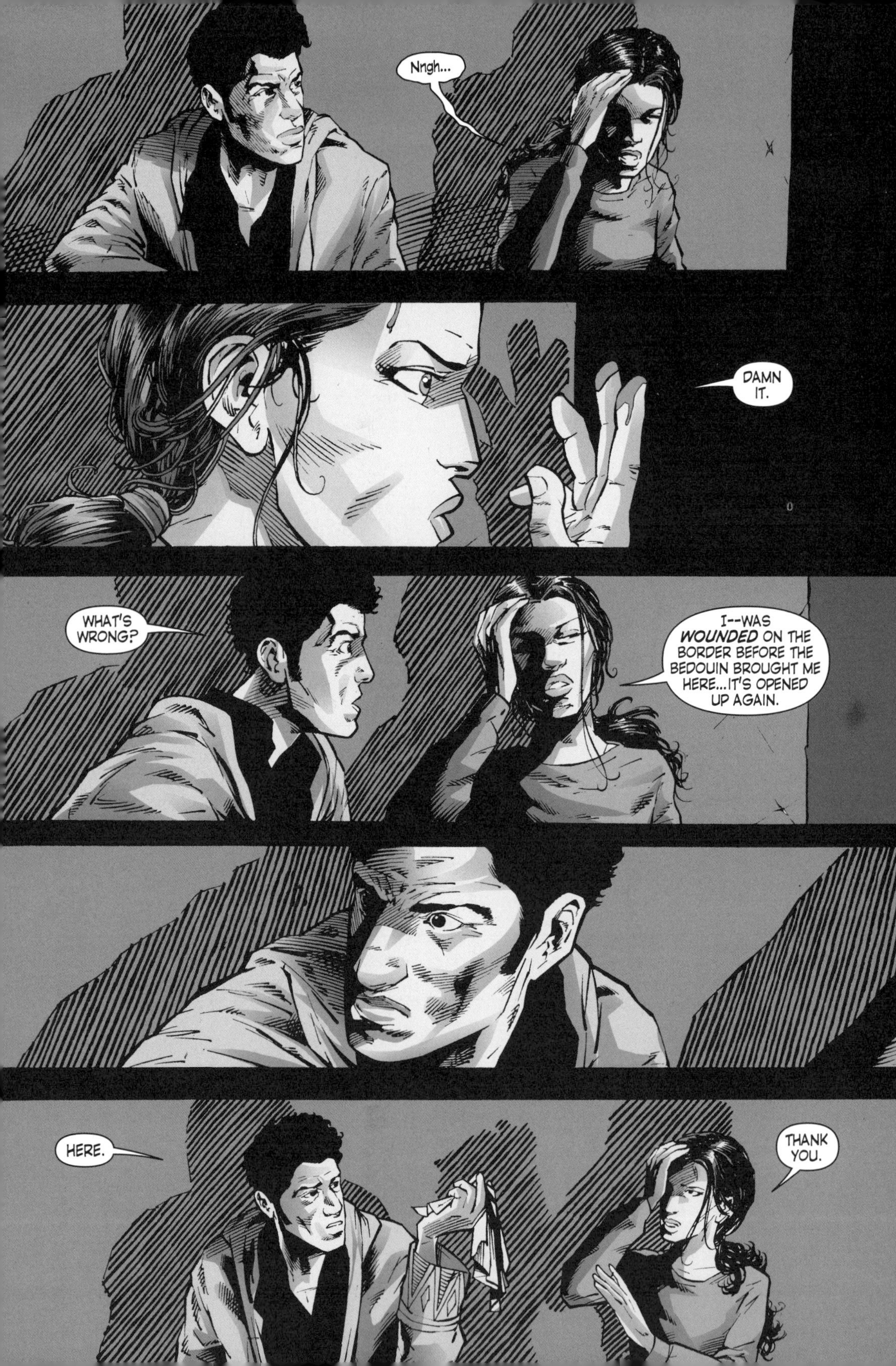
Nngh...
DAMN IT.
WHAT'S WRONG?
I--WAS WOUNDED ON THE BORDER BEFORE THE BEDOUIN BROUGHT ME HERE...IT'S OPENED UP AGAIN.
HERE.
THANK YOU.

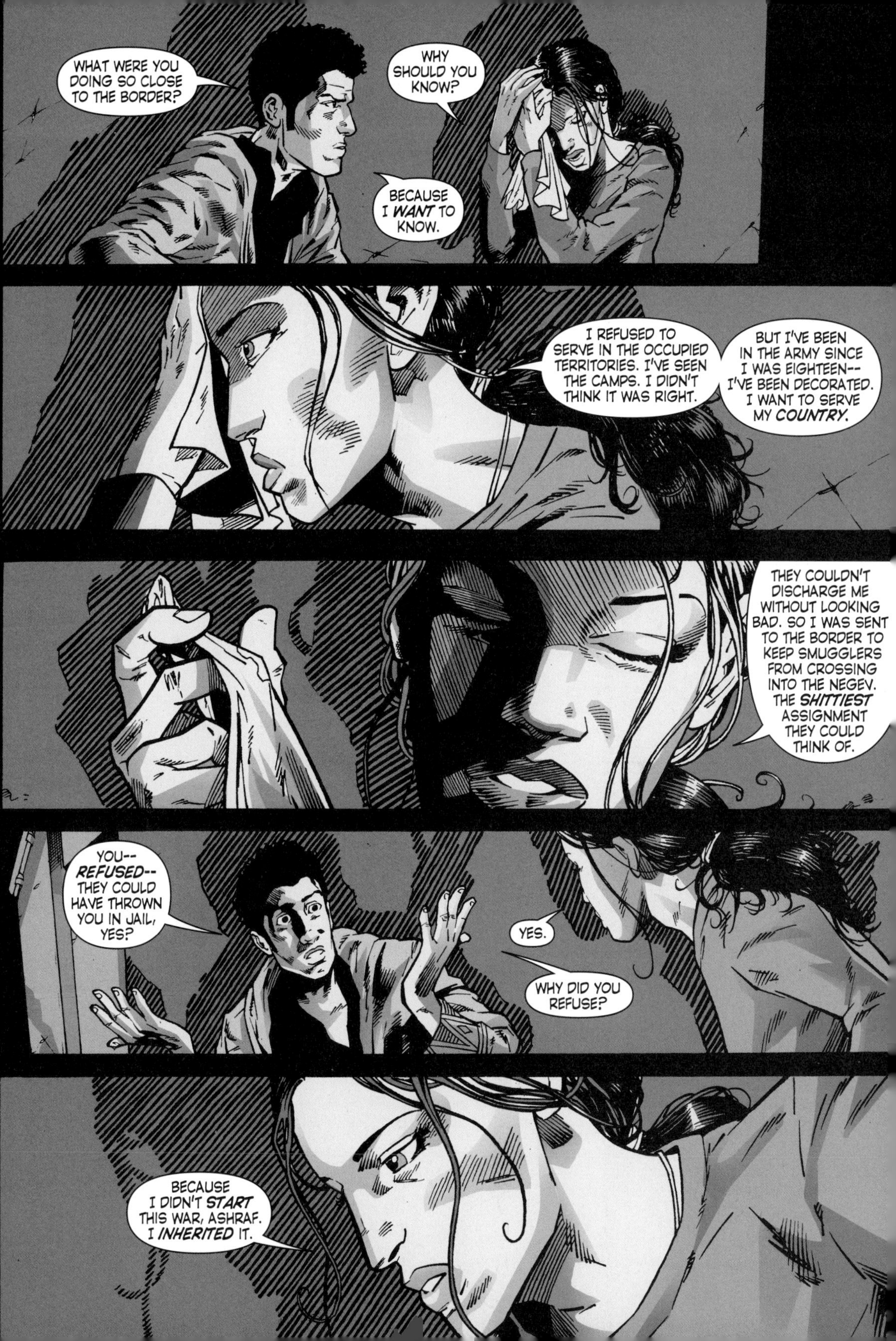
WHAT WERE YOU DOING SO CLOSE TO THE BORDER?
WHY SHOULD YOU KNOW?
BECAUSE I *WANT* TO KNOW.
I REFUSED TO SERVE IN THE OCCUPIED TERRITORIES. I'VE SEEN THE CAMPS. I DIDN'T THINK IT WAS RIGHT.
BUT I'VE BEEN IN THE ARMY SINCE I WAS EIGHTEEN-- I'VE BEEN DECORATED. I WANT TO SERVE MY *COUNTRY.*
THEY COULDN'T DISCHARGE ME WITHOUT LOOKING BAD. SO I WAS SENT TO THE BORDER TO KEEP SMUGGLERS FROM CROSSING INTO THE NEGEV. THE *SHITTIEST* ASSIGNMENT THEY COULD THINK OF.
YOU-- *REFUSED*-- THEY COULD HAVE THROWN YOU IN JAIL, YES?
YES.
WHY DID YOU REFUSE?
BECAUSE I DIDN'T *START* THIS WAR, ASHRAF. I *INHERITED* IT.

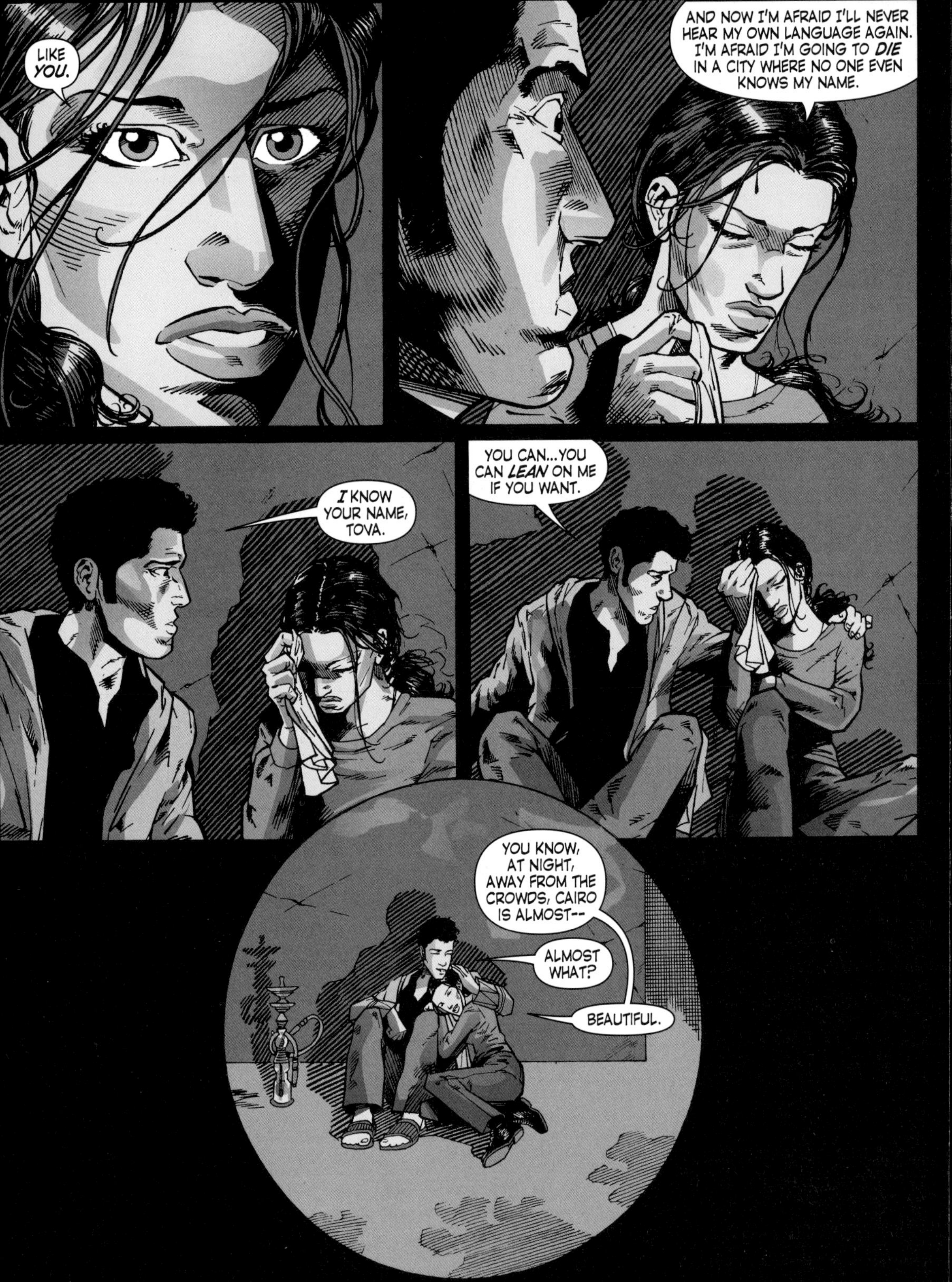
LIKE *YOU.*
AND NOW I'M AFRAID I'LL NEVER HEAR MY OWN LANGUAGE AGAIN. I'M AFRAID I'M GOING TO *DIE* IN A CITY WHERE NO ONE EVEN KNOWS MY NAME.
I KNOW YOUR NAME, TOVA.
YOU CAN...YOU CAN *LEAN* ON ME IF YOU WANT.
YOU KNOW, AT NIGHT, AWAY FROM THE CROWDS, CAIRO IS ALMOST--
ALMOST WHAT?
BEAUTIFUL.

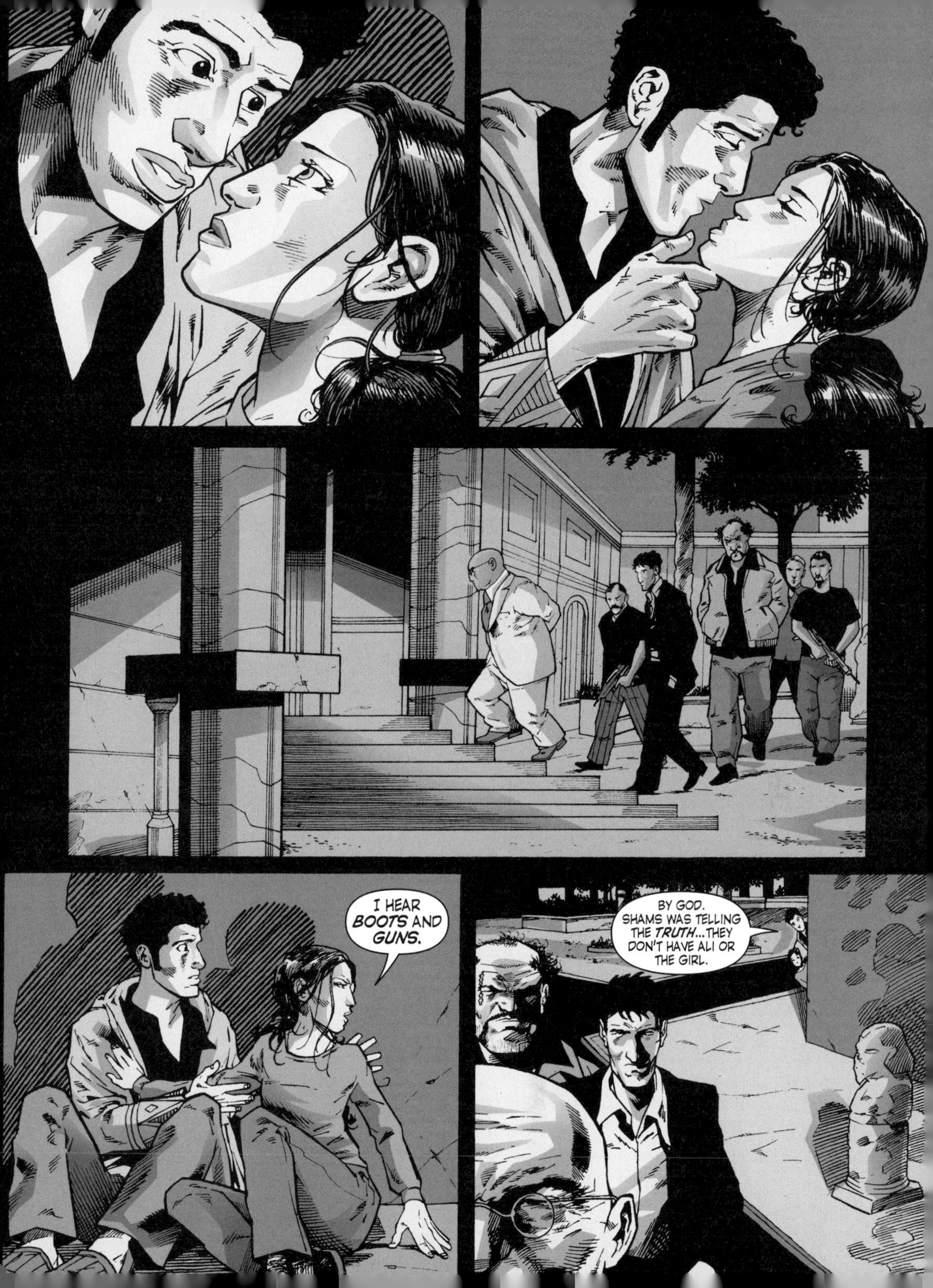
I HEAR *BOOTS* AND *GUNS*.
BY GOD. SHAMS WAS TELLING THE *TRUTH*...THEY DON'T HAVE ALI OR THE GIRL.

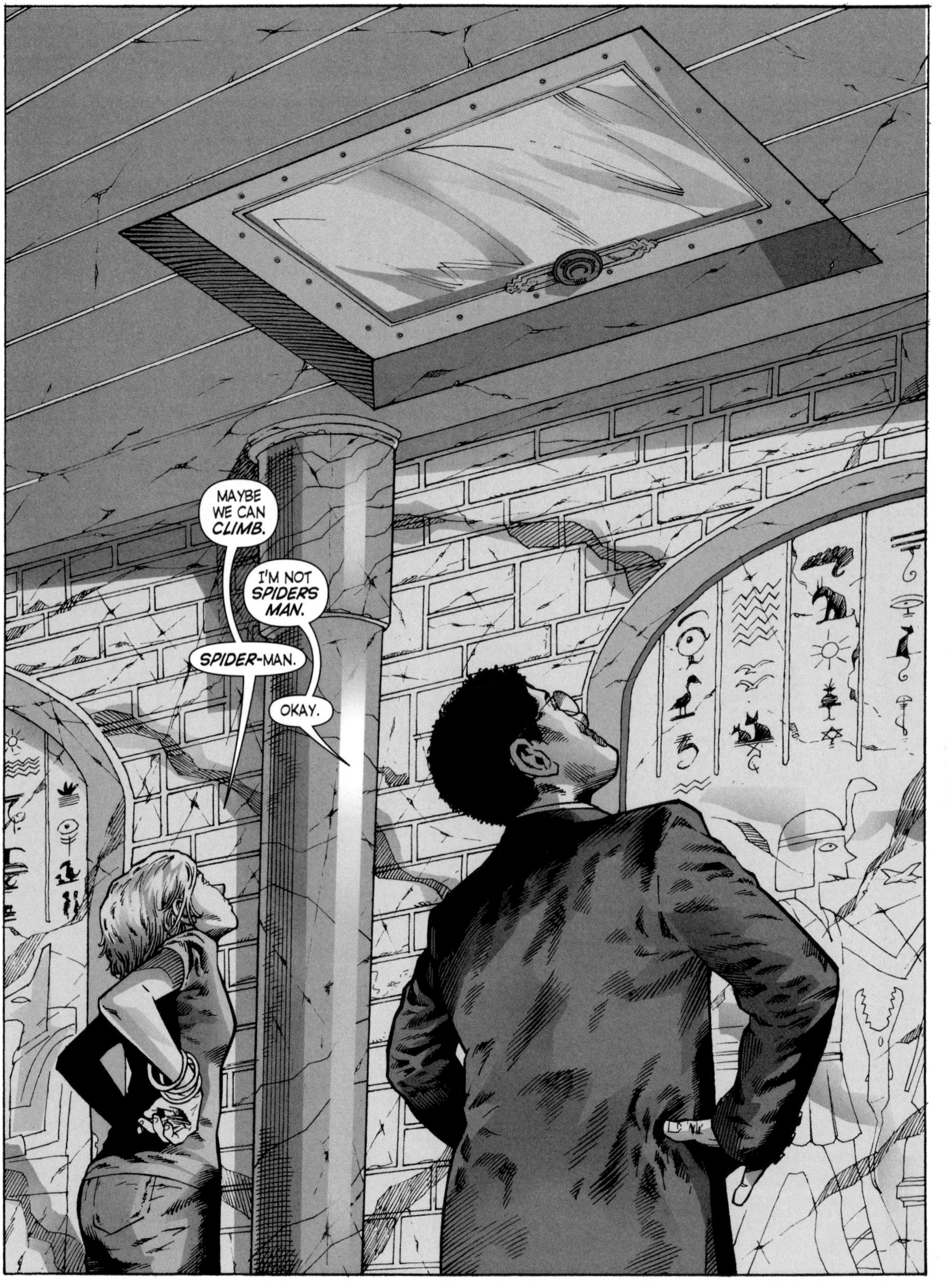
MAYBE WE CAN CLIMB.
I'M NOT SPIDERS MAN.
SPIDER-MAN.
OKAY.

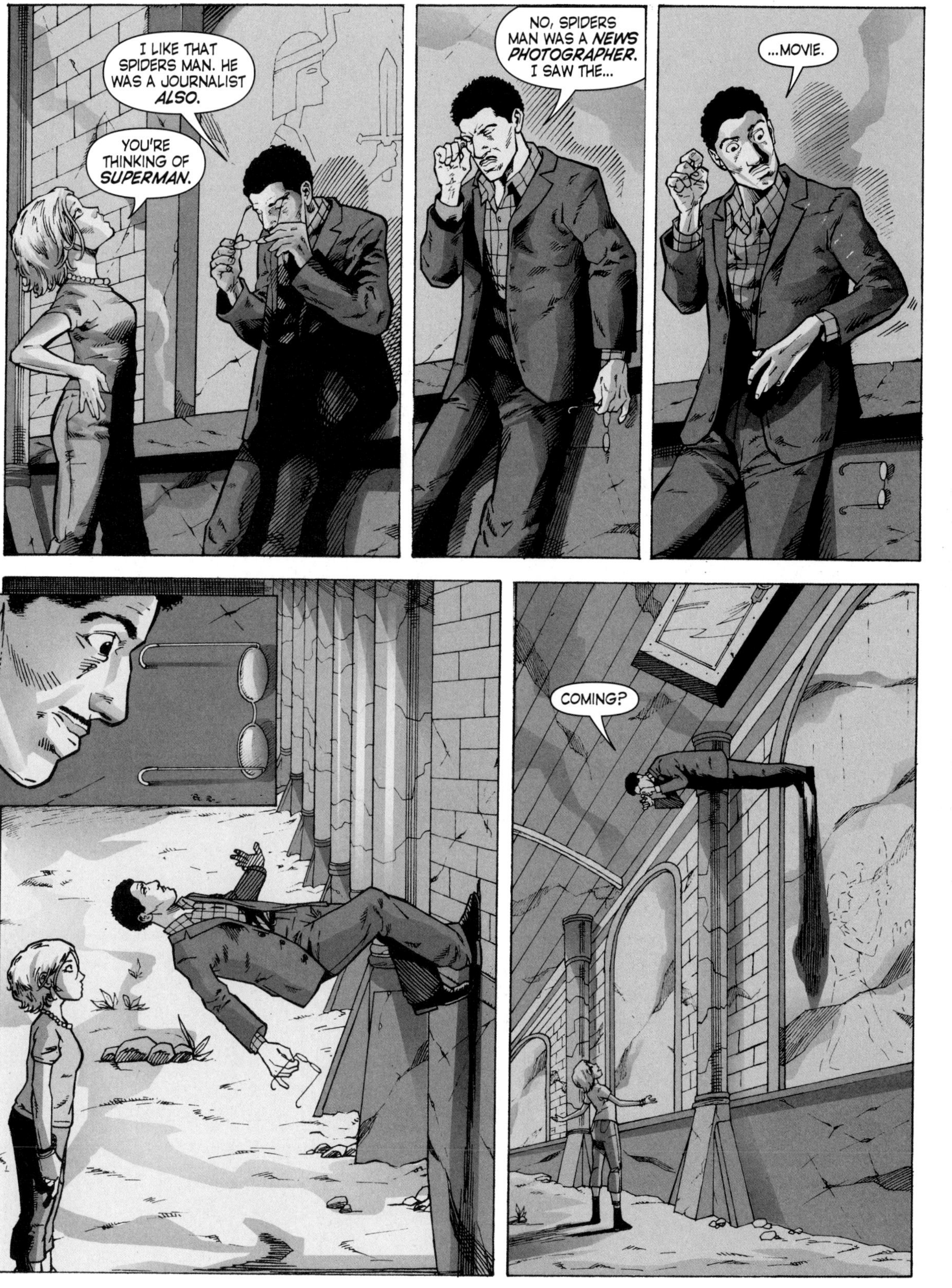
I LIKE THAT SPIDERS MAN. HE WAS A JOURNALIST ALSO.
YOU'RE THINKING OF SUPERMAN.
NO, SPIDERS MAN WAS A NEWS PHOTOGRAPHER. I SAW THE...
...MOVIE.
COMING?

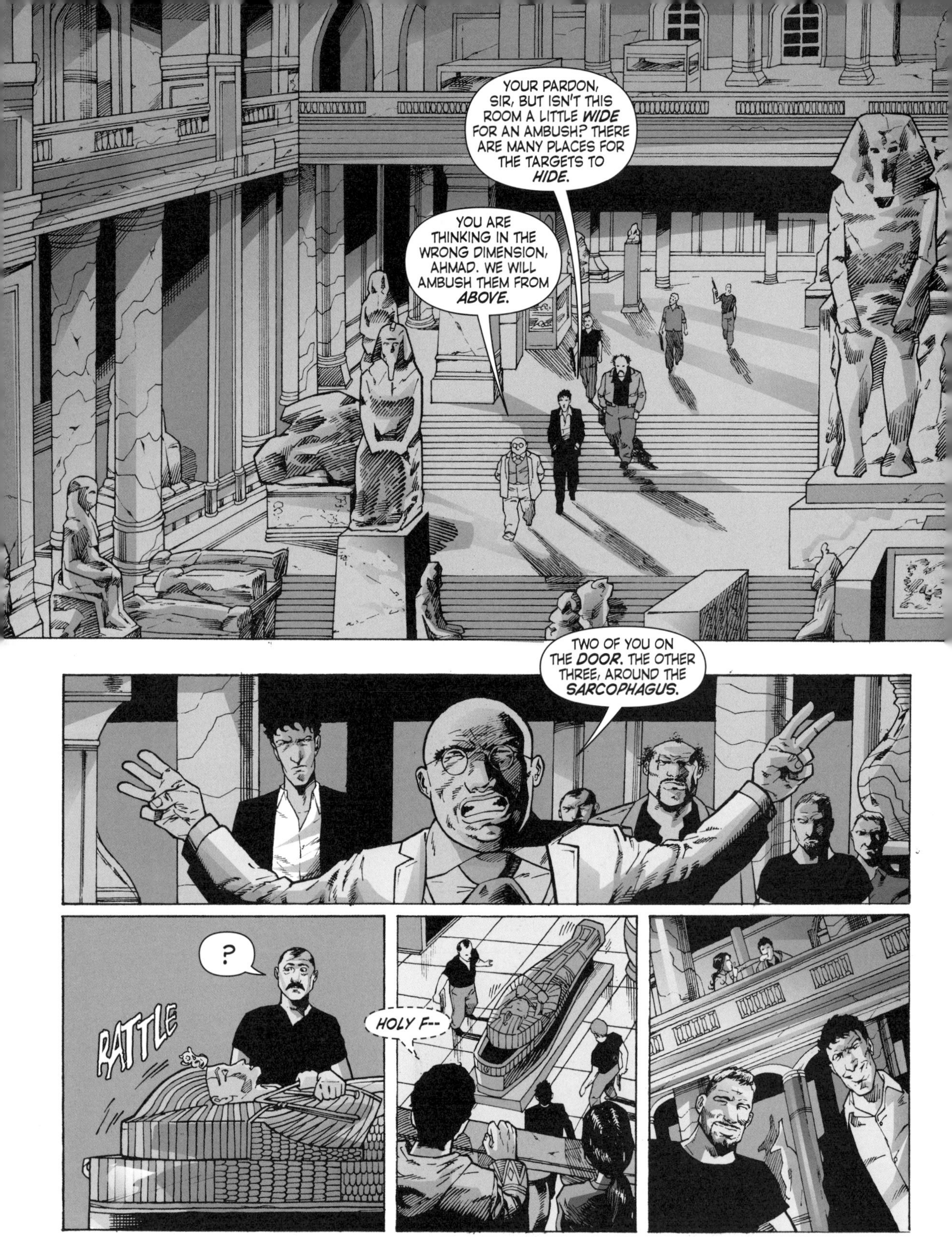

YOUR PARDON, SIR, BUT ISN'T THIS ROOM A LITTLE WIDE FOR AN AMBUSH? THERE ARE MANY PLACES FOR THE TARGETS TO HIDE.
YOU ARE THINKING IN THE WRONG DIMENSION, AHMAD. WE WILL AMBUSH THEM FROM ABOVE.
TWO OF YOU ON THE DOOR. THE OTHER THREE, AROUND THE SARCOPHAGUS.
?
RATTLE
HOLY F--

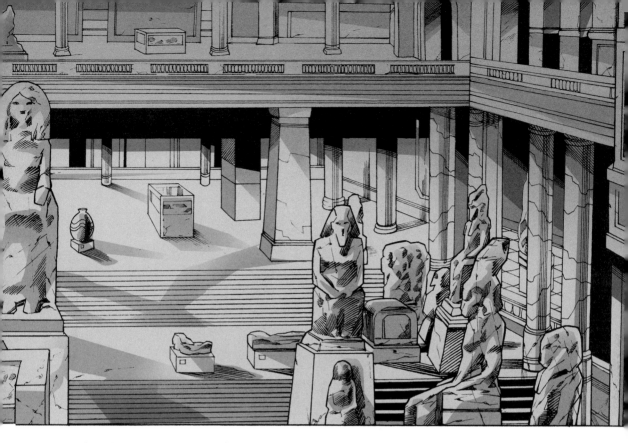

PRAISE GOD! WE'RE--

...SAFE.

RESPECTED SIR. WE MEET AGAIN.

YES! GOODBYE, UNDERNILE!

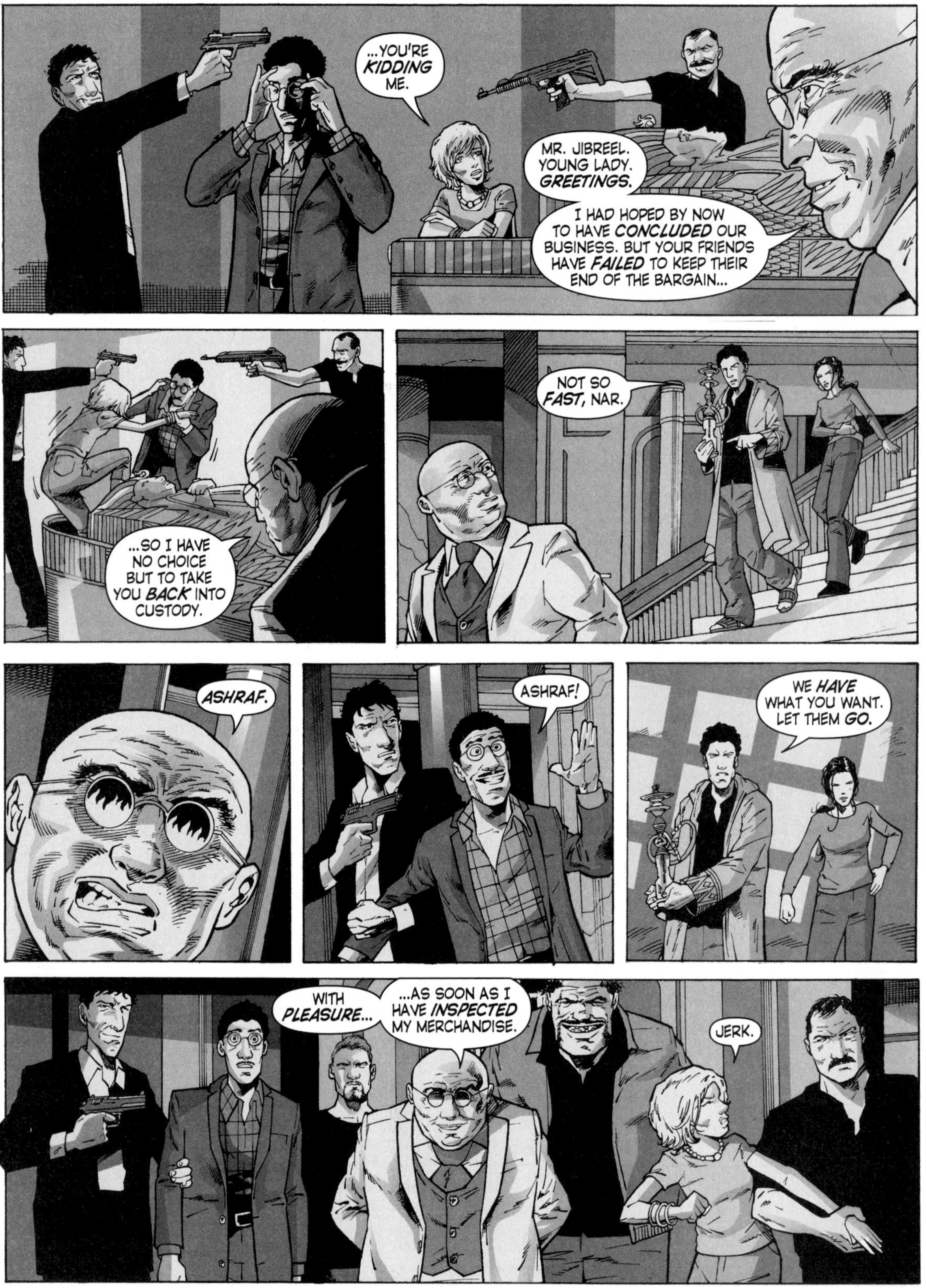
...YOU'RE KIDDING ME.
MR. JIBREEL. YOUNG LADY. GREETINGS.
I HAD HOPED BY NOW TO HAVE CONCLUDED OUR BUSINESS. BUT YOUR FRIENDS HAVE FAILED TO KEEP THEIR END OF THE BARGAIN...
...SO I HAVE NO CHOICE BUT TO TAKE YOU BACK INTO CUSTODY.
NOT SO FAST, NAR.
ASHRAF.
ASHRAF!
WE HAVE WHAT YOU WANT. LET THEM GO.
WITH PLEASURE...
...AS SOON AS I HAVE INSPECTED MY MERCHANDISE.
JERK.

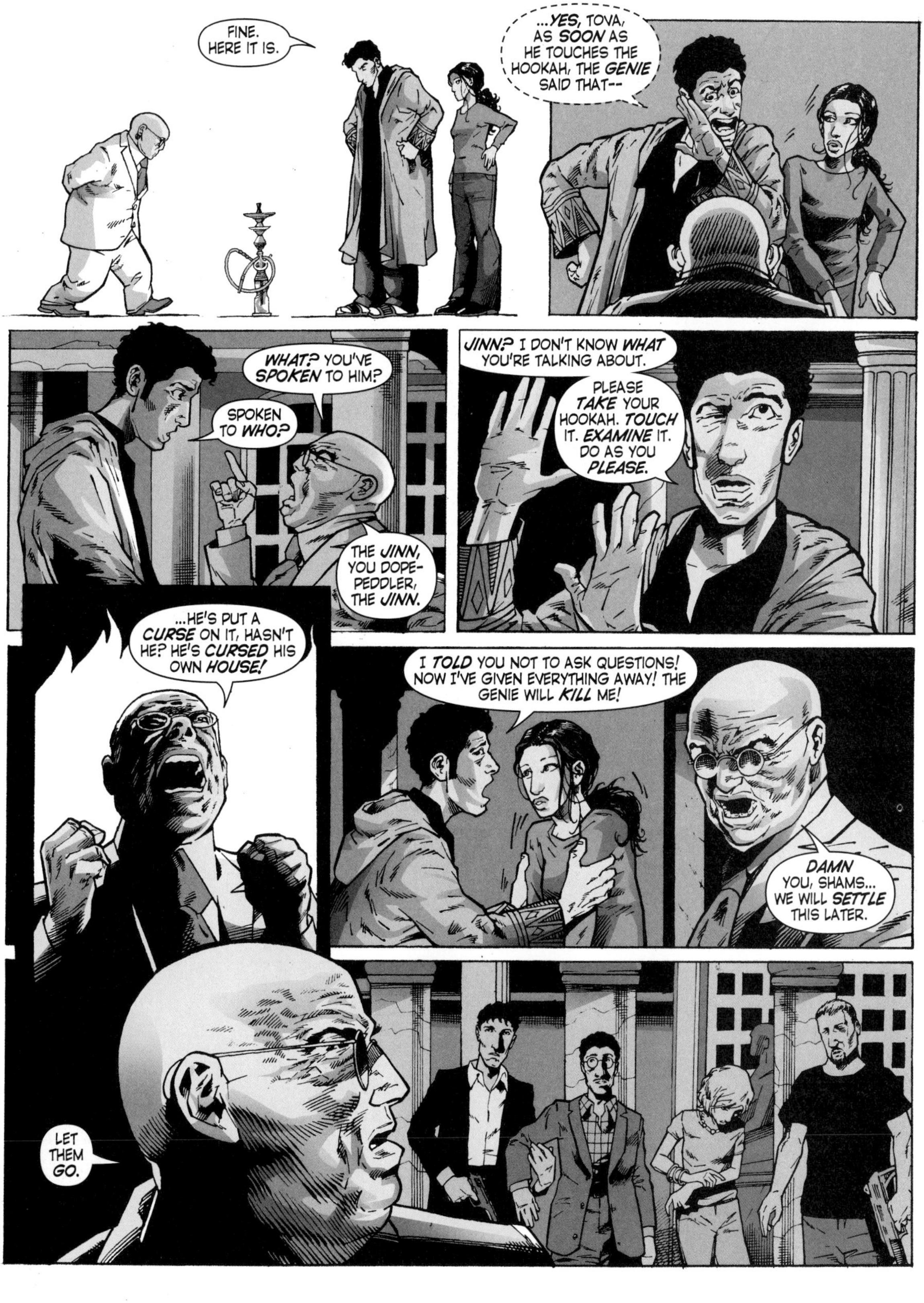
FINE. HERE IT IS.
...YES, TOVA, AS SOON AS HE TOUCHES THE HOOKAH, THE GENIE SAID THAT--
WHAT? YOU'VE SPOKEN TO HIM?
SPOKEN TO WHO?
THE JINN, YOU DOPE-PEDDLER, THE JINN.
JINN? I DON'T KNOW WHAT YOU'RE TALKING ABOUT.
PLEASE TAKE YOUR HOOKAH. TOUCH IT. EXAMINE IT. DO AS YOU PLEASE.
...HE'S PUT A CURSE ON IT, HASN'T HE? HE'S CURSED HIS OWN HOUSE!
I TOLD YOU NOT TO ASK QUESTIONS! NOW I'VE GIVEN EVERYTHING AWAY! THE GENIE WILL KILL ME!
DAMN YOU, SHAMS... WE WILL SETTLE THIS LATER.
LET THEM GO.

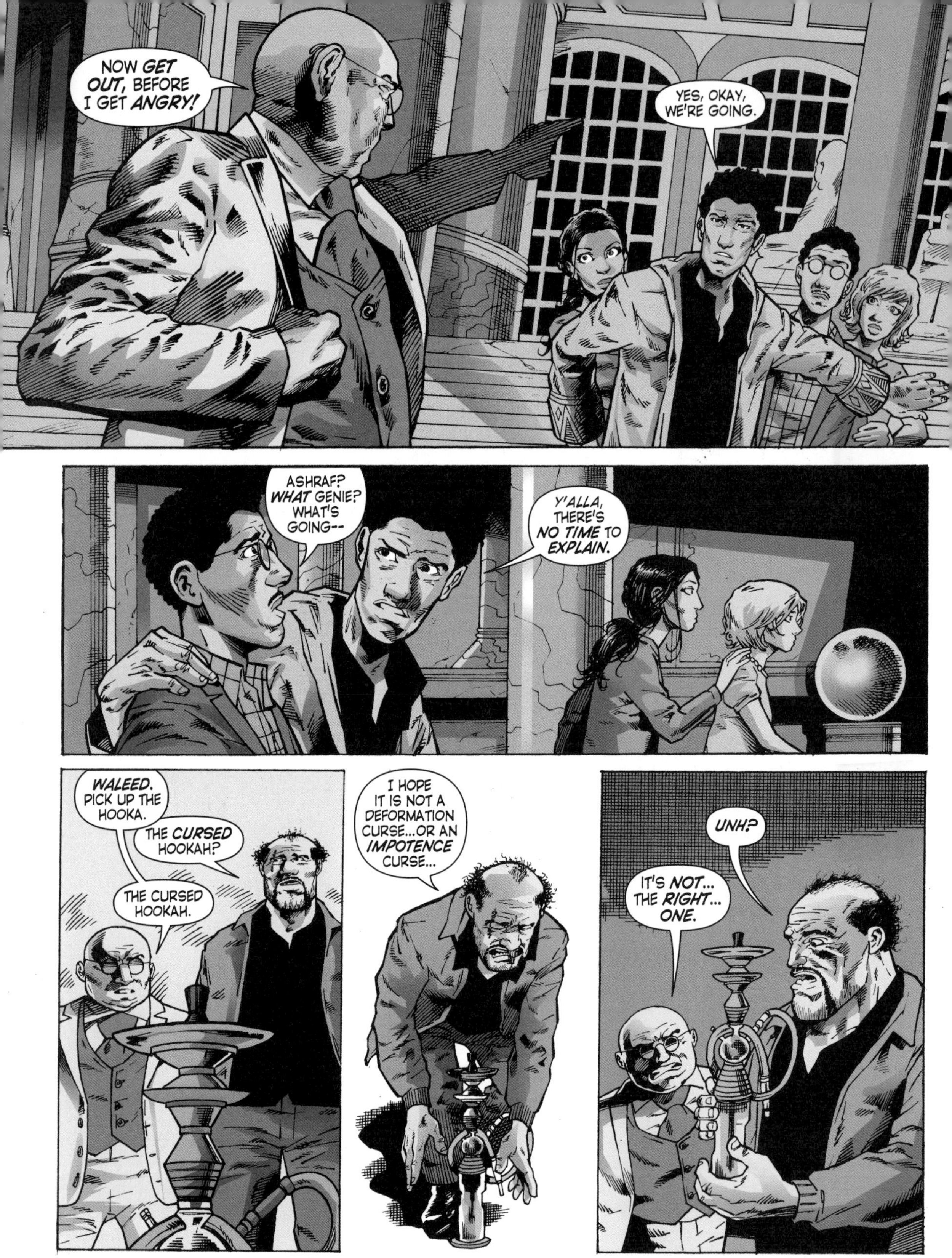
NOW GET OUT, BEFORE I GET ANGRY!
YES, OKAY, WE'RE GOING.
ASHRAF? WHAT GENIE? WHAT'S GOING--
Y'ALLA, THERE'S NO TIME TO EXPLAIN.
WALEED. PICK UP THE HOOKA.
THE CURSED HOOKAH?
THE CURSED HOOKAH.
I HOPE IT IS NOT A DEFORMATION CURSE...OR AN IMPOTENCE CURSE...
UNH?
IT'S NOT... THE RIGHT... ONE.

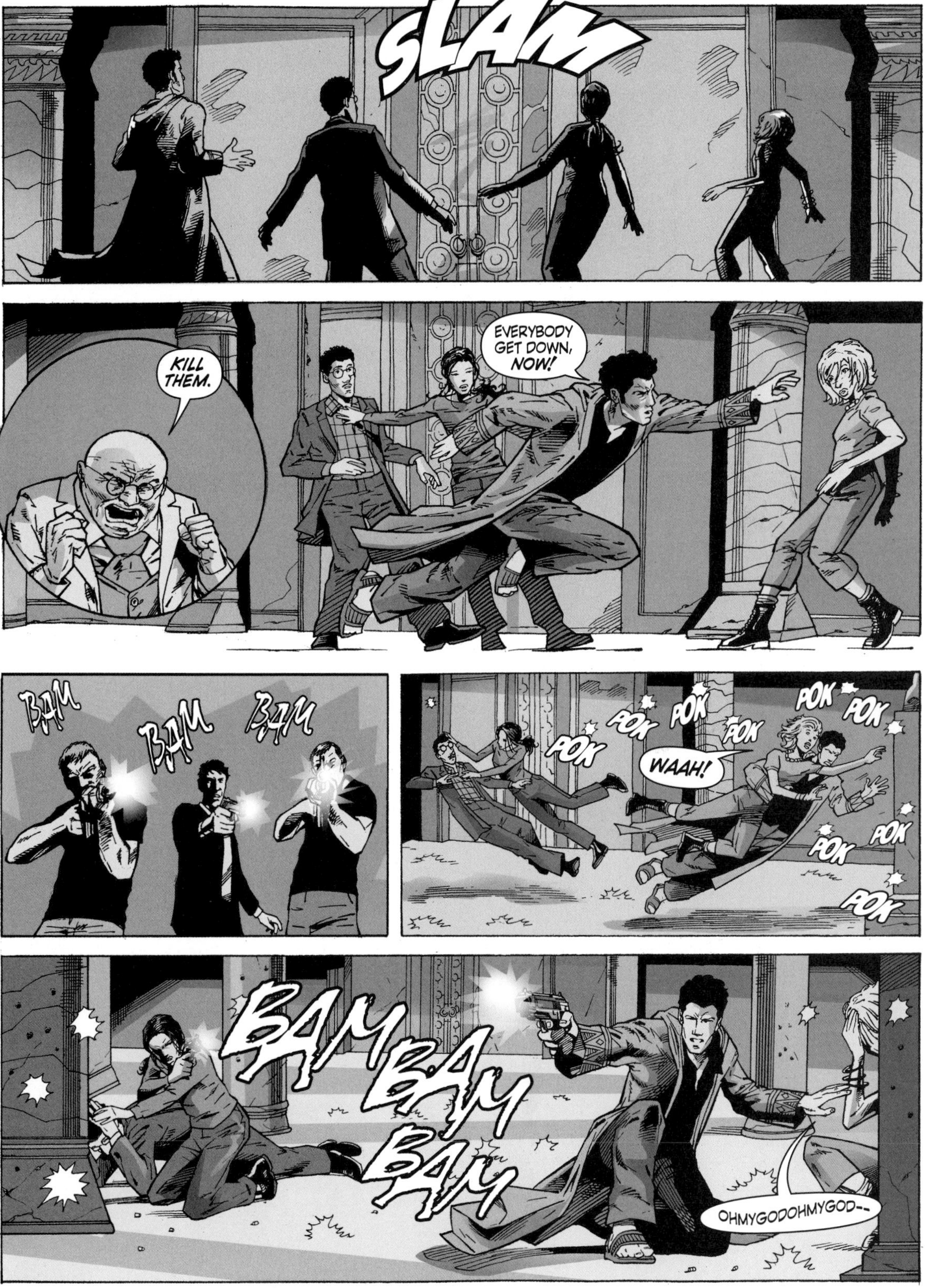
SLAM
KILL THEM.
EVERYBODY GET DOWN, NOW!
BAM
BAM
BAM
POK
POK
POK
POK
WAAH!
POK
POK
POK
POK
POK
BAM BAM BAM
OHMYGODOHMYGOD--

AH!

ASHRAF!

DAMN IT... Nngh...

STOP.

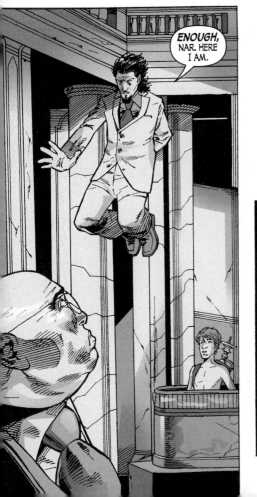

ENOUGH, NAR. HERE I AM.

THE MIGHTY SHAMS. *CLEVER*, BUT NOT CLEVER *ENOUGH*. ALL YOUR PLANS HAVE COME TO NOTHING. WE BOTH KNOW WHAT HAPPENS *NEXT*.

GIVE HIM THE HOOKAH, SHAHEED.

WHAT? NO--

IT'S ALL RIGHT. *GIVE* IT TO HIM.

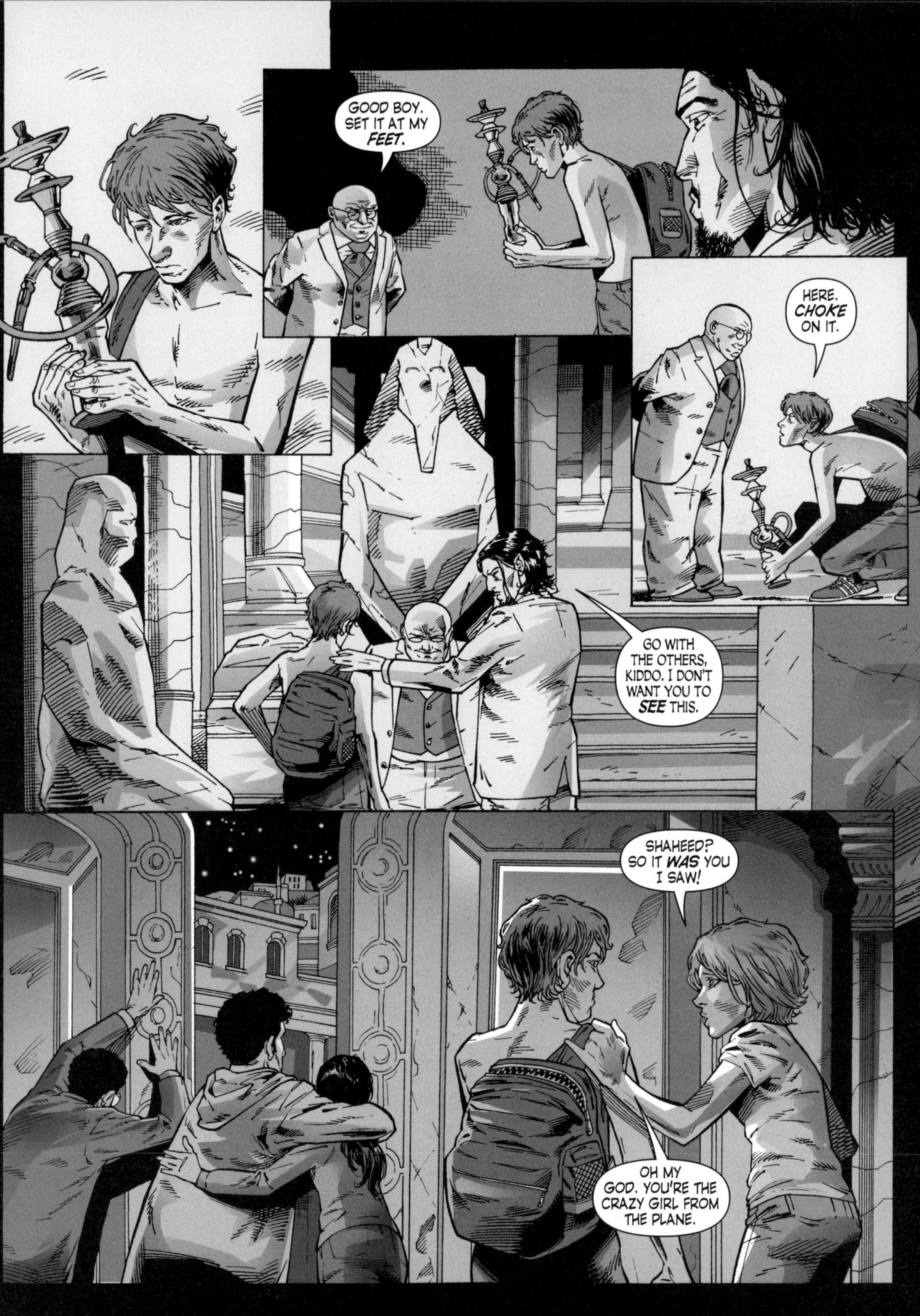
GOOD BOY. SET IT AT MY FEET.
HERE. CHOKE ON IT.
GO WITH THE OTHERS, KIDDO. I DON'T WANT YOU TO SEE THIS.
SHAHEED? SO IT WAS YOU I SAW!
OH MY GOD. YOU'RE THE CRAZY GIRL FROM THE PLANE.

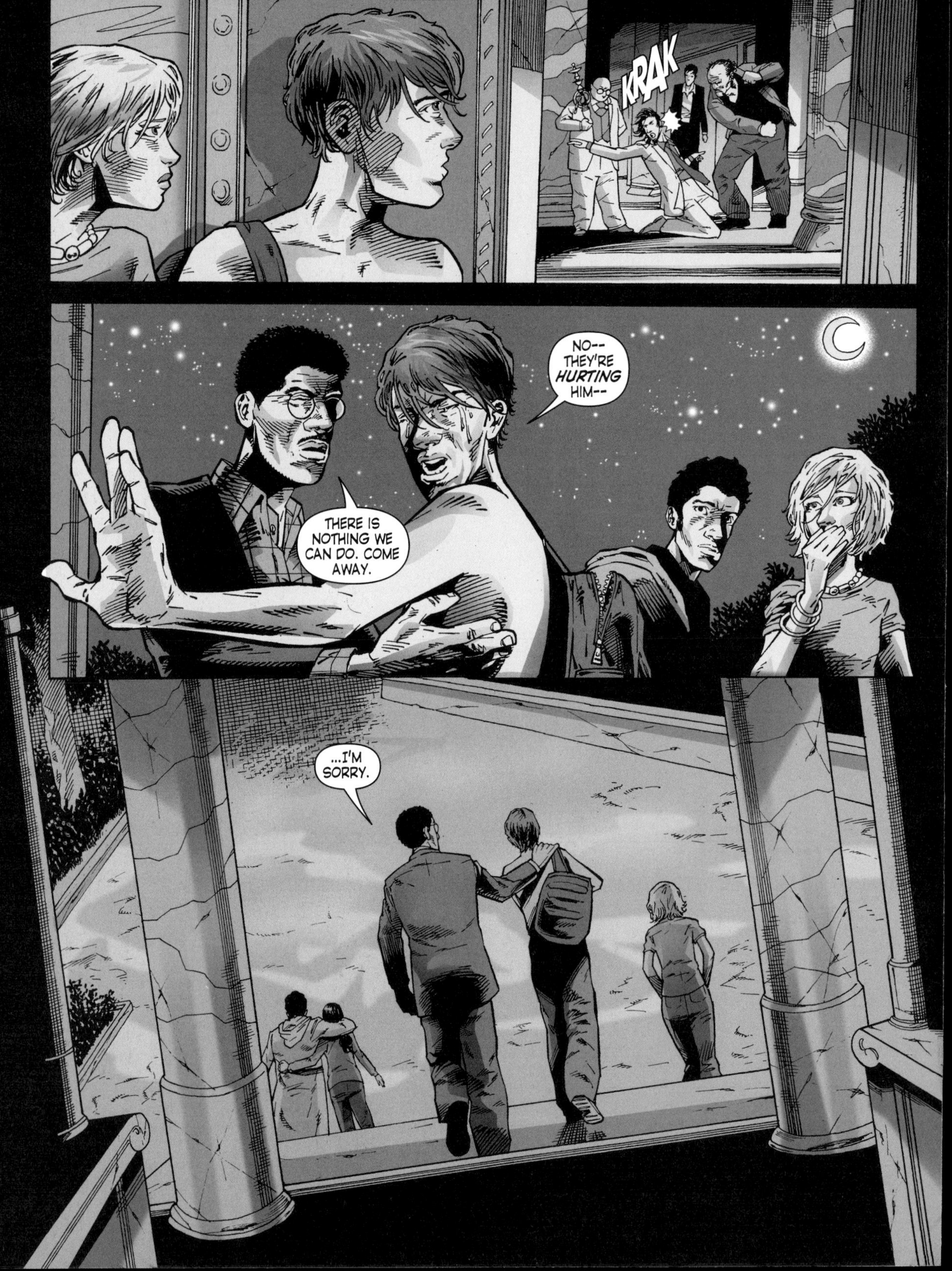
KRAK
NO-- THEY'RE *HURTING* HIM--
THERE IS NOTHING WE CAN DO. COME AWAY.
...I'M SORRY.

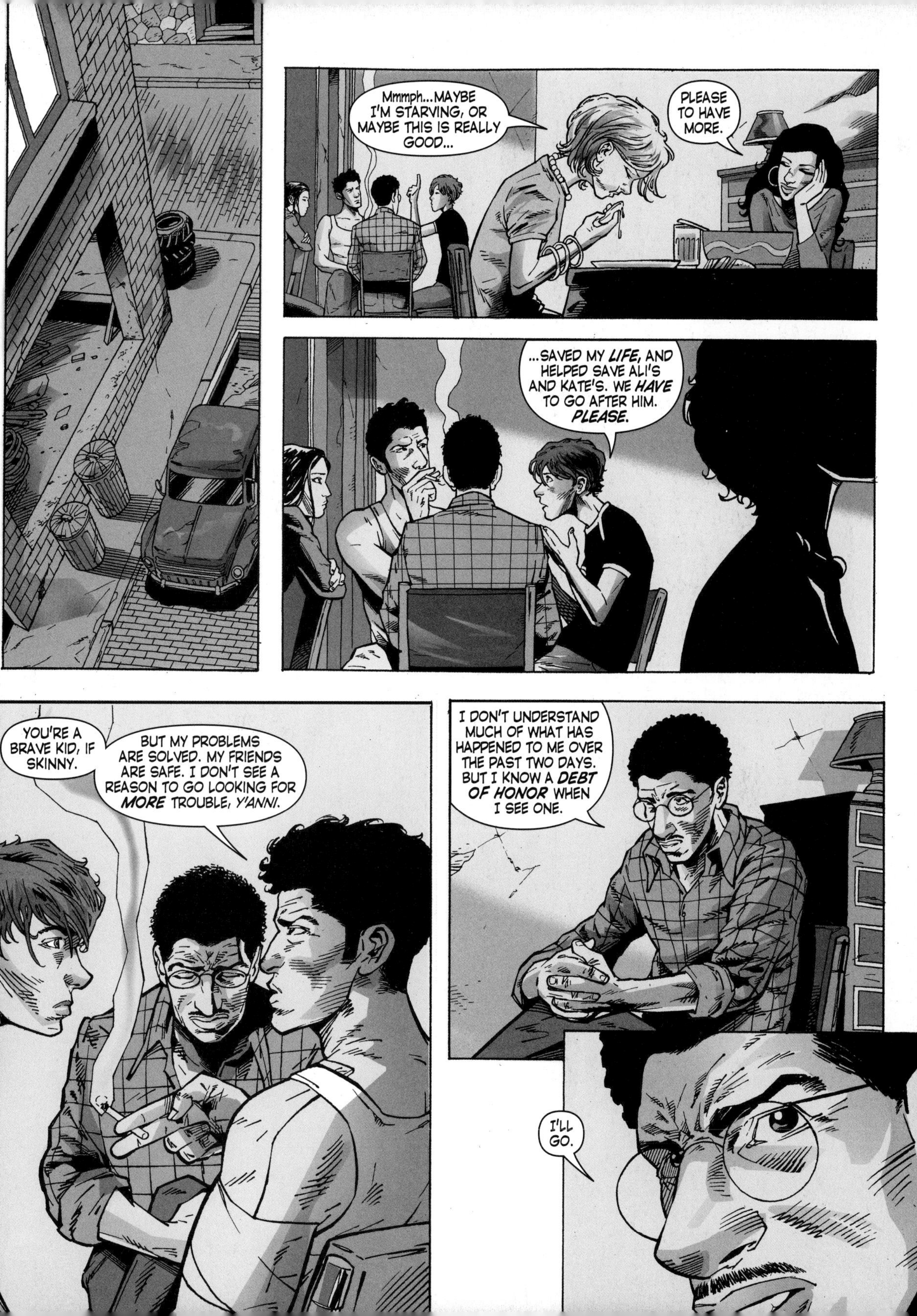
Mmmph...MAYBE I'M STARVING, OR MAYBE THIS IS REALLY GOOD...
PLEASE TO HAVE MORE.
...SAVED MY LIFE, AND HELPED SAVE ALI'S AND KATE'S. WE HAVE TO GO AFTER HIM. PLEASE.
YOU'RE A BRAVE KID, IF SKINNY.
BUT MY PROBLEMS ARE SOLVED. MY FRIENDS ARE SAFE. I DON'T SEE A REASON TO GO LOOKING FOR MORE TROUBLE, Y'ANNI.
I DON'T UNDERSTAND MUCH OF WHAT HAS HAPPENED TO ME OVER THE PAST TWO DAYS. BUT I KNOW A DEBT OF HONOR WHEN I SEE ONE.
I'LL GO.

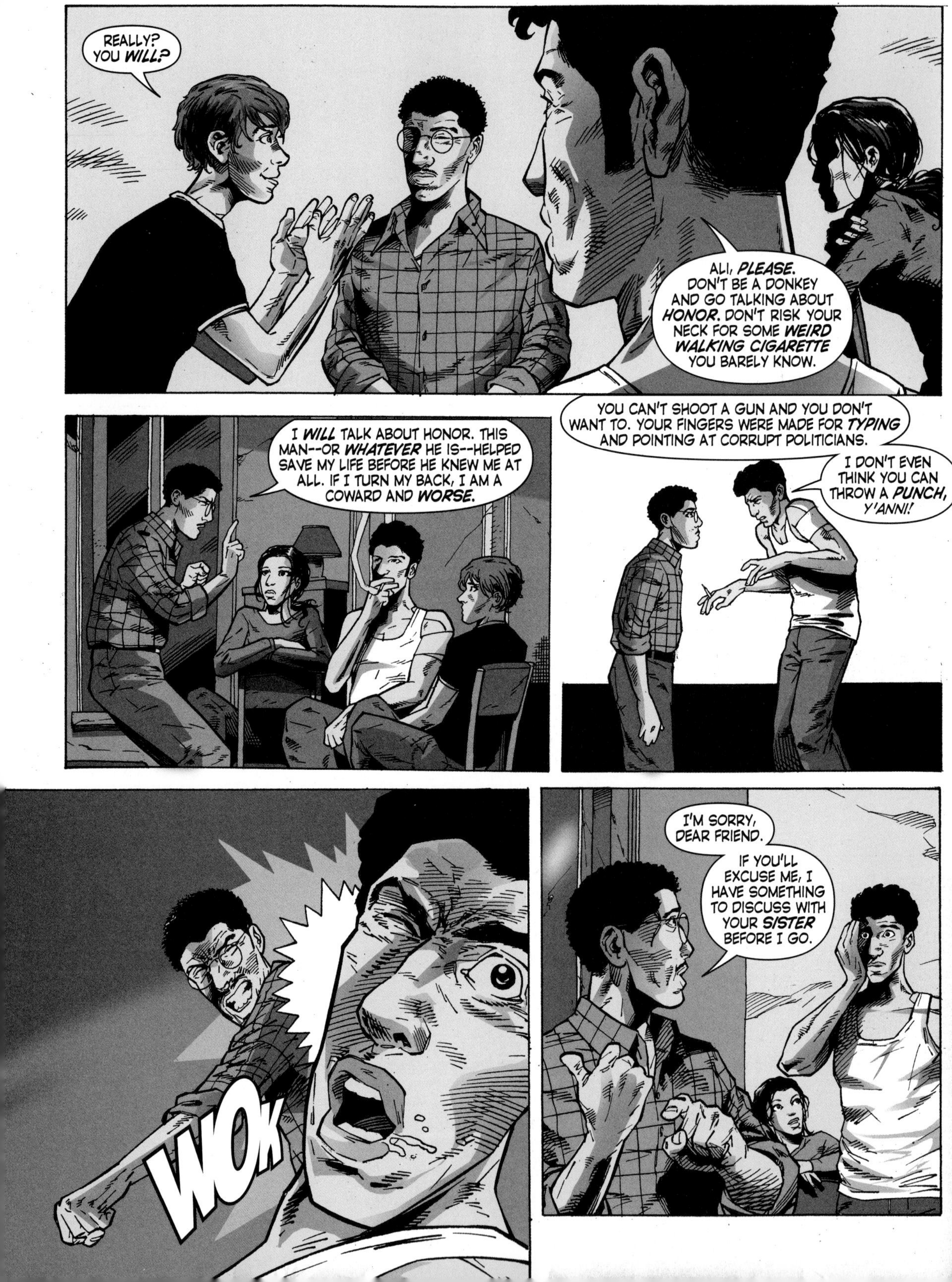
REALLY? YOU WILL?
ALI, PLEASE. DON'T BE A DONKEY AND GO TALKING ABOUT HONOR. DON'T RISK YOUR NECK FOR SOME WEIRD WALKING CIGARETTE YOU BARELY KNOW.
I WILL TALK ABOUT HONOR. THIS MAN--OR WHATEVER HE IS--HELPED SAVE MY LIFE BEFORE HE KNEW ME AT ALL. IF I TURN MY BACK, I AM A COWARD AND WORSE.
YOU CAN'T SHOOT A GUN AND YOU DON'T WANT TO. YOUR FINGERS WERE MADE FOR TYPING AND POINTING AT CORRUPT POLITICIANS.
I DON'T EVEN THINK YOU CAN THROW A PUNCH, Y'ANNI!
WOK
I'M SORRY, DEAR FRIEND.
IF YOU'LL EXCUSE ME, I HAVE SOMETHING TO DISCUSS WITH YOUR SISTER BEFORE I GO.

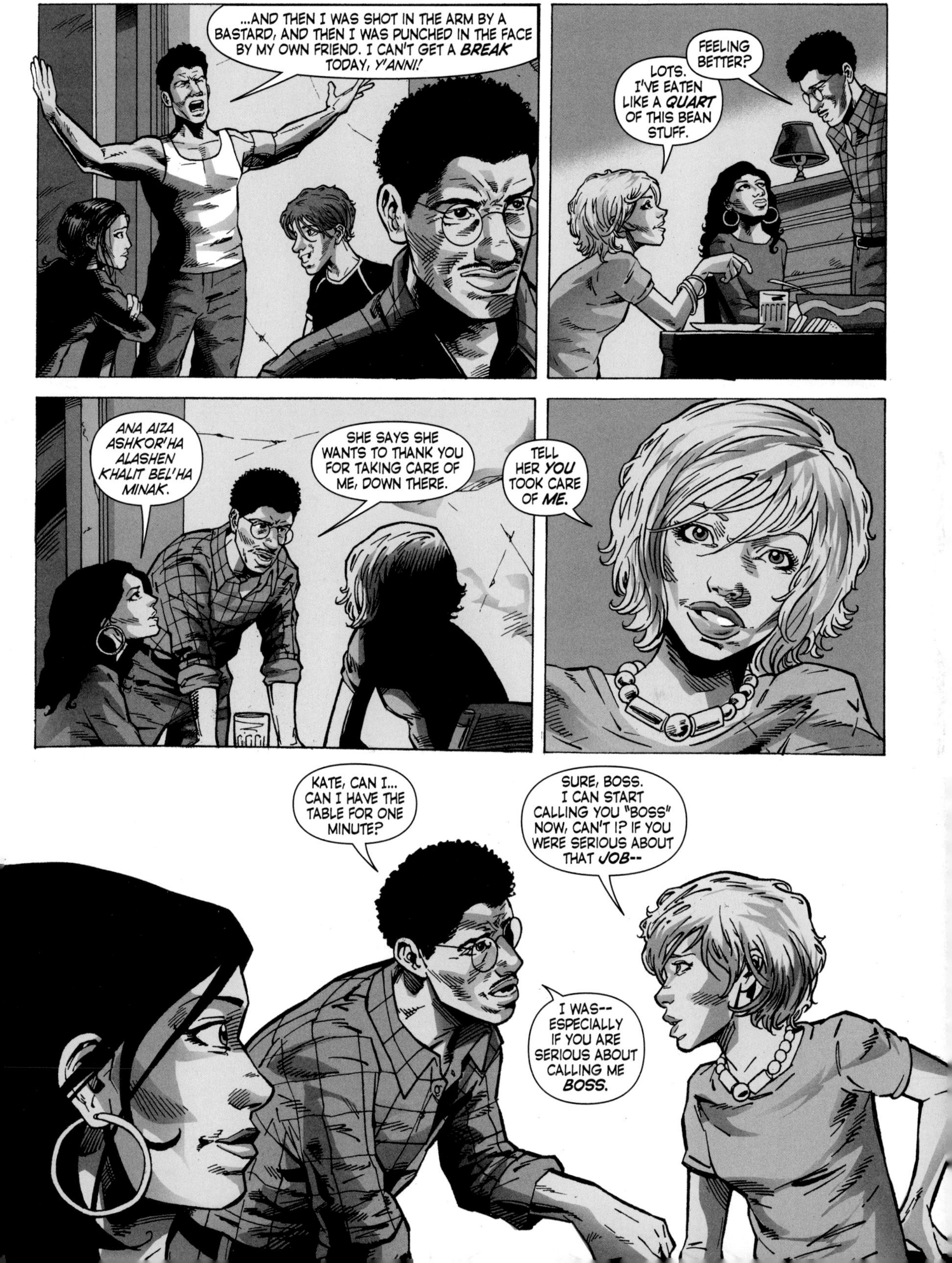
...AND THEN I WAS SHOT IN THE ARM BY A BASTARD, AND THEN I WAS PUNCHED IN THE FACE BY MY OWN FRIEND. I CAN'T GET A **BREAK** TODAY, Y'ANNI!
FEELING BETTER?
LOTS. I'VE EATEN LIKE A **QUART** OF THIS BEAN STUFF.
ANA AIZA ASHKOR'HA ALASHEN KHALIT BEL'HA MINAK.
SHE SAYS SHE WANTS TO THANK YOU FOR TAKING CARE OF ME, DOWN THERE.
TELL HER **YOU** TOOK CARE OF **ME**.
KATE, CAN I... CAN I HAVE THE TABLE FOR ONE MINUTE?
SURE, BOSS. I CAN START CALLING YOU "BOSS" NOW, CAN'T I? IF YOU WERE SERIOUS ABOUT THAT **JOB**--
I WAS-- ESPECIALLY IF YOU ARE SERIOUS ABOUT CALLING ME **BOSS**.

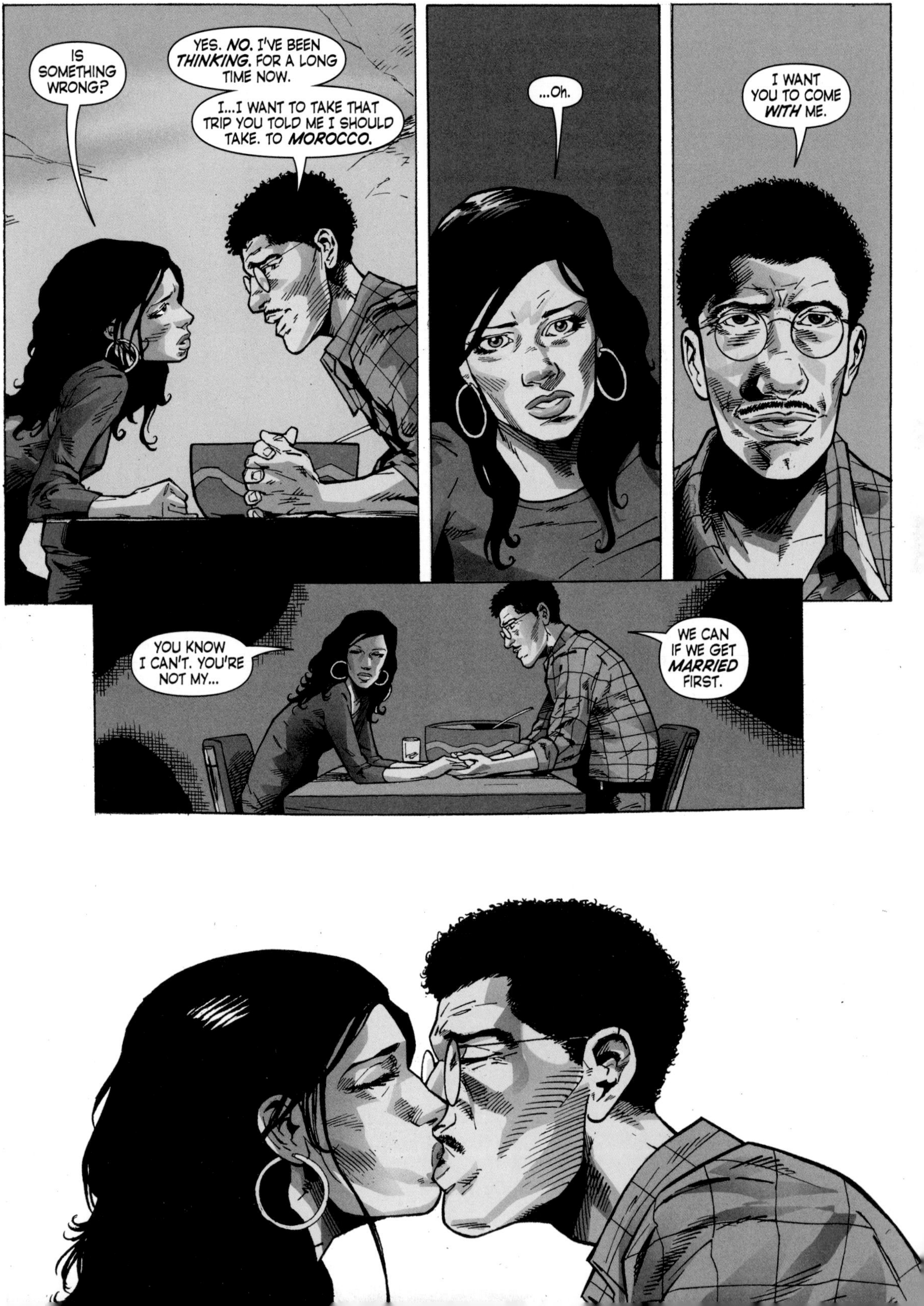
IS SOMETHING WRONG?
YES. NO. I'VE BEEN THINKING. FOR A LONG TIME NOW.
I...I WANT TO TAKE THAT TRIP YOU TOLD ME I SHOULD TAKE. TO MOROCCO.
...Oh.
I WANT YOU TO COME WITH ME.
YOU KNOW I CAN'T. YOU'RE NOT MY...
WE CAN IF WE GET MARRIED FIRST.

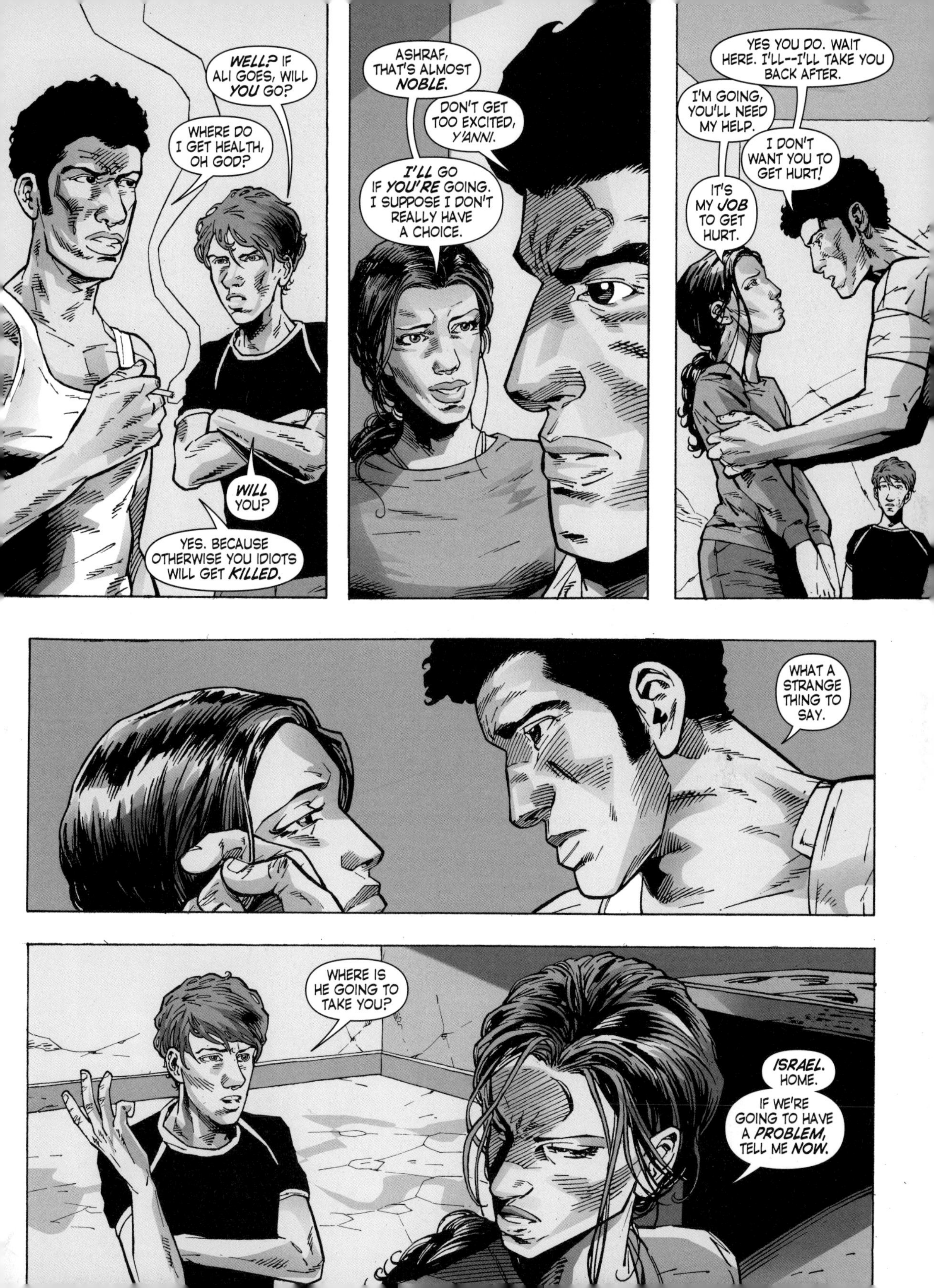
WELL? IF ALI GOES, WILL YOU GO?
WHERE DO I GET HEALTH, OH GOD?
WILL YOU?
YES. BECAUSE OTHERWISE YOU IDIOTS WILL GET KILLED.
ASHRAF, THAT'S ALMOST NOBLE.
DON'T GET TOO EXCITED, Y'ANNI.
I'LL GO IF YOU'RE GOING. I SUPPOSE I DON'T REALLY HAVE A CHOICE.
YES YOU DO. WAIT HERE. I'LL--I'LL TAKE YOU BACK AFTER.
I'M GOING, YOU'LL NEED MY HELP.
I DON'T WANT YOU TO GET HURT!
IT'S MY JOB TO GET HURT.
WHAT A STRANGE THING TO SAY.
WHERE IS HE GOING TO TAKE YOU?
ISRAEL. HOME.
IF WE'RE GOING TO HAVE A PROBLEM, TELL ME NOW.

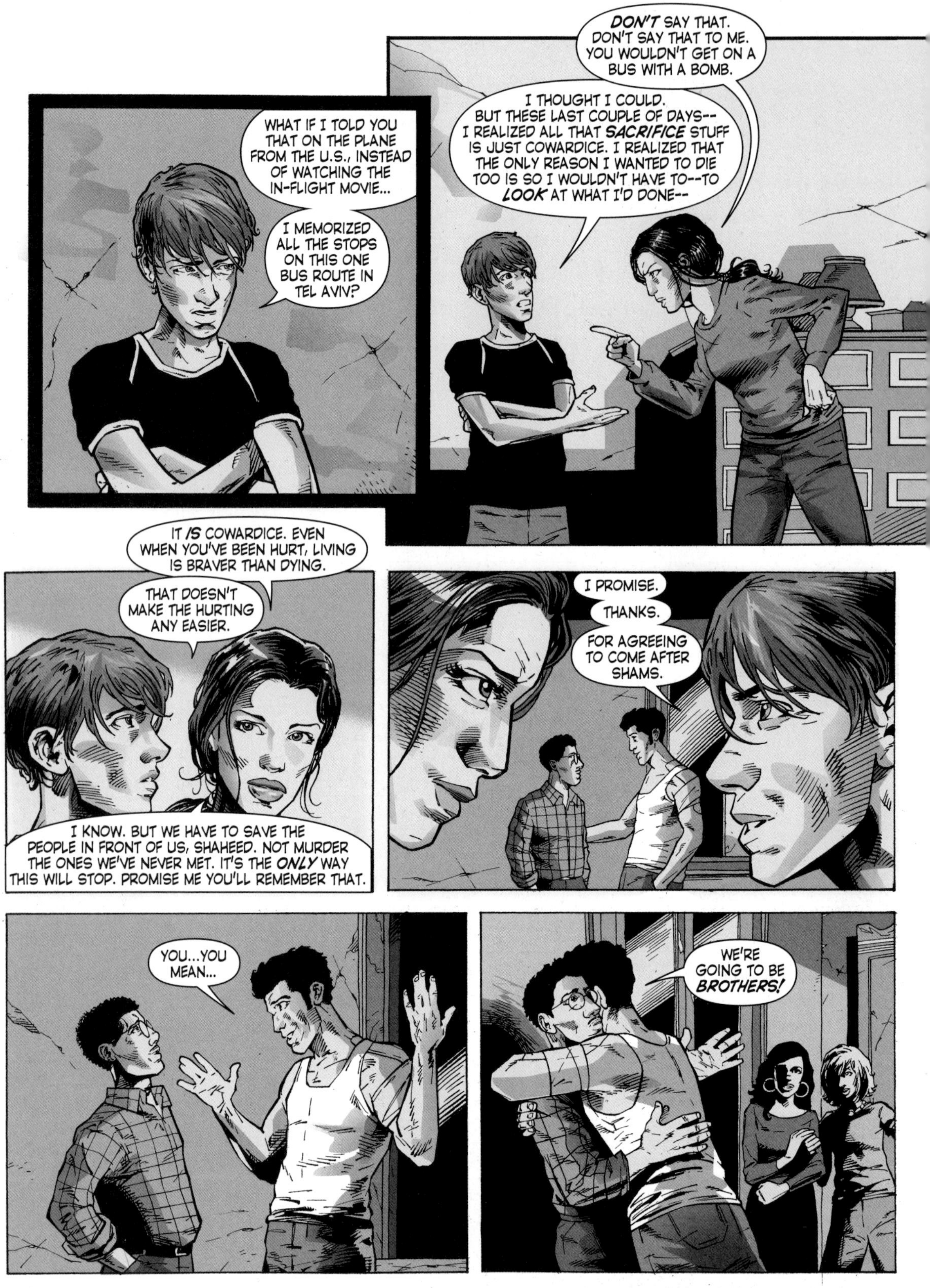
WHAT IF I TOLD YOU THAT ON THE PLANE FROM THE U.S., INSTEAD OF WATCHING THE IN-FLIGHT MOVIE...
I MEMORIZED ALL THE STOPS ON THIS ONE BUS ROUTE IN TEL AVIV?
DON'T SAY THAT. DON'T SAY THAT TO ME. YOU WOULDN'T GET ON A BUS WITH A BOMB.
I THOUGHT I COULD. BUT THESE LAST COUPLE OF DAYS-- I REALIZED ALL THAT SACRIFICE STUFF IS JUST COWARDICE. I REALIZED THAT THE ONLY REASON I WANTED TO DIE TOO IS SO I WOULDN'T HAVE TO--TO LOOK AT WHAT I'D DONE--
IT IS COWARDICE. EVEN WHEN YOU'VE BEEN HURT, LIVING IS BRAVER THAN DYING.
THAT DOESN'T MAKE THE HURTING ANY EASIER.
I KNOW. BUT WE HAVE TO SAVE THE PEOPLE IN FRONT OF US, SHAHEED. NOT MURDER THE ONES WE'VE NEVER MET. IT'S THE ONLY WAY THIS WILL STOP. PROMISE ME YOU'LL REMEMBER THAT.
I PROMISE.
THANKS.
FOR AGREEING TO COME AFTER SHAMS.
YOU...YOU MEAN...
WE'RE GOING TO BE BROTHERS!

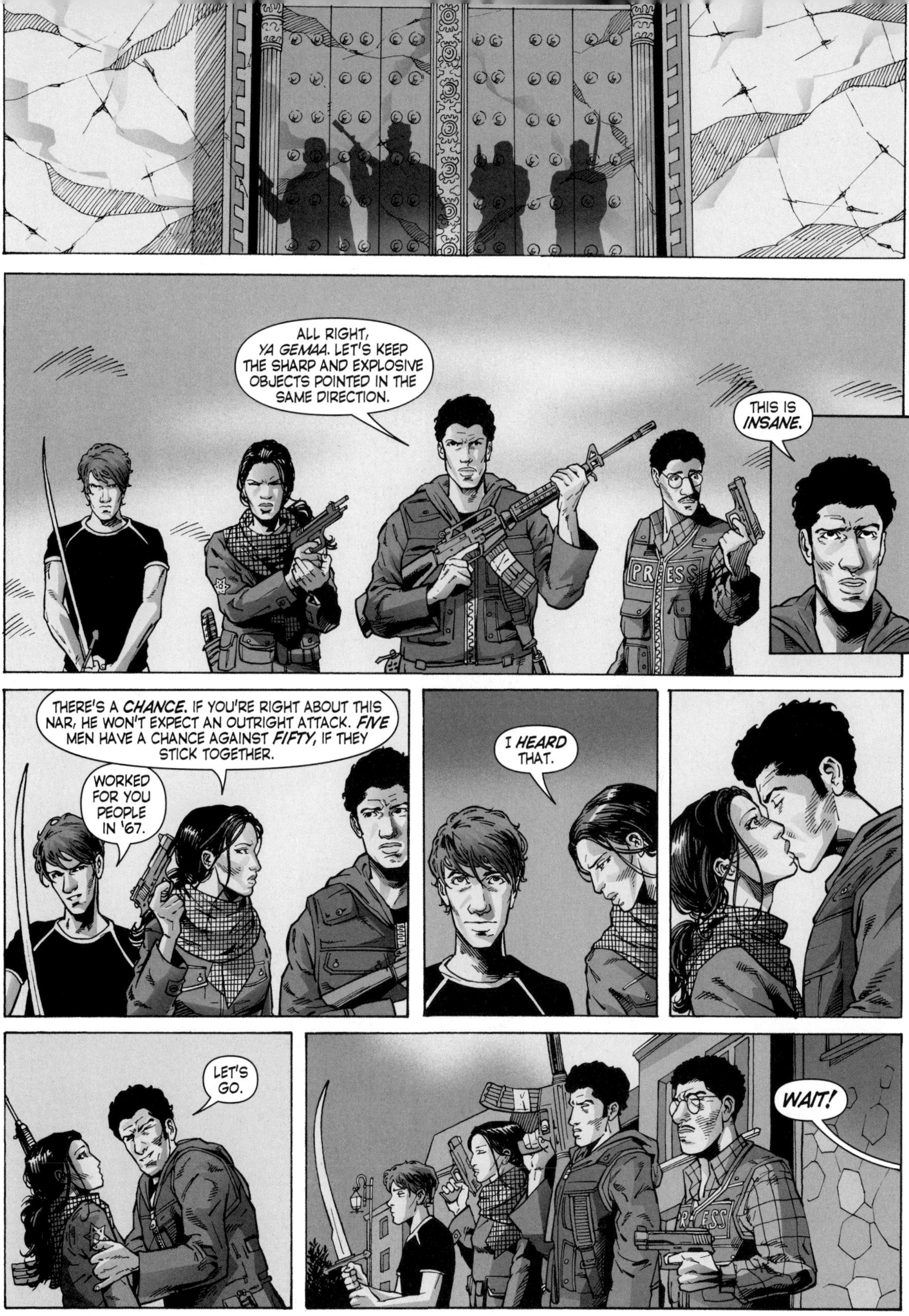
ALL RIGHT, YA GEMAA. LET'S KEEP THE SHARP AND EXPLOSIVE OBJECTS POINTED IN THE SAME DIRECTION.
THIS IS INSANE.
THERE'S A CHANCE. IF YOU'RE RIGHT ABOUT THIS NAR, HE WON'T EXPECT AN OUTRIGHT ATTACK. FIVE MEN HAVE A CHANCE AGAINST FIFTY, IF THEY STICK TOGETHER.
WORKED FOR YOU PEOPLE IN '67.
I HEARD THAT.
LET'S GO.
WAIT!
PRESS

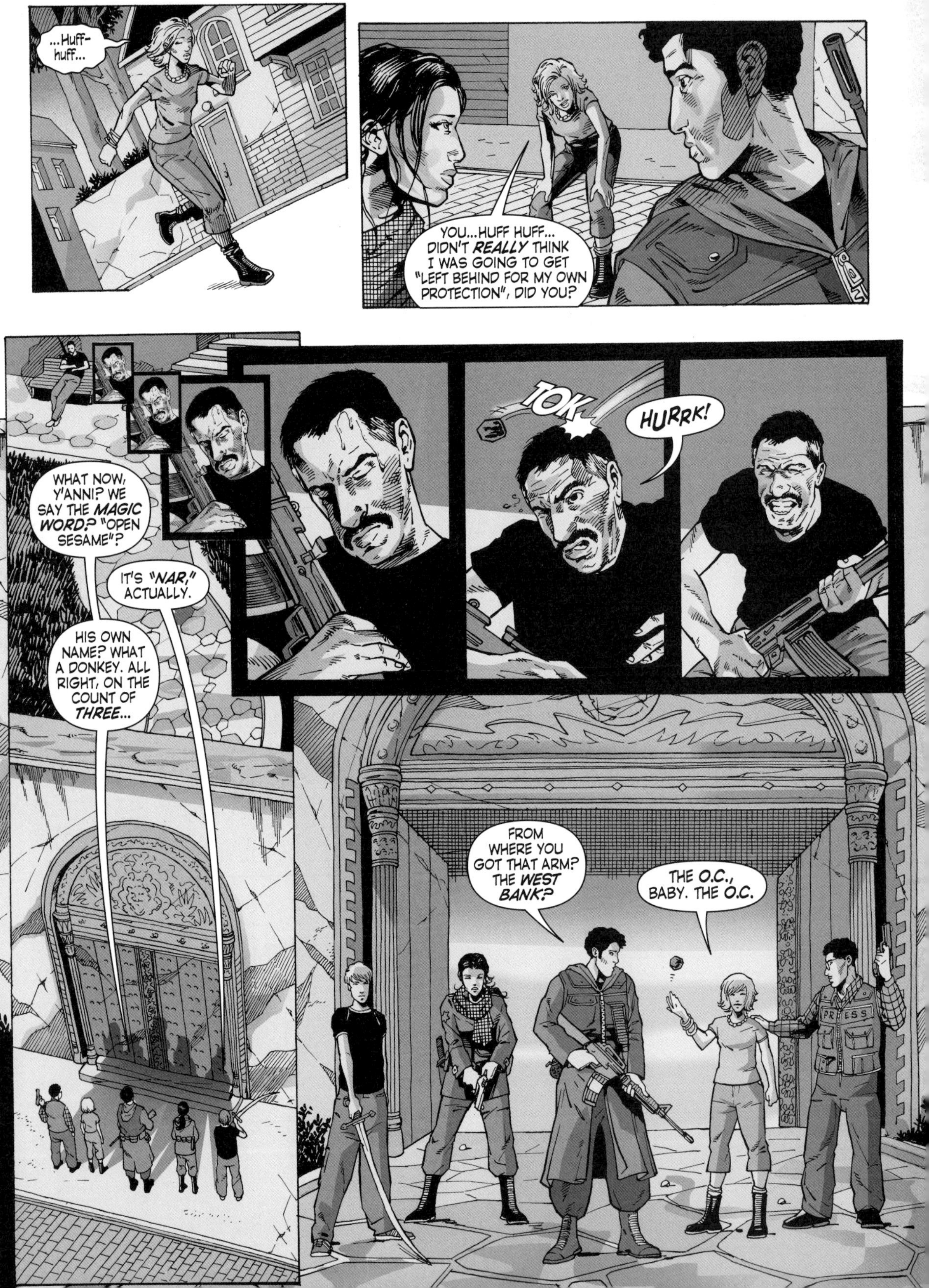
...Huff-huff...
YOU...HUFF HUFF... DIDN'T REALLY THINK I WAS GOING TO GET "LEFT BEHIND FOR MY OWN PROTECTION", DID YOU?
WHAT NOW, Y'ANNI? WE SAY THE MAGIC WORD? "OPEN SESAME"?
IT'S "NAR," ACTUALLY.
HIS OWN NAME? WHAT A DONKEY. ALL RIGHT, ON THE COUNT OF THREE...
TOK
HURRK!
FROM WHERE YOU GOT THAT ARM? THE WEST BANK?
THE O.C., BABY. THE O.C.
PRESS

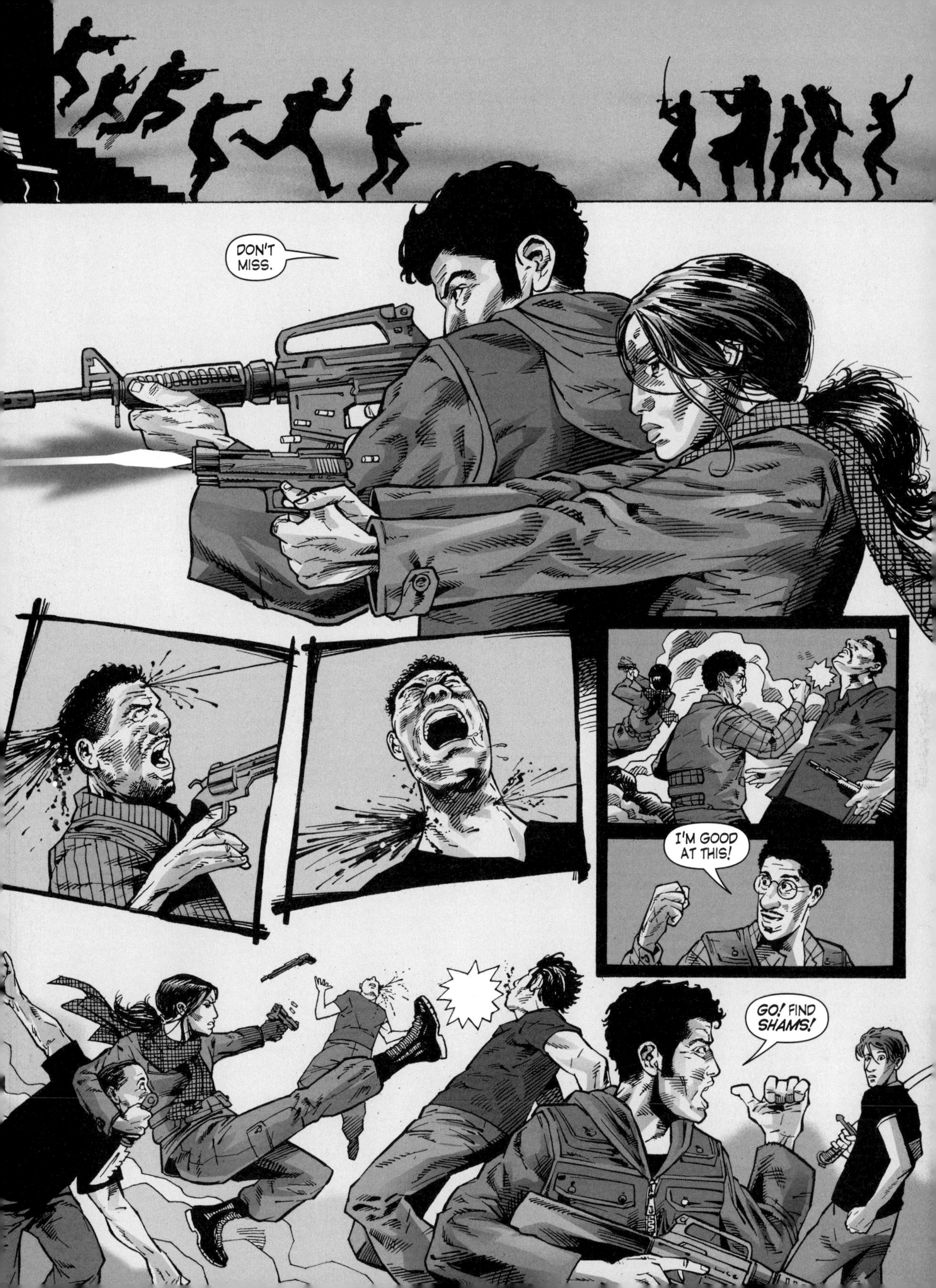
DON'T MISS.
I'M GOOD AT THIS!
GO! FIND SHAMS!

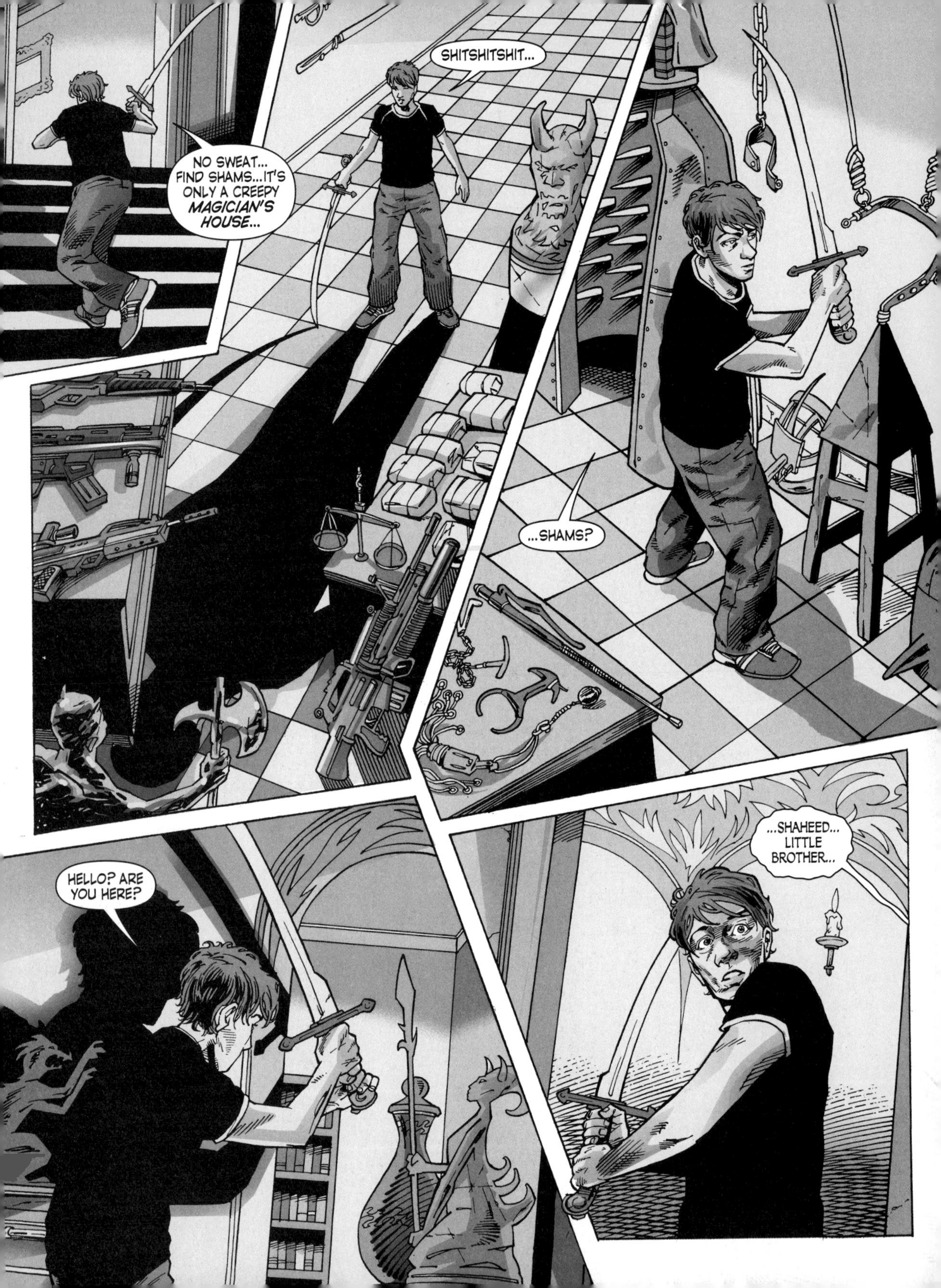
NO SWEAT... FIND SHAMS...IT'S ONLY A CREEPY *MAGICIAN'S HOUSE*...
SHITSHITSHIT...
...SHAMS?
HELLO? ARE YOU HERE?
...SHAHEED... LITTLE BROTHER...

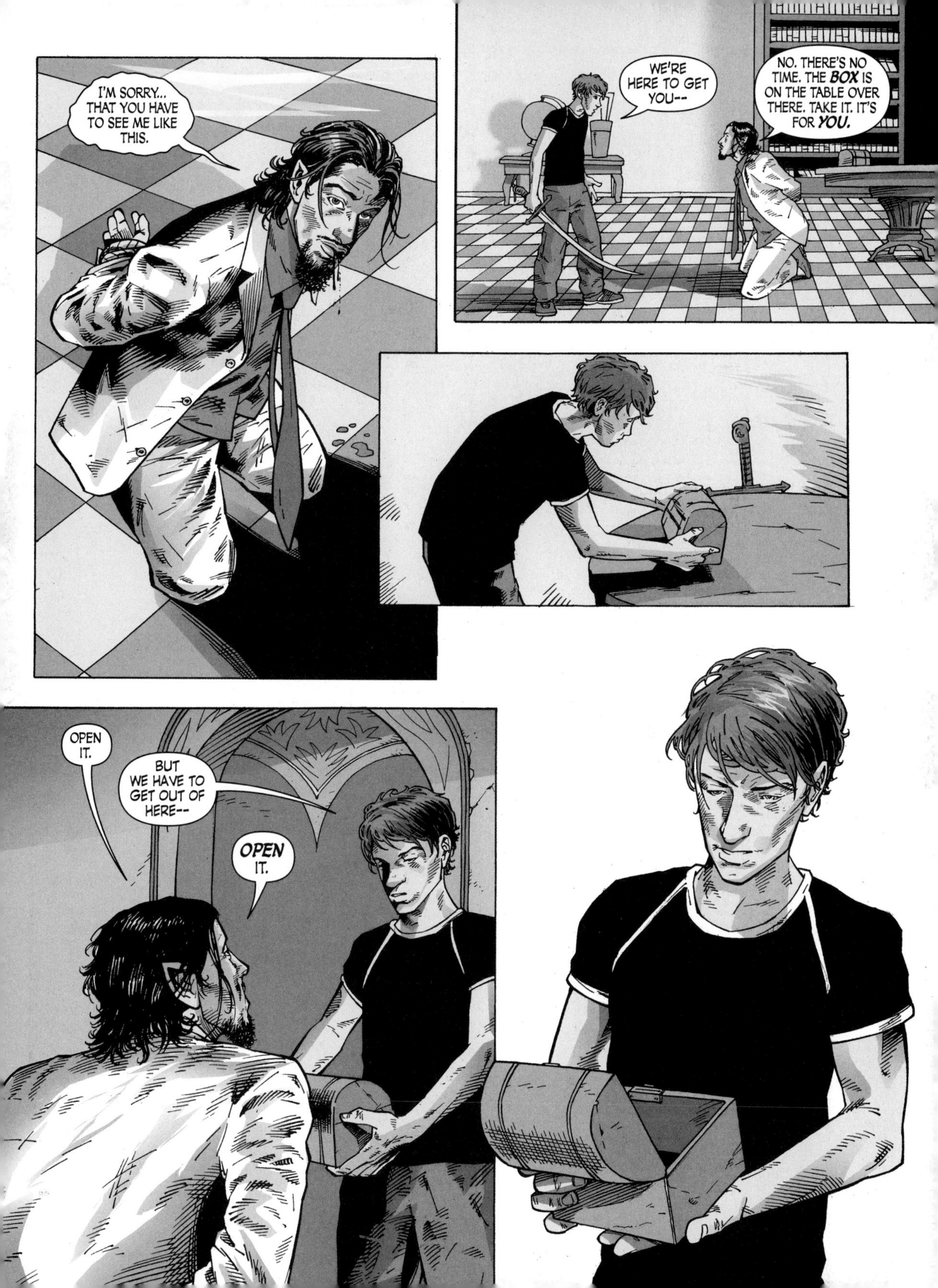
I'M SORRY... THAT YOU HAVE TO SEE ME LIKE THIS.
WE'RE HERE TO GET YOU--
NO. THERE'S NO TIME. THE BOX IS ON THE TABLE OVER THERE. TAKE IT. IT'S FOR YOU.
OPEN IT.
BUT WE HAVE TO GET OUT OF HERE--
OPEN IT.

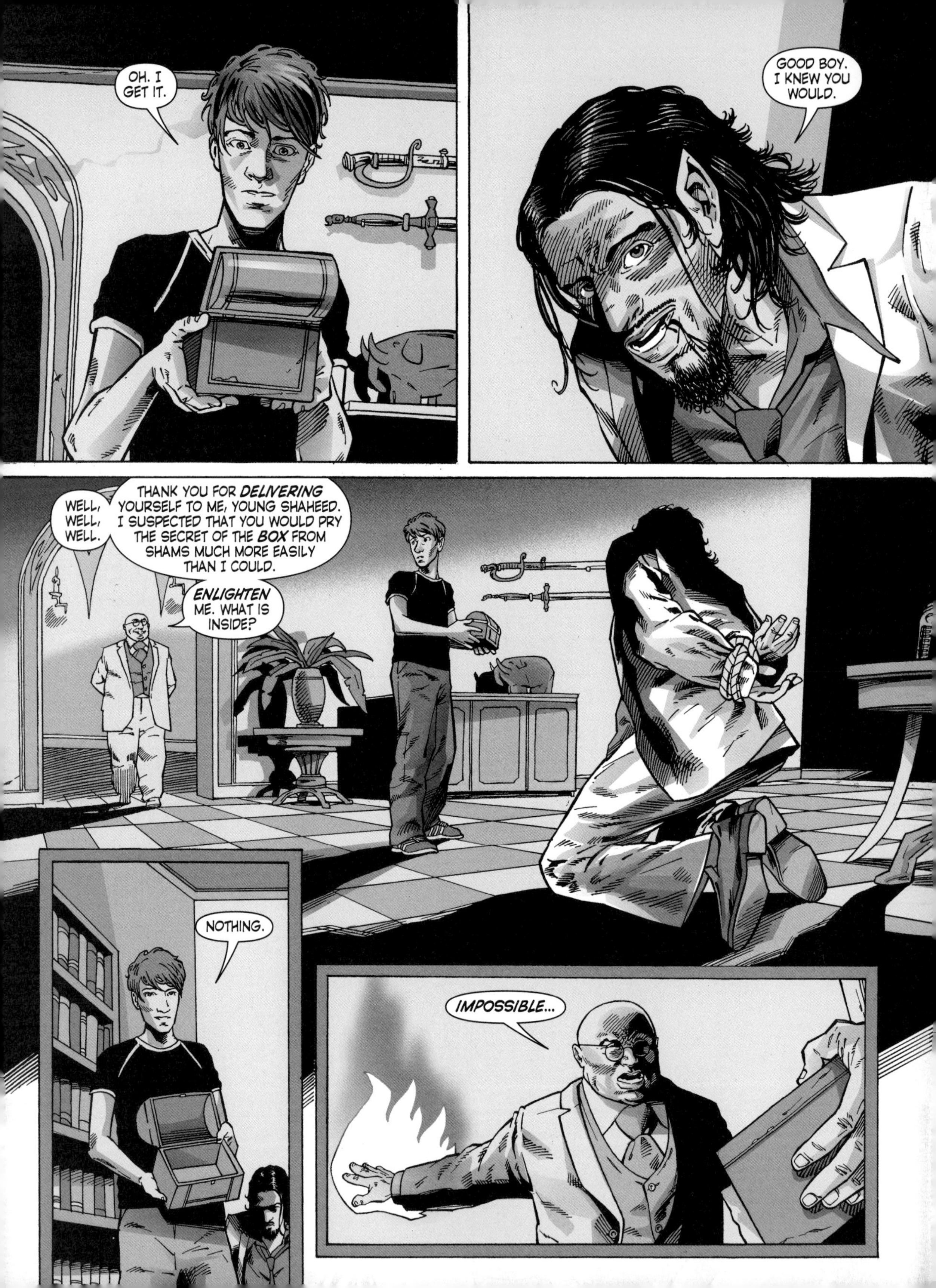
OH. I GET IT.
GOOD BOY. I KNEW YOU WOULD.
WELL, WELL, WELL.
THANK YOU FOR DELIVERING YOURSELF TO ME, YOUNG SHAHEED. I SUSPECTED THAT YOU WOULD PRY THE SECRET OF THE BOX FROM SHAMS MUCH MORE EASILY THAN I COULD.
ENLIGHTEN ME. WHAT IS INSIDE?
NOTHING.
IMPOSSIBLE...

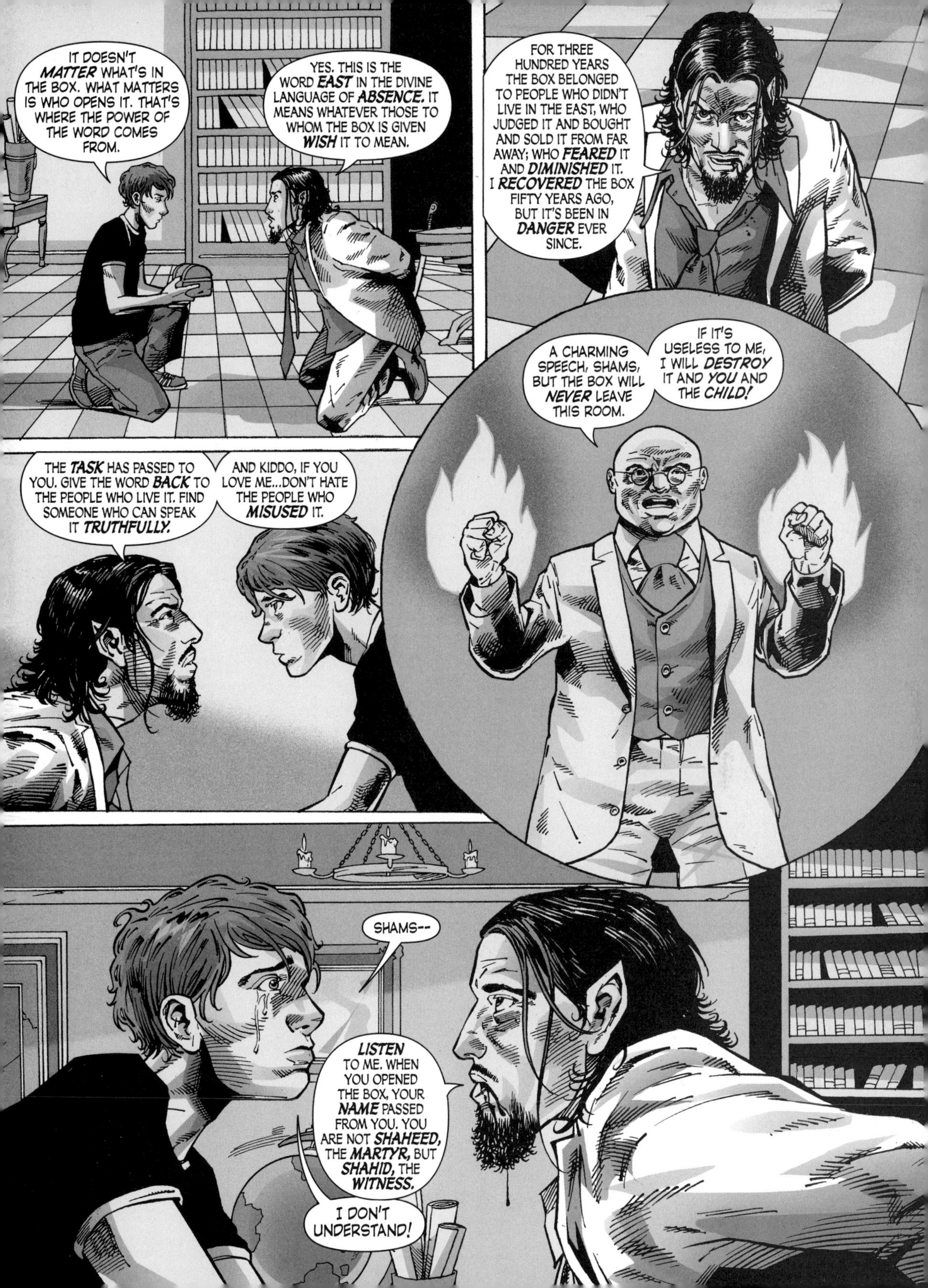
IT DOESN'T MATTER WHAT'S IN THE BOX. WHAT MATTERS IS WHO OPENS IT. THAT'S WHERE THE POWER OF THE WORD COMES FROM.
YES. THIS IS THE WORD EAST IN THE DIVINE LANGUAGE OF ABSENCE. IT MEANS WHATEVER THOSE TO WHOM THE BOX IS GIVEN WISH IT TO MEAN.
FOR THREE HUNDRED YEARS THE BOX BELONGED TO PEOPLE WHO DIDN'T LIVE IN THE EAST, WHO JUDGED IT AND BOUGHT AND SOLD IT FROM FAR AWAY; WHO FEARED IT AND DIMINISHED IT. I RECOVERED THE BOX FIFTY YEARS AGO, BUT IT'S BEEN IN DANGER EVER SINCE.
THE TASK HAS PASSED TO YOU. GIVE THE WORD BACK TO THE PEOPLE WHO LIVE IT. FIND SOMEONE WHO CAN SPEAK IT TRUTHFULLY.
AND KIDDO, IF YOU LOVE ME...DON'T HATE THE PEOPLE WHO MISUSED IT.
A CHARMING SPEECH, SHAMS, BUT THE BOX WILL NEVER LEAVE THIS ROOM.
IF IT'S USELESS TO ME, I WILL DESTROY IT AND YOU AND THE CHILD!
SHAMS--
LISTEN TO ME. WHEN YOU OPENED THE BOX, YOUR NAME PASSED FROM YOU. YOU ARE NOT SHAHEED, THE MARTYR, BUT SHAHID, THE WITNESS.
I DON'T UNDERSTAND!

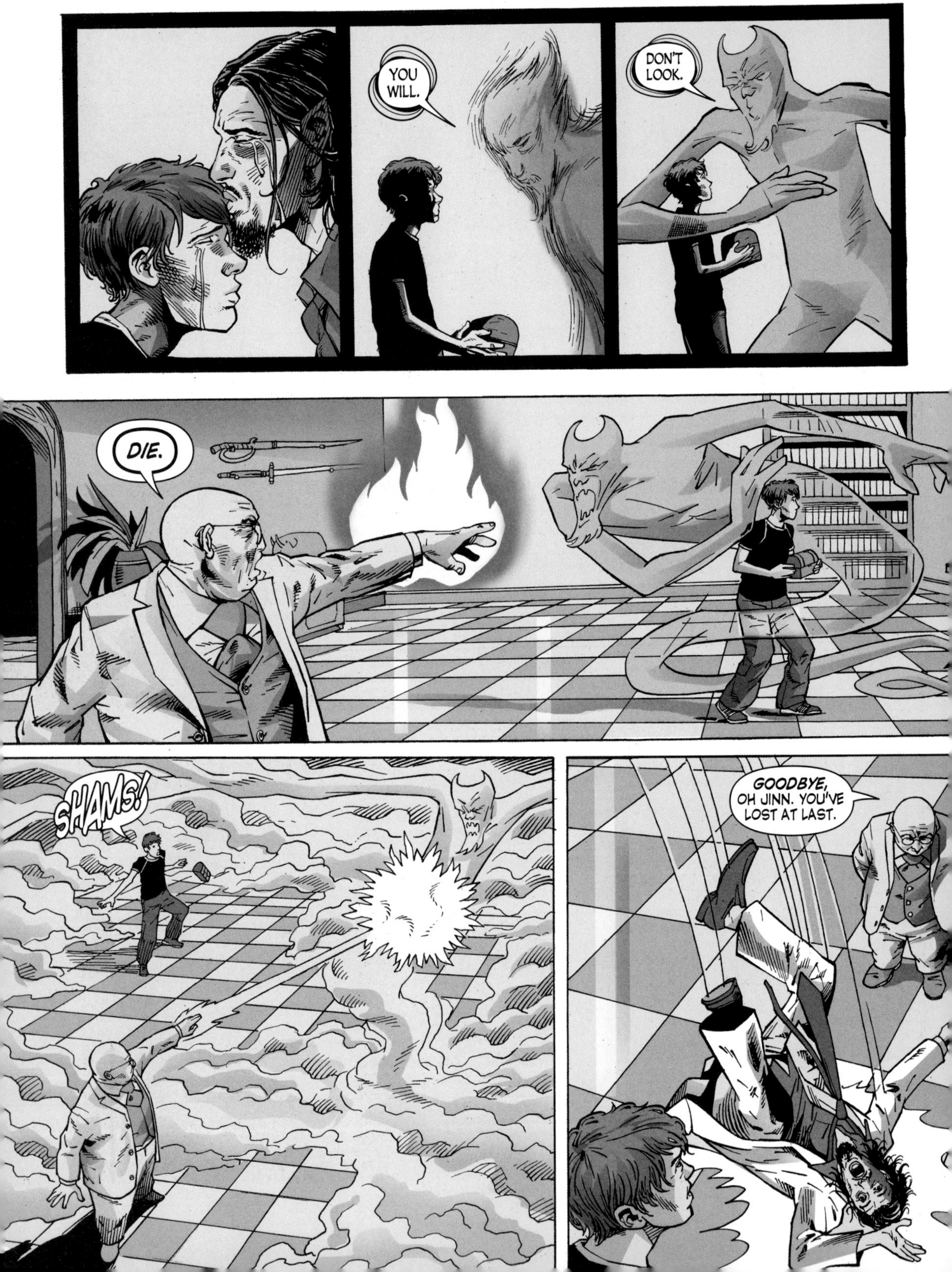
YOU WILL.
DON'T LOOK.
DIE.
SHAMS!
GOODBYE, OH JINN. YOU'VE LOST AT LAST.

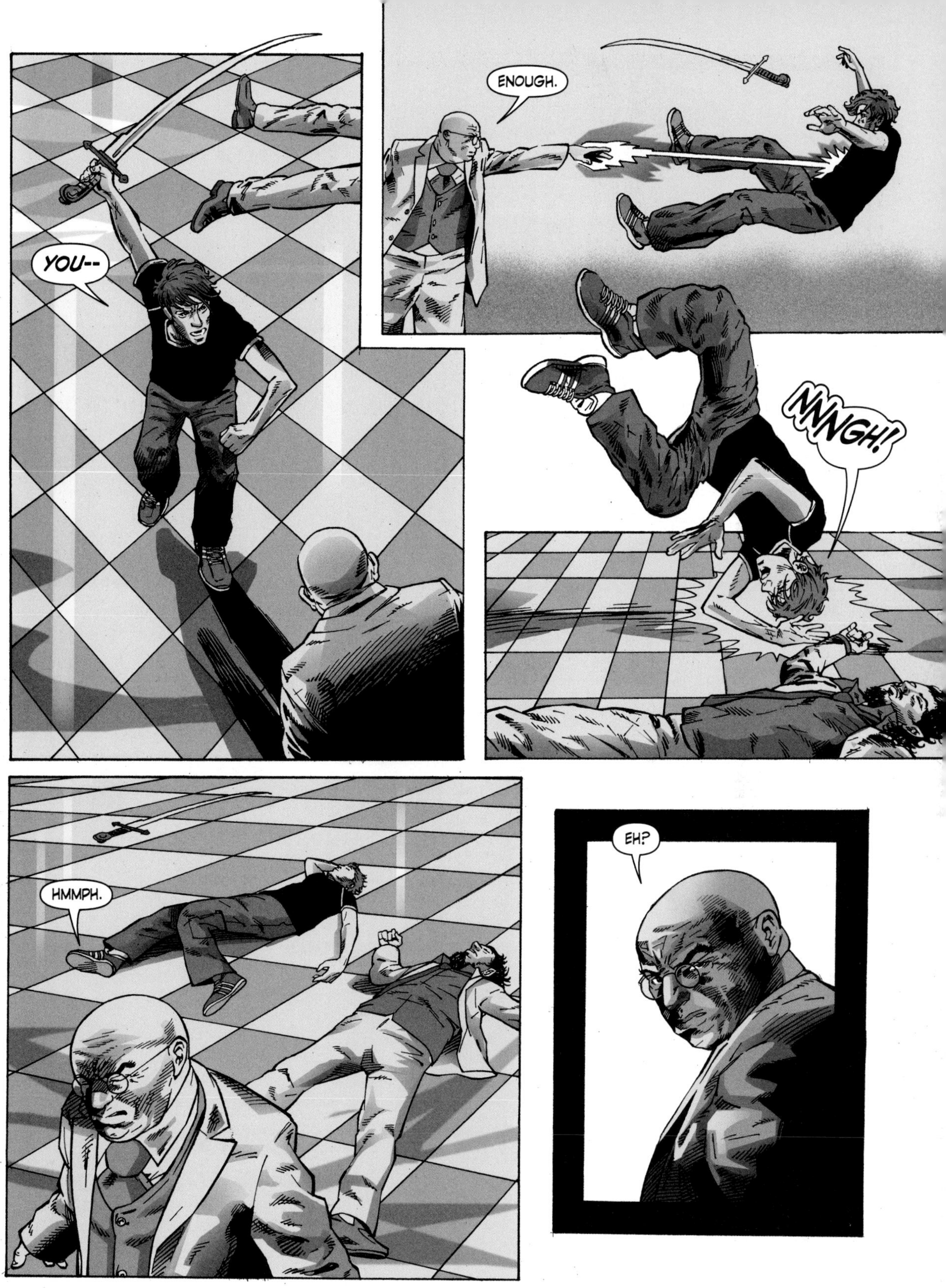
YOU--
ENOUGH.
NNNGH!
HMMPH.
EH?

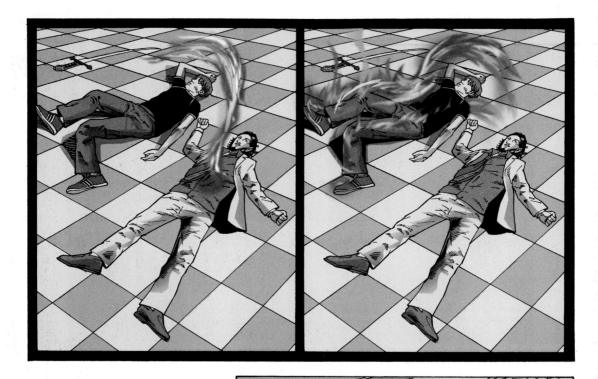

I...I DON'T BELIEVE IT.

A JUNAYN... A HALF-JINN... HE GAVE HIS *FIRE-SELF* TO THE BOY!

UNN...

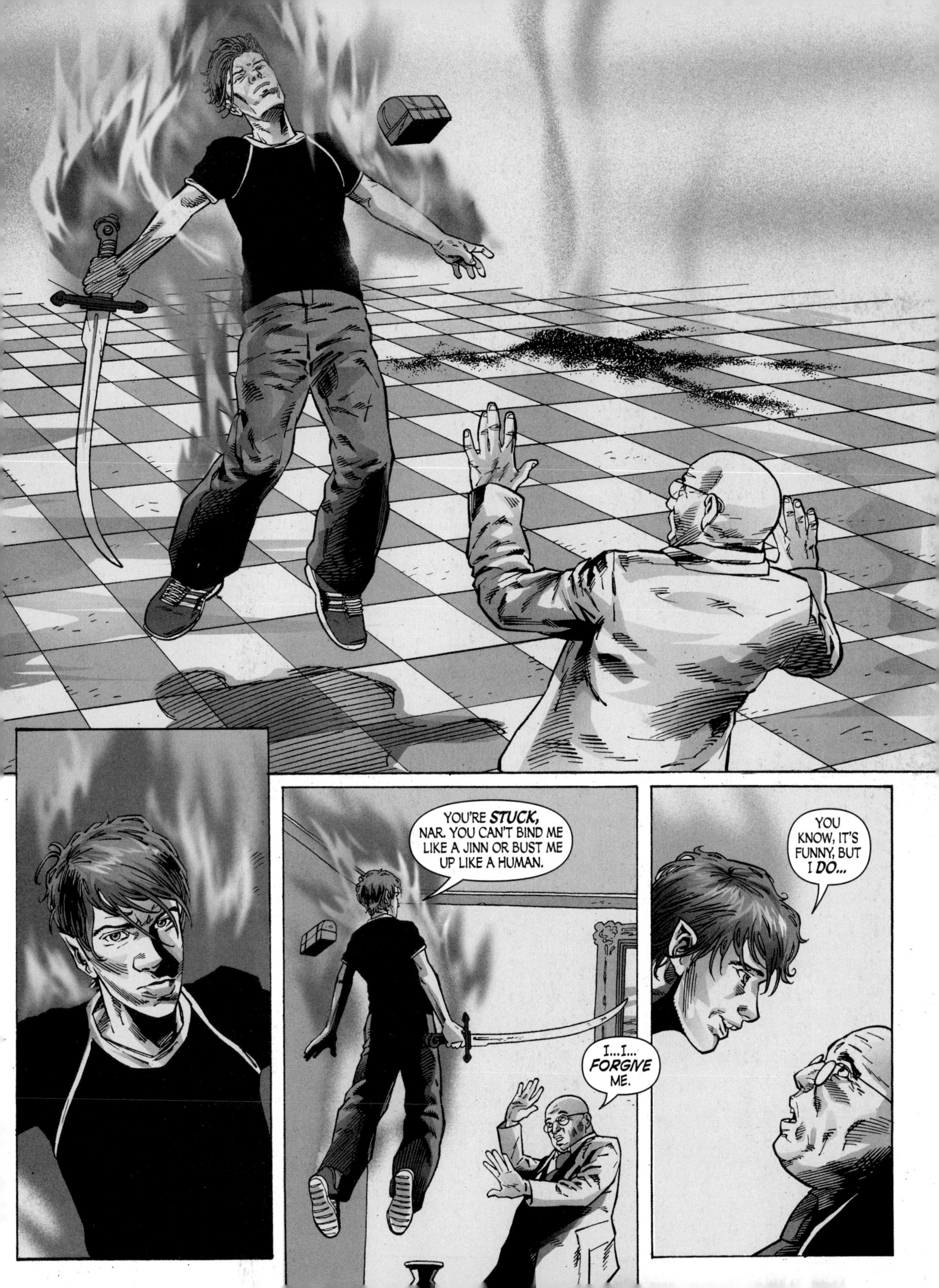
YOU'RE **STUCK,** NAR. YOU CAN'T BIND ME LIKE A JINN OR BUST ME UP LIKE A HUMAN.
I...I... **FORGIVE** ME.
YOU KNOW, IT'S FUNNY, BUT I **DO...**

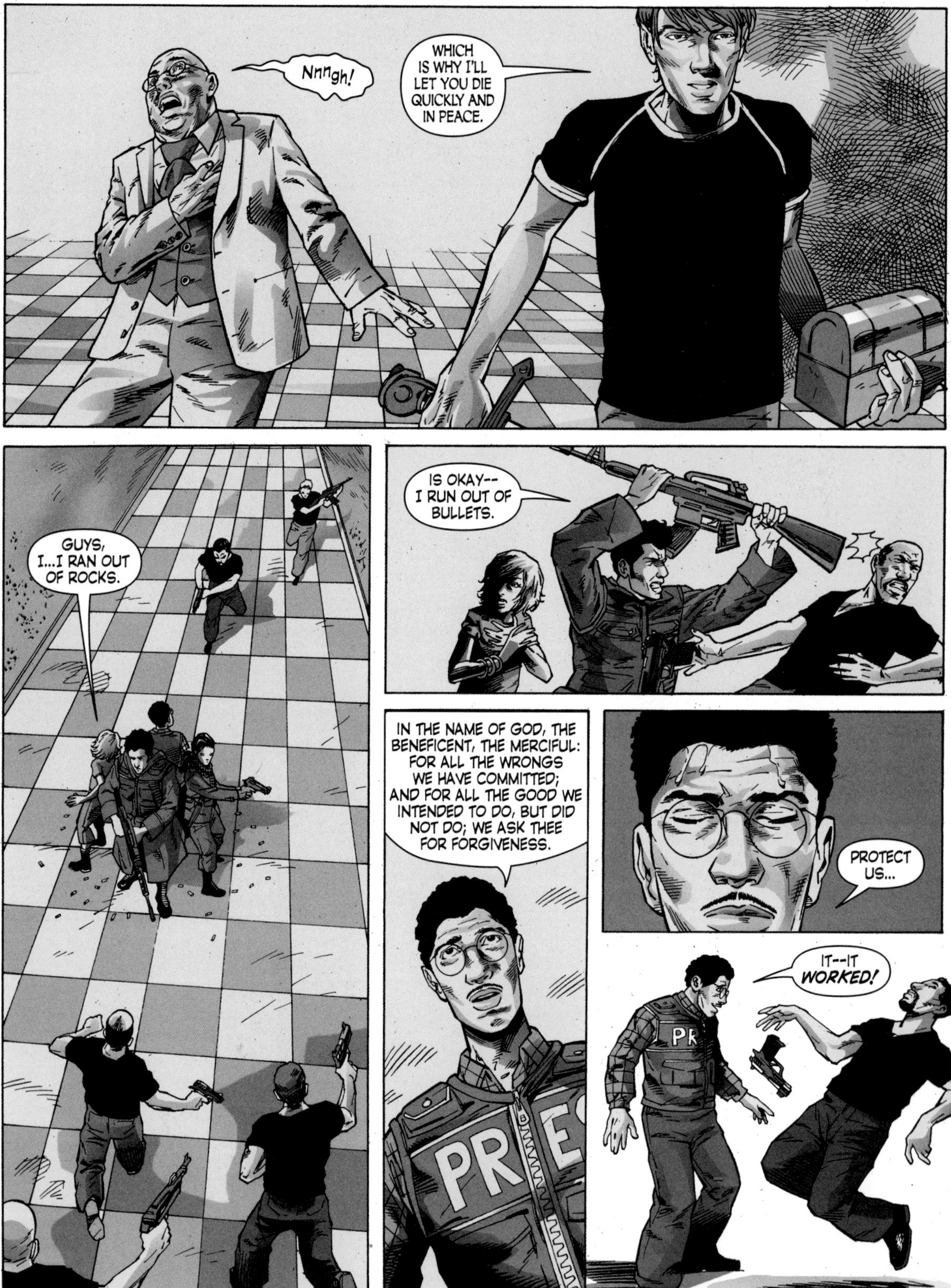
Nnngh!
WHICH IS WHY I'LL LET YOU DIE QUICKLY AND IN PEACE.
GUYS, I...I RAN OUT OF ROCKS.
IS OKAY-- I RUN OUT OF BULLETS.
IN THE NAME OF GOD, THE BENEFICENT, THE MERCIFUL: FOR ALL THE WRONGS WE HAVE COMMITTED; AND FOR ALL THE GOOD WE INTENDED TO DO, BUT DID NOT DO; WE ASK THEE FOR FORGIVENESS.
PROTECT US...
IT--IT WORKED!
PRES
PR

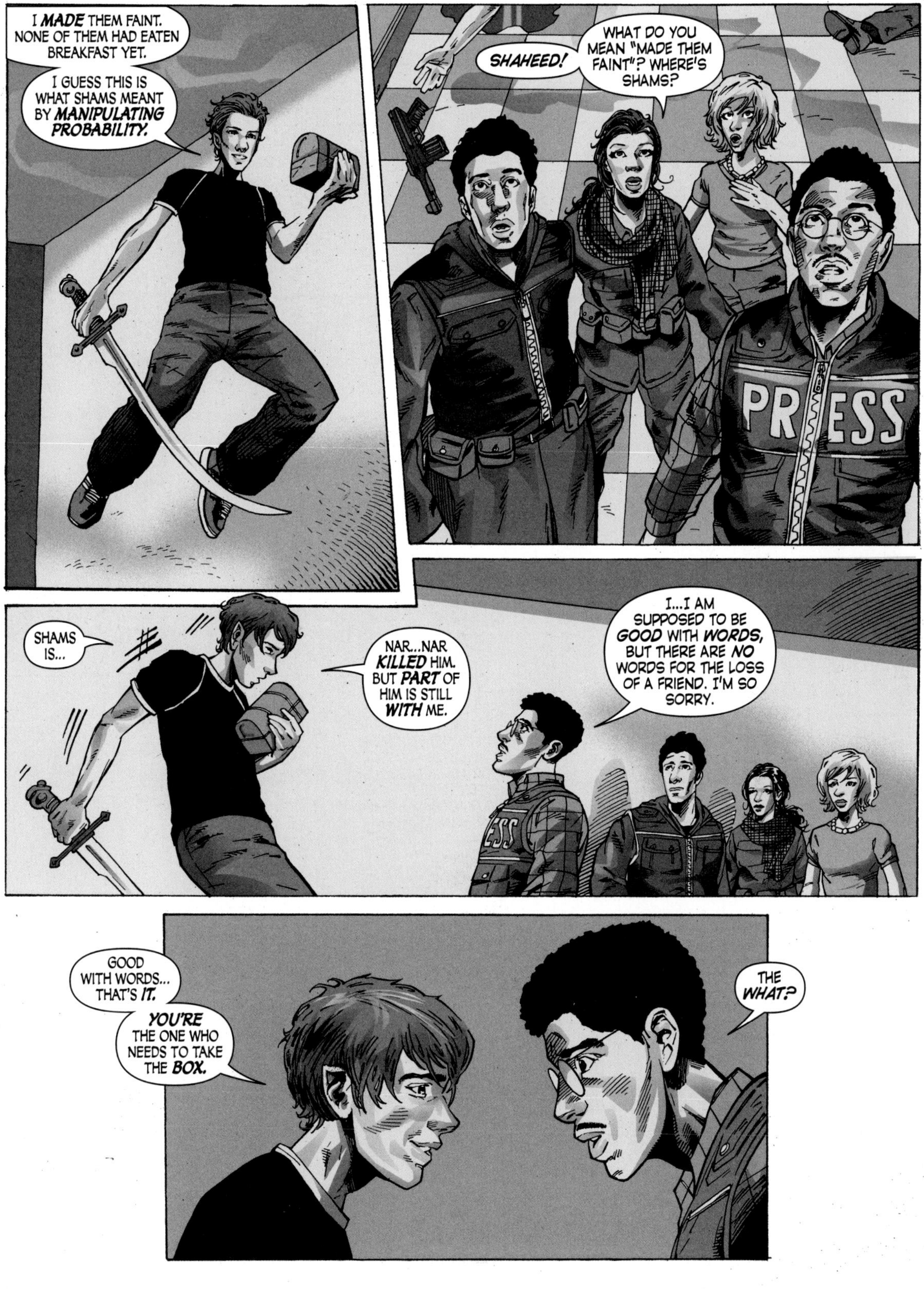
I MADE THEM FAINT. NONE OF THEM HAD EATEN BREAKFAST YET.
I GUESS THIS IS WHAT SHAMS MEANT BY MANIPULATING PROBABILITY.
SHAHEED!
WHAT DO YOU MEAN "MADE THEM FAINT"? WHERE'S SHAMS?
PRESS
SHAMS IS...
NAR...NAR KILLED HIM. BUT PART OF HIM IS STILL WITH ME.
I...I AM SUPPOSED TO BE GOOD WITH WORDS, BUT THERE ARE NO WORDS FOR THE LOSS OF A FRIEND. I'M SO SORRY.
GOOD WITH WORDS... THAT'S IT.
YOU'RE THE ONE WHO NEEDS TO TAKE THE BOX.
THE WHAT?

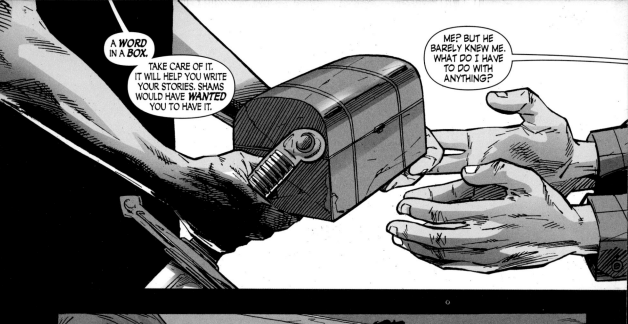

A **WORD** IN A **BOX.**

TAKE CARE OF IT. IT WILL HELP YOU WRITE YOUR STORIES. SHAMS WOULD HAVE **WANTED** YOU TO HAVE IT.

ME? BUT HE BARELY KNEW ME. WHAT DO I HAVE TO DO WITH ANYTHING?

I DON'T KNOW. DESTINY AND CHOICE ARE THE SAME THING.

YOU CHOSE TO BE HERE, SO IT COULDN'T HAVE HAPPENED ANY OTHER WAY.

...OH. I DIDN'T KNOW YOU MEANT **THIS** WORD.

CAIRO WILL **READ** AGAIN.

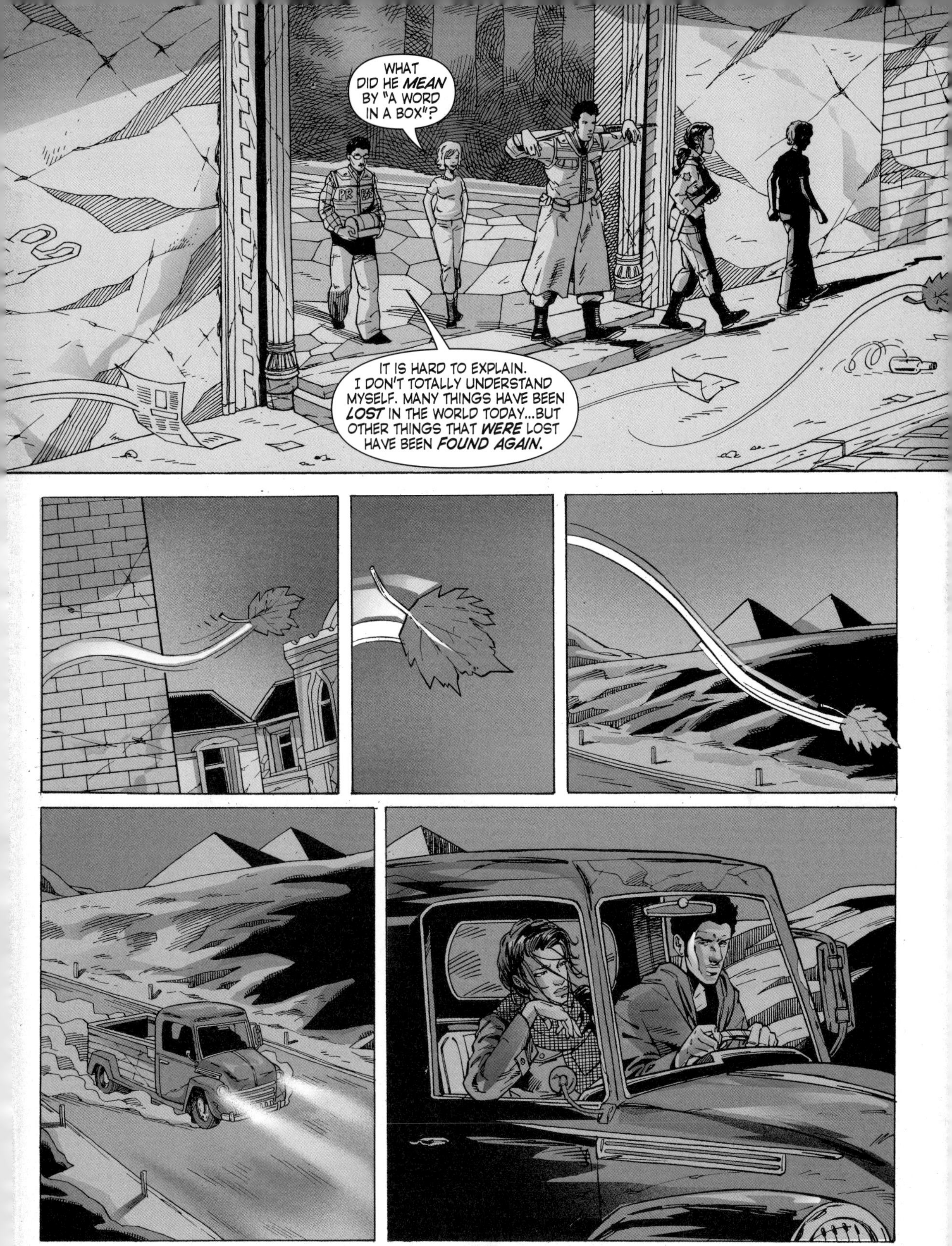
WHAT DID HE MEAN BY "A WORD IN A BOX"?
IT IS HARD TO EXPLAIN. I DON'T TOTALLY UNDERSTAND MYSELF. MANY THINGS HAVE BEEN LOST IN THE WORLD TODAY...BUT OTHER THINGS THAT WERE LOST HAVE BEEN FOUND AGAIN.

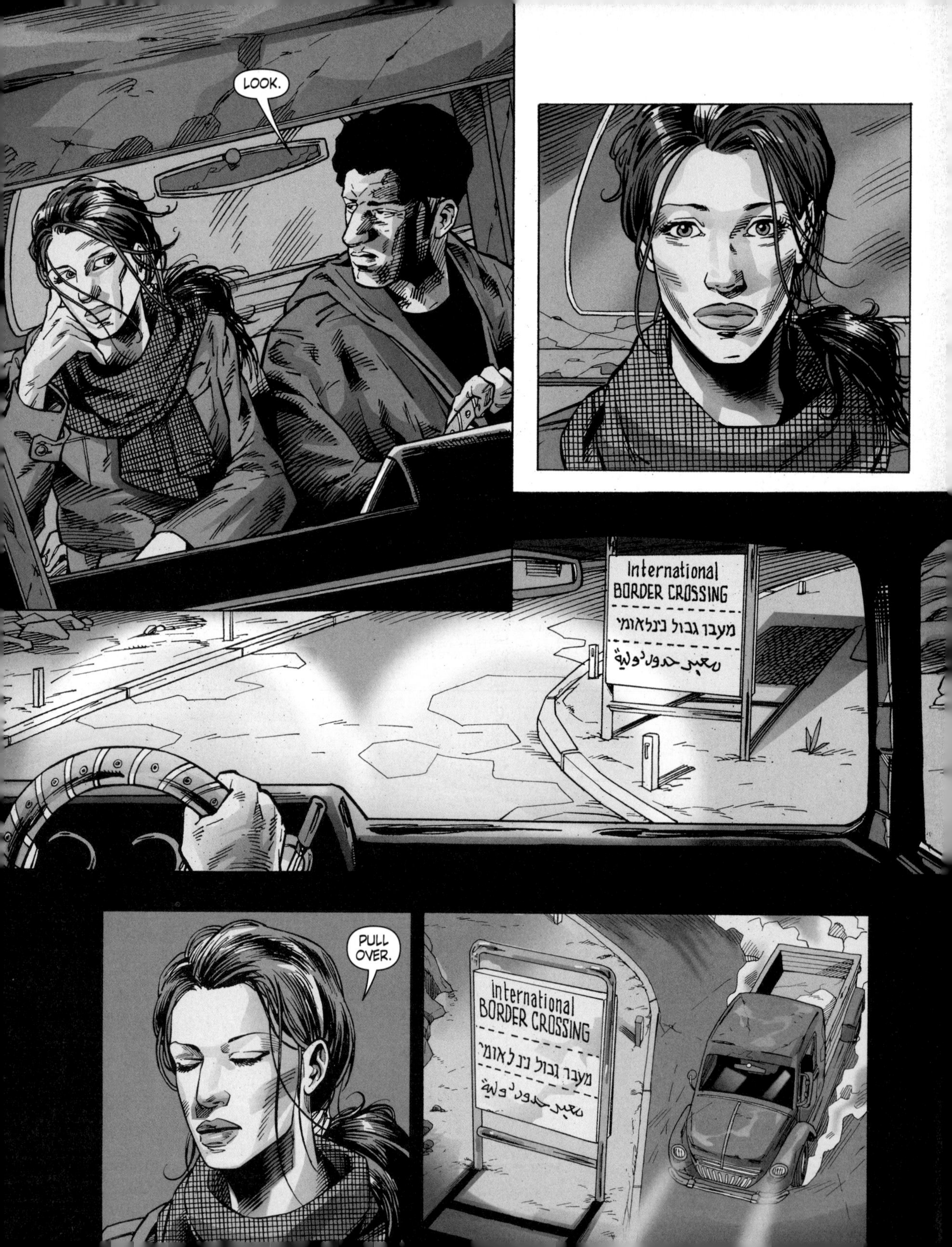
LOOK.
International
BORDER CROSSING
מעבר גבול בינלאומי
معبر حدود دولية
PULL OVER.
International
BORDER CROSSING
מעבר גבול בינלאומי
معبر حدود دولية

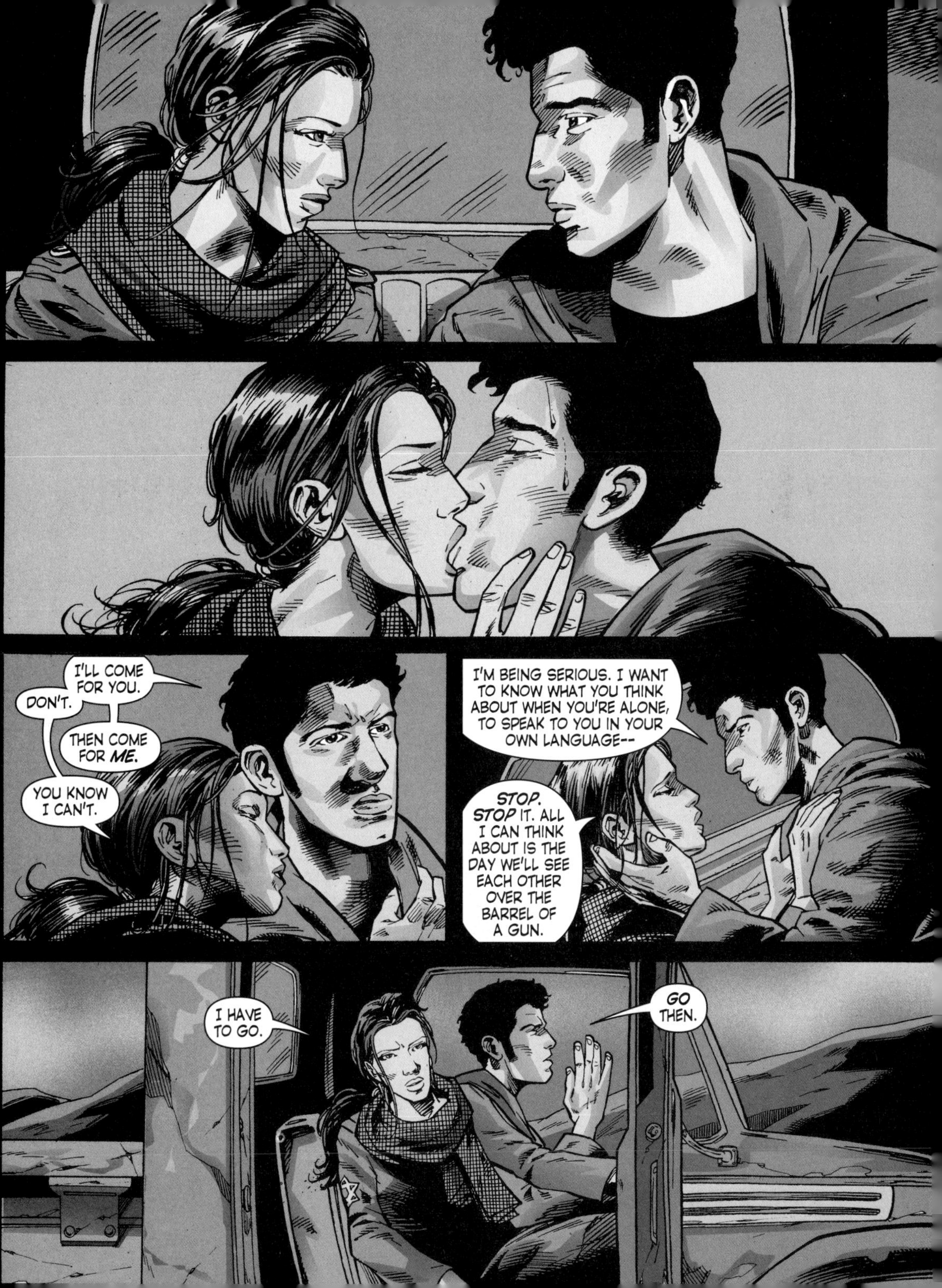

I'LL COME FOR YOU.
DON'T.
THEN COME FOR *ME*.
YOU KNOW I CAN'T.
I'M BEING SERIOUS. I WANT TO KNOW WHAT YOU THINK ABOUT WHEN YOU'RE ALONE, TO SPEAK TO YOU IN YOUR OWN LANGUAGE--
STOP. STOP IT. ALL I CAN THINK ABOUT IS THE DAY WE'LL SEE EACH OTHER OVER THE BARREL OF A GUN.
I HAVE TO GO.
GO THEN.

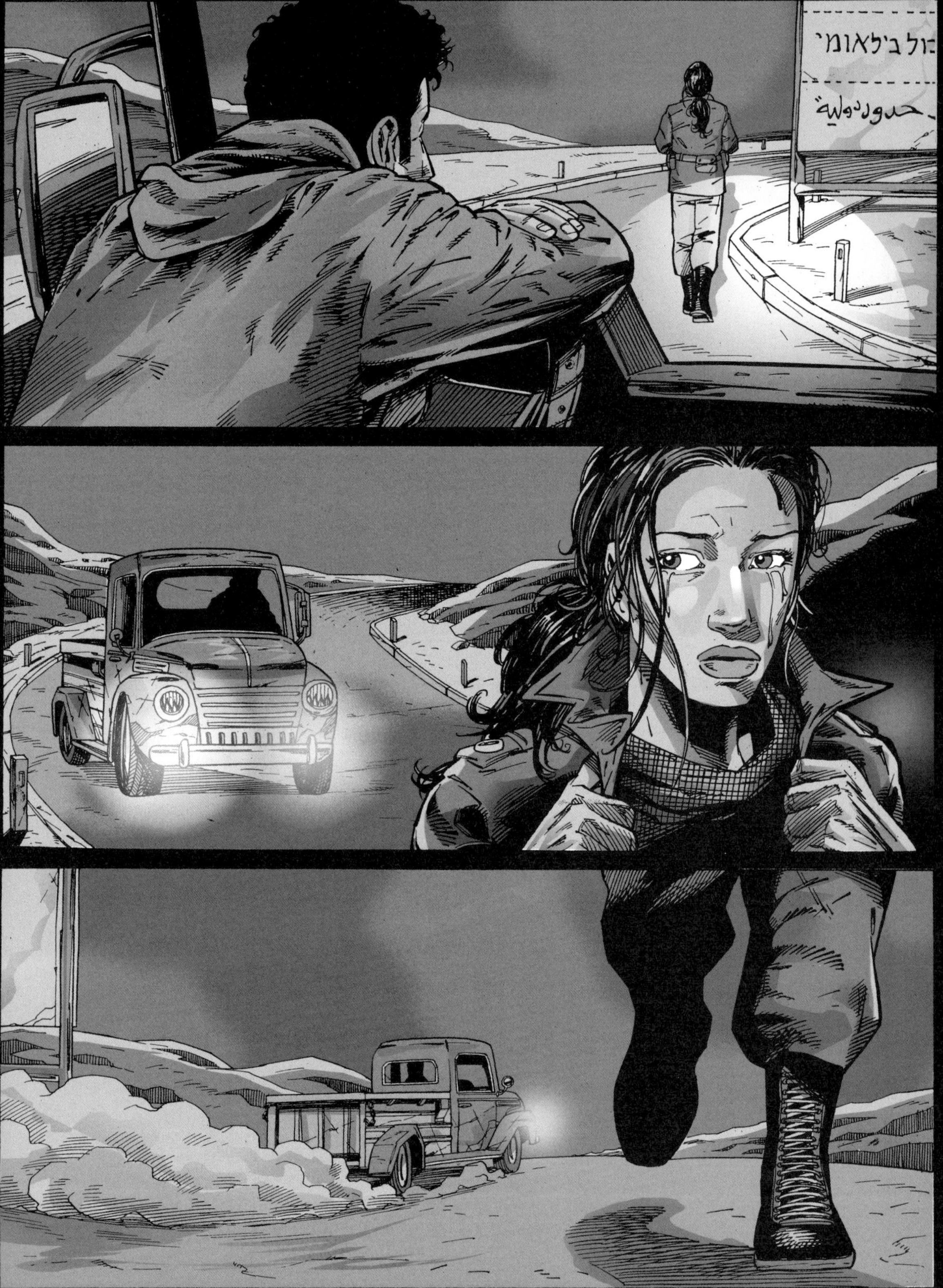

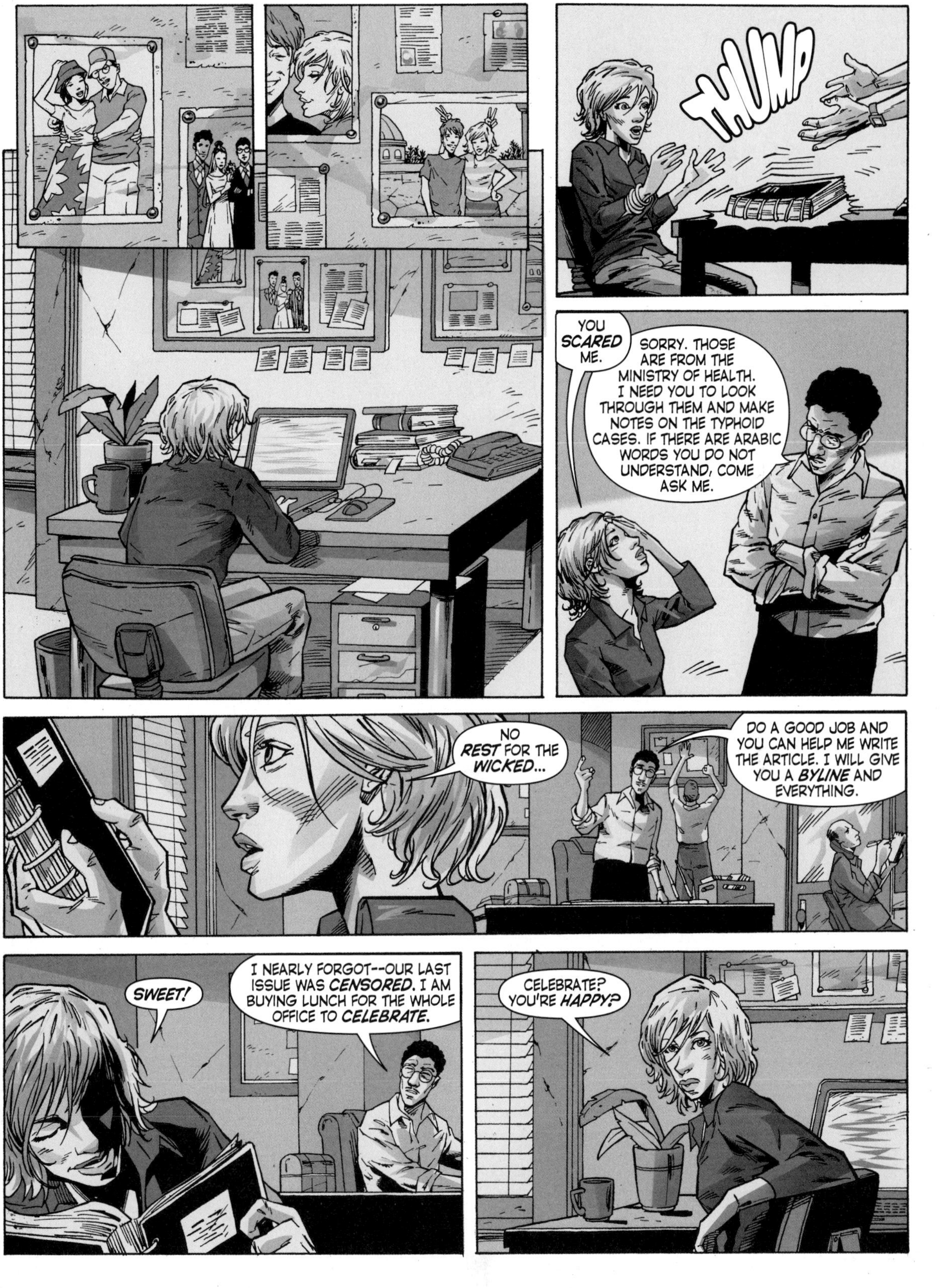
THUMP
YOU SCARED ME.
SORRY. THOSE ARE FROM THE MINISTRY OF HEALTH. I NEED YOU TO LOOK THROUGH THEM AND MAKE NOTES ON THE TYPHOID CASES. IF THERE ARE ARABIC WORDS YOU DO NOT UNDERSTAND, COME ASK ME.
NO REST FOR THE WICKED...
DO A GOOD JOB AND YOU CAN HELP ME WRITE THE ARTICLE. I WILL GIVE YOU A BYLINE AND EVERYTHING.
SWEET!
I NEARLY FORGOT--OUR LAST ISSUE WAS CENSORED. I AM BUYING LUNCH FOR THE WHOLE OFFICE TO CELEBRATE.
CELEBRATE? YOU'RE HAPPY?

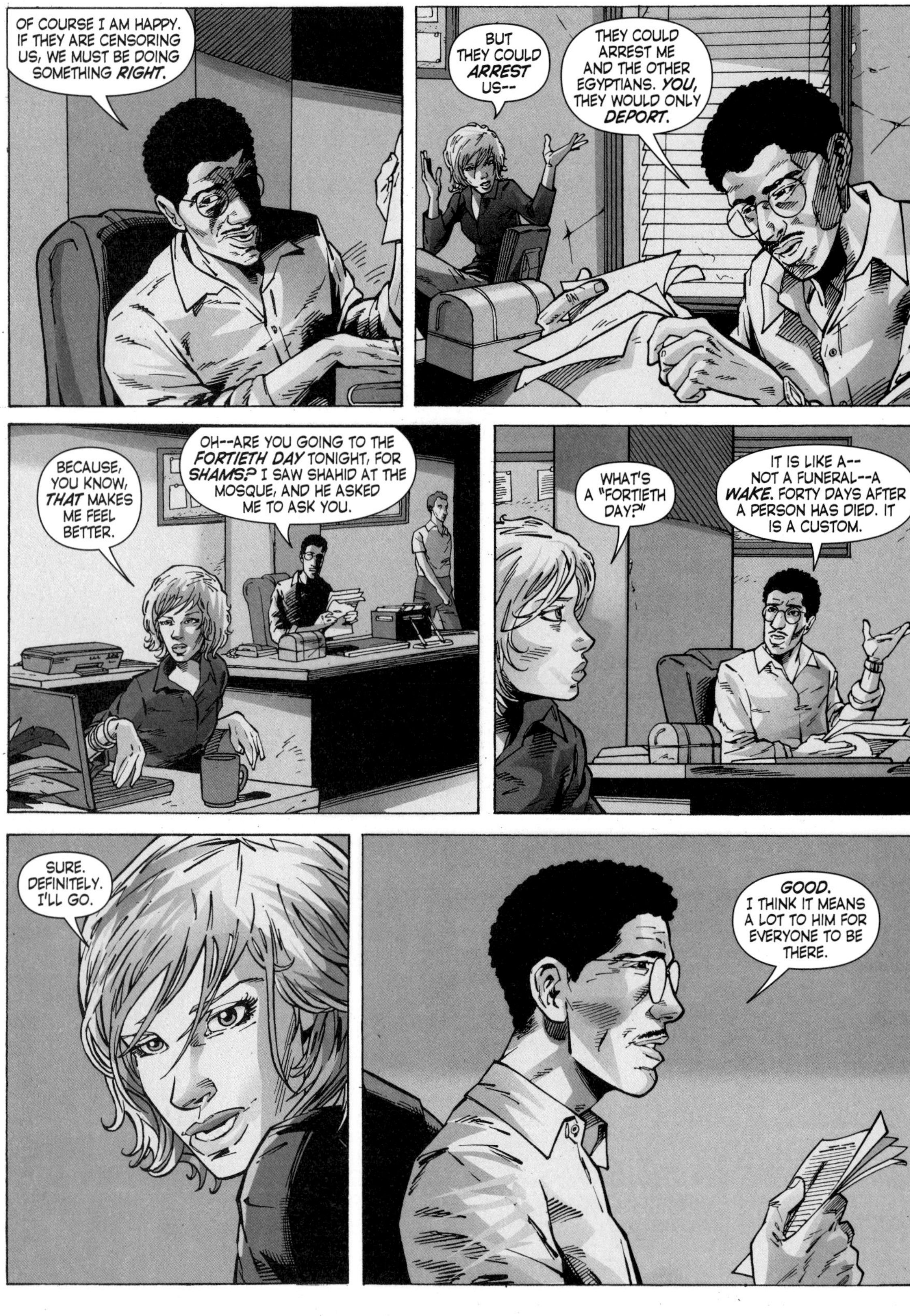
OF COURSE I AM HAPPY. IF THEY ARE CENSORING US, WE MUST BE DOING SOMETHING RIGHT.
BUT THEY COULD ARREST US--
THEY COULD ARREST ME AND THE OTHER EGYPTIANS. YOU, THEY WOULD ONLY DEPORT.
BECAUSE, YOU KNOW, THAT MAKES ME FEEL BETTER.
OH--ARE YOU GOING TO THE FORTIETH DAY TONIGHT, FOR SHAMS? I SAW SHAHID AT THE MOSQUE, AND HE ASKED ME TO ASK YOU.
WHAT'S A "FORTIETH DAY?"
IT IS LIKE A-- NOT A FUNERAL--A WAKE. FORTY DAYS AFTER A PERSON HAS DIED. IT IS A CUSTOM.
SURE. DEFINITELY. I'LL GO.
GOOD. I THINK IT MEANS A LOT TO HIM FOR EVERYONE TO BE THERE.

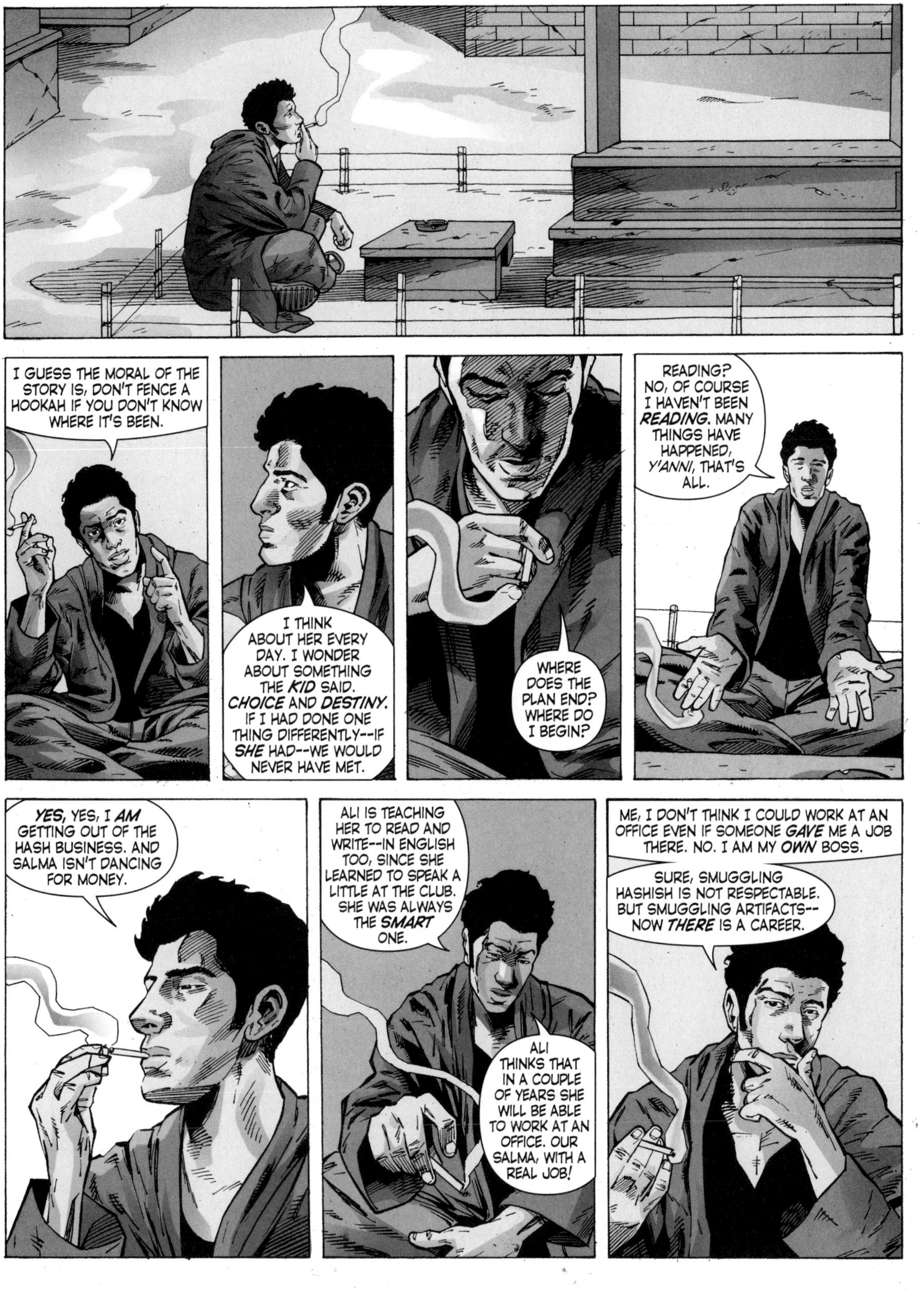
I GUESS THE MORAL OF THE STORY IS, DON'T FENCE A HOOKAH IF YOU DON'T KNOW WHERE IT'S BEEN.
I THINK ABOUT HER EVERY DAY. I WONDER ABOUT SOMETHING THE KID SAID. CHOICE AND DESTINY. IF I HAD DONE ONE THING DIFFERENTLY--IF SHE HAD--WE WOULD NEVER HAVE MET.
WHERE DOES THE PLAN END? WHERE DO I BEGIN?
READING? NO, OF COURSE I HAVEN'T BEEN READING. MANY THINGS HAVE HAPPENED, Y'ANNI, THAT'S ALL.
YES, YES, I AM GETTING OUT OF THE HASH BUSINESS. AND SALMA ISN'T DANCING FOR MONEY.
ALI IS TEACHING HER TO READ AND WRITE--IN ENGLISH TOO, SINCE SHE LEARNED TO SPEAK A LITTLE AT THE CLUB. SHE WAS ALWAYS THE SMART ONE.
ALI THINKS THAT IN A COUPLE OF YEARS SHE WILL BE ABLE TO WORK AT AN OFFICE. OUR SALMA, WITH A REAL JOB!
ME, I DON'T THINK I COULD WORK AT AN OFFICE EVEN IF SOMEONE GAVE ME A JOB THERE. NO. I AM MY OWN BOSS.
SURE, SMUGGLING HASHISH IS NOT RESPECTABLE. BUT SMUGGLING ARTIFACTS-- NOW THERE IS A CAREER.

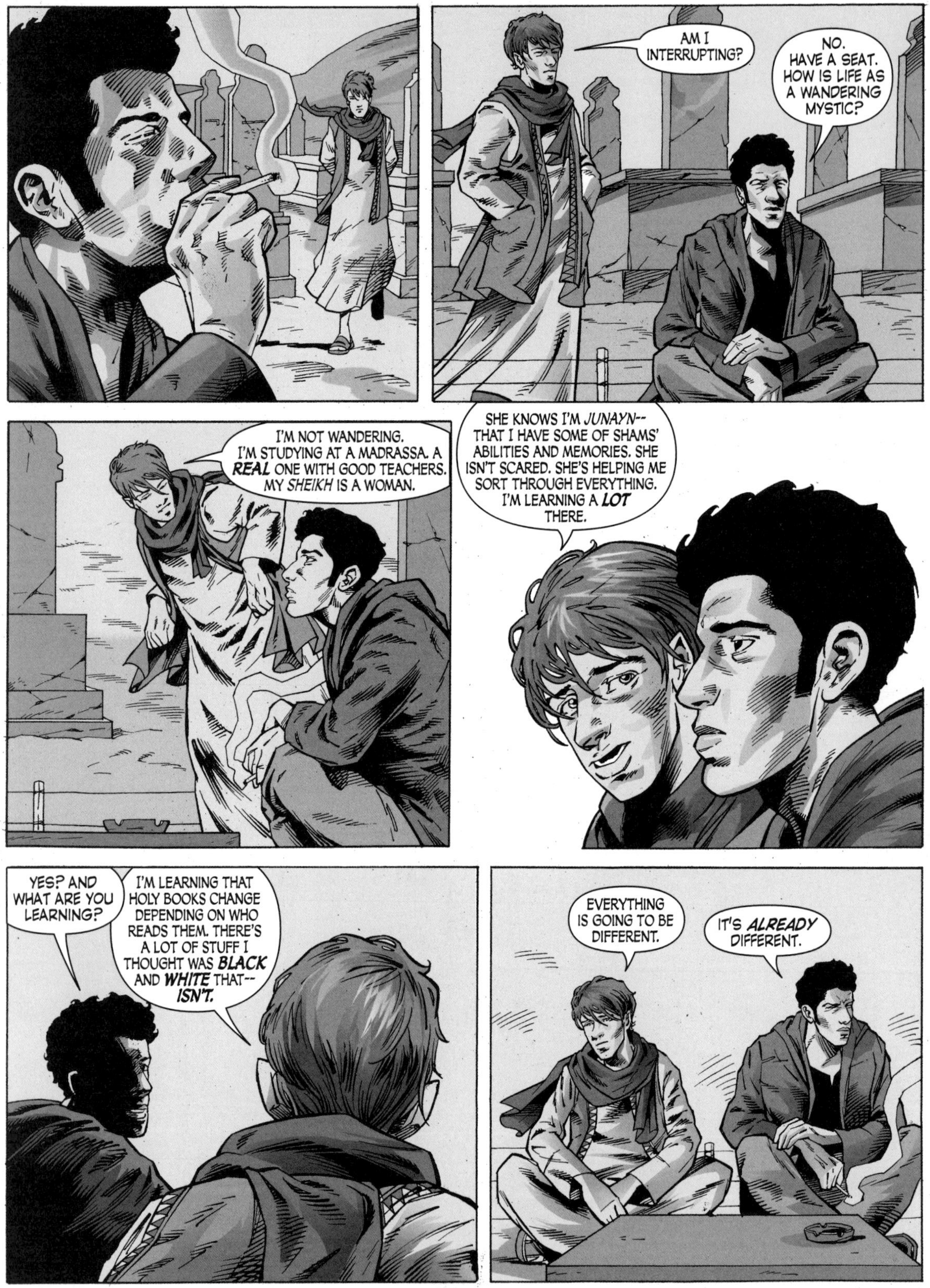
AM I INTERRUPTING?
NO. HAVE A SEAT. HOW IS LIFE AS A WANDERING MYSTIC?
I'M NOT WANDERING. I'M STUDYING AT A MADRASSA. A REAL ONE WITH GOOD TEACHERS. MY SHEIKH IS A WOMAN.
SHE KNOWS I'M JUNAYN-- THAT I HAVE SOME OF SHAMS' ABILITIES AND MEMORIES. SHE ISN'T SCARED. SHE'S HELPING ME SORT THROUGH EVERYTHING. I'M LEARNING A LOT THERE.
YES? AND WHAT ARE YOU LEARNING?
I'M LEARNING THAT HOLY BOOKS CHANGE DEPENDING ON WHO READS THEM. THERE'S A LOT OF STUFF I THOUGHT WAS BLACK AND WHITE THAT-- ISN'T.
EVERYTHING IS GOING TO BE DIFFERENT.
IT'S ALREADY DIFFERENT.

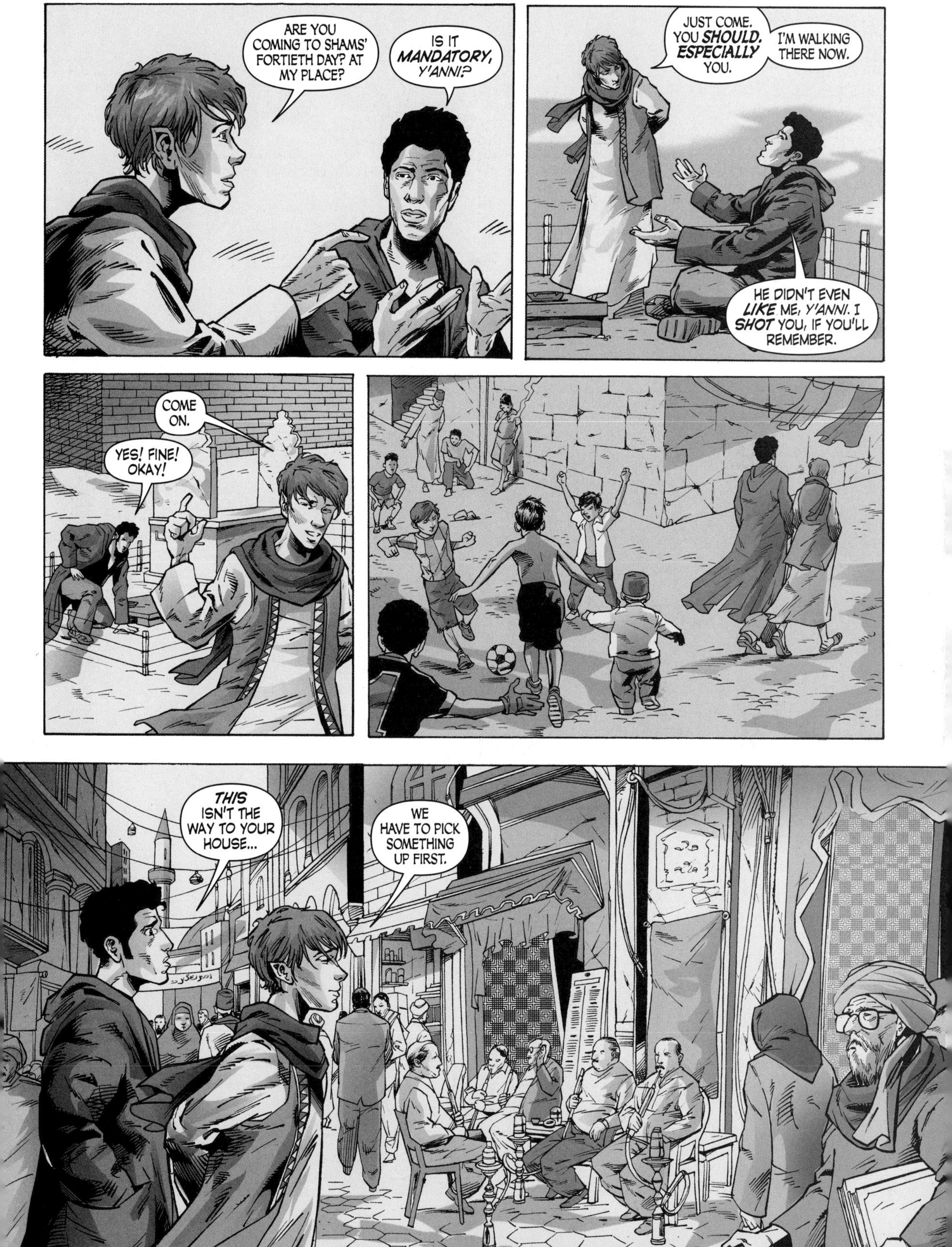
ARE YOU COMING TO SHAMS' FORTIETH DAY? AT MY PLACE?
IS IT *MANDATORY,* Y'ANNI?
JUST COME. YOU ***SHOULD. ESPECIALLY*** YOU.
I'M WALKING THERE NOW.
HE DIDN'T EVEN ***LIKE*** ME, Y'ANNI. I ***SHOT*** YOU, IF YOU'LL REMEMBER.
COME ON.
YES! FINE! OKAY!
THIS ISN'T THE WAY TO YOUR HOUSE...
WE HAVE TO PICK SOMETHING UP FIRST.

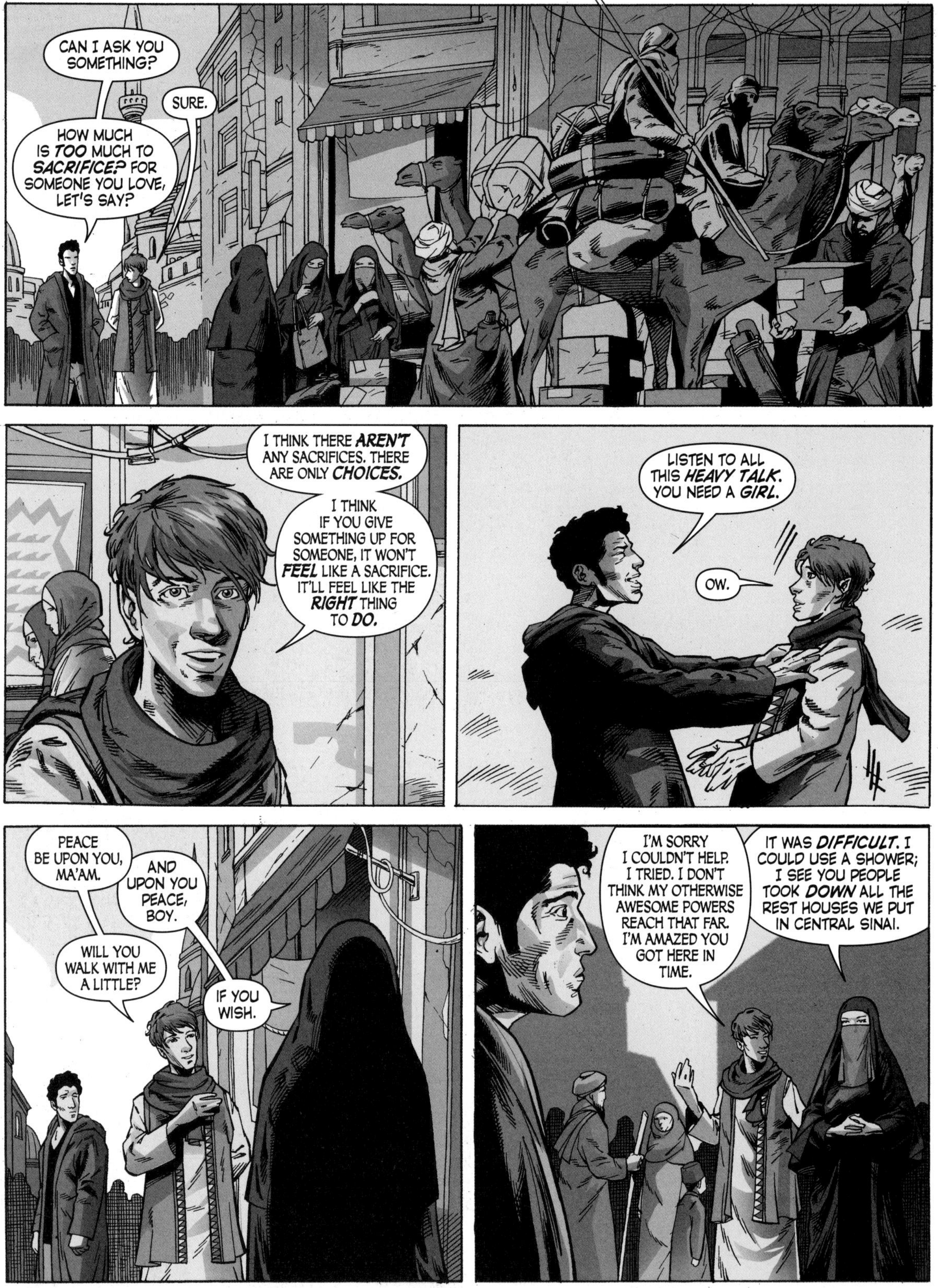
CAN I ASK YOU SOMETHING?
SURE.
HOW MUCH IS TOO MUCH TO SACRIFICE? FOR SOMEONE YOU LOVE, LET'S SAY?
I THINK THERE AREN'T ANY SACRIFICES. THERE ARE ONLY CHOICES.
I THINK IF YOU GIVE SOMETHING UP FOR SOMEONE, IT WON'T FEEL LIKE A SACRIFICE. IT'LL FEEL LIKE THE RIGHT THING TO DO.
LISTEN TO ALL THIS HEAVY TALK. YOU NEED A GIRL.
OW.
PEACE BE UPON YOU, MA'AM.
AND UPON YOU PEACE, BOY.
WILL YOU WALK WITH ME A LITTLE?
IF YOU WISH.
I'M SORRY I COULDN'T HELP. I TRIED. I DON'T THINK MY OTHERWISE AWESOME POWERS REACH THAT FAR. I'M AMAZED YOU GOT HERE IN TIME.
IT WAS DIFFICULT. I COULD USE A SHOWER; I SEE YOU PEOPLE TOOK DOWN ALL THE REST HOUSES WE PUT IN CENTRAL SINAI.

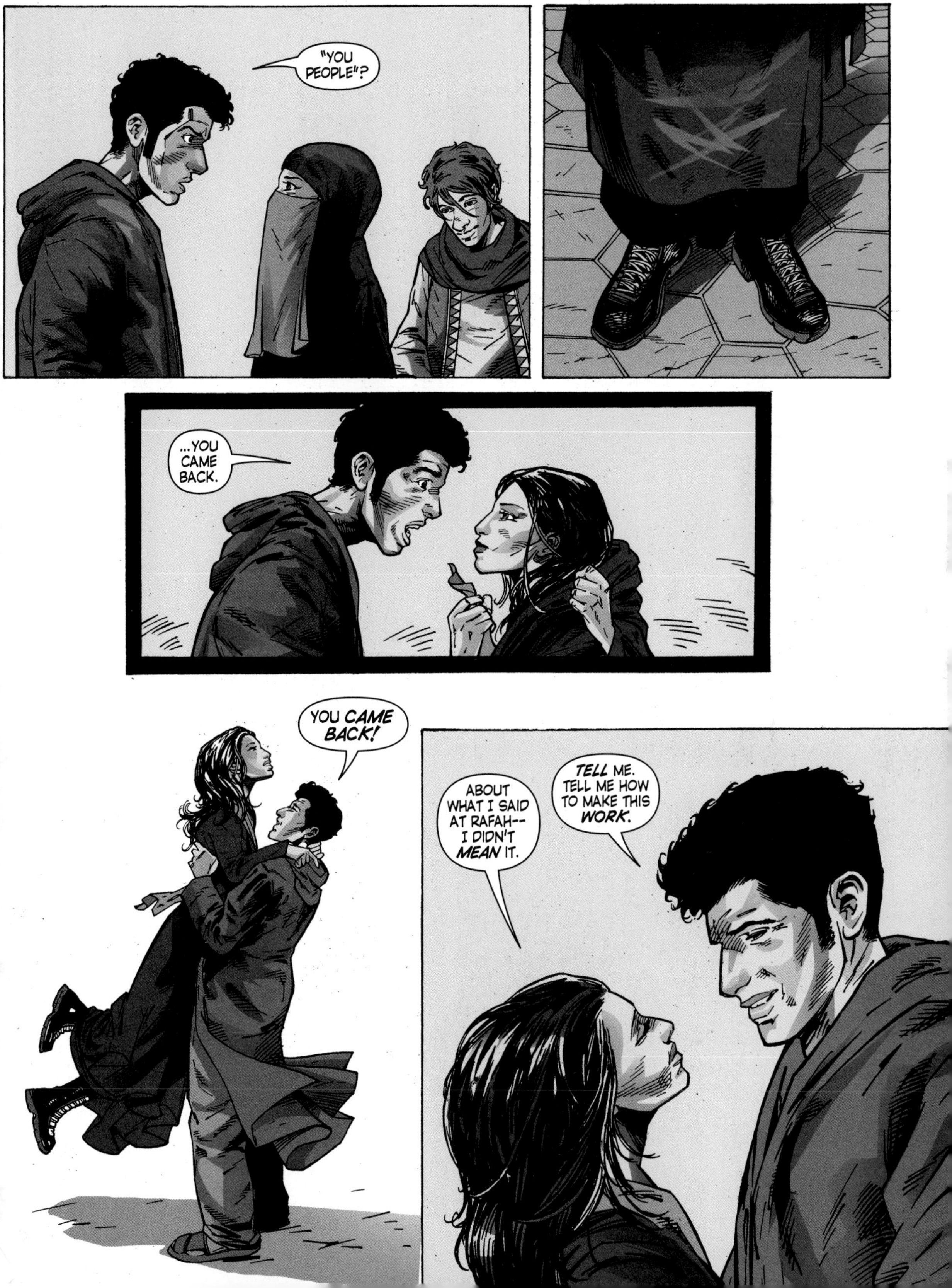
"YOU PEOPLE"?
...YOU CAME BACK.
YOU CAME BACK!
TELL ME. TELL ME HOW TO MAKE THIS WORK.
ABOUT WHAT I SAID AT RAFAH-- I DIDN'T MEAN IT.

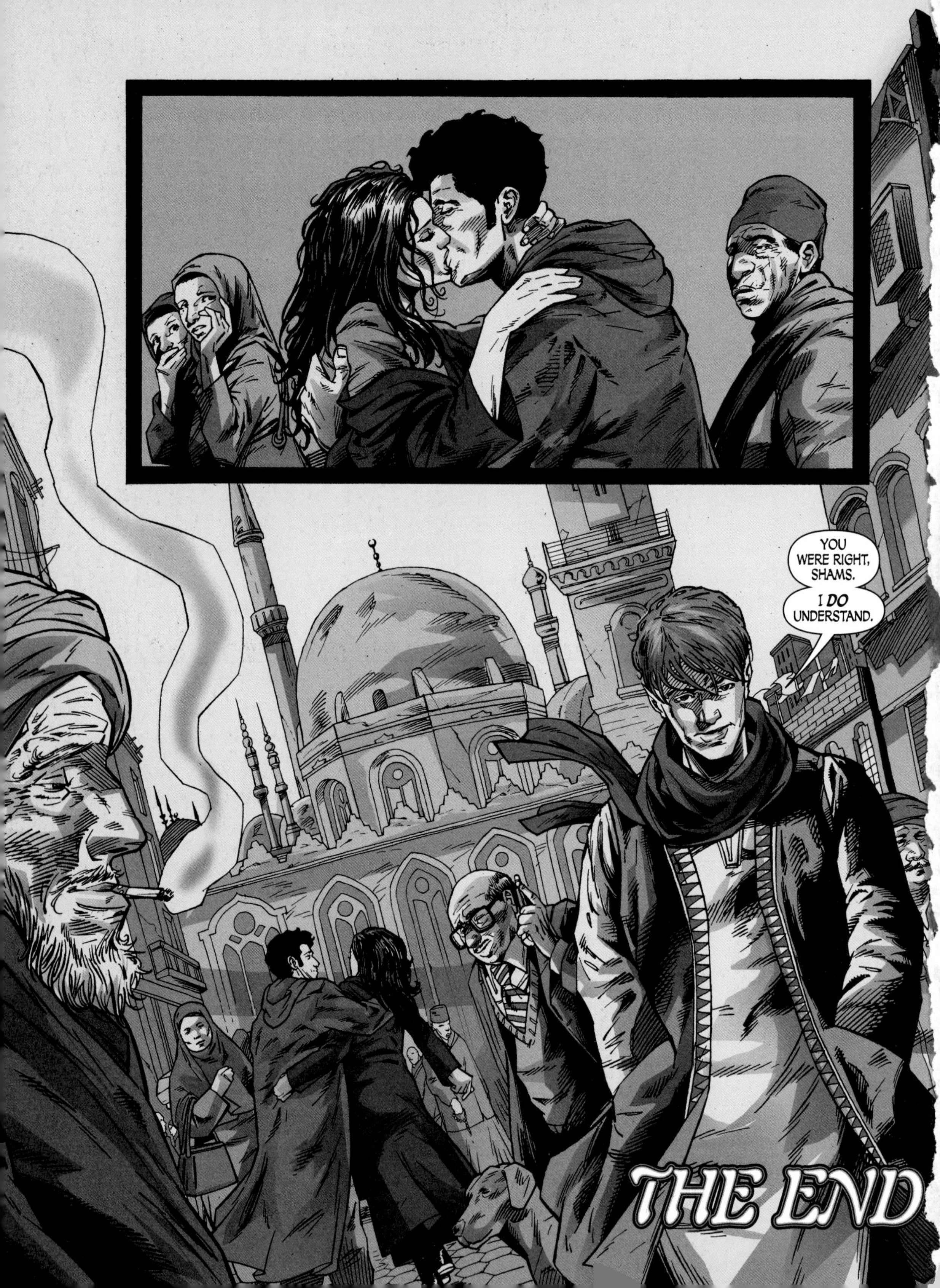
YOU WERE RIGHT, SHAMS.
I DO UNDERSTAND.
THE END